introduction to

psychological research

John Wiley & Sons, Inc., New York • London

introduction to

psychological

research

WILLIAM A. SCOTT and MICHAEL WERTHEIMER
University of Colorado

Preface

This book is based on a course for first-semester graduate students instituted in 1956 at the University of Colorado. The aim of the course was to acquaint beginners with the practicalities of doing original research. It had been our experience that students are all too frequently thrust ill-prepared into a situation which demands, but does not necessarily nurture, independent research. Most of the time the students in no sense suffered from lack of ideas, but the frequent frustrations encountered in the course of turning even a good idea into finished research often led to disenchantment with the entire process.

Certainly even the most seasoned investigator finds new and unforeseen complexities in any research project. This will probably always be true as long as the researcher's imagination and the scope of his inquiry extend beyond the range of the skills he has learned. But some problems are encountered time and again in various forms. Mastery of techniques for attacking them might free the newcomer's attention for more specific difficulties posed by his particular research project. If this mastery is based on a concern for principles and reasons behind the particular techniques, the researcher should be

v

able to think critically and creatively about the problems he encounters. He should also find himself capable of going beyond common practice (including the suggestions we offer here) to invent new techniques appropriate to his own research interests.

The recurrent problems include these. How can the research question be formulated so that it can be studied empirically? How do I find out what has already been done in this area? Shall I try an experiment or attempt less formal observations? What operational definitions should I use? How many subjects should I get? What kinds of statistics are required? How do I write up the findings for publication? What is an appropriate publishing outlet? And so on.

These are the sorts of issues on which we try to focus in this book. The student has, of course, met many of them before in his courses and laboratories. But all too often the techniques for solving such problems have been learned disjointedly and outside the context of the student's self-generated research interests. Further, all too often he has been left in the dark about how to handle the everyday practical matters encountered in doing research—there is a world of difference between following the manual's instructions for a laboratory exercise and actually inventing an experiment. Though one has had courses treating such things as statistics and experimental design, the philosophy of induction, and ways to search the library for references, he may not be able to apply this material to the formulation of a new problem of his own. So a typical student is likely to make several abortive attempts at research before he realizes how the various phases of the process relate to each other and that there is some "know-how" not taught in courses that he must pick up as best he can.

The material covered in this text is by no means intended as a substitute for advanced, intensive treatment of specialized topics, such as experimental methods, psychometrics, sampling, interview survey research, and statistical analysis. Many useful textbooks on these and other problems of psychological research are currently available, and we refer the reader to some of them at appropriate points in our discussion.

However, if the student's research training is obtained exclusively from any one or two of these specialized sources, he is likely to get the impression that there is only a single research methodology—or, at least, only a single "good" one. It is our intent to counteract this impression. By providing an extensive coverage, we hope to be able to give the reader some idea how various methodologies and research techniques can be helpful and also to indicate some relations among them which may not be apparent in discussions of any one considered in isolation. We trust that this scope of coverage will make up for deficiencies entailed in our brief treatment of any particular topic.

The limitation in topic treatment applies to our discussion of statistics as well. This is not intended to be a textbook in statistics. Rather, we attempt, at appropriate points, to present certain recurrent problems in data analysis, together with some relevant statistical techniques and their common-sense rationales. To go further than this would violate an ideological bias inherent in the entire presentation: namely, that statistics are here conceived as tools for research, not as techniques to be refined for their own sake. Though intensive treatment would certainly be appropriate in some contexts, we do not wish here to "let the statistical tail wag the research dog" (cf. Festinger et al., 1959; see references at end of Chapter 1).

To some, the ideological flavor of this book may seem to advocate a retreat from the high standards of research quality that we, as scientists, have been taught to respect. If so, then the contents will— unintentionally—prove controversial. We feel that the virtues of rigor and methodological sophistication are sufficiently emphasized in the current Zeitgeist. Though we agree with them fully, an exclusive focus on these standards may have an unfortunate side effect upon the creative process. Blind following of unrealistic dicta from above can only yield an unproductive caricature of research.

Although the research *product* should, of course, be as precise, elegant, and "clean" as possible, the creative research *process* is usually very different. It tends to be slow, back-tracking, informal, and, in its early stages, sloppy, woolly, and anything but rigid. Perfectionism, rigidity, and premature formalization may tend to stifle rather than nurture the creative spark which seems an integral part of any truly productive and significant research.

Some would maintain that "courses in how to do research before turning the student loose in the laboratory are like teaching a child to swim without letting him get near the pool" (Hebb, 1958). Although we agree, of course, that many aspects of research can be learned only by doing, a didactic presentation may help the student to anticipate recurrent problems and ways of solving them. This teaching should not, however, be such that "it simply produces a fear of making mistakes and the idea that one must swim with perfect style or not at all. . . . No research gets done by the man who must do only the experiments that are beyond criticism" (Hebb, 1958). Within the limits of producing convincing evidence, flexibility rather than rigidity should be the rule in all things associated with research.

The content of this book comes from many sources, but in most cases we would be hard put to specify just where. Much of it came from our own training, but perhaps more frequently it can be traced to our students, many of whom made us aware—sometimes unwittingly —of problems associated with the actual conduct of research. We planned the outline jointly, and all chapters have had some contributions from both of us. However, MW is primarily responsible for initially getting off the ground a book whose aim is to present an account of the practical, everyday problems encountered in doing research; WS is primarily responsible for the inclusion and formulation of the statistical material. We feel that, over-all, each of us contributed about an equal share to the final product; hence the alphabetical listing of authors' names. Each chapter benefited from careful reading by our wives, colleagues, and students.

We would be grateful if readers would let us know about inadvertent errors, and also if they would maintain a kindly tolerance toward any expressions of opinion that differ seriously from their own.

WILLIAM A. SCOTT
MICHAEL WERTHEIMER

Boulder, Colorado
March 1962

Acknowledgments

We are indebted to the following authors and publishers for permission to reprint copyrighted materials:

Professor Sir Ronald A. Fisher, F.R.S., Cambridge, Dr. Frank Yates, F.R.S., Rothamsted, and Messrs. Oliver & Boyd, Ltd., Edinburgh, for permission to abstract Appendix Tables C, E, and F from their book, *Statistical tables for biological, agricultural and medical research.*

Professor George W. Snedecor and the Iowa State University Press for permission to reprint Appendix Table A from their book, *Statistical methods* (Fifth Edition, 1956).

Professor Allen L. Edwards and Holt, Rinehart, & Winston, Inc., for permission to abstract Appendix Table B from their book, *Statistical methods for the behavioral sciences.*

Professor Quinn McNemar and John Wiley & Sons, Inc., for permission to reprint Appendix Table D and Figure 9-3 from their book, *Psychological statistics* (Second Edition, 1955).

Dr. Edmund T. Klemmer for permission to reprint Appendix Tables G and H from Attneave, F. *Applications of information theory to psychology.* New York: Holt-Dryden, 1959.

W. A. S.
M. W.

Contents

CHAPTER 1

The research process: an overview

Traditionally, the Ph.D. degree has been granted as a certificate of competence in research. Most Ph.D. programs therefore emphasize research training for the graduate student from the moment he enters the university. He is expected to undertake empirical studies so that by the time he receives his doctorate he will have acquired a work pattern in which the performance of research remains a major emphasis. The aim of this training, of course, is partly to equip him to prepare his doctoral dissertation, but primarily it is to help him become a scholar who will make research an important continuing part of his postdoctoral career.

Probably the only way to attain competence in research is to engage in it (cf. Festinger et al., 1959; Hebb, 1958). But other things may help, too. Candid talk with an experienced researcher may make the neophyte aware of many everyday problems which he has not personally encountered. Concrete examples of the history of success and failure, frustration and satisfaction, insight and puzzlement, which are a part of the process of actually doing research, generally produce a very different impression than the researcher's formal published report. There is a world of difference between the published product and the process of arriving at it. Many of the important decisions that the researcher must make in the pursuit of his goals are never mentioned in journal publications. The skills to overcome routine difficulties, such as finding references relevant to one's interest, turning an idea into researchable form, obtaining subjects, building and fixing equipment, writing a lucid report, and the like, must be acquired somewhere. At many institutions students have been expected to find this kind of information and learn these skills on their own. But increasingly, of late, courses are being developed and books written to help potential researchers master these often mundane but highly useful skills. The courses and books vary in level from the very sophisticated and analytical, presenting research designs and problems in an abstract, often idealized way, to the very concrete and down-to-earth, sometimes with a "how to do it" flavor. There are many useful references in the first category; some of them are listed at the end of this chapter (e.g., Cochran & Cox, 1957; Cox, 1958; Edwards, 1960; Lindquist, 1953; Underwood, 1957). The student should become acquainted with these books.

Not many volumes have been written with the more down-to-earth emphasis; it is one of the aims of this book to provide such a concrete approach. We take up various matters associated with the actual performance of research step by step as they are encountered, starting with the earliest phases of deciding on a problem and ending with the process of letting others know what was done and what was found. Statistics, equipment selection, philosophical issues, public relations, experimental design, and many other topics are touched on when they are relevant to the development of the typical research project.

The phrase "typical research project" is deceptive because every project has its own peculiar problems and every researcher his own style. There is no single formula for the ideal research approach; there probably is no single perfect study, either completed or contemplated. Research is a human product, and its producers are fallible human beings. This is something worth keeping in mind for the beginner, for whom the word "research" may have an other-worldly, awesome aura. It is, of course, desirable to aim at a competent product, but to remain practical there is no need to become discouraged when it turns out to be less than perfect. In the present stage of psychological knowledge even a relatively imperfect piece of research may well be better than none. Just because a particular project is not totally immune to criticism from all points of view does not mean that it must be discarded. The many pitfalls in research should not frighten the student away; with experience, he can probably handle them as well as the next person. These pages present some guides, suggestions, and techniques that we have found useful in our own research; this does not mean that there are not many alternative ways of meeting the problems we discuss. It is our hope that the reader will take whatever he finds useful here and apply it in his own way.

Research is a personal matter, performed by human beings, much as a work of art is the personal product of its creator. Individuals differ in their preferred modes of creation, and, as in art, there are many who feel that their style is the only correct one. It is perhaps fortunate for psychological research that there are many points of view, for this makes it possible to expose the neophyte to different approaches and to permit him to choose here and there, ultimately to develop his own idiosyncratic style. Certain basic principles, such as the need for controls, are, of course, common to virtually every approach; but about what to study and how to study it, whether to observe phenomena longitudinally through time or to obtain a cross-sectional view, whether to use randomization or counterbalancing, whether to study rats or college sophomores or natives of Trinidad, whether a particular problem is worth working on—about such issues there are disagreements, and often bitter ones. If one makes the assumption—which we do not question in this book but which also has two sides—that research is a "good thing," then an appropriate aim would be to let every researcher develop his own credo after due exposure to the array of existing methods. In the process, it is hoped, he may also acquire some respect and understanding for the methods of others.

We hope that our advice and suggestions will be taken in this vein. Almost anyone can perform research, and almost everyone can get a great deal of enjoyment out of it—mixed with considerable frustration as well.

WHY DO RESEARCH?

Perhaps what motivates most investigators is that using one's creative and intellectual powers to add something novel—something nobody else ever knew before—to the storehouse of human knowledge is an enormously rich and satisfying experience. Not that the average researcher is likely during his career to make a world-shaking discovery; a great deal of enjoyment can still be derived from the process of following an idea wherever it leads. Doing a difficult creative job well, according to one's own high standards, provides one of the greatest satisfactions that can be experienced, a depth of pleasure that can hardly be matched by anything else.

Research is done, then, for the hedonistic reason that often it is a highly pleasurable activity, which many people pursue simply because they "get a kick out of it." But there are many other related and unrelated reasons for doing research. One investigator may be hoping for immortality or looking for a grandiose world view. Another may want to satisfy his curiosity or to solve an immediate practical problem. Some individuals engage in research because they feel they want to help people and are convinced that in the long run new knowledge will make life more livable.

Then, for better or worse, there are more external reasons, which may nevertheless be compelling, reasons which do not involve doing research simply for its own sake. The realities of academic life being what they are, one generally has a hard time getting ahead unless he publishes—whether it is to obtain a job, tenure, a raise, or a promotion. Research may thus be used to enhance a person's own status—but also to help his department or university and perhaps even to gain acceptance of psychology as a science. Doubtless also many investigators are trying to establish and promulgate a belief or a theory to which they are strongly committed—to try to prove that they are right and their critics wrong. Since any behavior is likely to be multiply-determined, one should expect to find many different reasons combining to produce a given research endeavor.

Research is sometimes done for propaganda, sometimes for discovery, often for both. Ideally, whatever the underlying motives, the immediate goal is the acquisition of knowledge. Often knowledge is sought in a particular area by a special-interest group; doubtless the rapid development of science in fields such as public opinion, motivation, and human relations—not to mention such recent nonpsychological research foci as satellite and missile development—gains major impetus from public pressure for practical knowledge and skill in those areas.

PROBLEM-SOLVING, THEORY-DEVELOPMENT, AND THEORY-TESTING RESEARCH

As a tool for acquiring knowledge, research may be primarily directed toward one or another of three major but often overlapping goals: to solve specific problems, to develop or expand theories, or to test existing theories. Theories, whether explicit or implicit, virtually always play a role in research. Even so-called "shot-gun empiricism," in which the investigator seems to measure an almost random collection of variables, throw them in the hopper, and look for relations, is not entirely devoid of a kind of theory. The choice of one variable to measure, rather than another, implies an underlying hunch, hypothesis, or theory.

The designation of a research orientation as problem solving, theory developing, or theory testing is often somewhat arbitrary in any given case, since each fades into the others. Yet most projects can be fairly readily classified on the basis of how general and how explicit the theoretical statement is. Since both the explicitness and the generality of a theory are chiefly determined by the amount of knowledge already existing in a field, one cannot say a priori that any one of the three orientations is "superior" to the others. Psychology is a new enough and large enough discipline to provide room for people working with all of these goals; the three can and do supplement one another.

Problem-Solving Research

This kind of investigation is often directed toward a practical applied goal. For example, during World War II the Federal Government sponsored research on the relative visibility of blips on various designs of radar scope screens. The object here was to develop a screen design as error-free as possible. Another project had as its task the development of clearly discriminable knob shapes, so that an aircraft operator, with many different devices to manipulate, would not confuse one knob with another—possibly with disastrous consequences. Much research has been directed at assessing the relative efficacy of different teaching methods in schools and colleges. Other illustrations can be found in the development of tests to help in selecting and placing personnel, in the psychology of advertising, in assessing public attitudes towards major events such as the first earth satellites, etc. Less "applied" illustrations might include studies of the determinants of a particular perceptual illusion, of the social behavior of ants, or of certain adult personality patterns. Much of this research is not performed to test a general theory or to develop a theoretical formulation; the investigator is simply interested in finding the answer to a specific problem, or else he just wants to describe the phenomenon as precisely as possible. Often the work is of a kind characterized by the question, "I wonder what would happen if . . .", in which case the purpose approaches that of the next category.

Theory-Developing Research

Other studies are aimed at clarifying hunches. Perhaps most research performed by psychologists is of such an exploratory nature; if the study serves its intended function, one can begin to make a theoretical formulation. Generally, until the investigation is performed, the theory is so inexplicit in the researcher's mind that the study is carried out to determine not only whether a relation is positive, negative, or curvilinear, but whether any relationship exists at all. The researcher may have a feeling that a change in A should somehow affect B, but he has to perform a study before he can tell what kind of effect, if any. One investigator, for instance, believed that similarity between the personalities of psychotherapist and patient should affect the efficacy of therapy but that this effect might be facilitating, inhibiting, or both. A study was carried out to see which of these alternatives was most nearly correct. Another investigator has been spending several years exploring the physiological correlates of prognosis in schizophrenia, alternating between examination of data and the formulation of hypotheses, with the data suggesting further hunches as well as corroborating or disconfirming hypotheses that had already been formulated. Other research in social psychology, psychopathology, perception, learning, personality—virtually in any area in psychology—could be cited to illustrate the theory-developing goal.

Theory-Testing Research

No large step separates theory development from theory-testing research. The two orientations overlap considerably. The main difference between them lies in the precision of the formulations involved. The more precise they are, and the more rigorous the deduction which culminates in a hypothesis, the closer one is to theory-testing research. Much recent work in learning is of this variety, with Hull's, Spence's, and Estes' models providing fairly precise prediction of empirical outcomes. In the field of sensation, where highly specific and rigorous prediction is often possible, many theories can be stated in mathematical form; here we have perhaps the highest level of theory-testing research in psychology.

If theory is relatively advanced in an area, one may try to design a study so that its results will permit decision among several alternative formulations. Thus, whenever two or more positions can be interpreted unequivocally to make clearly different predictions about the same situation, a *crucial experiment* may appear to be in order. If theory A predicts that an increase in X should be accompanied by an increase in Y, whereas theory B predicts that it should be accompanied by a decrease in Y, a study is designed in which X is increased to see what happens to Y. If Y goes up as X does, theory A's prediction is supported, and one becomes convinced that (at least in the particular application represented by the experiment) it is superior to theory B; theory A has won the contest.

It would, of course, be ideal to have all competing theories stated in sufficiently explicit detail to permit crucial studies. In practice, though, such a strategy is possible only in relatively few fields in contemporary psychology. For a while some psychologists believed that the demonstration of latent learning was a crucial experiment supporting the tenability of Tolman's theory of learning as opposed to Hull's; but most of the time it was possible to show that an experiment which had initially been considered crucial had certain deficiencies that denied it this status. In fact, it is now widely believed unrealistic to try to perform truly crucial experiments in psychology because of the inevitable presence of at least *some* uncontrolled variables and because theories between which a crucial test is desired are usually too slippery—that is, are rarely stated explicitly and fully enough to make truly unequivocal predictions. In spite of utmost care in experimental design, alternative interpretations of any set of results are always possible; also, any theory can be expanded or modified to handle new data. (In fact this is one of the chief ways in which scientific progress occurs.)

Besides not being crucial, "crucial experiments" need not be experiments, in the technical sense of the term. Observational, correlational, or assessment techniques that do not involve explicit experimental manipulation may be used to help decide among theories; manipulation of independent variables—classically considered as the essence of experimentation—is not the only way to produce results relevant to a theoretical formulation. Strictly speaking, then, the phrase "crucial experiment" is paradoxical in that it refers to a study that is usually not crucial after all and that does not necessarily make use of the experimental strategy. Yet it points in the direction of a research design that, for many investigators, remains an ideal worth striving for.

Perhaps with this ideal in mind, psychologists in the younger and less well-developed areas have recently directed intensive effort at formulating theories precise enough to yield clear and unequivocal predictions. But all too often these theories exist only long enough to show that they are not supported by research findings. Perhaps such premature precision does serve an important heuristic function; but one might also suspect that efficient use of the theory-testing strategy requires at least sufficient empirical knowledge about the problem area to enable one to devise a reasonably applicable theory. It may be wasteful to use this approach if so little is known that theory-testing endeavors yield mainly negative or equivocal findings.

When clearly stated theories have successfully withstood repeated tests and a large amount of empirical information is available, a new and different kind of theory development may begin. This is a phase of parameter estimation, wherein one attempts to specify exactly the function relating independent and dependent variables, to establish the mathematical constants in the formulas which constitute the theory. Because of the crudity of most knowledge about psychology, this advanced kind of theory development is relatively rare. In some of the older areas, however, notably sensation, parameter estimation tends to be the rule rather than the exception. Thus much research with Helson's (1959) adaptation level theory has been directed at estimating the relative weights of different terms in an equation for predicting the neutral point of sensory dimensions; Stevens' (1957) recent discovery that a power function offers a better and more general description of the relation between physical and psychological magnitudes than is afforded by the traditional logarithmic function has led to research aimed at specifying the constants in the power law as it applies to many different sensory attributes. Because such precise formulations are just about impossible in most present-day behavioral science, not much attention is devoted in this book to research aimed at parameter estimation. Nevertheless, for many people it constitutes an ideal which, hopefully, all psychological research will eventually reach.

Research Goals in Relation to the History of a Field

The history of research in any area perhaps begins typically with a kind of problem-solving orientation, which may in turn produce some hunches. As these hunches are followed up and tested, a theory-developing phase begins, and as the theories and hunches become more and more refined theory-testing starts to play a major role. At certain stages in the accumulation of knowledge one approach may be more fruitful than another; problem-solving and theory-developing research may well be the most effective methods of gaining sufficient knowledge about the area to make theory testing profitable.

Although at different times and in different fields one or another strategy may be most congruent with the state of knowledge, the current intellectual climate in psychology seems to favor theory-testing research. Many university departments prefer dissertations that test theories to those that have the more ambitious aim (or the less ambitious aim, depending on one's point of view) of exploring a problem or developing a theory. This is not always true, but, when it is, the aspiring Ph.D. candidate might well take this preference into consideration. However, he should not permit himself to ignore the distinct advantages, and frequent necessity in some fields, of other kinds of strategy.

THE RESEARCH ATTITUDE

Although there are disagreements, and often bitter ones, about the kind of research an individual should emphasize, most people who accept the value of research would probably agree on the importance of developing a research attitude towards one's studies. This means that *every statement, every principle, every pronouncement by oneself or by another should be examined from two points of view: whether or not it is true and, even more important, how one could go about assessing its truth or falsity.* For many people, such an attitude is a new and strange one; our educational system often seems to instill an absolutistic view of knowledge (perhaps, after all, it is easier to teach dogmatically than to express all the necessary doubts, qualifications, and hesitations). Often the student wants to know "the truth" and becomes impatient with what he perceives as hedging by the instructor. A research attitude may therefore require a major reorganization in the student's concept of knowledge, a new view which permits uncertainty, vagueness, lack of clarity, and awareness of the relative, tentative character of scientific "truth." Recognition of the fallibility of present knowledge and conceptions is more likely to lead to further insights and progress than is an unquestioning acceptance of what can be found in books and in the minds of instructors and "experts." Cultivating such a research attitude may well be the most significant aspect of a graduate student's training, whether he expects to end up in clinical practice, in full-time research, in industrial consultation, or in an academic setting.

SOME EPISTEMOLOGICAL CONSIDERATIONS

The research attitude, then, includes an attempt to figure out how one can tell whether something is true or not. Most people would probably agree that the best way to check the validity of a statement is to subject it to empirical, scientific examination. Yet scientific examination is based on a series of unprovable assumptions. Espousal of a scientific approach involves accepting these assumptions at least tentatively. Most of them refer to the process of obtaining knowledge, and they form an interrelated system of beliefs about the nature of the world and of the scientific endeavor. A great deal has been written in recent years by and for psychologists about the nature of science. There seems to be a preoccupation, especially in the less well-developed areas of psychology, with "being scientific" and with specifying how one goes about being scientific; psychologists are almost militant in arguing that their discipline is a science. Perhaps this intense concern carries the flavor of protesting too much; if psychologists were more convinced of the scientific nature of their field, they might not have to be so insistent.

Science, we suggest, is one tool, and a powerful one, for producing conviction. There are others, such as intuition, mystical experience, suggestion, and acceptance of authority; but, for most Westerners, science, perhaps because of its superior objectivity and because it seems to work better than other tools, provides the most convincing information. If some scientific evidence becomes relevant to a statement, for most of us this evidence carries considerable weight in helping to decide whether to accept the statement or not. Yet science cannot yield absolute truth or certainty; every scientific "truth" has a probabilistic tag on it.

There is no a priori ground for maintaining that science is better than revelation. Depending on the culture, on a person's basic belief system, one set of epistemological tools may be more or less convincing than another. Nevertheless, we shall accept on faith (for it remains a faith, even though it seems based on reasonable and solid foundations) that science is at least one of the best ways to acquire "knowledge," "explanation," "understanding," or a belief in the truth or falsity of some proposition.

The rituals of scientific method, like those of the witchdoctor or of religions, are, in the last analysis, arbitrary. There are many assumptions one must make in order to play the game according to the rules [see, for example, Brown & Ghiselli's (1955) discussion].

Among the more important is the belief that *induction can provide information*—that one can find out about a vast number of things by looking at only a few of them—a belief that is itself based on many assumptions. Even though inductive knowledge is by nature incomplete, inductive procedure is basic to most (though not all) modern science. A belief that *deductive processes are valid* is another tenet of the scientist's catechism; one aspect of this belief is a faith in logic and mathematical reasoning. Further, science is generally considered to make the deterministic assumption that all events are caused, that *no event is capricious* (but there is currently a great deal of intense philosophical discussion about this issue, with some very capable arguments that this assumption, at least in a simple form, is both inadequate and unnecessary). It also assumes that *events in nature are,* at least to some degree, *orderly* and regular and that the order and regularity of nature can be discovered through the admittedly cumbersome activities of scientific procedure. Further, a *confidence in the dependability of scientific observers* is basic to scientific rituals; this involves reliance on the scientist's perceptual and sensory abilities and also on his memory, for there is always at least some time lapse, however brief, between an observation and the record made of it. Elaborate precautions may be taken in designing research to help justify the faith of others in the validity of a scientist's observations and judgment.

Operational Definition

Finally, the scientist's catechism includes the belief that *you cannot study something scientifically unless you can measure it.* The word "measure" here has a somewhat broader meaning than in common-sense usage. In the most general sense it means that the thing to be studied is perceptually discriminable, capable of being sensed and classified. Though the scientist may deal on a theoretical level with a variety of abstract concepts, such as learning, love, and limens, before he can study them empirically he has to designate some kinds of overt behaviors, stimuli, or events, which are directly observable by himself and others, to represent those concepts. This choice of a discriminable event to stand for an abstract concept is known as "defining the concept operationally."

An operational definition of a concept thus refers to the operations (including any instruments, manipulations, measurements, or recording procedures used in the process of observation) by which the researcher assesses the presence or absence (or magnitude) of the phenomenon denoted by a concept. In our use it is not really a "definition" in the sense of being exactly equivalent to the concept, for a variety of operational definitions might be chosen as indices of a single concept; furthermore, the sum total of all conceivable operations may not exhaust the potential meaning of any given theoretical concept. Yet, for the purpose of a particular study, the researcher chooses a single operational definition, or a limited range of them, and this provides the concrete meaning of the "thing" he is investigating.

Though common sense, logic, and the practices of other investigators provide some guide in choosing operational definitions, to some extent the definition of a concept, both theoretically and operationally, must be arbitrary. In a way, the scientific method might be considered as a tool for constructing telescopes for viewing nature. A particular telescope may be turned in one direction or another, and different telescopes will have different magnifications and different kinds of distortions built into their optical systems. It is unlikely that any single view will provide an even remotely adequate picture of the complex territory that we want to understand. Perhaps by piecing a large number of partial views together and making allowances for certain probable distortions, a rough "map" of the totality can be constructed. Even such an inexact representation may offer better understanding of the territory than no map at all. Of course, this position assumes that there *is* a "real" world "out there" and that the telescopes themselves are not just making it up. But philosophically naïve as such a belief may be, it serves as one reasonably practical way of handling the knotty philosophical problem of the nature of reality, without having to take the trouble to come fully to grips with it.

TYPICAL STAGES IN A RESEARCH PROJECT

Having touched briefly on some of the underlying epistemological problems, let us now consider what usually happens when someone engages in a concrete research project. No project can really be considered "typical"; each has its own peculiarities. Nevertheless, we shall present here a sequence of activities that is probably approximated in a large number of studies, to provide an overview of what is to come in succeeding chapters.

Selecting an Area (see Chapter 2)

The first step is to decide upon an area in which to work. For many novices, this is a very difficult decision—one on which it is hard to give advice, since the choice is inevitably a highly personal one. Often the decision seems to make itself; a beginner may start his work already knowing in which area of psychology he wishes to concentrate. But many students are overwhelmed either by the vagueness of their interests or by the myriad different possibilities for research; they have trouble assessing their allegiances to various fields and choosing that area in which they feel they will be most likely to maintain a deep and continuing interest.

Getting Ideas (see Chapter 2)

A wide gap separates initial interest in an area from specific ideas that can be turned into researchable form. This gap may be increased if the student has fallen into the habit of approaching the subject matter he is studying uncritically, with the intent of acquiring information and being able to reproduce it. Production of potentially workable ideas is perhaps best facilitated by cultivating a research attitude—turning every proposition encountered into a question. Immersion in the area, searching for criticisms or for new ways of viewing what others have done, may yield ideas that can form the basis for empirical investigation.

Using Previous Work (see Chapter 2)

Surveying the literature and becoming acquainted in other ways with what is already known serve to narrow and clarify the researcher's problem. A vague question may be turned into a clear, precise one; or, when the researcher initially has no specific idea other than general interest in an area, the literature may help provide hints which eventually lead to a specific problem. Careful survey of what is already known will avoid wasteful duplication of effort.

Defining the Scope of the Study (see Chapter 3)

As the concrete form of the research design slowly develops, the investigator explores different ways of narrowing down from the broad, perhaps vague, idea to specific questions that can be stated in operational terms. The particular operations he contemplates will limit the scope of the project in different ways; he must consider the conceptual universe in which he is interested and estimate how well the anticipated operations will represent this universe. Choice of particular subjects, variables, conditions, and operations determines the degree to which he can generalize his findings to other subjects, variables, conditions, and operations. The scope of the study, in terms of the generalizability of the findings, is defined by the specific research procedures employed.

Selecting the Research Strategy (see Chapter 4)

Certain problems require precise experimental control and manipulation; others may be more satisfactorily attacked via naturalistic observation or nonexperimental assessment. The over-all strategy should, of course, be chosen to fit best the problem under investigation. Choice of strategy, in turn, affects the details of design and of operations for measuring or manipulating variables.

Developing Measures and Techniques (see Chapters 5 to 8)

While developing the design and procedures, the investigator may jot down, uncritically at first as they occur to him, concrete techniques for measuring or manipulating the variables of interest. This helps him focus on specific variables and suggests alternative ways of manipulating or assessing them. Operational definitions begin to replace vague intuitive concepts; relatively precise hypothetical statements may become possible; the advantages and disadvantages of various designs and operations are clarified. Pilot work is undertaken in this process of narrowing down to specific techniques and of developing a preliminary design, to discover the concrete properties of various operations. The early pilot studies help clarify the feasibility of the study and the potential adequacy of alternative procedures. They also serve to raise in concrete form the problems the researcher must face in developing a final, detailed design proposal. This phase of the research work typically continues for a long time, with many revisions, reformulations, and changes in the instruments to be used in the later, more formal aspect of the project. The pilot stage generally ends with a detailed proposal for the design and conduct of the study and all of its component operations and includes as its last step a "dress rehearsal" or "dry run" of all procedures in their final form.

Obtaining Subjects and Assigning Them to Conditions (see Chapters 9 to 11)

Part of the process of developing the final, formal research proposal involves consideration of the subject population to be represented, how a representative sample of the desired population can be obtained both theoretically and practically, and how specific individual subjects are to be cared for and treated in order to assure their cooperation and in order to satisfy the requirements of the design.

Collecting the Data (see Chapter 12)

When the design is complete and pretested and final preparations have been made, the next phase is data collection. Although the problems up to this point have been chiefly those of concept, design, and apparatus, it is the more routine problems of scheduling, administration, record keeping, and public relations that become central at the time the data are actually obtained.

Analysis and Interpretation (see Chapters 13 and 14)

Then the data are analyzed. This involves both routine computational chores and speculative scrutiny of the data to integrate and interpret them adequately—to try to make sense out of what has been found.

Reporting (see Chapter 14)

The researcher's duties cannot be considered fulfilled until his methods, findings, and interpretations have been made available in an intelligible form to other interested workers. The tasks in this stage involve developing a clear, accurate, concise presentation and, eventually, the clerical job of seeing a report through publication.

Interweaving of the Stages

A linear development, going step by step successively through the phases just discussed, is probably fairly rare in the progress of research projects. A rising spiral might provide a better analogy. The investigator initially gets a hunch which sets him thinking about a problem. Then he obtains some information about what is already known. This usually alters his view of the problem, and he returns to generating somewhat different hunches than he began with. These new conceptions lead to a search of the literature in areas not previously considered relevant; this in turn may yield new hypotheses. While he is trying to develop operations to test his notions, further theoretical issues are likely to arise. The pilot studies, once begun, may suggest other relations and problems which will send the investigator back to the literature or the arm-chair of speculation. The results of the formal study itself are almost never exactly as predicted; this leads to more cogitation, literature search, and measurements. In this way, thinking, looking at the literature, and working with data are inextricably interwoven and succeed one another throughout the development of research and theory on a given problem.

There are, of course, occasional research projects in which the investigator starts with a hypothesis, takes a look at the literature, designs his study and runs it, obtains exactly the results he expected —or at least can interpret them readily—reports his findings; and that's that. But this is probably much less frequent than the slower, backtracking kind of development. Thus the decision whether to go ahead and publish what has been accomplished so far or to do more empirical or theoretical work may be difficult.

People beginning on research careers often misconceive the relative amounts of time consumed in the various activities associated with a study. The actual collection of data, for example, generally constitutes a much smaller portion of the total endeavor than one might think. How much time is spent in doing what, of course, varies with the problem and the investigator. But one must not, if he is to avoid frustration, underestimate the time involved in the initial planning and pilot phases and in the final analysis and reporting. Taken together, these may well take up anywhere from one half to nine tenths or more of the total time spent on a research project.

EFFICIENCY OF THE RESEARCH EFFORT:
THE INFORMATION/COST RATIO

Each of the stages of the research venture costs something. Though the investigator may not be responsible for large sums of money, his own time is valuable. If he spends time reviewing literature that has been adequately summarized already, if he takes several weeks to build a piece of equipment that his department might have purchased for him on short order, if he obtains a lot of unnecessary data, or if he wastes subjects and clerical time in administering a questionnaire that does not measure the right variables, clearly his efforts could more profitably have been spent otherwise. In order to make the best use of his time, and to make a maximal contribution to the over-all scientific effort, it is wise for the researcher to consider the return that each activity in the research process is likely to yield in relation to its cost.

A ratio of information to cost is useful in thinking about the efficiency of the total research project and of each phase within it. Thus the researcher may ask himself: Does the information gained from this activity justify the time, energy, and money expended on it? Will a slightly larger expenditure double the return from the study? Will the increment from another six months' work, from another 100 subjects, from another $5000 expense be so slight that it is not worth the trouble? Much of the material in later chapters about literature review, subject selection, study design, equipment maintenance, statistical analysis, and so forth is intended to help increase the information yield for a given cost or, conversely, to provide the same amount of information at less expense.

Estimating Research Costs

Aside from the energy the scientist devotes to his research (which is both a cost and a profit, considering the satisfactions that most investigators derive from their work), the price of a project can be considered under the overlapping headings of time and money. Studies have a way of costing more and of taking much longer than originally anticipated. Yet at least a crude estimate can usually be made by thinking through the successive phases of the contemplated project as vividly as possible. Even though the estimates are likely to be rough, it is worthwhile to consider the following categories, whenever they are applicable:

Time
Reviewing the relevant literature.
Thinking about the problem and conceptualizing it in research terms.
Designing the study.
Obtaining funds * and space.
Designing and constructing the necessary apparatus, questionnaires, etc., or obtaining them from commercial firms.
Redesigning the study and instruments; rethinking the theoretical meaning of the operations and the likely results.

* The chapter Supplement lists some sources of financial aid.

Selecting subjects and getting access to them.

Performing final pilot work.

Collecting the data.

Collating, coding, summarizing the data; getting them in shape for analysis.

Analyzing the data; pondering over their meanings.

Writing up a report of the project and making it accessible to others.

Money

Library fund—to cover costs of interlibrary loan or for purchase of journals and books.

Costs of equipment, questionnaires, etc., purchased or constructed.

Costs of expendables—e.g., paper, pencils, recording ink, food for animals.

Costs of machines—e.g., typewriters, shop equipment, desk calculators, IBM equipment, purchased or rented.

Costs of repairing any device that can break down.

Costs of analysis forms—e.g., IBM cards.

Costs of secretary, draftsman, in preparing manuscript.

Publishing cost (some journals charge this to the author).

Not every investigation, of course, will require all of these expenses. Some questions yield to very simple and inexpensive procedures; others can be "run on a shoestring," by dint of the investigator's slaving and scrounging and sometimes enlisting his colleagues' or students' free help. Very large projects may involve additional expenses, like research and clerical assistants, funds for consultants and for travel, rent or construction of suitable research space, maintenance, upkeep and janitorial service, etc.

Even in the most fortunately endowed study, one never seems to have enough money, time, or personnel to do all the things that are desirable. Whenever another subject is added to the investigation, the cost is increased well beyond what it takes to collect that extra bit of data. Contact must be made with the subject (or he must be bred and raised); measurements taken on him must be recorded, put in shape for analysis, and tabulated; a small increment is added to every subsequent phase of the research. Every time a new variable is added to the research design, additional instruments, observations, controls, analyses, and interpreting and writing time are likely to be required.

It pays to be realistic about time and money costs. Frequently a researcher must meet a deadline set by himself, his teachers or colleagues, a client, or an agency which has given him a research grant.

If he runs out of either time or money before his research is completed, both present and future projects are likely to suffer.

Estimating Information Yield

It is not easy to predict the costs of research accurately; it is even harder, if not almost impossible, to achieve a satisfactory assessment of the likely information yield, since many value judgments are involved.

However, there are several practical aspects of the research yield which help to define its worth. If the study is conducted to help in making a decision, its value might be judged by the number of alternatives that it helps to decide among. If ten different drugs are purportedly available for relieving certain psychiatric symptoms, a research project that compares all ten, and indicates which is most effective, could be regarded as more informative than one that merely compares the effectiveness of two of the drugs. Next, one might consider the precision of a result as a criterion for judging its value. If one's purpose is to estimate the mean IQ of students in a particular university, the smaller the sampling error of the estimate, the more useful the information. Further, on the practical level, it can be said that the more widely generalizable the research findings, the more valuable they are. Results that apply only to the residents of a single community are generally less valuable than those that apply to an entire species.

Another practical question is whether the proposed research is likely to yield clear-cut information or uninterpretable, useless data. Should the project be pursued at all? One must try, of course, to abandon hopeless cases early, yet at the same time not give up too easily because of difficult but surmountable obstacles.

Once one leaves the practical level and attempts to assess the theoretical import of research information, the criteria become far more vague and value-laden. Some psychologists feel that, other things being equal, studies relevant to a theory of large scope are more valuable than those relevant to a more restricted theory or to no theory at all. Also, it could be argued that the larger the number of meaningful relationships treated in a single investigation, the greater its value. Unfortunately, this argument must employ the word "meaningful," which is difficult to define independently of the investigator's own frame of reference. Another criterion suggests that the value of a study is greater if it yields information about new relationships than if it merely replicates previously known findings.

Considerations like these about information yield may eventually lead to the basic issue of whether the research is worth doing at all. One can question not only the scope or precision of the project but also the importance of the problem with which it deals. This is a challenge almost impossible to meet in an objective fashion. The question "So what?" can be asked of virtually *any* study. There is probably little consensus in the scientific community concerning even a vague, general definition of what is "important." Further, professional consensus itself would not necessarily provide a valid prognosis of the ultimate significance of a problem for future generations. Of course, subjective evaluations will continue to be made—by students, their professors, and the writers of this text—but they had best be interpreted broadly as reflecting the knowledge and prejudices of the evaluator as well as the merit of their target.

Some might wish to argue that the subjectivity of such evaluations can be avoided through the criterion of whether or not the results are publishable. But this does not really solve the problem, since it just changes the locus of the subjective criterion from the researcher himself or his professors or immediate colleagues to the editors of journals. Further, even treating the simplest, most trite problems (however defined), it could be argued that one would have grounds for glee if as many as one fourth of the research ideas he spawns lead to publishable findings. So the research yield—both "important" and "trivial"—from any single investigator is likely to appear disappointingly small in relation to the total effort expended.

Perhaps one can take solace from the oft-heard saying that progress in science is a slow process, with each additional finding adding but a small building block to the edifice of knowledge. Any single study is inevitably restricted in scope, so a variety of approaches to allocating energy among multiple tasks might be encouraged. One researcher may prefer to concentrate his efforts in a single, relatively limited research area, such as the mechanics of hearing, rat discrimination learning, psychopharmacology of tranquilizing drugs, or the measurement of prejudice. This professional strategy is perhaps more likely to produce a "breakthrough" in an area than is a single isolated study. Yet others may feel that endless variations on a single theme reach a point of sterility. They want a change of scene from time to time to freshen their thinking and maintain the pleasure of the research process.

The discussion of the last few paragraphs can perhaps be summarized by the statement that any criterion for assessing information yield from research must be considered only tentative and suggestive. No single one can be used unmodified to evaluate the quality or potential yield of any particular project. And there will be many occasions when one will choose to ignore those offered here in favor of some other consideration, like the sheer enjoyment derived from the process of doing the research, or one's own conviction that this particular project is something he wants to do, whatever anybody else says. The major point we wish to emphasize is that, somewhere along the line, the conscientious researcher will want to call himself to account for what is gained from his efforts. If pleasure is the objective, it might as well be derived inexpensively; if more general benefits are sought and appear likely, then one may wish to consider in advance the standards against which these benefits are to be assessed.

SUMMARY

Science involves a complex set of rituals, which must be learned by the novice before he can perform convincing research. The aim of this book is to provide a step-by-step introduction to some of these rituals, following the course of the typical research project.

There are many reasons for doing research, but even most of the personal ones usually involve a desire for knowledge. Depending on the state of the field in which the investigator wishes to work, a problem-solving, a theory-developing, or a theory-testing orientation may be appropriate; but whatever his strategy, he approaches the subject-matter with a "research attitude"; that is, whenever he encounters a proposition he wonders whether it is true and tries to think of ways in which he could check its truth or falsity. The most widely accepted way to undertake such checks involves a faith (but a critical and flexible faith) in the methods science designates for testing propositions. Science is only one way of obtaining knowledge or establishing conviction, but the communicability, objectivity, and pragmatic validity of its knowledge processes make it a powerful tool for producing conviction about the truth or falsity of empirical propositions.

The history of the typical research project includes the following phases, often concurrently and with frequent backtracking: selecting the area, getting ideas, finding what is known, defining the scope of the study, selecting the over-all strategy and developing methods and techniques, obtaining subjects and assigning them to conditions, running the formal study itself, analysis, interpretation, and reporting. The efficiency of the research endeavor can be enhanced by minimizing time and money cost and by maximizing the information yield, that is, by attempting to achieve as large an information/cost ratio as possible.

Judging the value of any study, proposed or completed, is a difficult, idiosyncratic, subjective matter. Although undoubtedly such evaluations will continue to be made on a wide number of different criteria, we feel it is wise at this stage in the development of psychology to adopt a "live and let live" view of the worth of any research project.

SUPPLEMENT

Sources of Financial Support

The psychologist nowadays can obtain financial help for his research through a wide variety of channels. Several branches of the Federal Government, including the National Institutes of Health of the Public Health Service, the Office of Education, the Air Force Office of Scientific Research, the Office of Naval Research, and the National Science Foundation, offer very substantial contributions to research in the behavioral sciences. Occasionally, large industrial concerns may also be interested in supporting certain kinds of projects. Various private foundations, such as the Ford Foundation, the Carnegie Corporation, the Social Science Research Council, and the Commonwealth Foundation, to name only a few, provide support for research on a wide variety of topics. Usually, however, such institutions prefer to consider requests only for relatively major grants to help with significant, long-term projects.

Information about fund-granting institutions, their fields of specialization, and requirements for application can be obtained through numerous sources. Many universities employ a person whose job it is to be well informed about such matters or who just happens to know about them. Periodically, there are discussions of government support for research in the *American Psychologist* (e.g., Alpert, 1957; Young & Odbert, 1960), and the National Science Foundation from time to time prepares a review on government sponsorship (e.g., National Science Foundation, 1958). Many private foundations prepare periodic reports (e.g., Ford Foundation, John and Mary Markle Foundation, John Simon Guggenheim Memorial Foundation, Social Science Research Council, Viking Fund, and Wenner-Gren Foundation), and various compendia of research foundations have been published (e.g., Rich, 1955). Often reference librarians or financial officers of the researcher's institution may be able to suggest further sources of information, the latter especially about local funds.

Most of the time the investigator must expect to wait quite a while before finding out whether or not he will receive the requested support. Generally a rather full formal research proposal must be submitted, and six months or more may pass before a decision is rendered. Partly for this reason, it is often wise to delay application for such a major grant until one has done more work than is represented by the typical preliminary research proposal. Although there are exceptions, grants of this kind are usually requested only after considerable research in the area has already been performed by the investigator,

Several agencies will consider smaller grants, usually for pilot studies or exploratory work, and the time between application and decision is often reduced in such a case. Among these are Psi Chi (psychology's honorary society), RESA (an affiliate of the national scientific honorary society, Sigma Xi), and the National Institute of Mental Health (which at present writing acts within a period of two months or less on requests for amounts up to $2000).

If the research is conducted within a university setting, the psychology department may have funds for minor financial assistance. These amounts may range anywhere from five or ten dollars up to several hundred, depending upon the university, the promise of the research project, and sometimes the academic status of the investigator. Often such grants are available to graduate and undergraduate students as well as to faculty members. There may also be a university agency whose function it is to allocate a research budget among individual applicants from the entire university staff.

On occasion the researcher can perform his study in an area for which his institution already has financial support. Then it may be possible to receive financial aid through an ongoing grant. This occurs mainly in research agencies and in the larger universities, especially in departments that have affiliated research institutes.

Sometimes, particularly if very small amounts are involved and if the investigator does not wish to go to the trouble of applying for a grant, he may decide to pay for his research needs out of his own pocket. This can save a lot of time and energy, and, though often frowned on in principle, may be the simplest and most efficient solution to a minor financial problem. The danger of such a procedure is that it sets a precedent which might in some situations jeopardize future requests for funds.

REFERENCES

Alpert, H. Social science, social psychology, and the National Science Foundation. *Amer. Psychologist,* 1957, **12,** 95–98.

Brown, C. W., & Ghiselli, E. E. *Scientific method in psychology.* New York: McGraw-Hill, 1955.

Cochran, W. G., & Cox, Gertrude M. *Experimental designs.* (2nd Ed.) New York: Wiley, 1957.

Cox, D. R. *Planning of experiments.* New York: Wiley, 1958.

Edwards, A. L. *Experimental design in psychological research.* (Rev. Ed.) New York: Rinehart, 1960.

Festinger, L., Garner, W. R., Hebb, D. O., Hunt, H. F., Lawrence, D. H., Osgood, C. E., Skinner, B. F., Taylor, D. W., & Wertheimer, M. Education for research in psychology. *Amer. Psychologist,* 1959, **14**, 167–179.

Ford Foundation Annual Report (Annual). Author: 477 Madison Ave., New York 22, New York.

Hebb, D. O. Alice in wonderland, or psychology among the biological sciences. In H. F. Harlow & C. N. Woolsey (Eds.), *Biological and biochemical bases of behavior.* Madison, Wisc.: Univer. Wisconsin Press, 1958.

Helson, H. Adaptation level theory. In S. Koch (Ed.), *Psychology: a study of a science.* Study I, Vol. I. New York: McGraw-Hill, 1959.

John and Mary R. Markle Foundation Annual Report (Annual). Author: 511 Fifth Ave., New York 17, New York.

John Simon Guggenheim Memorial Foundation Report (Annual). Author: 551 Fifth Ave., New York 17, New York.

Lindquist, E. F. *Design and analysis of experiments in psychology and education.* Boston: Houghton Mifflin, 1953.

National Science Foundation. *Federal funds for science: VI. The federal research and development budget, fiscal years 1956, 1957, and 1958. (A report of the National Science Foundation.)* Washington, D. C.: Government Printing Office, 1958.

Rich, W. S. *American foundations and their fields.* (7th Ed.) New York: American Foundations Information Service, 860 Broadway, New York 3, New York, 1955.

Social Science Research Council Annual Report (Annual). Author: 230 Park Ave., New York 17, New York.

Stevens, S. S. On the psychophysical law. *Psychol. Rev.,* 1957, **64**, 153–181.

Underwood, B. J. *Psychological research.* New York: Appleton-Century-Crofts, 1957.

Viking Fund Annual Report (Annual). Author: 14 East 71st St., New York 21, New York.

Wenner-Gren Foundation for Anthropological Research, Inc. Annual Report (Annual). Author: 14 East 71st St., New York 21, New York.

Young, Marguerite L., & Odbert, H. S. Government support of psychological research: fiscal year 1959. *Amer. Psychologist,* 1960, **15**, 661–664.

CHAPTER 2

Initial stages in a research project

There are so many different areas in psychology in which research can be performed that the beginning researcher often has a difficult time choosing among them. Reviewing his knowledge of psychology may help: "What do I want to know more about?" "Which topics fascinate me most?" "Which area do I want to be identified with in the long run?" Wherever the interest comes from—reading, a course, or a personal experience—if the student can find a field in which he is deeply and personally interested, his motivation is more likely to be maintained throughout the necessarily routine, and often frustrating, phases of research and he is more likely to derive the satisfactions the work can provide. The initial selection of an area, moreover, should not be taken lightly. One project tends to lead to another, so a line of inquiry "temporarily" set aside may never be returned to.

STARTING IN AN AREA AND GETTING IDEAS

To develop new ideas about a problem, it helps one not only to be interested in it but to be so engaged in the area that it, in effect, engages him. Familiarity with a field can be achieved by talking with others, reading widely, rethinking old ideas, and trying to summarize earlier findings in a few statements; if some relevant data or informal observations are accessible, exploring these sources may also help. Generally, the investigator's interest increases with immersion, and this makes the process of gaining familiarity with the area proceed quickly and painlessly. As familiarity is gained, the number of potentially researchable ideas may increase rapidly.

Becoming fully familiar with a field does not, of course, carry with it a guarantee that one is going to emerge with all kinds of research insights. Maintaining a research attitude helps, as does being explicitly on the lookout for new ideas. When one is reading, he may find himself getting vague hunches about new relationships, about difficulties in studies he is reading, or about alternative ways of interpreting findings. Such notions are often only on the fringe of consciousness and easily get lost if they are not followed up. Chances are that the typical graduate student, often without realizing it, generates a number of research ideas each day while reading for his courses. Almost all of these are likely to fade away, however, if he does not get around to writing them down; he may not at first even recognize the potential researchability of many of the fleeting undeveloped, preliminary notions that pass through his mind while he is reading.

In trying to understand where ideas which result in "scientific progress" come from, one might think that they arise through strict logical deduction from principles already known or postulated. This undoubtedly occurs sometimes, particularly in the final stages of theory testing. Mostly, though, new research ideas seem to come less from formal deduction than from some kind of intuitive process. The idea springs as something new into the mind of the investigator. Whether we call it illumination, a mystical insight, a divine inspiration, or rumblings from the unconscious—or try to find a more scientific sounding term for it—some such element seems necessary for the production of new thought.

The initial idea need be neither quantitative, nor operational, nor even researchable. Eventually the scientist must produce a formulation that can be attacked empirically; but this process can occur later. You cannot make an idea workable unless you have the idea first.

In the present stage of our knowledge about creative thought it is impossible to do more than speculate about the conditions that help to produce worthwhile ideas. Traditionally (e.g., Wallas, 1926), the problem-solving thought processes have been broken down into four successive stages; these stages may also be applicable to the problem of *finding* a problem. Trying to formulate a researchable question is a problem-solving endeavor much like trying to find the solution to an already existing puzzle. The first stage, *preparation,* involves immersion in the subject matter, becoming thoroughly familiar with the issues and facts, studying the ideas of others through their writings or through their talk, exploring data, trying out hunches—wild as they may seem—and being passionately committed to the problem area. The next phase, *incubation,* occurs, as it were, in the less conscious portions of the psyche; while the researcher is doing something totally unrelated to his research problem, the unconscious machinery of his mind is said to work with the material fed it during the preparation periods, sifting, sorting, analyzing, comparing. At some indeterminate time, the researcher may become aware of a solution, which creeps gradually or jumps suddenly into consciousness; this stage, *illumination,* signals the birth of the insight, tentative solution, or "creative idea." The final stage, *verification,* involves examining the idea from all sides to see whether it really is a solution, whether the new formulation actually is researchable.

This scheme is undoubtedly oversimplified. An orderly sequence from preparation through incubation and illumination to verification is probably the exception rather than the rule. Whether it is a matter of trying to find a problem to solve or trying to solve an already formulated problem, creative thought seems to be more a backtracking than a straight-line affair. Illumination may lead to more preparation in a different area, incubation may be required before a suitable way to verify an "insight" is found, and the result of a verifying process may well lead to further preparation and incubation. All of the stages tend to interweave in the history of a creative thought sequence.

Preparation and verification are activities in which the thinker can engage voluntarily, but incubation and illumination do not seem to be under conscious control. Some generally accepted rules of thumb have been formulated which may facilitate illumination (Gruber et al., 1962); they are based largely on arm-chair speculation, but even though most of them have not yet been tested empirically they may still prove helpful. An active looking for insights may make the potential idea scurry into hiding; one might try to maintain an unhurried frame of mind which is receptive to new notions but which is not too graspingly searching. This requires an ability to defer solution whenever an impasse is reached, while maintaining an immediacy of interest bordering on obsession. One must try to be committed to the area yet capable of objective detachment.

Sometimes the subject matter itself seems to point in certain directions; the researcher must permit himself to be guided by the requirements of the problem (cf. Wertheimer, 1959). At the same time that he lets the problem lead him by the hand, he should also be free enough not to be blinded by an immediate set toward the area; an ability to overcome current, accepted ways of looking at the issues may yield a radically new, potentially useful frame of reference.

Finally, the scientist should be free to learn from his mistakes. After following a particular line of inquiry and exploration, he may come to a dead end. Rather than being discouraged because no illumination occurs or because verification shows that the idea, which initially seemed so brilliant, is merely inadequate, the thinker can take advantage of his unhappy discovery. One useful device is to turn one's attention to seeking the link that led to failure: What false assumptions may have been made? What set uncritically adopted? What aspects intentionally or unintentionally ignored as unimportant?

The Research Diary

For making notes about such cogitations, and for many other purposes as well, a worthwhile practice is keeping a "research diary," in which the investigator can record his thoughts about the problem, including the various hypotheses he forms and the operations that occur to him for assessing and manipulating the variables. He can well permit himself to speculate rather freely and uncritically at certain points in this diary and return to re-examine the speculations with a critical eye later on. A whole notebook can profitably be devoted to any particular research project; if one gets in the habit of scribbling things in it—anything relevant to the research—he may be surprised to find how useful such a record can be. The diary is also likely to be valuable in later phases of the project—in making notes on literature and trying out ways to summarize it, preserving thoughts that could be used for improving operations, recording irregularities in procedure during data collection, and so forth.

MAKING USE OF PREVIOUS WORK

Sometimes the surest way to encourage development of a research idea is to look into the work others have performed. Too often the researcher is so enamored of his own inspiration that collecting original data forthwith seems the only appropriate way to consummate the affair. Yet it remains highly probable that if one psychologist has an idea today then somebody else had it yesterday. And it is likely that the fruits of previous encounters will have been recorded in the professional literature. Even if a study identical with the one the researcher has in mind has never been done, it will undoubtedly pay him to become acquainted with closely or even distantly related materials, since these often provide clues which will help to clarify his own thinking. Review of relevant literature may serve at least two functions: to avoid unnecessary work on worn-out problems and to make progress toward the solution of new ones. Even a successful investigator who knows only his own research is likely to be so out of step with his time that his contribution will be ignored.

Developing a Bibliography

Once a few beginning leads have been found in the literature, a bibliography in any area generally grows rapidly with little effort. The initial leads can be obtained by talking or writing to other people and by looking in secondary sources such as textbooks and the *Annual Review of Psychology*. The *Annual Review* includes chapters that summarize the research of the preceding year or two in most of the major areas in psychology. Certain topics may appear as chapters only every two or three years, but by looking at the last few volumes one can generally get a foothold in the literature which has the advantage of recency. Usually the more recent the first references, the easier the task, since the later ones frequently cite previous work.

Another major source of bibliographic information is the *Psychological Bulletin*, which publishes reviews of literature in various areas; with luck, one may be able to find a recent summary of the area in which he is interested. The relatively complete lists of references available in these articles greatly reduce the effort required of the next investigator.

By far the most useful tool for obtaining bibliographic information about psychological problems is *Psychological Abstracts*. Since 1927 the American Psychological Association has published, monthly (recently bimonthly), brief abstracts of books and papers of psychological interest from the world's journals. Coverage in *Psychological Abstracts* is almost complete for American journals and very thorough for other journals written in English; a sizable proportion of the foreign language literature is also included. The abstracts are numbered successively throughout any year, and in each issue the entries are topical and alphabetical, so that if one is interested in vision, for example, he will find all of the references relevant to that topic listed alphabetically by author in one place in the issue. Almost every listing consists of a full bibliographic entry, followed by a brief paragraph describing the contents of the entry. The abstract will generally make it possible to judge the importance of the paper for a problem; if it appears relevant, one can then go to the original publication.

A useful feature of *Psychological Abstracts* is the full index, published in December of every year. The *author index* is not generally so helpful in developing a research bibliography as the subject index; however, if one knows that a particular investigator has published research in an area, he can often find relevant papers by looking up the abstracts which are listed by number next to the author's name. The *subject index* contains a very large number of topics with their subdivisions; next to each indexed entry are one or more numbers of abstracts related to that subject. If subject headings are chosen judiciously, the numbers of appropriate abstracts can be found quite rapidly. Before entering the abstracts, one should consider which subject index terms might include relevant material. It is better to have too many than too few; one can always prune down by checking how appropriate the abstracts listed under a given entry are to his interests. Skill in using the *Psychological Abstracts* is to a large extent a matter of learning which subject index headings to sample.

To make the process of obtaining literature and bibliographic materials as painless as possible, one must, of course, be thoroughly acquainted with the routines of the library to which he has access. He should know where various kinds of collections are housed, how to go about making a request for interlibrary loan of journals and books not locally available, and which members of the library staff are likely to be helpful in routine matters such as taking out books or journals, using interlibrary loan, and getting access to microfilm readers, as well as in suggesting additional sources of relevant material. A few hours spent poking around a new library will pay off by greatly facilitating its use later.

Obtaining Recent Material

Textbooks, the *Annual Review, Psychological Bulletin* articles, reference lists at the ends of papers, and *Psychological Abstracts* are all useful for assembling a bibliography but are usually inadequate as sources for very recent material. Lags of a few months to two or even three years intervene between submission of a paper and its publication. Further, there is a considerable delay between the appearance of an article in print and its inclusion in *Psychological Abstracts* and an even longer one before the work is cited in a secondary reference. Thus the sources listed above may provide full bibliographic information only up to some three or four years before the current date. Other avenues must therefore be used to find out about recent research.

Sometimes a colleague or professor will be able to provide information about recent papers which have not yet been referred to in secondary sources or in *Psychological Abstracts;* he may also have some knowledge of unpublished materials and be able to furnish names of investigators currently engaged in the field. It is by no means presumptuous for the student to write or talk to researchers active in the area in which he wants to work and to ask them for reprints of their papers. Sometimes they may also be willing to provide some information about their current thoughts and research in progress.

Search of recent journal issues will often uncover up-to-date material which has not yet been abstracted or reviewed. But in order to peruse the recent literature efficiently, one must be acquainted with the typical contents of the journals that publish psychological material. First-hand familiarity with their coverage is, of course, best; Supplement A to this chapter presents brief descriptions of some of the more important journals.

Occasionally access may be gained to lists of current research grants made by major agencies; if a relevant title is found, one can write to the principal investigator for information.

Among the better sources for recent and ongoing research are psychological association meetings, one of the chief aims of which is to facilitate just this kind of interchange. Not only national, but also regional, state, and sometimes local conventions can help. The research papers or symposia may include material relevant to the potential worker's interest; he can also make personal contact for informal or formal discussions with researchers active in his area of interest. The July or August issue of *The American Psychologist* presents the detailed program, with abstracts, of the fall meeting of the American Psychological Association; a page near the end of each issue of that journal provides a calendar of national, international, and regional meetings, with dates, locations, and whom to write to for information. Programs of regional meetings (without abstracts) are printed in *The American Psychologist*, usually in the September issue. Copies of papers, or information about them, can often be obtained by writing direct to the author; some papers are available from agencies such as the Convention Reports Duplication Service, 1201 Worton Boulevard, Cleveland 24, Ohio.

Keeping Records While Obtaining Material

Compulsiveness in keeping notes while preparing a list of references saves time and frustration later. A widely used and effective technique is to make a file of small cards, one card for each article, book, or other entry. The full bibliographic reference should be written out (even though this may take a little time), so that it will not be necessary later to go back to the original source to fill in an omitted name, initial, page number, or title.

It is useful to learn early certain conventions in bibliography and to employ these standard forms in every single paper written, whether or not it is for publication. The details of these bibliographic practices are presented in full in the American Psychological Association's *Publication Manual* (1957); chapter Supplement B summarizes a few of them. Some of the other references at the end of this chapter (e.g., Alexander & Burke, 1958; Daniel & Louttit, 1953; Good & Scates, 1954; Latham, 1954; Louttit, 1932; Murphey, 1958) also provide a wealth of material on bibliographic techniques and sources.

Writing the Literature Summary

It is a good idea, while the references are being gathered, to develop and use a classification scheme so that right from the beginning references that logically belong together can be placed in the same category. This facilitates the process of integrating the information as it is obtained. Often there is a much larger amount of relevant material than was first anticipated, and unless one uses some system of classification he is likely to get lost in the sheer quantity of individual pieces of information.

Such a system is also very useful once the stage of writing the literature summary is reached. In the first phases of a search of the literature, new references are usually found at such a rapid rate that it is difficult to assimilate them, but as the search continues it will be discovered that many of the "new" references located are already in the list. The payoff, in terms of new material found per unit time spent in searching the literature, begins to diminish. Eventually a point is reached at which it is worthwhile to stop and take stock, to see what has been learned. Perhaps the best way to obtain perspective and an overview of the field is to write down the main findings in the form of a preliminary version of the literature summary. Very often, in an attempt to integrate what has been found by actually writing it down, the researcher may develop ideas about other matters to look into and achieve insights which will lead to research hypotheses.

New leads are especially likely to occur as discrepancies or disagreements become apparent in the literature. As one tries to summarize or integrate a series of studies, he may discover that they simply will not integrate—that some findings seem flatly to contradict others. Careful analysis of such inconsistencies may yield hunches about the reasons for the discrepancy, and often these hunches can form the basis for incisive progress. It is probably much more rewarding to the researcher and to the field if, in the face of contradictory findings, he sits down and really tries to come to grips with the reason for this state of affairs rather than merely adding one more study which, at best, tips the scales a couple of ounces in one direction or the other. The same goes for inconsistencies within one's own data, when he gets around to analyzing them, and for discrepancies between these data and those of others. An exception to a principle can be a more valuable finding than a corroboration because such an exception may provide clues to a more basic understanding, to a better principle. It is probably harder, but more significant, to pull together disparate or conflicting findings than to formulate and test routinely some straightforwardly deduced hypothesis.

The literature summary, then, should include integrated general statements, each statement containing as much information as possible. If one finds, say, five studies on a particular subtopic in the area, he might try to formulate a single sentence which will summarize them all. In this way, the major results in a given field can be surveyed in no more than three or four pages. The more condensed and brief the summary, the more perspective it provides and the more apparent the inconsistencies become. The form of articles in the *Psychological Bulletin* provides a useful model for the kind of précis to aim at.

When to Stop Reviewing

Although it is highly desirable to have available a complete bibliography and a thoroughly integrated, written summary of the entire literature, one should beware of overdoing the activities associated with this phase of the research endeavor. Pedantry for its own sake has little value. Of course, here, as elsewhere, researchers differ—and rightly so—in their styles; some give the literature at best a very quick, cursory overview, whereas others consider a thorough review of the field an end in itself, quite aside from its function in their more empirical research efforts. Compulsive summarizers serve a very useful function for the science as a whole, but not everyone needs to do this job as part of his own work. To mention but one reason against excessive attention to previous work, it is likely that any fresh approach the newcomer may have will be rechanneled into the more traditional ways of working in the area if he is too conscientious in cultivating his acquaintance with the literature. Certainly delving into literature can provide a useful way to develop research ideas, but one should not lose sight of the principle that such a search should remain a tool, like a knowledge of statistics, skill in electronics, or fluency in a foreign language. Tools are often indispensable, but the master should use the tool as he sees fit and not become its slave. It is all too easy to get sidetracked.

FORMULATING THE PROBLEM

There are degrees of refinement of knowledge. Generally the investigator tries to design his study to arrive at conclusions that are maximally informative. For some investigations this maximum may be a quantitative functional relation (such as $Y = 3X^2 + 14.73$), whereas for others it may be a correlation coefficient or only a statement that there is some relation between two variables beyond chance expectation. One should, of course, try to reach conclusions that are as refined as possible, but many researchers feel that in the present state of knowledge in psychology a crude, perhaps even somewhat faulty, conclusion may be better than none at all. It may also be more appropriate than an overly precise statement about variables which are themselves still fairly nebulous.

The job of turning the rather vague initial idea into a form that is amenable to reasonably refined empirical scrutiny is usually a time-consuming, frustrating task. This process constitutes the core of creative research. In the remainder of this chapter—and in most of the chapters to come—we consider some of the problems encountered in going from the first vague ideas to a more precise statement of what is to be done, why and how to do it, and the expected outcome.

The Necessity of Narrowing Down

While obtaining information from the literature and from colleagues, one may be tempted to make global speculations and to try in one fell swoop to solve all the major problems in the area. However, the beginner generally finds it almost impossible to design a study that will yield as much information as he initially intends; some restriction of focus is inevitable. The first reaction to this narrowing-down process is often a feeling that the significance of the study is lost, that the research becomes dull, pedestrian, too restricted, not worthwhile. Frustrating as it may be to the budding investigator, however, only rarely can a major portion of a given field be adequately treated in a single study. Skill in research is to a large extent a matter of judicious choice about what to study; deciding which of a series of possible ideas to pursue, or what aspect of a problem to focus on, may be an even more difficult problem than getting ideas in the first place.

It is thus worth keeping in mind that whatever the design of the eventual study it is aimed at accomplishing one particular class of objectives rather than some other. Only rarely, if ever, can a researcher find himself in the happy position of satisfying all possible aims by a given research design. Typically, some desirable objective must be sacrificed to further another, and this inevitably has the effect of restricting the study's implications to a narrower scope than might have been hoped initially. The significance of a research project is, in a sense, limited by its operational definitions, and since every step in the research design constitutes an operationalization of some idea lying behind the research the very process of choosing steps to acquire knowledge serves to limit the significance of that knowledge.

Let us illustrate with an investigator interested in the apparent speed of passage of time. At first he may wish to solve "the problem" of subjective time, but once he begins thinking about the area and reading in it he will soon realize how broad the problem actually is and how unlikely it is that any particular study would do more than add a modest increment to the information already available. As soon as he starts to become concrete, he finds it necessary to decrease the scope of his plan. As a first step he might decide to focus on the effect of abnormal conditions on subjective estimates of time. Even here the problem is far too broad, since there are many possible approaches to specifying "abnormal conditions"—such as administering drugs, assessing natural differences in metabolism, or using various groups of psychopathological subjects. He must narrow down further before he can perform an actual empirical study.

Suppose he chooses to study differences between schizophrenics and normals in the perception of time. By now he has sufficiently specified his independent variable, "abnormality," so that the focus of study is fairly clear. But the detailed operational definitions of "schizophrenic" and "normal" may still present knotty problems; it is in this stage of formulating concrete operational definitions that the final narrowing down occurs. How is one to measure schizophrenia? By test results? Psychiatric impression? A word on a hospital record? Will this include acute or chronic schizophrenics or a mixture of both? Will the study be limited to paranoids, to catatonics, or to hebephrenics, or will an attempt be made to obtain a representative sampling across all of the major subtypes of schizophrenics? Should they all come from a single hospital, or is a broader sampling of the schizophrenic population to be attempted? Must the sample of subjects be restricted to those patients who are not too deteriorated to cooperate in an experiment requiring complex verbal responses? Will they be males only or of both sexes? Is there to be some age limitation on the subjects?

The dependent variable in this study also needs further specification. How is "time perception" to be measured in the two groups? There are many different techniques that could be used, each with its advantages and disadvantages but each providing a narrower focus than "time perception" in general. One might, for example, ask the subject to hold a stop watch with its face away from him and to press the button on it once, then again when he thinks 30 seconds have passed, while the experimenter records the actual elapsed time shown on the watch. The researcher may present a 30-second interval to the subject and ask him to judge how long it is in seconds; or he may present the interval and ask the subject to reproduce it later. Times other than 30 seconds might be used; should there be one standard time or several? If so, which ones? Just what apparatus will be used? What, specifically, will be the responses required of the subjects? Before the problem is truly in researchable form, decisions of this kind must be made, and each specification reduces the scope, or generality, of the study.

Relations among Theory, Hypothesis, and Operational Hypothesis

The researcher may find some consolation in the thought that a narrow study on apparently trivial variables may acquire a far-reaching stature through its interrelation with other studies or through its consequences for some theory. This is probably why many people prefer research with clear theoretical implications. The process of turning a question, hunch, or theory into a specific research project inevitably involves narrowing down, but there is no reason why the specification should not be guided with an eye to eventual broad interpretation.

If the study is designed to test a formal, theoretical hypothesis, it is well to be as explicit as possible about the steps involved in going from the theory to the actual empirical operations. These steps and the possible deficiencies in them frequently provide the major point of attack when a critic tries to reconcile the results of a "crucial" study with the presumably disproven theory. Two main questions can be asked of any study purporting to test a theory: Does the hypothesis really follow from the theory? and Do the empirical manipulations actually provide an adequate test of the hypothesis?

If logical gaps intervene between theory and hypothesis and if the data do not support the hypothesis, the theoretical model from which it was presumably deduced would not necessarily be invalidated; or, conversely, the hypothesis may be supported, but if it was not rigorously deduced from the theory, one may not be able to say that the results strengthen the tenability of the theory itself.

Equally as critical as the derivation from theory to hypothesis is the translation of the hypothesis into empirical operations. It is here that experience and imagination become essential to the successful researcher. Although narrowing from theory to hypothesis can sometimes be a fairly logical, straightforward process, narrowing from theoretical hypothesis to operational hypothesis is largely—though by no means exclusively—an intuitive matter. Wide knowledge of available operations and an ability to invent new ones are the major skills required here.

The critical issue in assessing the adequacy of an operation is its validity: Do the operations really yield the desired information? How adequate is the "fit" between the concept and the measure of it? In devising the operational form of a hypothesis, the aim is to make the measures as objective and replicable as possible, as reliable as possible, without sacrificing their fit with the concepts they are intended to represent.

An illustration of poor fit is afforded by the following story, which appeared in TIME magazine: *

> The research director of a major agency was ordered to prepare a study about fleas. He put a flea on his desk and trained it to jump over his finger at his command. Then he pulled out two of the flea's six legs. "Jump," he ordered, and the flea still jumped. Two more legs came off. Again the flea jumped. Finally, he pulled off the last two. "Jump," he commanded. The flea did not move. With that, the research director wrote his report: "When a flea loses all six legs, it becomes deaf."

* November 25, 1957, p. 112; courtesy TIME; copyright Time Inc., 1961.

The obvious defect of this experiment is that the operational definition of "hearing" or "deafness" involves a response that is directly affected by the experimental manipulation. Thus the independent and dependent variables are hopelessly contaminated, and the results cannot help but confirm the expected relation between them. Although the inappropriateness of the operational definitions is readily apparent in this illustration, many less obvious examples could be found.

Suppose one wished to determine whether schizophrenics are more likely than other mental patients to have come from home environments where they received little love and attention as children. All too often such a problem is investigated by interviewing the patients about their early home environments; if the schizophrenics report less love, the hypothesis is considered supported. Yet clearly this test of the hypothesis is inappropriate, since it is the patients' present recollections of past events rather than observations of the events themselves that provide the operational definition of the independent variable. In this instance a longitudinal hypothesis has been translated into a cross-sectional operation to test it, with the consequence that the results of the study do not necessarily bear on the problem that impelled it.

Range of the Variables Represented

Narrowing down to operational definitions always involves decisions about which particular values of the variables are to be studied. If one suspects that Y is linearly related to X, and the operational definitions make it possible to manipulate or select along variable X, should one use two groups—one very low and one very high on X? Or would it be better to "take X as it comes," making Y measurements at whatever levels of X one happens to find? Should one sample extreme values or aim at representative sampling of X?

Consider a researcher interested in the relation between age and muscular strength in a certain psychomotor task. How should he go about selecting subjects? He might select on the basis of strength and then measure age; alternatively, he could use age as the "independent variable" and then systematically assess psychomotor strength. Should he use two extreme groups, perhaps one between 5 and 10 years of age and another between 75 and 95? Or should he select some other set of restricted ages? Should he try to *represent* the age distribution in the population to which he wishes to generalize, using, say, a stratified sample of ages?

Any of the methods of selecting subjects affects the way in which the variable, age, is operationally defined. It is necessary to keep in mind this operational definition when generalizing results from the study. If one found no difference in the strength of juveniles and octogenarians, this would not justify the conclusion that age and strength are uncorrelated, except in the very restricted definition of the age variable provided in such a study.

The argument for an extreme-groups strategy in psychological research is based on the notion that if X and Y are actually related then a wide or well-chosen difference in X should be more likely to produce a large measured difference in Y, hence making the relation of Y to X more "visible" than if a smaller or an ill-chosen difference were used. One is more likely to pick up the fact that metal expands as temperature increases if the length of a steel bar is measured under extreme temperature conditions (say $-250°$ F and $+800°$ F)— than if a smaller temperature difference (say $60°$ F and $65°$ F) is used. By analogy, then, if only a limited number of subjects or measures can be obtained, a difference in Y is most likely to be generated if a selection of subjects is made at a wide interval on X or if extreme conditions of the X variable are experimentally created.

The weakness of the argument is that it depends on a particular assumed form of the X–Y-relationship. If it happens to be curvilinear rather than linear, the extreme groups may not differ on the dependent variable, yet both of them may differ from a middle group. Prolonged breathing of 0% oxygen and 100% oxygen are both associated with relatively poor performance on virtually any task; children who are given excessive attention tend to become maladjusted, but so do children who are neglected. If information about middle groups is not available, the investigator cannot tell whether he obtains no difference between the two extreme groups because there really is no relation between X and Y or because the relation between them is nonlinear. Conversely, in the event that a difference *is* obtained, no inferences can be drawn concerning the shape of the relationship between the two variables—only that some relation exists. The same difference could be generated by an infinite variety of functions (see Fig. 2-1 for some reasonable and some fanciful functions which would be equally consistent with a given obtained difference).

This is only one particular example which shows how the form of a relationship may be obscured, distorted, or made inaccessible by an inopportune selection of a restricted range of the variables. Although each form of relationship may have its own peculiar areas of "sensitivity" or "insensitivity" to distortion, the general point remains: the ranges at which a variable is sampled or manipulated may affect the

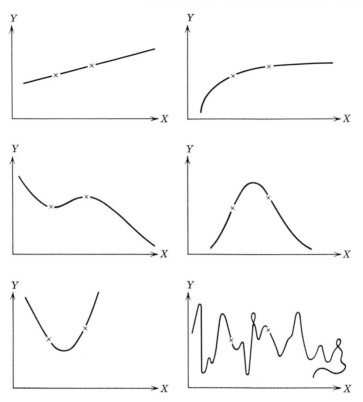

Fig. 2-1. Examples of functions equally consistent with a pair of empirically obtained points.

kind of relationship that is permitted to emerge. If one predicts, or wishes to explore the relation between X and Y throughout the entire available range of both, then representative sampling of these ranges would appear to be called for. If, on the other hand, one is really interested only in comparing certain selected values (perhaps extreme values) of a variable, then sampling at only those points is indicated. However, in this case the restricted operational definition of the variable should be kept in mind when any obtained relationship is interpreted.

PILOT STUDIES

While hunting for operational definitions of variables and while endeavoring to operationalize hypotheses, it can be very useful to try out various alternatives by working with some actual measures on a few subjects. Such crude try-outs may show inadequacies of the approach or may point to the kinds of things that need further work before definitions can be finally selected.

In addition to helping develop and refine operational definitions, the early pilot studies can serve a number of other functions. While searching for definitions, the researcher is often still somewhat undecided about the feasibility of the study and the likelihood that it will yield the information he wants. Early pilot attempts may give some indication whether the expected relationship will emerge and, perhaps more significantly, whether meaningful results of any kind are likely to be obtained with the anticipated measures. Quite aside from the function of forcing the investigator to face his hypothesis directly by turning his hunch into testable form, pilot work can point to new and crucial variables which were not even considered initially. Finally, in preparing to perform a preliminary test, one may find that his ideas are not yet clear enough to permit him to do so; it may show the need for further concrete thinking about the way a hunch can be operationalized.

THE PRELIMINARY RESEARCH PROPOSAL

At some time, either after crude preliminary studies have been attempted or while they are being conducted, the investigator should begin to consider writing out in detail just how he proposes to do the research. In the early stages the write-up will inevitably be only preparatory, since the design is likely to take specific shape rather slowly and to be greatly modified by further pilot studies and thought. Yet early attention to what will eventually be a polished, formal research proposal helps force the investigator to set his ideas down in concrete terms, in a form that he can criticize himself and that he can show to other people for criticism. The usefulness of writing out a detailed preliminary research proposal can hardly be overemphasized. Quite often one may feel that he is ready to run subjects, that his concepts, operations, and techniques are so clear that he need not go to the trouble of writing a proposal. But most of the time glaring gaps and errors will be found in a research program when an attempt is made to write out detailed plans for it. Thus a crude preliminary research proposal may help the investigator to avoid serious problems further on; it may also prevent his discovering several months too late that he has been wasting his time on a problem that is not, in its present form, really researchable.

A final research proposal generally cannot be written until much later, just before data collection is about to begin, but a preliminary proposal can at least aim at something approximating the final one. Thus, typically, even the preliminary proposal includes a brief discussion of the area in which the research is to be performed, a statement of the problem, specification of the method and techniques, description of the types of analysis to be undertaken, and a discussion of the anticipated results. The more detailed the proposal, the more useful is it likely to be. If the writing has been done conscientiously, it may be possible to use large parts of it—discussion of area, problem, research method, and techniques of analysis—as preliminary drafts of portions of the final proposal or even of the completed research report itself. Since writing is such a difficult and prolonged matter for most of us, the earlier in the project one begins on the task, the more time he is likely to save at the end.

A useful outline is one like the following:

Introduction

A brief discussion of the area in which the research falls can serve as an introduction to the proposal. It may well be accompanied by a condensed version of the main findings of the literature survey, if this is already far enough along.

Statement of the Problem

This section starts from the generalizations made in the introduction and narrows down to the particular problem with which the study is concerned. If appropriate, the theoretical assumptions are stated and the conceptual hypotheses derived from them. Generally, the researcher will try to end the section with a rather formal statement of the specific hypotheses to be tested.

Procedure

Method and technique probably should be discussed in that order; that is, the major strategy for attacking the problem is first described in broad terms, followed by a detailed presentation of techniques, with full specification of all operations. In the preliminary forms of the research proposal one can often be more detailed about techniques— and reasons for them—than in the final report. (Space limitations in journals usually make it impossible to give a description of the techniques as complete as one may wish.) Every little step taken in the study, including a verbatim record of instructions to subjects, the particular sequence and techniques of the measures, and details of apparatus construction, should be considered. Much later, in the final formal draft of the proposal, this portion is rewritten so that ideally someone who knows nothing about the study could carry it out exactly as the writer intends.

At the earlier stages, though, it may prove useful to try to justify every step of the technique. By forcing himself to account in writing for each portion of the procedure, the researcher will often find that various parts he had considered adequate can actually be performed much more efficiently or elegantly. He may also discover unnecessary steps or superfluities in the design.

Analysis

The anticipated methods of data analysis can profitably be thought through early. This step includes the possible procedures for coding or combining measures, the descriptive statistics which might be computed, and consideration of the advantages and disadvantages of various significance tests. The appropriateness of the statistics to the measures must be considered here.

Discussion of Anticipated Results

In the final part of the preliminary proposal, the investigator might well consider in turn each of the possible outcomes of his study—what they might be and how they could be interpreted. This may keep him from being taken aback, later on, by results different from those predicted.

For example, if a positive correlation between two measures is predicted and he happens to obtain a negative one, how might such a finding be interpreted? If neither a positive nor a negative correlation is obtained but either no relation or a curvilinear one emerged, how could these be accounted for? Such preliminary thinking not only helps avoid embarrassments later in the project but may also yield new insights into the problem which lead to further improvements in the way it is attacked.

SUMMARY

Ideas for research come partly by concentrated, assiduous searching and partly by fairly aimless reflection and rumination. Immersion in a problem area, which is achieved by reading, thinking, and talking about it, is likely to aid both the purposeful and accidental aspects of the idea-seeking phase.

Information about previous work can be obtained from reading and by talking or corresponding with other people doing research in the area. A literature summary based on a thorough examination of what is available can provide a useful overview of what is known to date. The references for such a purpose can be found by perusing *Psychological Abstracts*, the *Annual Review of Psychology*, and recent issues of journals in which material relevant to the topic is likely to appear. A uniform, efficient system for recording and filing bibliographic information will avoid confusion as the reference list grows and as the literature summary is written.

Formulating the problem in researchable form means going from a crude, vague conception to a more precise, refined design. Refinement of the proposed research involves narrowing down the problem to a scope that can be handled in an empirical study, specifying in detail how each variable is to be measured and how the study is to be run. Concepts must be restated in operational terms before they can be measured and manipulated. But the very nature of the operations chosen necessarily restricts the generalizability of the results or the meaning that can be attached to them.

The research proposal constitutes the final specification of the problem and how it is to be investigated. Early pilot studies are generally of value in arriving at this specification. The final proposal should include an introduction which sets the study in the perspective of earlier work, a statement of the problem (accompanied by specific hypotheses if appropriate), a description of the method, techniques, and proposed analyses, and a discussion of the possible outcomes and their interpretations.

SUPPLEMENT

A. The Psychological Journals

Twelve journals are published by the American Psychological Association. In brief, the A.P.A. journals and their coverage are as follows. (More thorough descriptions can be found in the A.P.A. *Publication Manual*, 1957.)

The *American Psychologist* (*Amer. Psychologist*) is the main journal for matters of professional concern to American psychologists. It carries articles that are of general interest to all, whatever their field of specialization, as well as articles relating to psychology as a profession. *Contemporary Psychology* (*Contemp. Psychol.*) reviews books and visual aids. The *Journal of Abnormal and Social Psychology* (*J. abnorm. soc. Psychol.*) is one of the major outlets for research articles in the fields of personality, abnormal psychology, and social psychology. Although almost all of the papers in this journal are research reports, occasionally some theoretical articles and case histories are included. Its coverage is so broad that often papers relevant to perception, learning, and other more classical areas in psychology appear in it. The *Journal of Applied Psychology* (*J. appl. Psychol.*) publishes papers primarily concerned with applied problems in fields such as human engineering, advertising, and personnel selection. The *Journal of Comparative and Physiological Psychology* (*J. comp. physiol. Psychol.*) concentrates, as its title implies, on research in psychobiological areas. Many papers concern rodent learning, but the majority of articles are about studies of other species and other processes. The *Journal of Consulting Psychology* (*J. consult. Psychol.*) is a major outlet for work in clinical psychology, paralleling to some extent the coverage of the *Journal of Abnormal and Social Psychology*, except that the contents of the *Journal of Consulting Psychology* tend more to be restricted to papers on testing, especially intelligence testing and projective techniques, and articles on psychotherapeutic processes. The *Journal of Experimental Psychology* (*J. exp. Psychol.*) publishes papers on learning, motor processes, and sensory psychology, with occasional articles in other fields such as motivation. In general, its coverage has not been quite so broad as its title implies. *Psychological Abstracts* (*Psychol. Abstr.*) is a journal which publishes one-paragraph summaries of most of the current world literature in psychology. The *Psychological Bulletin* (*Psychol. Bull.*) is psychology's review journal. The typical paper in it summarizes the status of research findings, theory, or methodology in a circumscribed area and provides an extensive, sometimes an exhaustive, list of references. *Psychological Monographs: General and Applied* (*Psychol. Monogr.*) is an outlet for papers that are too long for publication in one of the other journals. Contributions come from virtually any area of psychology. The *Psychological Review* (*Psychol. Rev.*) is not, despite its title, a review journal (the *Psychological Bulletin* serves this function); rather it is the A.P.A.'s chief outlet for theoretical contributions. Finally, the *Journal of Educational Psychology* (*J. educ. Psychol.*) publishes papers in the field indicated by its title.

A second major publisher of psychological journals is the Journal Press, edited until recently by Carl Murchison. Its *Journal of Psychology* (*J. Psychol.*) has served as a rapid publication outlet for investigators who are willing to pay for radically reducing the usual publication lag. Its issues contain empirical and theoretical papers on a variety of topics. The *Journal of General Psychology* (*J. gen. Psychol.*), the *Journal of Genetic Psychology* (*J. genet. Psychol.*), and the *Journal of Social Psychology* (*J. soc. Psychol.*) all tend to have relatively wide coverage. Perhaps because of the vagueness of boundaries among the various subareas in psychology, there is a great deal of overlap in their contents, although papers relevant to social psychology have been somewhat more likely to appear in the *Journal of Social Psychology*, whereas developmental studies are more likely to be found in the *Journal of Genetic Psychology*. All three have served as outlets for empirical research or theoretical discussions in almost any field of psychology.

Finally, *Social Psychology Monographs* (*Soc. Psychol. Monogr.*) and *Genetic Psychology Monographs* (*Genet. Psychol. Monogr.*), regardless of their titles, have published longer papers in almost any field.

The Southern Universities Press, with R. B. and Carol H. Ammons as editors, publishes two journals. *Psychological Reports* (*Psychol. Rep.*) covers the general field of psychology with some emphasis on theoretical discussions. *Perceptual and Motor Skills* (*Percept. mot. Skills*) is limited to studies of perception and of motor learning.

There are many other independent journals that the investigator cannot afford to overlook in developing a complete recent bibliography. An outstanding one is the oldest psychological journal in the United States, the *American Journal of Psychology* (*Amer. J. Psychol.*). This journal publishes experimental studies mainly in learning, perception, and sensation; most of them are on human subjects, though there are some exceptions to both these generalizations. The *Journal of Clinical Psychology* (*J. clin. Psychol.*) is another privately owned one, which has become a major publication outlet to parallel in part the A.P.A.'s *Journal of Consulting Psychology*. Its contents deal primarily with psychotherapy, clinical testing, and related problems. The *Journal of Projective Techniques* (*J. proj. Tech.*) specializes in research, theory, and reviews of the literature on the Rorschach and the TAT, with occasional articles about other projective tests. The *Journal of Personality* (*J. Pers.*) is a major non-A.P.A. outlet for research and theory in the areas of personality and social psychology. In addition to these sources, there are many more journals, such as the *Psychological Record* (*Psychol. Rec.*), the *Psychological Newsletter* (*Psychol. Nwsltr.*), and *Child Development* (*Child Develpm.*); relatively complete listings of journals that publish psychological material can be found in the index issues of *Psychological Abstracts*.

A number of journals in related areas often carry material of interest to the psychological investigator. Among them is *Educational and Psychological Measurement* (*Educ. psychol. Measmt*), which publishes, in addition to relatively applied papers, much material on statistics, testing, and scale construction. *Sociometry* includes social psychological articles, as do *Human Relations* (*Hum. Relat.*), *Conflict Resolution*, and *Public Opinion Quarterly* (*Pub. Op. Quart.*). *Psychometrika* is a journal that specializes in mathematical psychology, including statistics. The weekly journal, *Science*, published by the American Association for the Advancement of Science, covers many different fields, from astronomy to zoology, with a very short publication lag and relatively brief papers; quite often psychological material will be found in this journal. The interdisciplinary journal, *Behavioral Science* (*Behav. Sci.*), publishes papers aimed at integration (theoretical as well as empirical) of findings in such fields as anthropology, sociology, biochemistry, and psychology; it also abstracts publications of interdisciplinary interest and reviews recent developments in electronic computers applied to research on behavior. Journals in psychiatry, statistics, sociology, anthropology, vocational guidance, personnel work, and other related fields often contain material relevant to a psychologist's interests.

Many foreign journals are available in university libraries. Such periodicals as the *Canadian Journal of Psychology* (*Canad. J. Psychol.*), the *Journal of Mental Science* (*J. ment. Sci.*), the *Quarterly Journal of Experimental Psychology* (*Quart. J. exp. Psychol.*), the *British Journal of Psychology* (*Brit. J. Psychol.*), *Année Psychologique* (*Année Psychol.*), *Journal de Psychologie* (*J. de Psychol.*), the *Japanese Journal of Psychology* (*Jap. J. Psychol.*), *Zeitschrift für Psychologie* (*Z. Psychol.*), and *Acta Psychologica* (*Acta Psychol.*) may be mentioned as examples. Foreign language journals often publish papers in English or else carry summaries of their papers in two or three languages, including English.

B. Notes on Some Conventions in Bibliography

The A.P.A. journals' standard form of references is as follows. (If the researcher plans eventually to submit his paper to some non-A.P.A. journal, he can modify the form of his reference list to fit that journal's conventions.) For a *journal article:* the author's last name, followed by his initials (if the author is a female, the initials are replaced by the full given name), and then the full title of the paper. Only the first letter of the first word of the title is capitalized, and all the rest of the title is in lower case. Then appears the abbreviated name of the journal (see Supplement A), underlined, the year of publication of the journal, the volume number, and the number of the first page of the article followed by a hyphen, followed by the number of the final page of the article. If the reference is to a *book*, the name of the author comes first, followed by the underlined title of the book; only the first word of the title is capitalized. Next is the city where the book is published, followed by a colon; then a brief form of the name of the publisher and the year of publication. In references to *chapters of books*, when the author of the chapter is different from the editor of the book, the usual procedure is to cite the author of the chapter and the title of the chapter, followed by "In" and the full reference to the book, with "(Ed.)" after the editor's name.

If an item is referred to, but has not been seen, a convention is to follow the reference by "original not seen," placed in parentheses after the full bibliographic reference. Placed within the parentheses also is the source of the bibliographic information; for example, one might write "(original not seen; referred to by Jones, 1961)." This kind of reference should be used most sparingly.

References in the text of a paper to items listed at the end of the article are made by using the author's last name and the date of the publication, as, "(Jones, 1961)." We have tried to use the A.P.A. form throughout this book.

One further point concerns the difference between a *bibliography* and a list of *references*. It has become conventional to use "bibliography" only as the heading for a list of items that has some claim to completeness in the coverage of the literature in the field. Since most lists of references do not fulfill this requirement, it is usually safer to title the entire list not "bibliography" but "references" (of course, each item in the "references" list of a paper must actually be referred to in the body of the paper).

Additional details of bibliographic practice, as well as conventions concerning preparation of papers for publication, will be found in the American Psychological Association's *Publication Manual* (1957). The student is urged to study this booklet thoroughly and perhaps to purchase a copy of his own, since he will very likely want to refer to it frequently throughout his career.

REFERENCES

Alexander, C., & Burke, A. J. *How to locate educational information and data.* (4th Ed.) New York: Bureau of Publications, Teach. Coll., Columbia Univer., 1958.

American Psychological Association Council of Editors. *Publication manual of the American Psychological Association.* (1957 Revision.) Washington: American Psychological Association, 1957.

Annual review of psychology. Stanford, Calif.: Annual Reviews, 1950 ff.

Daniel, R. S., & Louttit, C. M. *Professional problems in psychology.* New York: Prentice-Hall, 1953. (See especially Chs. 3–5.)

Good, C. V., & Scates, D. E. *Methods of research, educational, psychological, sociological.* New York: Appleton-Century-Crofts, 1954. (See especially Ch. 3.)

Gruber, H. E., Terrell, G., & Wertheimer, M. (Eds.) *Contemporary approaches to creativity.* New York: Atherton, 1962.

Latham, A. J. Guides to psychological literature. *Amer. Psychologist,* 1954, **9,** 21–28.

Louttit, C. M. *Handbook of psychological literature.* Bloomington, Ind.: Principia Press, 1932.

Murphey, R. W. *How and where to look it up.* New York: McGraw-Hill, 1958.

Wallas, G. *The art of thought.* New York: Harcourt, Brace, 1926.

Wertheimer, M. *Productive thinking.* (Enlarged Ed.) New York: Harper, 1959.

CHAPTER 3

Conditions for
generalizing findings

Whatever the balance between practical and theoretical concerns, the research problem is typically one whose generality goes beyond the particular operations chosen to investigate it. Consider the researcher who wishes to find out what areas of a city have the highest rates of juvenile delinquency, to explore some factors related to difficulty in learning mathematics, or to test a hypothesis concerning the effect of drive level on resistance to extinction of a habit.

In the course of studying the first problem, he would have settled on just one or two operational indices of the juvenile delinquency rate —such as the number of crimes committed by minors during a given year or the number of minors involved in crimes in relation to the total population of the area. Nevertheless, he assumes that these operations represent the concept sufficiently well to permit him to draw conclusions about juvenile delinquency as a general phenomenon, broader than the particular measure he chose.

In exploring what it is that makes people have trouble learning math, the researcher cannot possibly study all people; he is necessarily restricted to just a sample of them. Yet he undoubtedly hopes that whatever the findings from his group of subjects they can be generalized to a much larger population of people, yet unstudied.

When investigating the relationship between drive level and resistance to habit extinction, not only must the experimenter settle on a particular group of human or animal subjects and some concrete measures of drive and resistance to extinction, he must also provide a set of standard conditions under which the experiment is performed —relatively constant temperature in the laboratory, standard diet and incentive, particular apparatus, certain specific skills for the subjects to acquire, and so forth.

All aspects of the research design are concerned with narrowing down from very general concepts and relations to particular operations, particular subjects, and particular conditions under which the measures are taken or the experiment is performed. This is because the task of performing all conceivable operations on the complete population of potential subjects under all possible conditions would be prohibitive; even if feasible, it would surely constitute a waste of time and effort which might well be devoted to other discoveries.

The strategy of scientific investigation, therefore, requires a careful selection of subjects, operations, and conditions for observation, so that they represent as well as possible the total class of events into which one is inquiring (cf. Brunswik, 1956; Churchman, 1948; Churchman & Ackoff, 1950). Then, by a process of induction, inferences are made about unobserved events on the basis of the observed. In everyday life inductive inferences are performed routinely: one concludes from a small sample of Karen's behavior that she is a friendly person; one decides from his own and his friends' experiences with a department store that it sells good but expensive merchandise; one determines after a disappointing love affair that "women are fickle." Such generalizations about enduring characteristics of people, groups, or things, on the basis of sampled experience with them, serve the same function in science that they do in everyday life; they enable one to react readily (and perhaps, but not necessarily, appropriately) toward new events of the same class, without having to find out about them individually.

The main difference between induction in science and induction in everyday life is, in the last analysis, only one of degree. The scientist is presumably more careful about how he samples the class of events to which he intends to generalize. Instead of judging a person friendly on the basis of one or two casual encounters, the psychologist will wish to observe a sample of his "normal" behavior or of his behavior elicited with a standard stimulus situation to which other people can be exposed for comparison. Although just *how* to get an adequate sample of events to observe is still largely a matter of individual preference, and subject to considerable disagreement among researchers, some aspects of the inductive process have been codified with sufficient rigor to gain currency in the field.

These standardized procedures deal mainly with the techniques of subject sampling, a topic treated in some detail in Chapter 9. The problem of induction is considerably broader than this, however, for it relates to sampling and inference over tasks, measuring instruments, and conditions of study as well as over people. There are similarities among the logical problems in each of these induction situations, and we shall try here to make these similarities clear. The precise techniques for dealing with them are likely to be quite different in various specific instances, and therefore we postpone discussion of details to later individual chapters.

SOURCES OF VARIABILITY AMONG BEHAVIORAL EVENTS

Behaviors, as observed and recorded by the psychologist (or layman), are influenced by a large number of factors. The most obvious determinant is, of course, the behaving person himself. Some people have difficulty learning mathematics, others do not; and the degree of difficulty experienced varies with the person. It is equally true that the observed behavior depends on the circumstances in which it occurs. For instance, with a great deal of distraction anyone is likely to experience more difficulty in learning new material than under conditions in which he can concentrate.

A third determinant of observed behavior is the method of observation itself. Since any phenomenon represents a joint product of the external event and the process by which it is perceived, even scientifically recorded behavior is affected by the techniques used to measure it. The fact that the measuring procedures of science are "objective" does not alter this consideration; "objective" usually means only that the procedure can be repeated, not that it is without influence on the thing measured. The observed behavior itself may be affected by the measurement process; thus a 3-year-old girl is likely to act differently in the presence of an adult observer than when alone.

Furthermore, the *measurement* may be affected even if the behavior is not. The mathematical ability of a 10-year-old boy, for example, may be judged quite differently by his doting mother and by his arithmetic teacher. Yet judgments like these frequently constitute behavioral data for the psychologist. Even if the teacher were to improve the objectivity of her judgment by basing it on a test, she would have quite a variety of tests to select from. Some of them might show the boy in the near-genius range; others as simply good. Variation among results of tests would stem largely from the fact that they include different kinds of problems, all considered in some way to measure mathematical ability. Obviously any one test cannot possibly include all relevant problems, and the results of its measurement will depend, in part, on the particular sample of items chosen for it.

These three general sources of variability in behavior—the behaving person, the conditions of his behavior, and the nature of the measuring instrument (including the human observer)—need to be taken into account by the psychologist in designing his research. He may wish to know what effect a particular teaching method has on mathematical ability, but clearly it can have no unique effect; people subjected to it will differ in measured ability, depending on who they are, how their ability is measured, and what the surrounding conditions are. In order to determine how much, if any, effect the teaching method has, he must make provision for sampling or controlling these other influences on the behavior being studied.

The research problem can thus be stated in a more refined way: Given a certain type of people (who, of course, vary within the type), a limited range of learning conditions (relating to class size, nature of school facilities, home environment of the pupils, etc.), and a particular way (or ways) of measuring mathematical ability—given all of these other conditions which might affect the behavior under study, does the method of teaching also affect it? These specified conditions of the research each serve to define the limits of generalization from the research findings. Conclusions can be drawn about the effectiveness of the teaching method only within the limits of the kind of subject studied, the kind of test used, and the range of teaching and assessment conditions represented.

All of these restrictions refer to *classes* of events, not to particular instances of the class. If the research is to have any general value, its implications must extend beyond the *particular* subjects, conditions, and instruments included in the study. But the extension can go only as far as the class boundaries which these particulars represent. The wider the classes, the more general the study's findings, and since general conclusions are usually preferred to restricted ones the researcher would do well to think out in advance just what range of people, measures, and conditions he wants to cover in his study. The illustrations in the remainder of the chapter are intended to clarify this point.

GENERALIZING OVER PEOPLE

Either explicitly or implicitly, the research problem refers to a population of people (or animals) of interest to the investigator. In posing the question: "What causes juvenile delinquency?" the researcher is referring to the behaviors of people within a certain age range—say 10 to 20. (Sooner or later he will have to be definite about this.) Although he does not say so, he is presumably concerned, for the moment, only with juveniles in this country or perhaps just with those in industrialized societies. The implicit geographical restriction may be narrower than that: he may have ideas about the problem that apply only to urban, not rural, youth.

The experimenter who hypothesizes that partially reinforced habits are more durable than those completely reinforced is also presumably thinking of some fairly sizable population for which this generalization might hold. Perhaps it is all animals, or all mammals, or only the species *Mus norvegicus albinus;* perhaps it is children in the United States with IQs greater than 70; perhaps it is all human beings on the planet.

Whatever the limits of this theoretical population, valid inferences about it presume an accurately representative sample of subjects. For almost any attribute one might conceive, members of the population would differ to a greater or lesser degree. Therefore, a single subject can rarely represent the population. If a group of subjects is to represent it accurately, the group must show the same distribution of relevant characteristics that the population does. For a study of the effect of reinforcement schedule on habit durability, a sample should be so chosen that its distribution of reactions to the schedule of reinforcement would be proportionately the same as the distribution of reactions that would be obtained if the entire population were studied. Obviously, this distribution is not known, since the entire population has not been, and will not be, studied on this attribute. But the situation is not hopeless, for one often has information about the distribution of the total population on characteristics that are *related* to the critical attribute. One might suspect, for example, that in the total population of children the predicted relationship would hold better in bright persons than in dull ones, better in children from middle-class homes than in those from lower-class homes, better in girls than in boys, and so on. (These are, of course, only illustrative guesses, not thoughtful hypotheses.) From such considerations, therefore, the investigator would want to be sure to include in his sample of subjects the proper proportions of bright and dull, rich and poor, male and female, in order to represent adequately the range of reactions to the experimental conditions. This is known as the principle of quota control,* widely used in obtaining samples of respondents from which to predict election outcomes. Just what constitutes an essential attribute for quota control will depend on knowledge of factors relevant to the problem being studied. And here is where the difficulty arises.

In the first place, one cannot know in advance all factors that are relevant, in the sense that they correlate with the dependent variable or interact with the relationship that is being investigated. The obvious characteristics, such as sex, age, genetic strain, and college major, may account for some variation among subjects, but usually not a sizable amount. In the second place, many of the attributes which are recognized as relevant to the problem under study cannot be assigned for quota control because there is no easy way of knowing how a potential subject stands on them. Whereas it is fairly simple to classify by sex and age, and perhaps even IQ (in a school where adequate records are kept), it would be almost impossible to know who was introvert and who extravert, who had a family history of mental disorder, who was afraid of heights, etc., without actually asking or otherwise testing the entire population. Although these might be the more critical attributes for control in sample selection, there would be no convenient way of establishing the appropriate quotas for them; so the quota method could not be applied to characteristics for which it was needed most.

It is therefore necessary in most cases to resort to a more primitive principle, *randomization*. A *random sample* (often called a *probability sample*) is one in which every member of the population has an equal † chance of falling in the sample of subjects to be studied. In other words, in the entire group of organisms to which results are to be generalized every single one must have a practical chance of being studied. If this condition holds true, then statistical theory can be used to make fairly good judgments of how representative the sample is on any attribute with which one may be concerned. If a random sample is selected from a known population, then it is possible

---

* Not to be confused with *stratified random sampling,* discussed in Chapter 9.

† Technically, "an equal or otherwise known chance (not zero) of entering the sample," for it is possible in disproportionate stratified sampling (see Chapter 9) to assign some people higher probabilities than others. As long as the exact probabilities are known, however, representativeness can be achieved by appropriate weightings of the various subgroups in the sample.

to use results from the sample to estimate any characteristic of the population—such as the age, sex, emotionality, or IQ distribution or the distribution of responses to an experimental variable—and also to determine the accuracy of the estimate within certain probability limits.

So, generalizing from a sample of subjects actually studied to a larger population of individuals is entirely defensible, provided the principle of representation by randomization is adhered to. This principle is exceedingly difficult to carry out in practice. Consider its implications: in order to say that every member of a population has a known chance of being studied, one must be able to specify exactly what that chance is. In order to know what population one is talking about, and to sample it, every member must be identifiable and potentially available for study. At some stage of the sampling process members of the population must be listed and numbered * so that a sample can be taken with a table of random numbers (see Appendix, Table A) or some other device which assures equal probabilities of selection. If any member of the population fails to appear on the list, then he cannot possibly fall in the sample and the sample, therefore, cannot be random.

Most of the populations that psychologists are interested in are not nearly so well defined as this. They say, "all animals," "all mammals," "all human beings," or "all juvenile delinquents in urban areas," with no intention of ever listing all the organisms eligible for study. Typically, they will pick a catch-as-catch-can sample of subjects who fall within the theoretical population but may not actually represent it very well. (Nobody ever really knows how well they do represent the intended population!) This makes generalizations from psychological studies necessarily fuzzy. Rather than say, "The results of this study would probably be replicated on a different random sample of juvenile delinquents—or of laboratory rats," the cautious researcher would say something like, "If I could get another sample of subjects like the one I just studied, the results would probably be replicated." How he would get another sample like that is often far from clear.

Some critics of research methodology would contend that little of scientific value comes from empirical findings of unknown generality. Our position is somewhat less severe: the problem of generalizing

---

* Although it may not be necessary to list all members, but only a part of them, as in multistage sampling (see Chapter 9), at least all *groups* have to be listed initially; then of the selected groups, all individuals within them must be listed for subsampling.

across people is in principle no different from that of generalizing across other populations represented in the research design—populations of measures, situations, or experimental operations. In the last analysis, the validity of generalizations depends on two things—consensus in the scientific community and empirical verification. Tentatively one can presume to generalize his results to populations not explicitly sampled for the study, provided neither he nor anyone else can think of a good reason why they should behave differently. Then, more convincingly, he can demonstrate their applicability to a new population by direct study of that group.

This seemingly lax way of treating the problem of generalization is not intended to encourage more careless induction than is now prevalent. Rather than proclaim that it is all right to generalize from samples of unknown representativeness, we would prefer to emphasize that, since most samples are likely to be nonrepresentative, it behooves the researcher to consider carefully just how their nonrepresentativeness might limit the generality of his conclusions. In most cases this amounts to a matter of thoughtful judgment rather than empirical technique. Quite often the nonrepresentativeness is assumed to be on characteristics that are not critical for the relation under study, but one never can be sure that this assumption is warranted.

One compromise between rigor and convenience might be recommended: out of the large and vaguely conceived theoretical population the researcher is interested in, he might try to define precisely an empirical population that seems to embody the essential characteristics and is completely accessible. A random sample can be drawn from this empirical population by one of the standard techniques presented in Chapter 9. Then statistical theory of sampling can be applied for rigorous generalization across the empirical population, and the researcher can rely on his best judgment for generalizing to the larger theoretical population. At least such a procedure would have the advantage of fairly rigorous restrictions on one aspect of the inductive process.

Sampling the Appropriate Unit

Although most attributes of interest to psychological research are found in individual humans or animals, some variables describe instead a larger, perhaps social, unit in which the individual organism is involved. If one refers to the effectiveness of psychotherapy, for example, he is talking about the consequences of a relationship between doctor and patient that is presumed to be generalizable over doctors as well as patients. If the researcher were to try to study the effectiveness of a given therapeutic technique by taking a random sample of clients of a single therapist, the study would not accomplish its intended purposes. It might tell him a great deal about how successful this particular doctor is with various kinds of patients, but this would not help much in generalizing over doctors concerning the therapeutic technique per se. Required instead is a representative sample of doctor-patient relationships.

As another illustration, suppose a social psychologist wanted to investigate the notion that deteriorated neighborhoods breed psychosis. What is needed here is a representative sample of deteriorated neighborhoods (compared, of course, with a sample of nondeteriorated neighborhoods) rather than just representative samples of people from two or three areas that fit the requirements. The reason for this is that the problem is not whether community A has a higher psychosis rate than community B but whether communities of a given class (deteriorated) tend, as a whole, to show disproportionately high rates. One should therefore sample adequately from this class rather than just pick a single example of it.

The general principle, then, is sampling of the appropriate units. First decide the primary locus of the trait to be studied. If it is an individual, then sample individuals for the research; if it is a pair or group or locale, then take a sample of these units as the objects of investigation. If it cannot be decided in advance what the primary locus of the attribute is, then it is better to play safe and sample the more inclusive unit.

GENERALIZING OVER CONDITIONS

In stating his problem or hypothesis, the researcher leaves unsaid a great many things about the conditions under which his findings are to be applicable. Then, in the course of designing his study, he necessarily accepts, or sets up, a particular set of conditions that was never explicit in the conceptual statement of his problem. Tests are administered to a group of subjects at a particular time of day, although there is nothing in the definition of the attribute they measure that suggests that one time would be more appropriate than another. An experiment on visual acuity is performed at a certain room temperature simply because the experimental room happens to be that warm rather than because that condition is judged to be the most appropriate for demonstrating the research hypothesis. On the day before a questionnaire is administered to students to determine their religious sentiments, anti-Semitic incidents break out on campus. In these ways—and in many others—a research project is performed under a particular set of circumstances which may never be replicated; and most of them, furthermore, go unrecorded.

Yet the generalizations to be drawn from the study invariably transcend most of these particular conditions, even though no one bothers to specify the limits explicitly. In many cases it may be legitimate to ignore "background conditions" of the research situation because the investigator (or anyone else, for that matter) cannot think of any reason why they might affect the outcome. Other conditions are not so innocuous; they may influence the level at which one of the variables operates, hence its relation with other variables in the study. If there is reason to suspect that a particular condition of the research could affect its outcome, then the investigator has two courses of action open to him. He can either specify the particular level of the condition that he will deal with and make sure that all observations are made at that level, or he can try to sample a range of conditions and see how his experimental variables behave under all of them. Failure to do one of these is like failure to obtain a representative sample of subjects or to note the relevant characteristics of the particular sample obtained; it leaves one at a loss to know how far to generalize the research findings.

Assuming that maximum generality is desired, there is still the problem of deciding just how to achieve it by appropriate sampling of conditions. It is usually very difficult to specify in advance just what the range of possible conditions might be, let alone to include an adequate sample of them in the research design. As a practical limit, one might reasonably decide to represent only the range that is normally encountered in the subjects' habitat.* In an investigation of the effectiveness of group-centered versus teacher-centered instruction, for example, a concern for adequate representation of various learning conditions might lead one to try the two methods out in various departments of the university in which the superior method is to be adopted but not to bother setting up synthetic courses that would never be taught there anyway.

The study of teaching methods is usually a case in which the critical attribute, effectiveness, resides not in the individual student but in the teacher-student relationship; hence the appropriate unit of anal-

---

* This restriction might, however, be quite inappropriate for a project explicitly designed to study a particular range of conditions, even though some of them may be unusual in the subjects' normal environment.

ysis here may not be the student but the class (or maybe even all classes of a given teacher). Thus one may wish to try to pick a sample of teacher-class relationships that will cover the range of subject matter conditions to which the results are to be generalized. Various techniques of statistical analysis (see Chapter 13) enable one to determine whether the method has the same effect in all classes or whether it really does depend on the subject matter being taught. Such statistical techniques can be of no help whatever, though, unless the research design provides for an adequate sampling of the relevant conditions in the first place. If it turns out on analysis that subject matter differences did not constitute a relevant condition after all, then nothing is lost; the over-all effect of the teaching method can still be demonstrated. But if one had failed to take these conditions of instruction into account and just tried out the method in a single department (or in those few which volunteered to participate), then there would be no way of knowing how far beyond these particular classes to generalize the findings; and common sense would make one hesitate to extrapolate very far.

Failure to sample adequately the full range of relevant conditions may sometimes lead to spurious results which depend on the particular conditions of the study rather than on the intended variable. Thus, if only volunteer instructors are used in the experiment on a new teaching method, it could appear effective simply because all the instructors happen to believe in it rather than because the method itself is inherently superior. In order to find out whether it works even for instructors without an initially favorable bias, such a condition has to be included in the experimental design.

Decisions concerning the conditions to sample must be based on the researcher's best judgment about what situational variables may affect the experimental outcome besides the one he explicitly manipulates. This judgment, unless performed with 20/20 hindsight, is bound to be faulty at any one stage in scientific development. So the history of empirical psychology is studded with instances in which an investigator with today's knowledge and insights demonstrates that yesterday's experimental outcome was simply a spurious result of failure to control a crucial contaminating situational variable. If the researcher is concerned about the validity and the generality of his conclusions (and presumably every researcher always is), then he should consider the range of conditions to which the results are to be applied and try to include a convincing sample of them in the conditions of his study.

GENERALIZING OVER OPERATIONS

The operations of research are the methods used to measure the concepts embodied in the statement of the research problem. The measurements may be crude subjective ones, for example, when a therapist judges whether or not a patient is "improved," or they may be refined and precise, when an experimentalist uses the method of limits to determine an auditory difference limen. A given research design may provide only a single operational characterization of a particular concept, but the concept virtually always carries broader meaning than the one operation, so it is theoretically possible to think of different operations that might have been used and that would presumably have yielded comparable results.

The problem faced by a psychologist in the early stages of his research is to pick an operation, or a sample of them, that adequately represents the concept he is trying to get at. For some concepts this is a fairly straightforward matter, and anyone would be expected to agree that the chosen operation is appropriate. Concepts such as time (duration) or distance can be readily operationalized with any one of a number of standard instruments, and the researcher can afford , to be reasonably confident that (within limits) no matter which instrument he chooses—a foot rule or a yardstick—and no matter who reads it—himself or his critic—the results will not vary appreciably. So he is free to pick almost any one of the standard set and use it alone without further checks.

Things are not this clear-cut for most psychological concepts. At best, a commonly accepted operation may be found which, though somewhat arbitrary, at least identifies the concept precisely for other researchers. Such is the case for the WISC, widely accepted as *the* (or at least *an*) appropriate measure of intelligence in children. Other concepts are defined so poorly or used in research so infrequently that no single operation for them can be universally accepted. This is true for notions like "personality rigidity" and "mental health," each of which has been measured by a tremendous variety of operations that often do not yield the same results. Even a concept like "ability to see" turns out to have no unique operational characterization. Rhesus monkeys with bilateral destruction of the occipital cortex can still solve problems involving brightness discrimination, but their performance in pattern vision and size discrimination tasks exhibits a marked deficit.

What to do when faced with noncorresponding operations of the "same" concept is a problem the researcher frequently meets at some stage in his project. But, first, the thing to do in planning the project is to consider, and even attempt, a variety of operations, giving non-correspondence a chance to occur. If only a single measure of a concept is tried, the investigator will not learn whether the results depend on that one measure or whether they can be generalized to the broader meaning of the concept he has set out to study. The difficulty in generalizing from a single measure is that it is hard to tell whether performance on that measure depends on the particular attribute of concern to the research or is the product of some irrelevant response tendency peculiar to that instrument.

Selection among multiple operations is handled somewhat differently by psychologists who use verbal test instruments and those who use experimental apparatus. The first group tends to combine a variety of imperfectly correlated measures in a test and to administer them all to the subjects, whereas the second group tends to select, after preliminary try-out, the one or two "best" measures of the attribute. Perhaps the difference in strategy is due to the relative ease in the first area of devising operations (test items) and administering a lot of them to subjects without undue fatigue, whereas operations involving apparatus are generally more costly to set up and take more time to perform. If one can feel confident that a number of different instruments will measure the same attribute, then it is a matter of option whether to refine the best of them so that it discriminates precisely among subjects or to use them all in short form and combine their results for a best estimate of the common attribute. The problem is how to develop the requisite feeling of confidence so that it can be shared by other investigators.

Specific techniques for sampling and choosing among operations are discussed in Chapters 6, 7, and 8. They differ somewhat, depending on whether test items, apparatus, or human judgments are used. All are aimed at the same end, however—to assure that a particular measure, or a sample of measures, adequately represents the intended concept. Whenever there are grounds for questioning the unique appropriateness of a single operation, it is advisable to attempt several that seem theoretically, or intuitively, appropriate. Their results should be intercorrelated, as a matter of course, before proceeding with the major portion of the study. If various definitions yield roughly equivalent results, then it is probably justifiable to use the most convenient one, or a combination of them. But if two different operational characterizations of the "same concept" fail to correlate appreciably, then the researcher should stop at this point and think things through before going on. Further examination may show one of them to be faulty in construction, so that it really does not measure the intended construct or so that its reliability is too low to permit sizable correlation with any other measure. If both instruments appear conceptually and mechanically adequate, one must consider the possibility that they tap not one but two (or more) distinct attributes. If so, at least some ground has been gained, for the study —and the theory behind it—can now be designed to take account of both attributes rather than just the one initially conceived.

WHEN TO SAMPLE AND WHEN NOT TO

Given all the sources of variability in empirical results—associated with subjects, research conditions, and measuring instruments as well as with the variable of central interest to the investigator—it is easy to see why the completely general study has never been performed and probably never will be. One can afford to be comfortable with fairly modest aspirations for a given piece of research. Realistically, the major problem in planning for induction beyond the scope of the particular research observations lies not in determining how to be as general as possible but in deciding where generality is to be attained and where it is to be sacrificed. Since psychologists have become acutely aware of individual differences as an unwanted source of variability, they typically take great pains to provide for these differences in their research design by assessing a heterogeneous sample of subjects and determining the average effect of a particular variable on them. The critical variable itself may be represented by only one instrument, and the various background conditions may be held as nearly constant as possible at a particular level.

If the operations and conditions are thus held constant, that is, if they are represented by a sample of one each, this may stem from different intents on the researcher's part. He may assume that any other operation and any other condition of assessment would lead to the same result and is therefore letting his sample of one stand for the entire population of instruments and conditions that might have been used. He may, more cautiously, be purposely holding constant these unwanted sources of variability in order to study better the critical effects in relation to intersubject variability alone.

But this is not the only way to do research. For a given problem one might conceivably just as well assess a single subject—pigeon, rat, chimpanzee, or human—under a variety of conditions and with a sample of instruments or research operations, all intended to determine the effect of an experimental variable on *him*. Most investigations are not designed this way, for the theories and practical problems of psychology generally deal with relationships obtaining over organisms in general rather than within a given organism, and most investigators are unwilling to consider any one person or animal a truly representative, "typical" exemplar of his species. It is clear, though, that whenever the conclusions from a given research project are intended to transcend the particular operations and particular conditions represented in it the researcher either must plan to sample enough of these to offer convincing empirical evidence of their commonality or be prepared to defend logically his choice of a single instance from which to generalize. In the absence of either an empirical or a logical defense, it might be wise tentatively to restrict his interpretations to the operations, subjects, and conditions actually represented in the study and to regard any more general interpretation simply as a hypothesis.

SUMMARY

Any single study is necessarily performed on a particular group of subjects, with selected instruments and under conditions which are, in some respects, unique. Yet the researcher wants the results of his study to yield information about a larger domain of organisms, conditions, and operations than were actually investigated. Thus a major objective of all research is induction from the observed to the not-yet-observed. In order to make the inductive leap reasonably convincing, some kind of assurance is needed that the sample of events actually studied represents, in essential respects, the larger population to which results are generalized.

In most instances the degree of representativeness of the sample is a matter of judgment rather than of clearly demonstrable fact. One needs to consider carefully what the essential characteristics of the theoretical population are and then attempt to duplicate them in the empirical study. Generalization over people (or other organisms) requires a representative sample of subjects; generalization to the complete theoretical meaning of a concept demands a representative sample of operations relevant to that concept; generalization to the population of conditions under which a particular relationship holds necessitates adequate sampling of those conditions. Just how to obtain a representative sample in each of these instances is far from established in present-day research technology. When a population can be explicitly defined, as is the case for some studies of humans, then it is possible to apply precise techniques of subject sampling whose validity derives from statistical theory. For vaguely conceived populations, however—such as populations of organisms with nervous systems or of operations and research conditions—there are no formal sampling techniques available. So the researcher must arrive subjectively at a set of research conditions, operations, and subjects that seem to him to represent adequately the essential features of the problem he is trying to understand. Subjectivity can be circumvented to some extent; in the last analysis it is replication of findings in slightly altered contexts that lends confidence to conclusions based on empirical studies.

REFERENCES

Brunswik, E. *Perception and the representative design of psychological experiments.* (2nd Ed.) Berkeley: Univer. California Press, 1956.

Churchman, C. W. *Theory of experimental inference.* New York: Macmillan, 1948.

Churchman, C. W., & Ackoff, R. *Methods of inquiry.* St. Louis: Educational Publishers, 1950.

CHAPTER 4

Control over
research variables

In 1951 a study was done at Worcester State Hospital (Wertheimer, unpublished) to determine the effect of prefrontal lobotomy on body weight. Reports of physiological experiments had suggested that damage to the frontal lobes of monkeys and chimpanzees often produced overeating and consequent weight gain. Lobotomy in human beings, perhaps a comparable operation, had also occasionally been reported to result in weight increases. The aim of the study was to check this observation by reviewing the weight records of all patients lobotomized between two and five years prior to the study.

Regular routine at the hospital included a monthly weighing of each patient. Complete records were kept for years afterward, so it was a simple matter to determine the amount of weight gained (or lost) each month after lobotomy. Omitting the details, and smoothing the curve, the expectation that weight should increase following lobotomy was amply confirmed. As Fig. 4-1 shows, there was a steady increase in mean weight as a function of months following the operation ("L" month).

So the study was complete and showed what it was intended to show. But was it and did it? Only if the weight gain could be clearly and unequivocally attributed to the lobotomy and if without lobotomy weight does not increase.

The next step, therefore, was to determine whether the weight of the patients over the period *preceding* lobotomy had not increased.

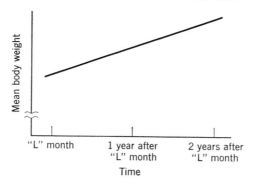

Fig. 4-1. Mean body weight after lobotomy.

The mean weight curve for the 12 months before lobotomy, together with the mean weight for two years following the operation, is shown in Fig. 4-2. Examination of the result showed that something was wrong. The same increase observed after the operation had already occurred beforehand; if the lobotomy had produced the weight gain, the curve should have been flatter before "L" month. Perhaps a pattern of gradual weight increase was typical of the patients on whom lobotomy was performed. Apparently the lobotomy, per se, did not increase the patients' weight.

A still more convincing control was provided by a second group. These were patients on whom the operation had been recommended but not performed because the parent or guardian had refused or could not be reached, or for some other reason. Mean weight for these patients was also plotted, "L" month being defined as the month at which the patient would most likely have received operation, had

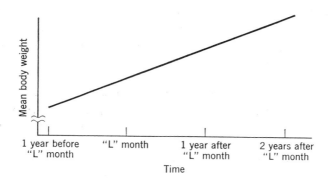

Fig. 4-2. Mean body weight before and after lobotomy.

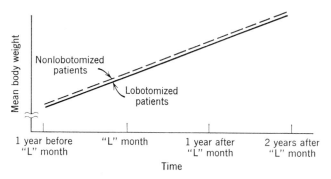

Fig. 4-3. Mean body weights for lobotomized and nonlobotomized groups.

permission been forthcoming (as estimated from the operated group). As Fig. 4-3 shows, the two curves coincided perfectly. The operated group (solid line) did not show any different relation between months and weight than the nonoperated controls (dashed line). Clearly the relevant variable producing the weight gain was not the lobotomy but some other factor. Perhaps better nutrition or decrease in activity was responsible; living in a hospital may tend to make people heavier —or simply the fact of getting older. A nonhospitalized control group would be needed to decide whether the hospital situation played a role in the weight gain.

THE FUNCTION OF CONTROLS

The point of this illustration is that the meaning of an empirical result is not always clear from a superficial analysis. One would like to interpret a given outcome as showing some sort of intrinsic relation between two or more variables—it might be a "cause-and-effect" relationship, in which one of them (the independent variable) influences the other (the dependent variable), or it might simply be a relationship of concomitance, in which two phenomena tend to occur, or not to occur, together. But acceptance of the desired interpretation implies ability to eliminate alternative explanations of the empirical outcome. This is the function of research controls. In the Worcester State Hospital study inclusion of the relevant controls showed that alternative explanations could *not* reasonably be eliminated; therefore there was little ground for inferring a cause-and-effect relation between lobotomy and weight gain.

In planning an empirical investigation, one of the things the researcher does is decide just what sort of relationship he wishes to demonstrate. Then he selects his operations and performs his study under conditions that will permit that relationship to appear. But that is not enough. He must also consider alternative interpretations that might be offered for the expected outcome and decide which of these he wishes to exclude as possibilities. The design of appropriate controls is then a matter of finding ways to eliminate "extraneous" variables, that is, variables on which the alternative interpretations depend.

The general purpose of controls, then, is to clarify the nature of the research variables and their interrelationships. This is an exceedingly broad function which is, in a sense, coextensive with the overall aim of scientific research itself. As a matter of fact, most of the things we say throughout this book have something to do with the problem of control in its broad sense. When the researcher selects a particular operational characterization of a psychological variable, one of his aims is to find an operation that can be interpreted as representing only the variable he is interested in and not some other. When he selects or constructs a situation in which to investigate the relationship between two variables, he tries to see to it that the situation itself does not spuriously contribute to the intended relationship. In picking subjects for study, it is important that they not have inherent, extraneous characteristics which could either exaggerate or mask the effect the researcher is interested in. And so on; one could conceive of each step in scientific research as aimed at clarifying intrinsic relationships by the control of extraneous influences.

Every study poses its own peculiar control requirements. Ability to think of particular contaminating variables comes in part through familiarity with the field; the researcher with experience in a given area can usually propose more alternative interpretations, and better ways of eliminating them convincingly, than the novice can. In addition to experience, one can also use a certain amount of imagination and ingenuity. Designing a study that is adequately controlled is one of the more creative aspects of research activity; the esthetic pleasure gained from a particularly elegant design can enhance the enjoyment of the process.

In this chapter we are chiefly concerned with a rather restricted meaning of the term control, referring to manipulation of the research variables themselves. Controls that are performed by subject selection, by construction of research instruments, and by statistical analysis of relationships are discussed in subsequent chapters. Here our main concern is with what is done to subjects, in the course of collecting data on them, to insure that observed variables and relationships are intrinsic rather than spurious.

THREE KINDS OF RESEARCH STRATEGY

Basically, there are three sorts of things that might be done to subjects in an investigation of their behaviors and the reasons for them. One might leave them alone and just watch what they do by themselves; one might try to elicit inherent behavior tendencies by exposing all subjects to a standard test situation; or one could attempt to influence their behaviors in diverse ways. These three levels of manipulation constitute the basis for one commonly used classification of research strategies: (1) naturalistic observation, (2) systematic assessment with controlled stimuli, and (3) experimental manipulation.*

Any classification of research strategies is bound to be somewhat arbitrary, since it highlights certain similarities and differences to the exclusion of others. The present classification focuses on the degree to which the research variables are actively controlled. In naturalistic observation there is no active control over stimuli or responses. All one can do is take certain precautions to see that extraneous observer variables do not contaminate the presumed relationships. In systematic assessment the researcher attempts to control subjects just enough to elicit responses that are assumed to reflect pre-existing characteristics of the subjects themselves; he deliberately tries not to affect the nature of the attribute on which the responses primarily depend. Control over extraneous variables can be achieved only passively by appropriate assessment and statistical analysis. In experimental research the investigator tries actively to influence the determinants of the response—to induce differences in responses by manipulating the conditions under which they occur. Simultaneously, he can achieve active control over potentially contaminating variables either by holding them constant or by varying them systematically.

* Often the "clinical method" is regarded as an additional research strategy. But we shall not consider it separately here because it seems less unitary than the other three and its research aim is less pure. In most clinical settings data collection is intended primarily to serve the ends of diagnosis or therapy and only secondarily, if at all, those of research. When clinical methods are used for research purposes, some may wish to class them with naturalistic observation procedures, but this gives insufficient attention to the diversity of clinical approaches. Depending on the clinician and the nature of the problem, the techniques used may combine features of the other two strategies as well.

The differences among these strategies may be represented in the following diagram, which indicates the extent of active control over research variables.

	Control Over		
	---	---	---
Research Strategy	Inde- pendent Variable	De- pendent Variable	Extra- neous Variables
Naturalistic observation	none	none	slight
Systematic assessment	none	some	some
Experiment	much	some	much

This is a rather abstract classification, and many research designs probably would not clearly fit any one of the categories. Moreover, any particular project may well combine features of each strategy. But the schema is fairly representative, and it serves to highlight the problem of controls.

There are those who claim that experimentation is the only road to the understanding of causal, or even functional, relations because only by manipulating an independent variable and observing its effect can one legitimately infer that the presumed dependent variable actually depends on it. We would certainly agree that the experimental strategy has superior features, particularly in providing for direct control over extraneous variables. This is not to say that it is without its own defects. In fact, as we shall see later, experimental manipulation may provide such refined control over the situation in which a relationship is established that the generality of the result becomes questionable. Precision of control is not the only consideration in designing a research project. Generality and applicability of the conclusions are others. In some ways, therefore, the aims discussed in this chapter are at odds with those presented in Chapter 3. The problem facing the investigator is to find an appropriate compromise that will afford control over certain unwanted influences, while at the same time adequately representing the complex interplay of circumstances he is trying to find out about.

NATURALISTIC OBSERVATION

Naturalistic observation is the oldest of the three research strategies and is, in a sense, basic to the others. Essentially, it is watching what happens in connection with the phenomenon being studied. No attempt is made to manipulate or, perhaps, even to measure in any refined sense; rather, the observer tries to record relevant events, always alert for instances of covariation from which he can abstract variables and infer relations among them.

Such an approach to acquiring empirical knowledge was used thousands of years ago by astronomers, long before the development of modern conceptions of science. Yet naturalistic observation continues to play an important role in contemporary research, including psychology and the other behavioral sciences. It is most frequently applied in an exploratory way to discover what sorts of phenomena and relationships merit more controlled study; but the method may also be combined with precise instruments of observation in a formal test of hypotheses.

Barker & Wright (1951), for example, have used such procedures to explore the natural habitats of children. The investigators simply followed a subject around unobtrusively to see what sorts of events he encountered and what he did in the course of his day's activity.

Another illustration is offered by the study of animals in their natural habitat. In Grand Teton National Park, Wyoming, Dr. Margaret Altmann (1956) has for a number of years been investigating the social and maternal behavior of large, free-ranging game animals. Her strategy is to find a herd of moose or elk and to follow it for weeks or even months at a time, keeping careful records of which animals seem to stick together and studying problems such as social organization as a function of age or the disruptive effect of a new calf on the relation between a yearling and its mother.

Sociologists and political scientists use a kind of naturalistic observation in their content analyses of communication media (e.g., Berelson, 1952) to detect propaganda lines or other cultural themes. Here, the object of observation is not the behaving organisms themselves, but the products of their behaviors. Ethnologists observe both behaving people and their products when they study primitive cultures (e.g., Whiting, 1954). A high order of statistical and analytic sophistication can be found in the naturalistic studies reported by Baldwin (1948). Behaviors of parents and children in the home and in free play were rated by observers according to a large number of attributes (e.g., "impatience," "curiosity"); these ratings were then factor-analyzed and the factors were correlated to determine which patterns of adult and child behavior were associated.

Such a strategy affords absolutely no control over the behaviors of subjects. In fact, if their behaviors were affected by the very process of being observed, the results would often be considered invalid. If children, wild animals, people in other cultures, or even adults in this society are aware that someone is watching them, they may act quite differently from the way they would under normal circumstances. For this reason, the naturalist often takes great pains to conceal himself; or he may try to stay among his subjects long enough and to fit in with their ways so unobtrusively that they will go on about their behaviors as they would in his absence. To prevent contamination by unwanted influences, the naturalist institutes controls aimed at *avoiding* rather than assuring manipulation of subjects' behaviors.

Another kind of unwanted influence in naturalistic observation may result from the observer's own expectations concerning what will occur. He typically observes a complex pattern of behaviors-in-situations and abstracts from them variables that appear to be related. If he is the only one doing the observing, or if his co-workers are trained to the same expectations that he entertains, then it is possible that any "observed relationships" are simply manufactured by his own set to observe them and do not reflect dependencies inherent in the phenomena. In order to guard against such contamination from an observer variable, it is prudent for the naturalist to provide some objective criteria for the variables he abstracts, so that another investigator, operating under a different set of expectations, would at least agree that a given overt behavior had occurred to a specified degree. Control, in this instance, consists in eliminating a built-in contamination among variables which results from their being filtered through the same measuring instrument, the human observer.

Secondary Records

Records of observations or measures made by others frequently provide the data for analysis by a new investigator. This amounts to a kind of "second-hand" naturalistic observation, since the present researcher has no control over either the independent or dependent variables, however assessed. He himself does not even see the behaviors referred to but relies on the records of someone else who did. The lobotomy study described at the beginning of this chapter is an example of this approach. Knapp & Greenbaum (1953), using lists of Fulbright fellows, U. S. Public Health fellows, etc., were able to explore the academic backgrounds of eminent scholars in the United States to see if they came disproportionately from certain colleges and universities. (They did.) Hollingshead & Redlich (1958) used hospital records to compare mental patients' diagnoses with data on their social classes to see if certain psychiatric groups tended to have distinctive class origins. (They did.)

There are many occasions on which the psychologist will do well to save time and expense by using second-hand data gathered by someone else. Studies of social, psychological, or physiological correlates of mental disorders, for example, sometimes do not require direct assessment of patients, but instead can be performed on records previously obtained by the hospitals. It is becoming more and more common nowadays for researchers to reanalyze interview survey data collected by others, or to review and combine the findings of several surveys, in an attempt to make wider and deeper interpretations than those provided in the original studies. [See, for example, Scott and Withey's (1958) survey of public opinion polls concerning the United Nations.] There are several sources of previously collected data, if the investigator feels they may serve his purposes. Raw data from published studies can sometimes be obtained from the American Documentation Institute in Washington, D. C., or by writing to the author himself. Various specialized data depositories often permit others to use the material in their files; among them are the Roper Public Opinion Research Center at Williams College, the Human Relations Area File at Yale University, the University of Chicago's National Opinion Research Center, and the University of Michigan's Survey Research Center.

When using second-hand records in this way, the researcher places himself at the mercy of those who collected the data in the first place, for they have already provided operational definitions of his variables for him. All he can do is interrelate the variables in new ways. He might very properly be concerned, therefore, not only with the accuracy of the records but also whether the very process of obtaining them might not have influenced the measures themselves. Often data on patients' psychiatric histories, for example, are collected during the intake interview, in which the patient, his spouse, parent, or some other responsible person is the informant. Under these particular circumstances, the informant's memory for past events may be unusually faulty; more seriously, it may distort these events in the direction of congruence with the present symptoms. So the researcher who attempts to establish a relation between psychiatric diagnosis and the patient's past history may find one in hospital records, but the relation may be largely artifactual.

Whether the subjects are clinical patients, school children, or other groups, reports of past behaviors which were recorded at the time they occurred are generally preferable to retrospective reports by the subjects themselves, or by another person, sometime later. Contemporaneous records are less influenced by the assimilating, distorting, and consistency-inducing effects of memory.

Often it is possible to find in the same records additional information about extraneous variables which may be responsible for an apparent relationship. This was the approach to controls used in the lobotomy study. In some instances of second-hand observation one may suspect that peculiarities of the particular institutionalized population, or diagnostic biases of the institution, account for a spurious relationship. This suspicion can sometimes be checked by replicating the study in another institution in which the particular population or diagnostic biases are not present. If the relationship were thought to reflect a temporary influx of certain kinds of patients or the idiosyncratic behaviors of certain personnel, one might replicate in two or more widely separated periods of the hospital's records.

The approach to control of extraneous variables in naturalistic studies is usually quite indirect. For any obtained relationship, it requires thinking of alternative interpretations which are to be explicitly excluded, then looking around for additional observations that will afford a check on the unwanted alternatives. This indirect, roundabout way of clarifying relationships is necessitated by the absence of direct control over the variables themselves.

SYSTEMATIC ASSESSMENT WITH CONTROLLED STIMULI

Aside from the limited control over extraneous variables which naturalistic observation affords, it has another serious disadvantage from a research standpoint. Some kinds of behaviors occur so rarely in the normal course of events that it would take endless observation if the behaviors were ever to be recorded. It would, for example, be impossible to discover whether upwardly mobile Americans feel hostile toward their parents by simply following subjects around and waiting for signs of hostility to appear. Occasions for its expression would arise so rarely and social taboos against that kind of sentiment are so strong that one would expect to see almost no hostile overt acts in the course of natural observation. Furthermore, even if the behavior appeared frequently enough to make its observation worthwhile, it could occur under such a variety of conditions that one would find it very difficult to know whether it had the same meaning for one person as for another. Any signs of hostility one did observe would be likely to vary greatly from individual to individual and from situation to situation. Some systematic device is needed to elicit the response more dependably and under standardized conditions, so that different subjects can be compared.

This is the principal function of psychological tests: to provide a standard stimulus situation that will elicit responses manifesting the attribute one is interested in. The stimuli used in this systematic assessment are conceived as response eliciting rather than response manipulating devices. It is assumed that the attributes they measure are inherent in the subjects themselves and are not just products of the testing situation. This conception is, of course, only approximately correct, since any response presumably reflects simultaneously the characteristics of the immediate situation and the responding organism. Because the researcher is interested in assessing characteristics of the organism, he tries to control the contribution of the stimulus situation by keeping it constant over all subjects. As long as the test items are constant, any variability among subjects' responses can presumably be attributed to the subjects' own characteristics. Thus systematic assessment provides somewhat greater control than naturalistic observation over the research variables: it controls the conditions under which they are manifest.

Psychometrics and Psychophysics

Modern development of controlled stimuli for systematic assessment has its historical and logical roots in the psychometric procedures that form the basis of the psychophysical methods. Although psychophysics typically makes use of an experimental approach, the methods basic to it can also be used in systematic assessment. The concern of psychophysics is the relation of physical characteristics of stimuli to psychological characteristics of responses; it considers such questions as the effect of the frequency of a sound wave on its perceived loudness, how different two lifted weights must be if a person is to notice the difference, how visual acuity is affected by certain background characteristics of the situation in which the stimuli are presented, and so on. These are truly experimental questions, for it is possible to manipulate the stimuli directly; and they are not primarily concerned with individual differences, since their major aim is to relate variations in common, or average, responses to variations in stimuli.

It is a somewhat unfortunate historical accident that the measuring procedures used to study such problems have come to be known as the *psychophysical* methods because this terminology has led to some confusion. It is perhaps more accurate to say that the science of psychophysics gave rise to a series of *psychometric* methods, whose elaborations and applications nowadays go far beyond the classical psychophysical problems; that is, the psychometric methods of psychophysics can be used not only to determine how psychological attributes vary as a function of changes in physical stimuli but also how people differ in such broad personality and cognitive characteristics as intelligence, aptitudes, motives, and attitudes. Further, the stimuli need not be specifiable in precise physical terms but may be words or symbols whose values are difficult or impossible to assign independently of people's responses to them. Subjects' responses can be used to "calibrate" the stimuli, much as physical devices are used for calibration in classical psychophysical studies.

The core problems of psychophysics and of using stimuli in systematic assessment are, in a sense, obverse. In psychophysical experiments one generally studies the effect of variations in stimuli on the responses of an average observer; in systematic assessment the aim is usually to study individual differences in response to an unchanging set of stimuli. Whereas interindividual variability is the focus of systematic assessment, it is deliberately masked in most psychophysical studies. To the extent that responses are constant over individuals, they provide psychophysical information; to the extent that people's responses differ, they provide information about the people themselves.

Thorough descriptions of the psychometric methods can be found in many sources, such as the Guilford (1954), Osgood (1953), Torgerson (1958), or Woodworth & Schlosberg (1954) texts listed at the end of this chapter. Since current usages of the terms "psychometrics" and "psychophysics" are somewhat confused, it may be necessary to consult both headings in these books in order to find discussions of what we here have called psychometrics.

Psychological Tests

The most common form of psychometric device for systematically assessing individual differences is the verbal test. A test typically consists of a series of questions designed to elicit verbal manifestations of an underlying attribute. The attributes assessed may be various—general intelligence, knowledge of particular topics, attitudes toward specific or general issues, motives, values, or defense mechanisms. There is no intrinsic reason why a test must be verbal, for the same trait could result in a variety of overt behaviors which may or may not require words. Nonverbal tests of intelligence and a host of other attributes have been devised; but it is often convenient to take advantage of the symbolic skills of human subjects, since these afford an efficient avenue for eliciting a number of traits. It is also possible to assess any particular trait with only a single test item rather than several. However, single-item assessment is generally cruder and less reliable; furthermore, it permits less clear identification of the relevant psychological characteristic. So it is now common practice in psychological research to administer multiple-item tests, in which performance on all items is scored to yield a composite index of a common underlying attribute.

Free Response Techniques

One difficulty with standardized assessment stimuli—particularly if they provide a set of fixed alternative answers or require some other specifically defined behavior, such as marking a line to designate how one feels about a particular issue—is that the subject may never have considered the matter before, so that he is, in effect, asked to make discriminations along a dimension he would not normally use. Thus the very intent of assessment techniques—to measure attributes without affecting them—may be subverted by the measuring procedure. In order to reduce the extent to which the test stimulus itself contributes to the response, *open-ended* or *free-response* questions might be used. In these the subject may simply be asked to report anything that comes to mind when he is confronted with some situation or concept. He is free to use any categories or dimensions he wishes rather than forced to state where along some predetermined dimensions his opinion or impression would fall. Such an approach provides information about the relative "salience" of various aspects of the subject's impression, which would not be obtainable in a fixed-alternative test. Further, it does not force him to use dimensions or categories that appear artificial to him. On the other hand, the investigator may often have a difficult time in classifying such free responses for subsequent analysis (cf. Berelson, 1952), and it is quite unlikely that all of them could be conveniently placed along a single dimension. So, in choosing between a fixed alternative and an open-ended test item, one needs to weigh the potential gain in validity of the data against the cost of analyzing and interpreting them.

Interview Survey Research

A widely used application of some techniques of systematic assessment methods is interview survey research—sometimes called public opinion polling. Here the "test" for an attribute is administered orally rather than with paper and pencil; and in the same interview a wide range of attributes may be assessed by means of both open and closed questions. During the last few decades psychologists and other behaviorial scientists have devoted a great deal of attention to developing the techniques of interview surveys (see, e.g., Campbell & Katona, 1953; Hyman, 1955; Stephan & McCarthy, 1958). They are mainly used for determining attitudes in large populations—states, regions, or an entire nation. Besides aiming to predict election outcomes, survey researchers have applied their techniques to such varied ends as forecasting national economic trends, assessing the prospects of government bond sales, determining the level of employee morale in large industrial organizations, and sounding out the public on enacted or anticipated foreign policy.

Typically, the central variables for such investigations are *attitudes* about socially controversial issues. So, for various reasons, the subject may distort his response to an opinion question in such a way that it reflects not his own attitude but some other attribute which is imposed by the assessment situation. If the assessment device measures the amount of *information* that a subject possesses, then he is presumably not motivated to distort the measure downwards and he is unable to distort it upwards. But a subject may be quite capable of feigning an attitude that he does not actually possess, simply to please the interviewer or to make himself appear more "normal," etc. If this happens, then the assessment procedure has not achieved its purpose of finding out what the subject is like without disturbing the nature of the attribute being studied.

In order to avoid purposeful distortion by respondents, careful interview survey researchers generally go to great pains to reduce the motivation for it and to enhance the opposite motivation to give accurate answers which reflect the respondent's true feelings. Considerable attention is devoted to establishing rapport in the interview situation, so that the person will enjoy the relationship and the task he is requested to perform. Anonymity of replies is guaranteed in order to reduce the subject's potential fear of other people's finding out what he has said. Controversial issues are presented in a permissive context so that any opinion is made to seem socially acceptable. Great use is made of open questions, which do not suggest particular directions of response. Standard nondirective probes (such as, "Can you tell me a little more about what you mean by that?") are used in preference to probes that suggest a particular attitude (such as "You mean you favor the Democratic position on this issue?"). The interviewing situation is strongly flavored with the principles of nondirective counseling (see Kahn & Cannell, 1957). Throughout, its purpose is to elicit responses that reflect essential characteristics of the subjects and yet are comparable from person to person because they are elicited with standard stimuli.

Indirect Assessment Techniques

Numerous research situations arise in which there are reasons to believe that even the most permissive assessment procedures will not elicit true, undistorted reflections of subjects' characteristics. Perhaps there are such strong, pervasive pressures in their culture toward giving socially desirable responses that no amount of assurance will induce them to admit deviance. It would be unusual indeed for people in contemporary American society to report a preference for homosexual over heterosexual relations, or for communism over capitalism, even if they felt that way. Other characteristics cannot be reported directly because psychological defenses or lack of insight hinder the subject's awareness.

To measure attributes such as these, the researcher often resorts to indirect techniques, in which the true purpose of assessment is disguised. Typically, the subject is confronted with a task under the pretext of assessing one attribute, whereas the researcher is really interested in another. Thus in Hammond's (1948) "error-choice" method of attitude assessment the subject is presented with what is ostensibly an information test, but both alternative answers are incorrect; his choices are scored to yield data about his attitude toward some controversial issue. [Sample question: "Russia's removal of heavy industry from Austria was (1) legal, (2) illegal."] The Rorschach inkblots and the Thematic Apperception Test are among the better known methods for indirectly assessing personality traits; others are word association, sentence completion, finger painting, and doll play. (See descriptions of these and other techniques in, e.g., Anderson & Anderson, 1951; Bell, 1948; Goodenough, 1949; Rapaport, 1945, 1946; Schafer, 1948; Stern, Stein, & Bloom, 1956.) Often these are called *projective* techniques because they were initially based on the psychoanalytic notion that the individual projects his own unacceptable impulses onto ambiguous stimulus material. For many indirect measures such an assumption is not necessary; people caught unaware may reveal a variety of traits in ways that do not necessarily require the mechanism of projection. If, for example, a subject were asked to give his name, and the interviewer recorded not the response itself, but the response latency, this would constitute a "projective" or indirect test in the broader sense, since the subject is not made aware of the dimension by which his response is to be analyzed.

For some of these procedures, formal scoring systems are available. But often the examiner gives his impression of the subject on the basis of an intuitive, global analysis of the response protocol; in this case the "instrument" used is not really the test alone. Rather, the test and the interpreter together constitute the device for assessing personality.

A great deal of current research is aimed at improving the various indirect methods and at assessing the validity of behavioral inferences and predictions made from them. The researcher wishing to use such techniques should be warned that to date the results of validity studies have generally been quite disappointing, whether global impressions or more precise scores are used. This holds for the Rorschach and the TAT as well as for the newer techniques; predictions based on responses in indirect assessment do not often do better than chance.

One can only guess about the reasons for such poor validity. Perhaps the techniques are not yet sufficiently well developed, and further refinements may lead to better prediction. Or perhaps the methods are not really "indirect" enough; maybe they do not, after all, manage to circumvent the ego-defensive processes which make direct study of emotional areas difficult. Also, responses in an indirect test can be readily influenced by factors other than the particular characteristics of the subject in which the examiner is interested. The nature of the testing situation, of the stimuli, of the examiner, and of the subject's attitudinal set can all affect responses profoundly, so that the protocol by no means provides a pure reflection of the critical characteristics of the subject. For that matter, subject characteristics quite different from those in which the examiner is interested may be largely responsible for his response pattern.

Controls in Systematic Assessment

The various techniques for systematic assessment reviewed here are intended to afford some degree of control over the process of eliciting intrasubject variables. This kind of control has two aspects, standardization and unobtrusiveness. By standardization we mean that all subjects are assessed under comparable conditions, so that variations among their responses can be attributed to characteristics of themselves rather than to characteristics of the stimulus situation—as is likely to be the case in research that depends wholly on naturalistic observation. By unobtrusiveness we refer to the aim of affecting minimally the attribute that the instrument is designed to assess. These two aims of control can usually be only partly attained in any concrete research situation; furthermore, they are likely to work against each other, so that the more standardized the stimulus, the more obtrusive it becomes; and the more freedom of response permitted, the less the testing situation is really standardized.

Try as he may to devise a standard set of stimuli with which to confront all subjects, the researcher will have difficulty in demonstrating that their meaning—that is, their "subjective stimulus value"—remains constant for all people. This is particularly troublesome for verbal stimuli, whose meaning depends so much on the common or idiosyncratic language system that the subject uses. Nearly all standardized verbal tests are culture-bound, applicable only to the population on which they were developed; if one wishes to assess the "same" attribute in a different culture, he generally has to devise a new set of test items that will reflect that attribute appropriately in the new context. The problem is most apparent for cultures with entirely different languages; but the same difficulty arises in comparing different subgroups within the same society, whose symbol meanings may differ just enough to make objectively identical verbal stimuli subjectively incomparable. Some attempts have been made to increase the comparability of different subject groups by using nonverbal test stimuli; but even with this approach the general problem is far from resolved.

With respect to the aim of unobtrusiveness, this too can be achieved only approximately, for one must always disturb subjects at least enough to elicit a response; and this may be sufficient to distort the very attribute being measured. For instance, a researcher might wish to find out if people who are well informed about an issue are more likely than others to hold strong attitudes toward it. If his interview schedule is designed so that the information questions come first, then ignorant respondents may be intimidated by them to the point that they are unwilling to commit themselves on the subsequent attitudinal question, whereas their opinions before the interviewer came along were as strong as those of the well informed. If this happened, then a positive correlation between information and attitude strength might be spuriously generated by the research procedure itself.

One way to avoid this particular kind of contamination would be to separate the two sets of questions in the interview; or, better yet, two different questionnaire forms could be used, one in which the attitude questions came first, and the other in which the information questions came first. Then it would be possible to tell whether any obtained relationship was wholly the result of a particular order of presentation.

Another problem of research control faces the investigator who uses the strategy of systematic assessment. This is control over extraneous variables which might contribute spuriously to a relationship that is erroneously interpreted as essential. If, for example, one were to assess the strengths of the motive for affiliation and the motive for achievement by means of imaginative stories, using the technique developed by McClelland, Atkinson, and their associates (see McClelland, et al., 1953; Atkinson, 1958), one might find that the two sets of scores were positively correlated. This could lead to the conclusion that achievement and affiliation motives tend to go together. The problem is that both of these measures of motive strength depend, to some extent, on the lengths of stories the subjects write. So the correlation between the two measures may simply be due to the fact that people who write long stories tend to score higher on both than people who write short stories. In order to infer an intrinsic relation between the two motives, it is necessary to control this extraneous variable by comparing scores with protocol length "held constant" or "partialled out." (See discussion of partial relations in Chapter 13 for a description of analysis techniques appropriate to this problem.)

Assessment studies, which involve no direct manipulation of the independent variable, generally cannot provide very convincing evidence for causal relations. Even if a direction of causation could be logically established on theoretical grounds, it is usually impossible to demonstrate it unambiguously by the correlational procedures available in assessment research. Returning to a previous example, suppose one entertained the hypothesis that people tend to become well informed about those issues concerning which they hold extreme attitudes. A positive correlation between attitude extremity and amount of information is certainly required by this hypothesis; but it would not constitute sufficient evidence for it because the same correlation could result from the opposite direction of causation, namely that people who acquire a great deal of information about an issue tend to develop extreme attitudes toward it.

Control over extraneous variables, to the extent that it can be achieved in assessment research, requires the investigator to think of them in advance so that he can try to hold them constant or obtain relevant measures of them at the time data on the principal variables are collected. This is a big order, for there are often many competing interpretations of a single relationship, and the investigator is likely to think of only a few of them; therefore, many relevant control variables will be omitted from any particular study. Perhaps the best that can be expected is that one will include a few obvious measures of potentially contaminating factors and see if the essential relationship holds up even when these factors are controlled statistically. Then, if he thinks of another extraneous variable later (or if a journal editor points it out to him when he submits his manuscript for publication), it can well be included in a subsequent study that is intended to help clarify the remaining ambiguities. There is probably no study that is perfectly controlled for all time, so one need not be paralyzed at the thought of a relevant control variable which might have been omitted from a given battery of assessment instruments.

EXPERIMENTAL MANIPULATION

The main shortcoming of assessment research, from the point of view of control, is that it requires one to think of so many potentially contaminating extraneous variables that must be held constant, or controlled statistically, before he can conclude with certainty that there is an intrinsic relation between X and Y. Particularly, to make some statement like "X causes Y" requires much more evidence than the mere fact that the two variables are found to covary across a sample of subjects. For such an inference one must be able to discredit the interpretation that some third variable is responsible for the observed relationship. Although this possibility can never be absolutely excluded, one can, with an experimental strategy, obtain more convincing evidence for causal propositions than is available from assessment studies or from naturalistic observation. This is because the effects of extraneous variables in an experiment are controlled by the experimental conditions, and the presumably causal independent variable is directly manipulated to determine its effect on the dependent variable.

To illustrate the difference between an assessment and an experimental approach to the same research problem, consider the hypothetical research question whether anxiety has a facilitating or inhibiting effect on examination performance. One way of tackling the problem via systematic assessment would be to administer a test of anxiety at the time of an examination, then correlate grades on the exam with scores on the anxiety test. The limitation of such a strategy would be that one could not necessarily conclude from a positive correlation, for example, that anxiety *produced* an improvement in exam performance. Both sets of scores may have been influenced by the same third factor, such as intelligence (stupid students may not know enough to be anxious), attitude toward scholarly pursuits, study habits, amount of sleep the night before, and so forth.

An experimental approach to the same problem might consist of administering the exam under two different conditions which are identical in every respect except that one is anxiety arousing and the other neutral. The same subjects could be exposed to both situations, or, alternatively, two equivalent groups could be constructed and one assigned to each condition. If the "aroused" group performed better than the "neutral," it could reasonably be concluded that anxiety (at least this particular method of inducing anxiety) had a facilitating effect on test performance (at least on this particular exam).

The essential features of an experiment are manipulation of the independent variable, control of pre-existing intersubject differences, and control of extraneous factors in the experimental situation itself.

Manipulating the Independent Variable

This is achieved by assigning subjects to conditions intended to represent two or more values of the independent variable. Sometimes there is an actual temporal manipulation, in which subjects are exposed to a changing stimulus situation, and one looks for systematically associated changes in their responses. In other experimental designs different subjects may receive different values of the independent variable, and their responses are compared to see if they vary systematically with the experimental conditions. In either case the appropriate conditions of the independent variable are presented directly to the subjects. This feature contrasts with assessment research, in which the investigator can only try to ascertain whether or not subjects have been, or are being, exposed to the relevant conditions.

Controlling Intersubject Differences

In the assignment of subjects to the conditions of an experiment they themselves have no voice in the selection of the condition they are exposed to. This is decided for them by the experimenter. Basically, there are three ways of assigning subjects to conditions—by simple randomization, by randomized matching, and by using subjects as their own controls. All three procedures are aimed at assuring equivalence among the groups that are exposed to the various experimental situations. In this way one can be fairly certain that any postexperimental differences can be attributed to the conditions of the experiment rather than to pre-existing intersubject differences.

If subjects are randomly assigned to the various experimental conditions, it can reasonably be assumed that, within the limits of sampling error, all characteristics associated with them, whether relevant to the dependent variable or not, have likewise been randomized. Statistical tests for the significance of experimental effects (see supplement to Chapter 10) help one to decide whether the observed differences among conditions are sufficiently larger than what would be expected from sampling error. An alternative assignment procedure is to match individual subjects, before random assignment to the experimental conditions, on as many extraneous variables as one can think of which might affect the dependent variable. If .the groups are adequately matched on these, then there is even greater assurance that any postexperimental differences can be attributed to the independent variable that was directly manipulated. Finally, it is sometimes possible to assign the same subjects to all conditions. This, essentially, provides optimum matching of the various experimental groups; but there are some circumstances in which such a *treatment-by-subjects* design is not feasible (see Chapter 10).

Controlling Situational Differences

The researcher constructs his experimental conditions to represent values of one or more particular independent variables. If he is to conclude that the intended variables are responsible for the experimental effect, then he must see to it that some further, extraneous, factor does not covary with them in the experimental conditions. Suppose that, in our previous illustration on anxiety and test performance, the situation constructed to arouse anxiety involved a big, scowling dean of students presenting a mathematics test with instructions that those who failed would be flunked out of school, whereas in the neutral group the same examination was presented by a friendly innocuous-looking graduate assistant who simply said that he wished to see how students would do on the test. Although intending to manipulate anxiety, the researcher has probably also manipulated a number of other attributes, such as hostility toward the test administrator or motivation to do well. Any differential test performance between the two groups could then just as readily be attributed to hostility or motivation levels as to anxiety.

Another common research situation in which an extraneous situational variable may be unintentionally "tied" to the independent variable occurs in a treatment-by-subjects design in which all subjects receive all experimental conditions. If the conditions are administered in an order that is constant for all subjects, then any observed differences among them might result, in part, from the particular order in which they appear. If, for example, the same subjects were tested first under neutral and then under anxiety-arousing conditions, the experimental effect might be inflated (or masked) by the order of presentation—that is, the subjects might do better in the second test simply because of practice on the first. A difference between the two conditions could not certainly be attributed to differences in anxiety (nor could a lack of difference be taken to mean that anxiety level had no effect), for the two variables, anxiety and order of presentation, are experimentally confounded.

There are three basic approaches to the control of such potentially contaminating situational variables. One can hold them constant, randomize them, or manipulate them systematically and separately from the principal independent variable. Holding extraneous variables constant means that all subjects in each experimental group are treated exactly alike except for their differing conditions on the independent variable. This is often more difficult to achieve than it may sound, but in the test-anxiety experiment, for example, an approach to this ideal would consist in having the same person (e.g., the dean) administer the test to both the neutral and the aroused groups, so that at least differences in the personalities and roles of the administrators could not affect the outcome.

Such a "hold constant" approach to controlling extraneous situational variables is the one commonly adopted because it is cheaper and more convenient than the others, but the experiment suffers in loss of generality. If one studies the relationship between an independent and dependent variable when all other relevant factors are held constant at particular levels, then the relationship can be demonstrated for those levels alone. If only the dean administered the test to the neutral and aroused groups, there is no assurance that a comparable relation between anxiety and test performance would hold when someone else administered it.

A different attack would consist of subdividing the two major groups into several smaller groups and having a number of different people administer the test in both the anxiety-producing and the friendly way. This is one way of randomizing certain situational variables, so that a variety of extraneous conditions is represented, yet not allowed to affect the dependent variable systematically. Though more laborious and expensive, such an experimental design helps to meet the criteria of generality discussed in Chapter 3 as well as those of control which are of chief concern here.

Finally, it is possible to achieve control over extraneous situational variables by varying them systematically. For example, the usual way of controlling the order in which experimental stimuli are presented is by *counter-balancing;* half the subjects may receive them in order AB and the other half in the order BA.* This design not only serves to remove the possible contaminating effect of order, but it can provide an estimate of the size of the order effect by determining whether the average A and B values obtained in the two sequences are different. If a number of stimuli are presented to each subject, or if the same two stimuli are presented over and over, the variety of sequences increases greatly. Unless all possible arrangements can be used, it is necessary to select some particular set that seems unlikely to contaminate the experimental relationship. For instance, if A and B are to be repeatedly presented, one might wish to counterbalance in such a way that the average serial position of both is the same for all subjects—for example, by giving half of them the sequence $ABBAABBA$ and the other half $BAABBAAB$. (The orders $ABABABAB$ and $BABABABA$ would not suit the purpose because the average positions of the As and Bs are not identical in the two sequences.)

Other kinds of extraneous situational variables can be systematically manipulated in treatment-by-levels designs (see Chapter 10). Any of these methods of systematic control amount to the same thing as adding more independent variables to the experiment. Though the complexity of the study may be greatly increased by such an arrangement, it has the advantage of representing a range of conditions under which the experimental effect is demonstrated; furthermore, it enables one to detect the effect of the independent variable more easily because a more powerful significance test can be used.

Preliminary and Systematic Designs

In many experimental designs only two values of the independent variable are represented—"high" and "low," or an "experimental" and "control" condition. The first group receives the experimental treatment (and therefore has some value above zero on the independent

* An even preferable arrangement might be $ABBA$ and $BAAB$, since a given ordered difference, such as $B–A$, could thereby be assessed both early and late in the presentation sequence.

variable), whereas the control group, which does not receive the experimental treatment, is essentially at zero on the independent variable. The second group provides a base line against which to compare the first to see whether the independent variable had any effect. This is a *preliminary design* in that it only establishes the presence or absence of an experimental effect. If a greater number of values of the independent variable is represented, a *systematic design* is approached, and it becomes possible to specify more precisely the nature of the function relating the independent and the dependent variables.

Thus, in a preliminary experiment, if the investigator wishes to know whether the relation between X and Y is positive or negative, he might use a high and low value of X to see whether Y goes along with it. Or, he may have the hunch that there is a curvilinear relation between two variables, in which case he may use three values of the independent variable, a high, a low, and a medium, to see whether the medium behaves differently on Y than the high and the low. Essentially, a preliminary design samples a few points along the range of the independent variable to see whether the dependent variable changes concomitantly.

In a systematic or functional design enough different points along the dimension of the independent variable are studied to permit one to determine not only whether there is a relation between X and Y but also the nature of the relationship. At the highest level of functional design, the exact curve relating X and Y can be specified by means of a graph or a precise mathematical equation. Such functions have been established in many areas of psychology, especially the older ones like sensation. For instance, to plot the shape of an *equal loudness contour,* the subject is presented with two tones, one standard and the second variable. The standard tone is presented at a fixed frequency and intensity, whereas the frequency of the variable tone is systematically manipulated. The subject's task is to set the intensity of the variable so that its loudness sounds equal to that of the standard tone. By using some 15 or 20 values of the independent variable (frequency of the variable tone) and asking the subject to set the dependent variable (intensity of the variable tone), the precise shape of the curve containing all tones that sound just as loud as the standard tone can be plotted on a frequency-by-intensity graph.

In the history of a field preliminary experiments may be expected to give way to later functional designs. It would seem premature to perform a detailed systematic experiment relating two variables without knowing whether there is any relation between them in the first place. When the investigator starts work in the area, he first tries in broad outline to find out which independent variables seem to be important. For such purposes, it is often strategic for him to choose values of the independent variables that seem most likely, on an intuitive or any other basis, to produce the most dramatic differences in the dependent variable. Sometimes he may wish to use only extreme values, even those rarely encountered in real life; a positive experimental outcome depends, in part, on how well chosen these values are. Once the field has been staked out with preliminary or exploratory studies which have demonstrated the relative importance of several variables, it becomes strategic to begin a systematic attack on the more important ones.

However, there are assumptions in the preliminary strategy which are formally equivalent to those implicit in the "extreme groups" design (see Chapter 2, pp. 38–41). When only two values of the independent variable are represented in an experiment, the researcher is implicitly assuming a linear (or at least a monotonic) relation to the dependent variable. If the expected experimental effect emerges, then only by extrapolation (or interpolation) can he conclude that X has a general effect on Y comparable to that obtained in the experiment. Conversely, if no difference between the two conditions appears, then to conclude that X and Y are unrelated is to ignore a variety of curvilinear relations that could have made these two points come out the same on the dependent variable. A preliminary experiment provides a particular restricted operational definition of the independent variable, representing it by two or three points on what is generally conceptualized as a continuum. In interpreting the results, then, one should keep the restricted operational definition explicitly in mind and only with caution generalize to the full range of the variable.

PRINCIPLES OF CONTROL COMMON TO THE THREE STRATEGIES

Although naturalistic observation, systematic assessment, and experimentation differ in the *degree* of control they afford over research variables, the *kinds* of control permitted by the three strategies are, in a sense, similar. Repeatedly in the foregoing discussion we have referred to randomization, systematic variation, and holding constant as methods for eliminating unwanted influences on the essential research relationships. It is in the means used for maintaining control over extraneous variables that parallels among the strategies become apparent. In order to highlight these parallels, we shall briefly review here the three general approaches to control.

Holding Constant

In nearly every research design some extraneous variables are controlled by holding them constant. This is frequently true, for example, of the observer variable. Although refinements in instrumentation are intended to make measures less dependent on human observers, some dependence may remain even in the most mechanized study. One way of eliminating variance in results due to this effect is to use just one observer. So in field studies a lone ethnologist or ethologist may do all the recording of events and of the relations among them; in small-scale experiments and interview surveys one investigator may gather all the data himself.

The research conditions or location of observations are also commonly controlled by holding them constant. An experiment is conducted in a particular room where noise, illumination, temperature, arrangement of apparatus and of furniture, smudges on the wall, and other surrounding features are maintained at an approximately constant level. Interviewers in a national survey typically interview respondents in their homes—perhaps more often at night or weekends. Although "home" is not quite such a constant condition for all people as is a single experimental room, it nevertheless represents some limitation in the range of background stimuli confronting subjects. The naturalist, too, is generally restricted to a particular set of observing conditions—for example, daytime, humanly tolerable weather, and reasonably accessible locations. He may even choose to control background conditions further by observing his subjects in just one location or activity, such as the salt lick or playground or conference table.

The instruments of experimentation and assessment are always, to some degree at least, held constant for all. The same instructions are presented to all subjects, and each subject may be uniformly asked to respond "yes" or "no," to turn a knob right or left, or to keep his head in a chinrest and fixate on a point of light while watching the visual stimuli. Degree of deprivation and sequence of maze turns may be kept the same over all subjects. Verbal stimuli in assessment studies are usually presented in constant order. Part of the standardization procedure, which permits comparison among subjects, requires a fixed sequence of questions or problems within the test.

Finally, it is possible, at least in principle, to control even miscellaneous subject variables by holding them constant. This would amount, in the extreme, to doing an entire study on just one organism. Such an approach has been used in a few important psychological studies [e.g., Ebbinghaus' (1913) memory experiments and some of Skinner's (see, e.g., Ferster & Skinner, 1957) studies of learning in pigeons]; but it is not common, probably because psychologists usually aim to generalize over organisms and do not ordinarily regard a single member as representative of his species. A less extreme control over intersubject variability can be attained by restricted selection of subjects. Thus an investigator may use a particular strain of albino rats, a sample of college sophomores, or adults who fall within a "normal" range of intelligence and psychiatric adjustment. The reason for such restricted sampling is not always explicit and deliberate, but it might well be simply to limit contamination from unknown variables.

Randomizing

If one wants to avoid the limitation on generality that such hold-constant procedures afford, he can use randomizing as a method of control over extraneous variables. (It is clearly impossible to randomize every extraneous variable; some control by holding constant—e.g., the test form, experimental apparatus, or geographical locale—is inevitable. So the investigator will typically single out only those variables for which generalizability is crucial and randomly sample them while holding the others constant.)

This method of control is most frequently applied to subject selection, but it can often be conveniently applied to other aspects of the research design as well, whenever the investigator wants to make sure that his research outcome does not depend on a particular fortuitous selection of measures. For instance, a group of interviewers (or experimenters or observers) might be assigned to subjects at random, in order to offset a possible biasing effect from one of them alone. Also it is possible to randomize the times at which measures are taken, to keep from introducing a systematic bias. For instance, physiological measures on hospitalized patients might be taken at various times during the day; a time sampling of children's behavior in nursery school might be arranged so that at each half hour a random child in the class is observed; or in interviewing applicants for jobs one might purposely try to randomize the order in which various traits are judged, so that a single one of them cannot exert a dominant halo effect by always being judged first.

In administering a series of perceptual stimuli to a subject, it is common practice to randomize them to reduce any systematic effect that a particular fixed order might impose. In the psychophysical method of constant stimuli, for example, the subject is presented with randomly ordered variable stimuli, which he is to judge as greater than, less than, or equal to a standard. The purpose of this presentation is to provide assurance that the judgment of any one variable stimulus will not be systematically affected by the judgments of those which preceded it, as could be the case if a constant order were used for all subjects. Although it is not often done, verbal instruments, too, could be arranged so that the various questions (stimulus items) would appear in random order, some subjects responding to them in one sequence, some in another. Such an arrangement would permit control of possible sequence effects.

In all of these randomizing techniques, the subjects, observers, time intervals, or stimulus orderings are selected, not just haphazardly, but by a table of random numbers (see Table A in the Appendix). The reason for using this mechanical method is that humans, unaided, are not capable of generating truly random number sequences. They tend to have built-in preferences and aversions, either for certain numbers or for certain ways of ordering them. Tables of random numbers can be routinely generated by digital computers in such a way that any conceivable bias is negligible.

Systematic Variation

Any extraneous variable that can be randomized can, in principle, be systematically varied as well—though the cost and effort may be prohibitive. Two reasons for preferring this method of control are (1) that it provides an unequivocal, readily analyzed set of data on the influence of the systematically varied factor and (2) that it permits a more powerful test of statistical significance by reducing within-groups variance among scores. Thus the treatment-by-subjects design of an experiment is a method of systematically varying intersubject differences by assigning all subjects to all experimental conditions. A treatment-by-levels design applies the experimental variable within each of several predesignated classes of subjects or conditions, controlling extraneous variables associated with the classification by systematically varying them. (Chapter 10 presents descriptions of these experimental designs and the methods of statistical analysis by means of which their increased precision can be taken into account.)

Counterbalancing of experimental treatments provides a clear-cut way of systematically varying the extraneous variable, order of presentation. The treatments are presented to the same subjects repeatedly in several sequences or each sequence is assigned to a different group of subjects. This is a special instance of a treatment-by-levels design, which is especially useful when each subject is to get all experimental treatments and one wants to make sure that no treatment is systematically contaminated by the effects of those preceding it.

It is also possible to vary systematically such things as the material to be learned (e.g., mazes, puzzles, or nonsense-syllable lists), background conditions (e.g., temperature, light, time of day, or geographic location of study), and the person who collects the data. One would simply assign a different group of subjects to each different value of the extraneous variable (or, alternatively, assign the same subjects successively to all different conditions). Sometimes it is profitable to *confound* two or more extraneous variables by making them vary together. Thus, if there were two different experimenters, E_1 and E_2, and two different problems, P_1 and P_2, with which to investigate the effect of fatigue on performance, it might be advantageous to let E_1 present P_1 and E_2 present P_2 each to a different group of subjects. This would presumably make the performances within groups as homogeneous as possible, so that the effect of fatigue could be more precisely detected. [Of course, such a design demands that the effect of the main independent variable (fatigue) be comparable in both groups. If it were not, then one would never know whether the experimenter or the problem accounted for the difference.]

The principle of systematic variation can be applied to observational and assessment research as well as to experiments. Public opinion pollsters frequently use the split-ballot technique to make sure that the particular form in which a question is asked does not distort the replies to it; they simply administer a different form to each of two or more subsamples of respondents and look for comparable response distributions within each subsample. Similarly, an observer of children's natural behaviors could compare the amounts of ascendancy shown by boys and girls in a number of different types of situations to make sure that any apparent sex difference was not simply a reflection of sex-role differentiation in one particular situation.

OTHER COMPARISONS AMONG THE THREE STRATEGIES

We have devoted considerable attention in this chapter to contrasting and comparing the three research strategies with regard to the amount and kind of control that can be exercised within each. But control is not the only desideratum to take into account when designing a research project. It is well to consider other advantages and disadvantages inherent in various strategies before deciding on a particular one or a combination of them. For the sake of perspective, it might be well to review briefly some other criteria that have been alluded to in passing.

Precision

A research design is precise to the extent that it permits accurate measurement of the variables under study and specific statements concerning their functional interrelations. Naturalistic observation is likely to be rather weak, according to this criterion, and experimentation relatively strong. In experimental work the independent variable is under the control of the investigator, and he can vary its magnitude in a systematic fashion, which is not possible in either the naturalistic or the assessment procedures. If the researcher must take his subjects as he finds them, their present characteristics and past histories may not be amenable to neat distribution along any particular set of dimensions. When assessment of past events depends on the subject's own recall, this is likely to correspond only roughly with the true facts of the case. Precise measurement of the dependent variables is also likely to suffer in naturalistic observation, more than in non-experimental assessment or experimentation. In their natural settings responses tend either to occur or not to occur, with little room for variation in magnitude. Thus restaurant owners are found either to admit or not to admit a colored clientele, and from such a dichotomous classification it is difficult to measure a variable such as "extent of discrimination."

Functional relations among variables may be stated with different degrees of precision. If the maximum in precision is to be possible at all, one must be able to assess all values of X and Y within the range covered by the empirical proposition. In an experiment these values can usually be made to occur more dependably than they can be found in nature.

Repeatability

A finding is more convincing if someone else can repeat the observations and come up with the same results. A difficulty with the intuitive judgments that frequently enter into naturalistic observations or clinical predictions is that it is very difficult to define the bases on which these judgments are made, so that another investigator might obtain the same impressions independently with similar evidence. Refinements of assessment instruments and other elaborations of research design are often accompanied by clearer specification of the steps that another investigator must go through in order to reach the same conclusions as those resulting from a previous study.

The three research strategies are *potentially* subject to comparable degrees of repeatability, given adequate sampling and stability in the phenomenon under study. It is possible to specify the conditions of observation as well as of manipulation and to develop quantified, reliable check lists or assessment instruments that will permit another investigator to replicate studies in any of these categories. Certain practical limitations, however, may intrude to decrease repeatability. Natural observation procedures are frequently applied to complex, multiply determined phenomena which occur rarely or, perhaps, only once—such as a lynching mob or a mass delusion. If these do occur again, their conditions are likely to be so different that another set of principles must be found to account for them. This is not, of course, a necessary limitation on naturalistic observation, for the method can be applied equally well to recurrent phenomena, such as church services, animal rearing, or traffic violations. But the observations made in experiments are, in general, the most clearly specified, hence more easily duplicated by a different investigator.

Generalizability

When it comes to generalizing research findings to the normal, everyday behavior of the organism, naturalistic observation would appear to enjoy a clear lead over the other methodologies—assuming, of course, that it is based on an adequate sampling of the behaviors under study. Not only can the investigator be sure that the relationships he has observed occur in the subjects' natural habitat, but through time-sampling of behavior he can determine the relative frequencies with which the events appear. This can provide an index of the "importance" of a functional relationship to the organism in its natural ecology. In laboratory studies, on the other hand, the particular functional relationship observed may be in large part a product of the special, artificial conditions of the experiment. Such a restriction in generality is likely to be particularly serious in those "hold constant" experiments in which control of extraneous variables artificially places them at levels that would hardly be encountered in the subject's normal activity. A given experiment may show conclusively a relationship between the independent and dependent variables, which, however, is demonstrated only under such peculiar circumstances that the result is uninteresting, except as a curiosity.

Controlled assessment procedures are also liable to challenge on grounds of nongeneralizability. Although, typically, the subject is observed under somewhat less artificial circumstances than in a laboratory experiment, the very nature of the instruments used requires that the response under study be elicited out of context of the subject's "normal" behavior. A statement by a respondent in an interview that he is "for" a particular political candidate in itself evidences a kind of attitude, but it may not be the same sort of attitude that would impel the respondent to vote for the candidate in an actual election. Inferences concerning determinants of attitudes expressed in an interview may not apply to the corresponding attitudes expressed in overt action.

A more critical problem may arise in assessment research if the nature of the psychological attribute itself is affected by the process of measuring it. The respondent may not have entertained an attitude toward a candidate in a forthcoming election until the interviewer came along and requested him to express one. Further, the manner in which the attitude is expressed may be conditioned by the respondent's concern over the "right thing" to say. The principles of nondirective interviewing are aimed at reducing the potency of such "situational" determinants of responses, but they are likely to be only partially successful in any given case. Thus, when unusual stimuli are injected into the research situation to elicit responses, it is difficult to know the extent to which the responses reflect previously existing psychological attributes and the extent to which they are "forced" by the measuring procedure itself. Such a concern is critical for both experimental and controlled assessment research. It is, by contrast, unlikely to come up at all in naturalistic observation, particularly when the subjects are unaware that their behavior is being recorded.

Choice Among the Strategies

There is no justification for assuming, a priori, that one research strategy is better than another. Controlled assessment makes it possible to elicit responses and measure them precisely; but it only permits inferences concerning correlations, not "causes," and it may influence the very phenomenon being studied. Experimentation can provide more convincing evidence about "causal" relationships by virtue of its better control over extraneous influences, but it may distort the attribute under study, and elaborate controls may impose an excessive degree of "unreality" on the phenomenon. Further, experimentation in some areas may be out of the question on practical or ethical grounds. Naturalistic observation techniques have the advantage of providing "rich" records of behaviors and relationships in their natural habitats; but causal or even correlational inferences from them are often exceedingly tenuous, and many kinds of relationships cannot be studied in this fashion at all because the critical stimuli and responses are not normally observable.

Choice of design must therefore depend to a large extent on the stage of investigation, the resources available, and the specific goals of the research. In the earliest phases of a study it is perhaps wise to "get a feeling" for the phenomenon by observing it in its natural habitat. Systematic assessment and experimentation can then follow to help clarify the critical variables and relationships. The conceptual scheme derived from this work can again be referred to a natural setting to determine its applicability there.

Experimentation on a large scale is expensive, as is systematic assessment, especially if the theoretical population is to be sampled adequately and the experimental conditions are to be made as similar as possible to those of the natural habitat. So perhaps over-all research efficiency is initially furthered by small pilot studies on selected groups, until sufficient confidence can be developed in hypotheses and measuring procedures to warrant the considerable expense of a large-scale study.

Finally, the goal of the researcher is an important factor, perhaps the chief one, in making a selection among the various available strategies. Virtually any goal can constitute, from one point of view or another, a legitimate objective for psychological research. It would seem inappropriate to legislate the objective or restrict the method; rather, an adequate meeting of the two should be encouraged, so that whatever the investigator's goals they can be substantially furthered by his research design.

SUMMARY

The aim of control is clarification of variables and the relations among them. This can be accomplished in a variety of ways, but the procedures of major concern in this chapter have been those that involve either manipulation or systematic assessment of psychological attributes. Both research strategies are antedated by the methodology of naturalistic observation. Though in its highly developed forms naturalistic observation may provide for certain refinements in control and measuring procedures, it is commonly used by psychologists today just to get a rough, rich, impressionistic view of a phenomenon before undertaking more systematic study. There are, however, many kinds of research problems that are not amenable to study by other methods, and the strategy of passive observation and recording may be the only one available. This is necessarily true in studying records of past behaviors which occurred under conditions that can no longer be directly measured.

Systematic assessment with controlled stimuli is a strategy aimed at measuring attributes by intentionally eliciting behaviors which reflect them. As in naturalistic observation, the aim is to measure variables without influencing them. Typically, standardized stimuli are presented to subjects and differences in the way they respond are interpreted as stemming from characteristics of the subjects themselves. Relations among the variables of focal interest are clarified by a kind of passive control over extraneous influences. This may be achieved by appropriate subject sampling, by arrangement of stimuli, and by assessing additional attributes. The "independent variable" is allowed to fluctuate naturally, measures of it being taken as they are found.

In addition to the controls available in naturalistic observation and systematic assessment, experimental research provides for direct control over the independent variable by the assignment of subjects to conditions of the experiment. This permits more certain exclusion of extraneous influences; hence experimentation is the most convincing method for demonstrating the effect of one variable on another.

Each of the three research strategies offers advantages and disadvantages that should be carefully considered in choosing among them. When control of extraneous variables is paramount, the experimental method is generally preferred, but its superiority in this regard may be offset by loss of generality. Moreover, it is unrealistic to hope that any study can ever be so perfectly controlled that all possible interpretations save one are certainly eliminated.

REFERENCES

Altmann, Margaret. Patterns of social behavior in big game of the United States and Europe. *Transactions of the twenty-first North American Wildlife Conference,* 1956, 538–545.

Anderson, H. H., & Anderson, Gladys L. *An introduction to projective techniques.* New York: Prentice-Hall, 1951.

Atkinson, J. W. (Ed.) *Motives in fantasy, action, and society.* Princeton, N. J.: Van Nostrand, 1958.

Baldwin, A. L. Socialization and the parent-child relationship. *Child Develpm.,* 1948, **19**, 127–136.

Barker, R. G., & Wright, H. F. *One boy's day.* New York: Harper, 1951.

Bell, J. E. *Projective techniques.* New York: Longmans, Green, 1948.

Berelson, B. *Content analysis in communication research.* Glencoe, Ill.: Free Press, 1952.

Campbell, A., & Katona, G. The sample survey: a technique for social science research. In L. Festinger & D. Katz (Eds.), *Research methods in the behavioral sciences.* New York: Dryden, 1953.

Ebbinghaus, H. *Memory: a contribution to experimental psychology.* (Engl. trans. by H. A. Ruger & C. E. Bussenius.) New York: Teachers College, 1913.

Ferster, C. B., & Skinner, B. F. *Schedules of reinforcement.* New York: Appleton-Century-Crofts, 1957.

Goodenough, Florence L. *Mental testing: its history, principles, and applications.* New York: Rinehart, 1949.

Guilford, J. P. *Psychometric methods.* (2nd Ed.) New York: McGraw-Hill, 1954.

Hammond, K. R. Measuring attitudes by error-choice: an indirect method. *J. abnorm. soc. Psychol.,* 1948, **43**, 38–48.

Hollingshead, A. B., & Redlich, F. C. *Social class and mental illness.* New York: Wiley, 1958.

Hyman, H. *Survey design and analysis.* Glencoe, Ill.: Free Press, 1955.

Kahn, R. L., & Cannell, C. F. *The dynamics of interviewing.* New York: Wiley, 1957.

Knapp, R. H., & Greenbaum, J. J. *The younger American scholar: his collegiate origins.* Chicago: Univer. Chicago Press, 1953.

McClelland, D. C., Atkinson, J. W., Clark, R. A., & Lowell, E. L. *The achievement motive.* New York: Appleton-Century-Crofts, 1953.

Osgood, C. E. *Method and theory in experimental psychology.* New York: Oxford, 1953.

Rapaport, D. *Diagnostic psychological testing.* Chicago: Year Book Publishers, 1945, 1946. 2 vols.

Schafer, R. *The clinical application of psychological tests.* New York: International Universities Press, 1948.

Scott, W. A., & Withey, S. B. *The United States and the United Nations: the public view.* New York: Manhattan, 1958.

Stephan, F. F., & McCarthy, P. J. *Sampling opinions: an analysis of survey procedures.* New York: Wiley, 1958.

Stern, G. G., Stein, M. I., & Bloom, B. S. *Methods in personality assessment.* Glencoe, Ill.: Free Press, 1956.

Torgerson, W. S. *Theory and methods of scaling.* New York: Wiley, 1958.

Whiting, J. W. M. The cross-cultural method. In G. Lindzey (Ed.), *Handbook of social psychology,* Vol. 1. Cambridge: Addison-Wesley, 1954.

Woodworth, R. S., & Schlosberg, H. *Experimental psychology.* (Rev. Ed.) New York: Holt, 1954.

CHAPTER 5

Developing quantitative measures

Most psychological research is aimed at finding relations among variables. At a very general level, one can say that variables X and Y are related if a knowledge of the classification of subjects on one of them helps to predict their classification on the other. In an experiment the independent variable is manipulated by the researcher; he determines how his subjects are to be classified on this attribute by arranging to have each experimental condition represent a particular level of the independent variable. Then he assesses his subjects on the dependent variable to see how, if at all, their status on this is predictable from the experimental conditions. In research by systematic assessment the investigator merely elicits responses intended to represent two or more variables, then relates them by classifying his subjects simultaneously on both. Likewise, naturalistic observation may involve classifying subjects on two or more attributes at once, to see if there is a tendency for certain values of one to go with certain values of the other. In either type of assessment study, systematic or naturalistic, the distinction between an "independent" and a "dependent" variable may not be meaningful, since often there is no theoretical or empirical reason for treating one of them as "cause" and the other as "effect." Nevertheless, these terms are sometimes used anyway, simply to denote the direction of prediction—from subjects' statuses on the independent variable to their statuses on the dependent variable.

No matter what the research design, the dependent variable must always be assessed. Sometimes the independent variable is assessed, sometimes manipulated; but even in the latter case, the experimenter must have some way of determining—either formally or informally—what level of the variable is represented by each of his experimental conditions. These levels may be determined by reference to the condition itself, as when hunger is defined according to the number of hours of food deprivation; or the independent variable may be assessed by means of responses elicited from the subjects, as when hunger is defined from peoples' reports of their own feelings. Thus assessment of some kind is at the core of every psychological investigation.

When the magnitude of a variable is reported as a number, this kind of assessment is sometimes dignified by the term "measurement." We use the words assessment and measurement interchangeably, however, since the process of determining a subject's status on a variable is in the last analysis a judgmental one, regardless of whether numbers are used. Moreover, the precision of a numerical score may be more apparent than real, since the way in which it is arrived at may severely limit the interpretations that can be placed on it. Occasionally one encounters a distinction between qualitative and quantitative assessment, with the implication that quality refers to differences in kind, whereas quantity refers to differences in degree. We do not regard this distinction as a fundamental one either, since a qualitative measure can be seen as representing two levels of a variable—its presence and absence—whereas a quantitative measure simply provides for more refined discrimination within the former category by representing the degree to which the variable is present. A qualitative measure can be seen as a first crude attempt to define a variable which can perhaps subsequently be assessed with greater precision.

The development of precisely quantifiable measures of variables has occupied the attention of researchers in all fields of psychology. This is an exceedingly important preoccupation, since the precision with which variables are measured determines the exactness with which relations between them can be specified. It is ordinarily not enough to conclude that variables X and Y are related in the population from which the sample was drawn, for the word "relationship" can mean too many different things. One usually wants to know not simply that classification on one *can* predict classification on the other but more importantly just *what* predictions can be made and with what degree of certainty.

The quantitative specification of variables and their relationships is aided by statistics. Stated oversimply, statistical measures can serve two main functions, descriptive and inferential. A *descriptive* statistic is used to represent something about the data actually obtained, such as a sample mean, a standard deviation, or a correlation between two sets of measurements; an *inferential* statistic is used to infer something about the population from which the particular sample was drawn, such as a population location, dispersion, correlation, or difference. The second use is discussed in later chapters; here we are concerned only with statistics descriptive of location and dispersion.

DESCRIBING DISTRIBUTIONS

When measures of a variable are obtained from a sample of subjects, a number of different characteristics of these data can be described statistically. A simple one would be the number, or proportion, of subjects who fall in each category of the variable. One might also want to describe concisely the average category of classification or the most frequent. Somewhat more complexly, one could represent the degree to which this average value typifies the distribution—that is, the degree to which all measures fall close to it. Also one might want to know how the nontypical scores are scattered over the remaining categories—that is, evenly or disproportionately. It is often convenient to represent these abstract characteristics by numbers whose meanings can be interpreted even without seeing the entire distribution. Descriptive statistics serve just this purpose. They make it possible to describe and compare total distributions of scores in summary fashion without a laborious score-by-score reporting. Of course, as with any process of abstraction, the abstraction of a statistic or combination of statistics leaves out some characteristic of the original data. In that sense statistics can distort as well as represent distributions. The popular adage, "figures don't lie, but liars sure can figure," expresses a general distrust of statistical measures because some of them are inappropriately abstracted, obscuring significant aspects of the data they are purported to represent. Researchers bear a serious responsibility in their use of quantitative and statistical measures, for they are in a position to choose appropriately or inappropriately, and the users of their findings are frequently in no position to see the flaws.

NUMBERS AND THEIR MEANINGS

At the root of much quantitative misrepresentation of data lies a failure to consider carefully the meanings of the numbers used. Since numbers are so often associated with counting, it is tempting to treat them always as if they bore the relationships to one another implied by the counting operation: $3 + 4 = 7$, twice 6 is 12, etc. In general, these relations among numbers for counting can be stated as follows: the difference between any two numbers represents a standard difference in the attribute (numerosity) they measure; and the ratio of any two numbers represents the ratio of the attributes they measure. The 2 obtained by subtracting 5 from 7 is identical with the 2 obtained when 11 is subtracted from 13. Also $8 \div 4 = 2 = 12 \div 6$. The operations of addition, subtraction, multiplication, and division are meaningful whenever the numbers represent relative quantities of an attribute in the manner specified here. When this condition obtains, we have what is known as a ratio scale—that is, the ratio of the numbers represents the same ratio of the attribute.

Few psychological variables can be measured on a ratio scale. One has to look to the fundamental measures of physics—such as numerosity, distance, and weight—to find measures that clearly satisfy this requirement. The absurdity of a ratio-scale interpretation of the attribute intelligence, for example, is clear when one examines the statement, "Mark, with an IQ of 120, is twice as intelligent as Peter, with an IQ of 60." Although the numerals 120 and 60 bear a known ratio to each other, nothing in the measurement of IQ permits one to assert that the first index represents twice as much intelligence as the second. Students will readily agree that passing 30 items on a psychology test does not necessarily represent twice as much knowledge of the field as passing 15 items—if for no other reason than that the items themselves do not require equal amounts of knowledge.

The second assumption involved in the use of numbers for counting—that equal differences between numbers represent equal differences in the attribute—does not necessarily require the first; that is, one can establish meaningful units of difference without having equal ratios. We are quite willing to accept the interpretation that 1965 and 1960 are as many years apart as are 1865 and 1860, though no one would pretend that the year 1960 was 5% later than the year 1860. Similarly, we are accustomed to treating the difference between 100 degrees Fahrenheit and 101 degrees as equal to the difference between 50 and 51 degrees Fahrenheit; but it would be meaningless to suggest that 100 degrees is twice as hot as 50 degrees. The reason that ratio comparisons cannot be used on this kind of scale is that there is no absolute zero point. Instead, an arbitrary zero point is established by convention—such as the freezing point of water in the Centigrade temperature scale or the birth-year of Jesus in the Gregorian calendar—and equal units of the attribute (temperature or time) are measured on either side of the arbitrary zero. Such a standard of measurement is called an interval scale; equal differences between numbers represent equal differences in the amount of the attribute represented. (Note that the magnitudes of the *differences* can be treated as a ratio scale: for example, the difference between 20 and 10 degrees is twice as large as the difference between 10 and 5 degrees; or the time between breakfast and lunch is about two thirds the time between lunch and dinner.)

It is even difficult to find psychological variables that can be measured on interval scales. The Weber-Fechner fraction, $\Delta I/I$, was intended to represent subjectively equal intervals of stimulus difference in psychophysical experiments; but this unit is not the same for all subjects; moreover, within the same subject it holds constant only within a certain range of stimulus variation. Nor can measures of intelligence, knowledge, attitudes, and other personality traits be treated legitimately as interval scales. There is no way of knowing, for example, if the "favorable" end of an attitude scale is subjectively as far away from the "neutral" point as the "unfavorable" end is. Here the researcher usually steps in and defines equal intervals by fiat or on the basis of some questionable assumptions about the distribution of the attribute being measured. In order to average subjects' positions on his scales, or to compare movements from different initial positions, it is necessary to treat the scale as if it had equal units of measurement. So an expedient solution is chosen, with the consequence that the measure of average position or average movement may be somewhat difficult to interpret, once it has been obtained.

About the best that can be done in much psychological measurement is to represent an attribute by an ordinal scale. This is one in which the categories of the scale can be ordered according to the relative amounts of the attribute they represent, even though the absolute amounts are unknown. For instance, it is reasonably safe to assume that, for all subjects who understand the English language, the category "very favorable" represents a more positive attitude toward an object than the category "favorable" and that "favorable" represents a more positive attitude than "neutral"; and so on for the responses "unfavorable" and "very unfavorable." In other words, these five categories of attitudinal response can be ordered according to the attribute, "degree of favorableness toward X" (or, conversely, "degree of unfavorableness toward X"). For the sake of convenience, the researcher may assign the numbers 1 through 5 to these categories; but note that under such a rule of assignment the numbers can strictly be treated in an ordinal sense only, not as representing specifiable amounts of the attitude, as would be the case if they measured quantities such as time, length, or temperature. The meaningful operations that can be performed on such numbers—and indeed any numbers—are therefore limited by the rule of assignment.

Another common way of measuring psychological attributes such as intelligence, attitudes, or personality traits is to combine responses to a number of questions into a single composite score. For instance, some measures of intelligence are arrived at by counting the number of problems the subject gets right. The relation among scores obtained by such a method is not at all clear. Although one is tempted to believe that a score of 140 represents more of the attribute, intelligence, than a score of 135, such an interpretation involves certain assumptions about the intersubstitutibility, or relative difficulties, of items; for two subjects may obtain the same score by passing quite different sets of problems. Here, again for the sake of convenience, it is conventional to assume that a given numerical score represents a standard amount of the attribute, regardless of how it is obtained. It is rare that the researcher bothers to verify this assumption directly; he makes it for reasons of expediency rather than of demonstrated empirical validity. Having gone this far in interpreting his measure as an ordinal scale, he will usually take the next step and assume equal intervals between adjacent scale categories as well—for example, that the difference between the scores of 39 and 40 is equal to the difference between 59 and 60. This assumption then permits him to compute various statistics to represent his distribution of scores, such as the mean and the standard deviation, both of which are based on the assumption of an interval scale.

Finally, many psychological attributes are assessed according to sets of categories which are qualitatively rather than quantitatively distinct. For instance, in an experiment on learning as a function of incentive one group of animals may be given a solution of sugar-water, another group saccharine-water, and a third group plain tap water. The independent variable, "kind of fluid," is represented by three categories which, though different, are not ordered on any particular continuum representing amounts of an attribute. Similarly, college students may be classified according to their major fields of study. The categories of the variable, "college major," are treated only as different, not as representing relative amounts of any particular attribute. Such a category system is called a nominal scale. Numbers might be assigned quite arbitrarily to the groups, in order to distinguish them conveniently, but clearly such numbers would have no meaning even as an ordered set, for they could be interchanged quite freely without destroying their significance for the purpose of distinguishing categories.

In all this discussion the term "scale" refers to a set of categories into which objects are classified, not to the objects themselves. Only when the number of objects is small does one attain the limiting case of one object per category—as, for instance, when eight children can be completely ranked according to height or when each player on a football team is identified by a different number. The normal case is to have several objects in each category. This is often simply for the sake of convenience because one wants to work with a smaller number of categories than there are objects to be studied. It can also be a necessary condition, given enough objects, if the tools of measurement are not precise enough to permit indefinitely refined discriminations. Even though a person's age might be specified down to the minute, there will still be someone else in the world who appears to be exactly the same age, simply because the available measures are not sufficiently exact to distinguish between them.

For this reason, the categories of most scales must be considered as having some breadth. The numbers designating them should be regarded as average values for the categories, not as precise measures. There is nothing wrong, therefore, with classifying measures into fairly broad categories if this will aid tabulation. Age, for example, might just as well be classified into five-year as one-year intervals, provided the total span to be represented is a wide one. Some precision will necessarily be lost by coarse categorizing, particularly when the resulting number of categories is small, but this is quite often unimportant compared with the saving in time and expense.

SCALES OF MEASUREMENT

The presentation up to this point has been mostly intuitive and illustrative. Now let us recapitulate this material in somewhat more formal terms, so that some differences among the scale types can be made explicit. The four scales—nominal, ordinal, interval, and ratio (Stevens, 1951)—by no means exhaust the possibilities (see Coombs, 1950, 1953; Siegel, 1956), but they are the ones most frequently used in current psychological research, so we restrict attention to them. More extensive and technical treatments can be found in sources listed at the end of this chapter—for example, Senders (1958) and Torgerson (1958).

Beginning with the most primitive, a *nominal scale* is characterized by a single defining property:

a. the categories are mutually exclusive. (Any object can be placed in only one of them; objects that are alike on the variable are assigned to one category, and different objects are assigned to different categories.)

The scale is invariant (i.e., the relations among categories are not changed) under any symbol translation (transformation) that preserves this property of *unicity*. Thus the variable X defined by the categories

$$1 \quad 2 \quad 3 \quad 4 \quad 5, \quad \text{may be transformed to}$$

$$X': \quad 7 \quad 3 \quad 18 \quad 4 \quad 6, \quad \text{or to}$$

$$X'': \quad D \quad X \quad W \quad A \quad Z, \quad \text{or to}$$

$$X''': \quad * \quad = \quad + \quad \& \quad \%, \quad \text{but } not \text{ to}$$

$$7 \quad 2 \quad 3 \quad 2 \quad 8,$$

since two different categories would then be given the same designation.

Obviously, the categories represent neither absolute nor relative magnitudes of any attribute; they have no natural ordering but may be transposed in any way one wishes. It is therefore meaningless to talk about a mean or a median, or any other measure of central tendency, since "central" by one arrangement of categories could be peripheral by another arrangement. Rather we may speak of the *location* of a distribution of nominal scale measures, indicating their typical value regardless of how the categories are arranged. This is the *mode*, the category with the greatest frequency of scores.

In order to tell how well the mode represents the entire distribution, one might want some measure of dispersion or variability among the scores. Clearly, group B in Table 5-1 has a greater dispersion than group A, for its members are more evenly distributed among the categories. One way of looking at this fact is to note that, given a subject who is a freshman, one could guess his major field (i.e., "undecided") with greater certainty than one could for a junior. The degree of uncertainty of one's guess is a direct function of the dispersion of scores over the set of nominal-scale categories. One pos-

TABLE 5-1

Numbers of Freshmen and Juniors Majoring in Various Subject-Matter Areas (Fictitious Data)

Major (Nominal-Scale Variable)

Group	Physical Sciences	Social Sciences	Human- ities	Other	Unde- cided	Total
A. Freshmen	10	10	10	20	50	100
B. Juniors	25	20	20	20	15	100

Measures of Dispersion

Uncertainty

Group A: $H = \log_2 n - \dfrac{1}{n} \Sigma n_i \log_2 n_i = 6.64386 - \frac{1}{100}(33.21928 + 33.21928$

$$+ 33.21928 + 86.43856 + 282.19281)$$

$$= 1.96097$$

Group B: H $\qquad = 6.64386 - \frac{1}{100}(116.09640 + 86.43856$

$$+ 86.43856 + 86.43856 + 58.60336)$$

$$= 2.30371$$

Relative Entropy

$H_{max} = \log_2 100 - \frac{1}{100}\Sigma(20 \log_2 20) = 6.64386 - 4.32193 = 2.32193$

Group A: $R = \dfrac{H}{H_{max}} = \dfrac{1.96097}{2.32193} = 0.845$

Group B: R $\qquad = \dfrac{2.30371}{2.32193} = 0.992$

sible measure of dispersion, therefore, is the index of uncertainty, H, used in information theory.*

A somewhat more easily interpretable measure is obtained by expressing H in ratio to the maximum H possible with this number of categories. ($H_{\max}$ is obtained when all categories have equal frequencies.) Such a ratio is designated as R, the *relative entropy* of the distribution. It varies between 0.00 and $+1.00$, regardless of the number of categories. The calculation of both H and R is illustrated in Table 5-1. These computations are aided by the use of Appendix Tables G and H, which present, for various ns, the values of $\log_2 n$ and of $n \log_2 n$. The reader should consult Attneave (1959) for the rationales of these measures and for other uses to which they can be put.

An *ordinal scale* includes the essential property of a nominal scale, plus one more:

a. the categories are mutually exclusive;

b. they are ordered according to the amount of the attribute they represent. (If $A \neq B$, then either $A > B$ or $A < B$; if $A > B$ and $B > C$, then $A > C$.)

Such a scale is invariant under any order-preserving transformation. A great many algebraic transformations are order preserving; for example, multiplying each score by a constant does not change their order of magnitude, nor does squaring each number or taking its logarithm. However, transforming each number into its reciprocal is not order preserving, since large values are thereby converted into small, and vice versa. Many order-preserving transformations cannot be represented by simple algebraic equations. For example,

$$X: \quad 1 \quad 2 \quad 3 \quad 4 \quad 5$$

$$X': \quad 1 \quad 3 \quad 16 \quad 17 \quad 21$$

$$X'': \quad 20 \quad 21 \quad 983 \quad 1000 \quad 2006$$

$$* H = \Sigma p_i \log_2 \frac{1}{p_i}$$

where p_i is the proportion of cases that fall in the ith category. Instead of computing proportions, one can insert raw frequency data into the following equivalent formula:

$$H = \log_2 n - \frac{1}{n} \Sigma n_i \log_2 n_i$$

where n is the total number of scores and n_i is the frequency in the ith category.

Any of these transformations involves some kind of stretching or compressing of the scale (imagine it as a rubber band), but relative amounts of stretching need not be the same over all parts. It can readily be seen that the magnitudes of numbers used in an ordinal scale have no absolute, but only relative, meanings. If one category is assigned a larger number than another, this merely implies that it represents more of the attribute; it does not indicate how much more. Since the sizes of the intervals between categories are not known, any descriptive statistic that assumes equal intervals is not appropriate for an ordinal scale distribution. Though a mean or a standard deviation might be computed, its value would depend almost entirely on what numbers happened to be assigned to the categories—on how the scale happened to be stretched when the computations were made.

An appropriate measure of location is provided by the *median*, which is simply the category in which the middle score of the distribution falls. This can be ascertained by counting off 50% of the cases from either end. The median of a distribution would clearly be changed if all the numbers assigned to categories were increased or if all of them were decreased, but if the upper half were increased and the lower half decreased in any manner whatsoever, this transformation would still leave the median unchanged. This relative stability of the median is particularly advantageous when one is faced with a distribution containing some very extreme scores. For example, the dependent variable in a learning experiment may be the number of trials it takes subjects to memorize a set of nonsense syllables. It turns out that two of them are too stupid to learn the set even after several days' practice. What is their score to be? Infinite? One thousand? The maximum required by any subject who did learn the set? Clearly this decision would have to be an arbitrary one, and it would make a difference in the *mean* score of all subjects combined, but it would not affect the median in the slightest, as long as the number of deviant subjects is less than half.

Similarly, it is desirable to have a measure of dispersion for an ordinal scale which is relatively insensitive to scalar transformations. One such measure is obtained by simply counting the number of categories required to include the middle 50% of the distribution (or it could be the middle 25%, or the middle 95%, or any other proportion). Regardless of how the numbers designating the categories are changed—as long as it is an order-preserving transformation—the size of this measure of dispersion will remain the same.

An *interval scale* is characterized by three basic properties, including the two listed previously:

a. the categories are mutually exclusive;

b. they are ordered according to the amount of the attribute they represent;

c. equal differences in the attribute are represented by equal differences in numbers assigned to the categories.

Such a scale is invariant under any linear transformation of the form $X' = aX + b$. A constant, b, may be freely added to (or subtracted from) all quantities, for the relative distances among them are preserved by this operation—though the zero point (an arbitrary one) is moved. Moreover each category value may be multiplied (or divided) by a constant, a, without affecting the relative distances between them. Thus Centigrade measures of temperature (X) can be converted to Fahrenheit measures (X') by the equation, $X' = 1.8X + 32$. The Japanese Showa calendar (X) can be converted to the western calendar (X') by the transformation, $X' = X + 1925$.

Here for the first time the common measures of location and dispersion, the mean and the standard deviation, become appropriate as representing something about the underlying attribute which the scale is designed to measure. One can readily see why equal (or known) distances between categories are required for these measures, when one considers their definitional formulas. The mean can be defined as that point around which the sum of the deviation scores is zero $[\Sigma(X - M) = 0]$. A deviation of 3 is treated as half the size of a deviation of 6, and so on, for all deviation scores. Clearly such a treatment would not be meaningful with an ordinal scale, since the relative distances could be changed simply by stretching or compressing the scale differently along various parts of its range. The standard deviation also, defined as the square root of the average squared deviation around the mean $[\sigma = \sqrt{\Sigma(X - M)^2/n}]$, for the same reason requires intervals between categories that are of constant size relative to one another.

Once the scale intervals remain fixed, other characteristics of the distribution besides its location and dispersion can be meaningfully described—such as its general shape or the way in which objects are distributed among the categories. One idealized shape, which is approximated by some empirical distributions, is the normal curve. This curve can be defined by a mathematical equation, which specifies the frequency of any score as a function of its distance from the mean, in σ-units. The normal curve can be characterized roughly as symmetrical and bell-shaped. Actually, very few empirical distributions coincide well with this idealized form, but it provides a standard from which to measure departures. Two kinds of departures are of special interest, and descriptive statistics have been developed for them. Skewness refers to the degree to which measures are piled up in one tail of the distribution to a greater extent than in the other; kurtosis refers to the degree to which measures are piled up in the middle to a greater (or lesser) extent than in the normal distribution. Statistical measures of these characteristics can be found in most standard statistics texts, such as McNemar's (1955). Figure 5-1 shows some examples of normal, positively skewed, platykurtic, and leptokurtic distributions. Note that any of these characterizations of distribution shape would be meaningless with ordinal-scale data, for one shape could readily be converted to another simply by squeezing or stretching appropriate parts of the scale.

Finally, a *ratio scale* can be said to exist when

a. the categories are mutually exclusive;

b. they are ordered according to the amount of the attribute they represent;

c. equal differences in the attribute are represented by equal differences in the numbers assigned to the categories;

d. numbers assigned to the categories are proportional to the amounts of the attribute represented by them.

The last criterion is the essential one; it presupposes all the others, and in addition says that a ratio scale is invariant only under multiplicative transformations of the type $X' = aX$. No constant may be added or subtracted, since the zero point must remain fixed. Thus length measured in feet (X) can be converted to length measured in inches (X') by the equation $X' = 12X$ or to length measured in centimeters (X'') by the equation $X'' = 30.48X$.

Given a known zero point, it is meaningful to talk about the magnitude of one statistic in relation to another. For instance, one can

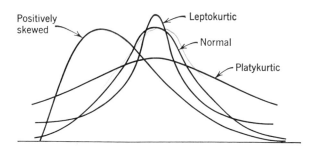

Fig. 5-1. The "normal curve" and some departures from it.

interpret the coefficient of variation V $(= \sigma/M)$ as the amount of variability among measures relative to their average size. Another statistic which can be interpreted only on ratio scale measures is the geometric mean, the kth root of the product of k numbers (e.g., the geometric mean of 3 and 12 is $\sqrt{3 \times 12} = 6$; see Chapter 6, p. 149 for an illustration of its use). Perhaps the most common use of ratio scale properties is in the direct ratio-comparison of two measures, as when one says that one board is twice as long as another. Since few psychological attributes can be measured as ratio scales, the reader is cautioned against uncritical attempts to make comparisons of this kind.

One can easily see that the meaningfulness of any statistic computed to describe distributions of data depends upon the scale type which the measures represent.* Here we have discussed only those statistics which describe one attribute-distribution at a time. Similar considerations apply to statistics, such as the correlation coefficient, which characterize relations between two (or more) variables. In Chapter 13 we describe certain commonly used statistics of relationships. There we emphasize again that the statistic one selects depends on two things, the kind of relationship hypothesized and the scale type embodied in the measures. Since a major purpose of research is to describe relationships among variables, it is important to anticipate the analysis phase early in the process by considering precisely what relationships are to be sought and by collecting data in such a way that the appropriate statistics can be used. The kinds of relationships are ordinarily specified in the research hypotheses. In the remainder of this chapter we discuss data-collection procedures that yield particular scale types. The interested reader can find additional materials on them in Coombs (1956), Edwards (1957), Ekman (1958), Green (1954), Guilford (1954), Gulliksen & Messick (1960), Messick & Abelson (1957), Rosner (1956), and Torgerson (1958).

SCALES AND MEASURING PROCEDURES

When one claims that his data represent a particular scale-type, this is an abbreviated way of saying that the objects (e.g., people)

---

* What is meaningful and what is not depends, of course, on one's purpose. Here we are referring to characteristics of the attribute in terms of distances between scale points. For another purpose, such as inferring a sampling distribution (see Chapter 9), a mean or standard deviation computed from ordinal-scale data, for example, might be quite "meaningful."

being studied can be placed in categories that bear a relationship to one another required by the formal properties of the scale. Even this statement needs to be made a bit more explicit by the elaboration of two points. First is the matter of how one knows that the objects can be placed into categories of a given scale-type. This involves the question whether the data-collection procedure permitted the scale *not* to appear or whether the relations among categories were necessarily imposed by the task set for subjects. Methods of data collection differ in permissiveness,* or the degree to which they allow "nonscalar" response patterns to emerge. At the extreme of rigidity, or nonpermissiveness, judges could be instructed to classify all objects into a predetermined set of categories that fits the criteria for a given scale. An extremely permissive method, on the other hand, would be to ask judges what kind of scale would appropriately classify the objects. This extreme, however, represents a question too unfocused for most people to answer (they would not know what the researcher meant by "scale"). So various indirect techniques of data collection have been devised which, though providing a specific task for the subject, nevertheless do not impose on him judgments that necessarily yield a particular scale. It is worth knowing whether the claimed scale-type resulted from a rigid or from a permissive method of data collection.

The second point that requires clarification when one claims a particular scale-type is the nature of the population of judges (or subjects) for which the scale has been demonstrated. If, for example, all the data are collected on one subject, they may yield an arrangement of categories suitable for him, but this gives no assurance that the same scale will fit someone else. It is necessary to distinguish group (or common) scales from individual (or unique) scales. Moreover, some procedures for data collection may be quite appropriate for studying one or two individuals but entirely too cumbersome for administration to large groups. Short-cut techniques are frequently used to determine scale-types on an entire group of subjects at once. Still, one should be prepared to find that a particular scale found in one population may not be exactly duplicated in a different population of subjects. The two groups may, in fact, see the objects of judgment quite differently and therefore use two different scales for classifying them. This means that one would do well to define explicitly the population to which the measure is eventually to be applied and to develop the scale on a representative sample from that population.

* Coombs (1953) has called this "searchingness."

Obtaining a Nominal Scale

A nominal scale may be imposed on a sample of objects by simply providing judges with the set of categories and instructing them to classify the objects accordingly.   For instance, an investigator might start with a conception of democratic, authoritarian, and laissez-faire group atmospheres and attempt to classify groups into one of these three categories.   As a check on his own judgment, he could have one or more people repeat the classification independently.   If the agreement among them is very poor, one would be forced to conclude that the sample of groups investigated could not be represented by a set of nominal scale categories common to all judges.   Thus what is a rigid method of data collection for a single judge is transformed into a more permissive method for a group of judges, since it allows a common scale *not* to appear.

A somewhat more permissive task for a single judge might involve his being presented with successive pairs of the groups with the instruction to rate them as "similar" or "different" in leadership style. A test of the basic requirement for a nominal scale could be performed quite directly:

If groups A and B are judged similar, and
$\qquad$ A and C are judged similar, then
$\qquad$ B and C must be judged similar.

If groups A and B are judged different, and
$\qquad$ A and C are judged similar, then
$\qquad$ B and C must be judged different.

If these relationships hold for all pairs of groups, then one is justified in asserting that a nominal scale has been established.   If exactly the same categories are provided by several other judges, then it is safe to conclude that a common nominal scale exists for all of them. Of course, a nominal scale derived from such a task may be quite different from one established a priori, as by the previous instructions to classify groups as "democratic," "authoritarian," or "laissez-faire." This is precisely the consequence of seeking to discover if a scale type exists rather than deciding in advance that it does and imposing it on the objects of study.

Obtaining an Ordinal Scale

One can impose an ordered classification on a set of objects by assigning them to a preordered set of categories.   For instance, in interviewing job applicants, a personnel manager might rank order a group of applicants on adjustment (with ties permitted); alternatively, he could rate each person on the following scale of social adjustment:

1. Very well adjusted, friendly, and poised.
2. Moderately well adjusted; no outstanding inadequacies.
3. Some evidence of maladjustment; apparently not incapacitating.
4. Exceedingly inept and ill-at-ease socially.

Both procedures would yield an ordinal scale because the ranks or categories are defined to represent successively decreasing amounts of the attribute *adjustment*. One might wish to investigate more permissively, however, whether the personnel manager is able to discriminate adjustment in a consistently ordinal fashion without the help of this a priori scale. A way of doing this would be to present him with all possible pairs of job applicants and for each pair require one of three judgments: A is better adjusted than B; B is better adjusted than A; or A and B are equally well (or poorly) adjusted. By comparing all pairs, one could determine if transitivity, the basic requirement of an ordinal scale, is met by these judgments.

If A is better adjusted than B, and
  B is better adjusted than C, then
  A must be better adjusted than C.

If A and B are equally well adjusted, and
  A is better adjusted than C, then
  B must be better adjusted than C.

If the number of objects is so large that the judge cannot keep in mind some assumed total order but instead has to treat each pair independently as he sees it, then it is quite likely that some intransitivity will creep into his orderings. This could occur for many reasons, but the commonest one is that his criterion for "adjustment" shifts somewhat through the judgment series. In other words, "adjustment" does not represent a single, unidimensional attribute but several of them. Judgment of adjustment depends on a number of different behaviors and impressions that might not have the same effect in successive appearances of a single object in different pairings. So the ordinal scale created by definition in the preceding instructions may have been deceptive in that it served to gloss over potential inconsistencies in relationships among categories which derived from the fact that they represented not one but several dimensions.

The method of paired comparisons is exceedingly laborious if the number of objects is sizable, and it is usually not a feasible technique for large groups of subjects. Instead, certain short-cut procedures may be used to determine whether a given ordering of categories is common to a group of judges. One simple way would be to intercorrelate their ratings of a single sample of objects on an a priori scale similar to that for adjustment illustrated above. To the extent that the average intercorrelation was less than 1.00, this would suggest that a common group scale did not exist.*

Another widely used method for determining a common group scale is the Guttman scaling technique (see Guttman, 1950; Borgatta, 1955). It is applicable for sets of monotone items,† such as tests of ability, in which every subject can be scored as passing or failing (alternatively, as accepting or rejecting) each item. If the items constitute a set uniquely ordered in difficulty along a single dimension, then the patternings of responses to them should be such that if any subject passes item C he should also pass all easier items; if any subject fails item C, he should also fail all items more difficult. (The "difficulty" of an item is determined by the number of people who fail or reject it.) If we represent passing an item by plus ($+$) and failure by minus ($-$), then only the following patterns of response are possible from a uniquely ordered set of five items:

Item Difficulty

Easy				Hard
A	B	C	D	E
$+$	$+$	$+$	$+$	$+$
$+$	$+$	$+$	$+$	$-$
$+$	$+$	$+$	$-$	$-$
$+$	$+$	$-$	$-$	$-$
$+$	$-$	$-$	$-$	$-$
$-$	$-$	$-$	$-$	$-$

Any other pattern of response (such as $--++-$ or $+---+-$) would imply that for the particular subject the items do not fall in the same order of difficulty as for other subjects; hence they cannot

---

* The measure of correlation appropriate here is not the Pearson product-moment r, since the categories do not represent an interval scale, but rather an index of order association. See Chapter 13, pp. 346–347.

† A monotone item is one which a subject is more likely to "pass," or "accept," the more of the relevant attribute he possesses. It is distinguished from a non-monotone item, which demands a certain optimal amount of the attribute for acceptance; subjects with either less or more of the trait will be less likely to accept the item.

represent the same unidimensional attribute. (In practice, a limited number of nonscalar patterns are permitted; rather than saying that they violate the scale, one treats them as "response error.")

In a Guttman scale the test items provide the boundaries of the categories in the ordinal scale representing the attribute, and subjects are classified according to the number of items they pass. A group that passed three items of the above set would fall between items C and D on the scale, since they must have passed A, B, and C and must have failed D and E. Thus Guttman scaling accomplishes the simultaneous ordering of items and people along a dimension, according to the relative amounts of the attribute they represent. In common parlance the people are said to possess the attribute and the items to measure it; but a Guttman scale is indifferent to this distinction.

Obtaining an Interval Scale

This approach of using subjects to scale stimuli while using the stimuli to scale the subjects has seen other variations even in pre-Guttman times. In the techniques of attitude scaling developed by Thurstone (1927; see also Guilford, 1954) the scale values of non-monotone opinion statements are determined by groups of judges; after that, the scale position of any subject can be ascertained from his responses to the set of statements. He will presumably accept the statement closest to his own attitude and reject all others.

In one of its cruder forms a Thurstone scaling procedure requires judges to sort a large number of opinion statements into eleven piles representing "equal appearing intervals" along a dimension of "attitude toward X." Such a technique provides for the imposition of an interval scale on the items, for a judge's decisions are treated as if he has understood, and can follow, the instructions to "make the intervals between piles equal." The same task is assigned to a number of judges, and only those opinion statements on which they all agree fairly well in category placement are included in the final set of items that constitute the scale.

A somewhat more searching investigation of the scale-type represented by an individual's judgments might involve something like the following procedure. He is given a standard unit of difference between items—such as "the smallest difference that it detectable" or "the amount of difference between statements X and Y." (Since the unit of measurement in an interval scale is arbitrary, it does not matter what standard is provided.) Then he is asked to judge every pair of opinion statements and to tell how far apart they are in terms of this standard. Such a procedure yields a large number of difference-measures, one for each pair of statements. It is a fairly simple matter, then, to see if these differences are algebraically consistent. For instance, $B - A$ should be equal to $(C - A) - (C - B)$; it should also equal $(D - A) - (D - B)$ and so on, for all pairings. To the extent that the distance between a given pair of items is not the same when calculated in different ways, one must doubt that the subject was using an interval scale when judging the set, for the size of his interval evidently did not remain constant over the total range. It is thus possible by this relatively permissive method of data collection to find out if a set of items does constitute an interval scale for any particular subject.

An economical but nevertheless fairly permissive method for arriving at a group interval scale is that elaborated by Thurstone from the method of paired comparisons (see Edwards, 1957; Guilford, 1954). Instead of having judges estimate scale distances directly, this is done for them by a normal-curve interpretation of group difference-judgments. If items A and B are presented with instructions to decide which is "greater" (i.e., represents more of the attribute), it is assumed that the greater the consensus among judges, the greater the distance between A and B on the scale. If 50% say A is greater and 50% say B, then the items are assumed to coincide in position. (The judgment $A = B$ is not permitted.) Under Guttman scaling procedures, such an outcome would be considered either as response error or as evidence for the lack of a unidimensional scale. But what is "error" for Guttman constitutes the essential basis for scale construction in Thurstone's system. Complete consensus among judges (i.e., no "error" in judgment of the stimuli) would make it impossible to tell how far apart the items were (see Coombs, 1958).

Given relatively discriminable items—that is, when there is less than 100% consensus regarding which in the pair represents more of the attribute—the distance between them is determined by reference to the normal distribution. For example, if 70% of the judges say $A > B$, then that σ-distance from the mean (i.e., .52) which divides a normal distribution 70/30 is taken as the distance between items A and B. The distance between every other item pair (except those for which consensus exceeds an arbitrary 95%) is determined in the same way. This yields a set of difference scores, the algebraic consistency of which can be checked by simple subtractions (as in the task described for a single judge). Thus one can ascertain whether a fixed-interval scale will account for all the obtained differences. A number of rather far-fetched assumptions are implicit in such a test, however, so it is rarely applied stringently.* Instead, the Thurstone scaling procedure averages the various difference-scores obtained for adjacent items in order to arrive at a single "best" estimate of the scalar distance between them. This expediency accomplishes by fiat what could not be demonstrated by the permissive technique of data collection. When faced with inconsistent estimates of distances among items, the researcher should doubt not only that an interval scale exists but even that a single ordinal scale can adequately describe his data; for nothing in this scaling procedure assures transitivity of the items.

Obtaining a Ratio Scale

For most research purposes interval scale measures are sufficient, for they permit one to describe functional relations among variables and to use statistics that are quite powerful and informative. In some cases, though—particularly in psychophysical research—it is desirable to establish relationships that describe exactly how much of one variable is associated with a given quantity of the other. The specification of absolute (as distinct from relative) quantities requires a ratio scale, in which one can tell at what point the attribute is absent. People are used to thinking of physical attributes such as length, weight and intensity in ratio terms, so it is fairly easy to get them to make judgments of the form, "A is n times as heavy (or loud or rough or bright, etc.) as B." (Depending on the task definition, any one of the three essential components—A, n, or B—could be provided by the subject after the experimenter gave him the other two components.) Judgments from a given subject relating all possible pairs of a set of stimuli provide a psychological variable for him, which can be functionally related to the actual physical characteristics of the objects. More important to the present illustration, they provide a check on the consistency of his ratios and, consequently, a method of determining whether he actually uses a single ratio scale in the set of judgments.

---

* The assumptions of this procedure (Thurstone's case V) include (1) normal distributions of discriminal processes, (2) equal standard deviations of these distributions, and (3) independence of the discriminal processes associated with different items. (A discriminal process refers to the act of judging the location of a stimulus, or an item, on an attribute dimension.) The distribution of a discriminal process or, more generally, an *item operating characteristic*, refers to the distribution of probabilities that any particular item will be seen as falling in any particular location. A normal discriminal distribution implies that the item is most frequently judged to be where it "actually is," and the proporton of subjects who see it in other positions decreases rapidly as these "other positions" depart from the "true position."

As in other scale-types, it is usually of interest to discover whether a common scale exists for a group of subjects. This can be investigated laboriously by having each subject judge ratios for every pair of stimuli. More efficiently, though, one could assign different sets of pairs to different subjects and determine the consistency of the entire set. Lack of consistency could, of course, be attributed to either of two circumstances: the subjects, individually, may not make consistent ratio scale judgments, or, though individual subjects use their own ratio scales, the scale intervals may not be the same from one subject to another.

PURISM AND PRAGMATISM

In the foregoing discussion we have tried to make a distinction between methods of data collection that impose a desired scale on the measures and methods that permit one to ascertain whether, in fact, the scale is appropriate for them. In practice, an absolute distinction between the "rigid" and the "permissive" technique is hard to arrive at, for any particular technique is likely to be only relatively permissive in comparison with some other. Moreover, the reader should not get the impression that in all cases the more permissive data-collection procedure is necessarily preferable. This may depend a great deal on one's purpose in doing the research. Many investigations are specifically aimed at discovering the nature of psychological attributes, how they appear subjectively to the individual, or how people differ in the manner in which the "same" attribute is structured. With these sorts of goals, it would seem that maximally permissive tasks would yield the most information, since measures obtained from them are likely to reflect characteristics of the subject more than characteristics of the task. If one wants to know what an attribute is like, he should try to avoid imposing qualities on it and then treating these impositions of the measuring process as if they were discoveries.

On the other hand, a great deal of research is performed which requires only that the measures represent the intended attribute approximately. Some hypotheses do specify a precise functional relationship between two variables; but, much more commonly, one wants to know only if they are related and will accept any sort of roughly linear or even monotonic relationship as verifying his hypothesis. Given these modest demands of the research outcome, one can sometimes afford to substitute assumptions for data, in determining a scale of measurement, particularly if similar assumptions have in the past led to useful results. There is plenty of pragmatic justification in psychological experience with personality assessment, for instance, for treating one's measures as if they constituted interval scales, even though the data-collection procedures themselves do not warrant it.

The main thing is for the researcher to be aware of the implications of his decision when he chooses either to explore a given scale-type or to assume it. Too often one intends to explore but uses tasks which assume instead, for example, when a rank-order task is used to determine whether a set of categories is transitive. Then, finding an interesting result in his data, he assumes that this reflects some characteristic of the phenomenon being studied rather than a necessary consequence of the way it was measured. The limitations of either the pragmatist or the purist orientation to measuring attributes are apparent: if a lot of unassumable things are accepted in order to attain a pragmatically justified end, then one may not learn as much as he might about the actual nature of the phenomena he intends to study. On the other hand, if one tries to explore his data thoroughly to discover just what assumptions are warranted, then the analysis is likely to get terribly complicated and—worse yet—the research may never get done.

SUMMARY

The purpose of quantifying research variables is to permit more precise description of attributes and the relations among them. When psychological attributes are conceived and measured as continuous, quantitative variables rather than as qualitative, "either-or" characteristics, one can make finer discriminations among subjects and thus gain more information from the research data.

However, the method of data collection imposes limitations on the quantifiability of a variable. Some research procedures permit one to distinguish only the presence or absence of an attribute; others permit more refined comparisons among objects. The kinds of comparisons possible can be conveniently summarized under the definitions of scale-types. In this chapter we have described four major scale-types —nominal, ordinal, interval, and ratio—and some data-collection procedures by which they might be established.

In actual research practice the scale-type is often assumed or imposed by fiat rather than empirically established by a permissive method of data collection. Psychometric procedures for ascertaining the empirical nature of a scale are generally laborious, especially for the more powerful scales. The researcher may not wish to demand such tedious tasks of his subjects, or he may prefer to focus his main attention on other phases of the research project. By short-cutting the scale-development phase and substituting arbitrary imposition for empirical search, one runs the risk of distorting the nature of his variables and of misinterpreting the descriptive statistics applied to them. Nevertheless, such a course may frequently be the most efficient one in the light of over-all research aims.

In order to arrive at a realistic interpretation of his measures, the researcher would do well to understand the technical requirements for any scale he assumes) and consider the adequacy of his data-collection procedures against the theoretically required standards. If the discrepancy is great, this does not necessarily mean that he must discard the measure; rather he should maintain a skeptical attitude toward it. He could restrict himself to interpretations that are clearly warranted by the method of data collection. If a technically unjustified interpretation is to be made, he would do well to find some independent way of checking it. When such a check is not possible, safe shelter can usually be found in a primitive operationism: the researcher may cautiously conclude that when variable X is measured by thus-and-so procedures, the following results appear; whether or not they would appear under a different procedure is an open question.

REFERENCES

Attneave, F. *Applications of information theory to psychology.* New York: Holt, 1959.

Borgatta, E. F. An error ratio for scalogram analysis. *Pub. Op. Quart.*, 1955, **19**, 96–100.

Coombs, C. H. Psychological scaling without a unit of measurement. *Psychol. Rev.*, 1950, **57**, 145–158.

Coombs, C. H. Theory and methods of social measurement. In L. Festinger & D. Katz (Eds.), *Research methods in the behavioral sciences.* New York: Dryden, 1953.

Coombs, C. H. The scale grid: some interrelations of data models. *Psychometrika*, 1956, **21**, 313–329.

Coombs, C. H. On the use of inconsistency of preferences in psychological measurement. *J. exp. Psychol.*, 1958, **55**, 1–7.

Edwards, A. L. *Techniques of attitude scale construction.* New York: Appleton-Century-Crofts, 1957.

Ekman, G. Two generalized ratio scaling methods. *J. Psychol.*, 1958, **45**, 287–295.

Green, B. F. Attitude measurement. In G. Lindzey (Ed.), *Handbook of social psychology.* (Vol. I.) Cambridge: Addison-Wesley, 1954.

Guilford, J. P. *Psychometric methods.* (2nd Ed.) New York: McGraw-Hill, 1954.

Gulliksen, H., & Messick, S. (Eds.) *Psychological scaling: theory and applications.* New York: Wiley, 1960.

Guttman, L. The basis for scalogram analysis. In S. A. Stouffer et al., *The American soldier: Studies in social psychology in World War II*. Vol. 4: *Measurement and prediction*. Princeton: Princeton Univer. Press, 1950.

McNemar, Q. *Psychological statistics*. (2nd Ed.) New York: Wiley, 1955.

Messick, S. J., & Abelson, R. P. Research tools: scaling and measurement theory. *Rev. educ. Res.*, 1957, **27**, 487–497.

Rosner, B. S. A new scaling technique for absolute judgments. *Psychometrika*, 1956, **21**, 377–381.

Senders, Virginia. *Measurement and statistics*. New York: Oxford, 1958.

Siegel, S. A method for obtaining an ordered metric scale. *Psychometrika*, 1956, **21**, 207–216.

Stevens, S. S. Mathematics, measurement, and psychophysics. In Stevens, S. S. (Ed.), *Handbook of experimental psychology*. New York: Wiley, 1951.

Thurstone, L. L. A law of comparative judgment. *Psychol. Rev.*, 1927, **34**, 273–286.

Torgerson, W. S. *Theory and methods of scaling*. New York: Wiley, 1958.

CHAPTER 6

Instrumentation:
verbal measures

So far we have dealt with general considerations of design and quantification which are relevant to most empirical research in psychology. Yet clearly the specific research techniques employed will differ widely, depending on the aims of the study and on the general strategy of investigation. This is especially true for the measurement of research variables. The operations by which a variable is assessed cannot be considered independently of its theoretical conception. Nor can they be reasonably separated from the practical limitations of the research context. What is a meaningful and feasible approach to measuring an attribute in one setting may be completely inappropriate in another. The amount of anxiety manifested by a subject might be measured by a questionnaire, by muscle tension, or by the amount of defecation, depending on whether the subject is human or animal and whether he is in the classroom or the laboratory.

Thus problems of instrumentation—that is, the operational assessment and manipulation of psychological variables—will be largely peculiar to a given study. Nevertheless, there are certain common approaches to instrumentation which can be applied with appropriate modifications to a variety of related problems. In Chapter 4 we discussed three basic ways of obtaining scientific knowledge—naturalistic observation, systematic assessment with controlled stimuli, and experimental manipulation of the independent variable. Historically, these three strategies have tended to be associated with different tactics of instrumentation. The experimentalist is more likely than other researchers to use "brass instruments" or their modern counterparts, complex electronic gadgets; the systematic assessor tends to employ paper-and-pencil tests; the observer of naturally occurring phenomena is generally forced to rely more heavily than others on his own judgment of variables. Hence the methods of instrumentation applied to hardware, to verbal tests, and to subjective judgment have tended to develop quite independently of one another. It is the rare psychologist who has general expertise in all three domains; rather, the typical researcher is likely to feel more comfortable with only one class of instruments—say verbal tests—and to be fairly ignorant of the others.

Yet there is more commonality in the basic problems of these various methodologies than would be apparent from their diverse terminologies and techniques. So we shall try, in these three chapters on instrumentation, to treat some common techniques in parallel fashion. It is convenient to begin with the methodology of systematic assessment, as elaborated in the field of psychological testing (see, e.g., Anastasi, 1954; Cattell, 1948; Cronbach, 1960; Gulliksen, 1950; Stern, Stein, & Bloom, 1956), since workers in this area have been most keenly aware of problems of validating their procedures and have developed fairly sophisticated techniques for assessing and refining them. Their methods of test construction and validation are by no means ideal in every case, but they do illustrate some tentative approaches to problems that are common to all research methodologies.

THE FUNCTION OF PSYCHOLOGICAL TESTS

A psychological test is basically a stimulus, or set of stimuli, designed to elicit responses which are presumed to reflect fairly enduring characteristics of the subject. Thus the test items ("stimuli") are generally constructed and presented in such a way as to disturb minimally the attribute they are intended to assess. Usually this aim can be only partly attained, since one must disturb subjects at least enough to attract their attention to the test. But as an objective, at least, it is quite distinct from that of experimentation, in which the explicit intent is to manipulate a variable that will affect the attribute to be assessed.

One of the easiest ways of eliciting responses of human subjects is by verbal questioning. Hence the contents of tests and the responses they elicit are most frequently verbal. This is by no means a necessary characteristic. There is a variety of primarily nonverbal tests, such as the Rorschach inkblots, the TAT pictures, and certain other "projective" instruments. Also, it is quite possible to assess psychological attributes from nonverbal responses, as when emotionality is inferred from blushing, GSR, or other manifestations. Such nonverbal tests, too, could be handled within the same framework as the verbal instruments discussed here. The techniques of analysis would be structurally similar. But for simplicity we present our discussion as if a test item were a question and the subject's response a verbal statement; it should not be difficult for the reader to make appropriate translations to nonverbal tests.

WHAT TO LOOK FOR IN SELECTING A TEST

Hardly a month goes by in the life of a psychologist without someone's coming to him with the question, "Where can I find a test of personality?" Before sending the inquirer to Buros' *Mental Measurements Yearbook* (1959), one really ought to recommend that he read a few books on theories of personality. For even a casual glance at most of them would convince the reader that "personality" is not a single measurable attribute but rather a configuration of them. Just what attributes are included in the configuration depends, to a great extent, on the theoretical orientation of the author. In order to make personality assessment a worthwhile venture, it is necessary first for the researcher to develop a pretty clear idea of what specific traits he wants to measure. Once he has translated a global term like "personality" or "motivation" into some simpler, more unitary concepts, such as, perhaps, "tolerance for ambiguity," "achievement motivation," or "self-control," he may be in a better position to decide what test to select.

In other words, the first criterion for selection of a test—whether of "personality," "attitudes," "aptitudes," or whatever—is represented by the question, "Does *it* measure what *I* want to measure?" The name attached to the test is not necessarily helpful in this regard. Just because the test developer has decided to label his instrument a "Test of Introversion" or a "Test of Self-Acceptance," there is no assurance that it measures what the researcher has in mind by the concepts "introversion" and "self-acceptance." Such terms as these generally have no unique meanings; instead, the conceptual meaning of any theoretical construct has to be defined by the theory in which it appears. If the test constructor's theory is different from that of the test user, then the meaning of a concept, as embodied in the test items, may be quite inappropriate to the user's research problem.

In order to gain some assurance that a particular test measures what he intends, the researcher should study the items to see if they appear to represent the trait he has in mind. Then, he might determine how it is to be scored—what responses or combinations of responses are used to define the attributes being assessed. Finally, if this has not already been done by someone else, he should examine those correlates of test performance which might show whether the intended construct is being measured. If the theory that defines the attributes suggests that certain kinds of subjects should score differently from others or that certain conditions of testing will produce differences in test results, then these implications should be studied. Failure to verify them may very well mean that the test does not at all measure the intended attribute.

The test purveyor should be able to provide empirical evidence about these kinds of relationships to enable the researcher to tell whether the test is appropriate to his needs. In addition, some tests require information about homogeneity and stability (see below) to permit one to judge the extent to which they measure unidimensional attributes and the degree to which scores are duplicated from one administration to the next. Finally, for any standardized test there should be published norms developed by representative sampling of the populations for which it is intended, on the basis of which the researcher can see how his subjects' scores compare with those in the standardizing population.

USING AVAILABLE TESTS VERSUS
CONSTRUCTING NEW ONES

If an available test measures the desired attribute and if sufficient information regarding homogeneity, stability, and test norms is available to determine its adequacy for the intended purpose, then there are marked advantages in the use of a standard instrument. Besides the time and effort he saves, the researcher gains certain advantages from the continuity of testing procedures. The results of his assessment can be interpreted in relation to those of other researchers who have used the same instrument. Thus his own data gain more meaning and contribute more to the main stream of psychological research;

other psychologists are less likely to raise questions about whether the intended attribute was indeed measured.

But the value of using standardized tests depends entirely on their adequacy with respect to the criteria. It is not uncommon for a test constructer to develop his test norms on a population quite different from that which the researcher plans to study. If, for example, hospital patients were used to develop a test purporting to distinguish manic from schizophrenic tendencies, there is no guarantee that its norms are applicable to a general population of nonhospitalized persons. A college entrance examination standardized on students at a small private college with a restricted enrollment may be quite inappropriate for a large state university.

Aside from inadequate standardization or test-retest stability, the most common deficiency of available tests for any particular research purpose is their failure to measure the attribute in which the investigator is interested. With the great variety of research problems and the diverse ways of defining any given psychological attribute, one is not likely to see the day when he can simply refer to a catalogue for an adequate test of the particular trait that concerns him. Rather than use a patently inadequate test which happens to be available, it is probably better to construct one's own. Even a crudely designed instrument which appears to measure what is wanted may well be preferable to an elaborately standardized one that does not.

TESTING SUBJECTS AND TESTING THE TEST

The manifest purpose of psychological testing is to assess attributes of people. But before one can safely use a test to this end, some kind of convincing evidence is needed to show that the test measures what it is intended to. Often, when one has to construct his own measures, this requires repeated trials, modifications, and discards before a satisfactory instrument is developed. In fact, a major preliminary phase of any large-scale research project is frequently devoted to instrument construction. This means that, at least in the early stages of research, one may administer a test with the main purpose not of measuring characteristics of subjects but of assessing the adequacy of the test itself.

Just how much time and effort must be devoted to instrument development will depend on the over-all research objectives. If the aim is to measure individual subjects accurately or to establish precise functional relationships among variables, then refined instruments are necessary. For instance, one would not attempt to use an intelligence test for grade-placement unless he were convinced that it would yield reasonably accurate scores for almost all pupils. And it would be useless to develop an elaborate equation relating the magnitude of a physical stimulus to the magnitude of a psychological judgment unless the latter could be measured with nearly the precision of the former.

However, many investigations are aimed simply at seeing if two variables are related at all or if two groups tend to differ on an attribute in a predicted direction. Though such primitive questions characterize research that is exploratory rather than definitive, the vast majority of present-day psychological research does not go beyond them. For these less refined aims, it is often quite appropriate to make do with fairly crude instruments. In fact, disproportionate refinement of one feature of the research while the others remain primitive constitutes a waste of effort since the value of the total product depends on the quality of the weakest link. So there will be numerous occasions when the researcher will decide to be content with a fairly superficial appraisal of his instrument's worth—maybe even letting it pass on the basis of an intuitive impression of validity —provided this appears efficient in the light of over-all aims. The main thing is that it result from a deliberate decision, rather than an ignorant oversight, for the researcher will then be in a better position to know what to do next if his results do not come out as expected.

In case one does decide to take the instrument development phase seriously, various techniques of construction and appraisal are useful to know about. We cannot begin to cover all of them here, for they could well take up several books. Instead, we offer illustrative solutions to a few common problems and suggest references for more thorough discussions.

All of the techniques are aimed at establishing the adequacy of a test in assessing the intended trait. Most of them stem from the notions of reliability and validity, long used by psychometricians (see Gulliksen, 1950; Tryon, 1957). These characteristics of tests have traditionally been conceptualized as if they could be determined independently of the content of the test and of what it was intended to measure. A test was described as reliable or valid or neither, and this statement was supposed to convey some information to the user. Actually, such a description can mean nothing without at least an explicit reference to the criteria and operations employed. Reliability under some conditions may not insure reliability under others, and validity by one criterion does not necessarily say anything about other criteria. Moreover, before one can tell how reliability and validity should be assessed, or even whether such considerations are appropriate, one must know what kind of attribute is being measured and how it should, on theoretical grounds, be manifest in test behavior.

Therefore, our discussion proceeds chiefly within the context of the construct validity of a test—the degree to which it measures the intended attribute (see American Psychological Association, 1954; Cronbach & Meehl, 1955). Instead of referring to reliability and validity, we use somewhat more precise terms, like homogeneity, stability, and correlation with other variables. These notions should not necessarily be regarded as permanent and definitive, either. Perhaps in time they too will be replaced by others which have still clearer conceptual and operational meanings. But it is a safe guess that the general problem with which they deal—the convincingness of research operations—will remain an enduring concern for many generations of psychologists.

SINGLE STIMULI AND MULTIPLE STIMULI

An answer to a question is a verbal response and, like other responses, it presumably reflects characteristics of the person and of the stimuli to which he is responding. The aim in testing is to infer characteristics of the person, rather than of the test, and every effort is made to limit the extent to which the test itself contributes to responses, or at least to hold this amount constant over all subjects. This is the main reason for using standard questions (though even the same words may mean different things to different people, hence may affect verbal replies differentially).

A test item is an operation for getting at a hypothetical attribute. Sometimes there is very little doubt about whether the operation is appropriate—as, for instance, when one uses a subject's reply to the question, "Did you see the light spot?" as evidence for his subjective response of seeing or not seeing. One might ask a respondent in an interview survey, "How do you feel about the Republican Party?" and treat his response, coded on a five-point pro–con scale, as representing the affective component of his attitude toward that party. The first illustration represents a closed question, in that the subject's reply is limited (at least implicitly) by the nature of the question. The second example is an open question, to which the subject replies in his own words, and his response is subsequently coded for the attribute in which the researcher is interested. In both cases, though, an attribute is being assessed by a single stimulus, which is treated as a unique and unambiguous operation.

This is all right as long as the subject understands the question in the way that the researcher intends it and as long as the researcher's colleagues will accept his operational definition of the attribute. But there are many attributes for which these assumptions should be treated as problematical. "Do you love your country?" and "Would you die for your country?" represent alternative ways of assessing the attribute, devotion to one's country. Neither is necessarily a uniquely appropriate operation, and the two questions could quite conceivably elicit different responses from the same subject.

Most psychological attributes can be measured by alternative, or multiple, operations; this is particularly evident for attributes measured by verbal tests. Every different question or test item that is conceived to get at the trait constitutes a different operation; if all are indeed measuring the same attribute, then there should be some degree of similarity among the responses they elicit. The fact that they do not all yield identical responses indicates the need for multiple assessment; it also gives rise to test theory, which is aimed at systematically accounting for patterns of differences. In a more fundamental sense, multiple-question assessment is required in order to ascertain whether responses to any single question reflect some particular attribute of the subject. Without a second method of measuring the presumed attribute, one cannot be sure whether responses to the first measure really reflect that attribute or whether they stem from some other characteristic of the particular operation. A "yes" reply to "Would you die for your country?" might reflect the respondent's longing for death rather than his patriotism. So one would not want to use the question in a test purporting to measure patriotism without evidence that it elicited responses somewhat comparable to those elicited by another question aimed at the same trait.

SELECTING TEST ITEMS

The researcher should beware trusting his judgment alone in determining what a test item means to respondents—that is, what common attribute their responses to it reflect. Often a meaning which seems obvious and unique to him turns out to be only one of many possible interpretations. The selection of appropriate items to represent an intended trait is a tricky business involving both conceptual and empirical considerations, not all of which can at this time be completely reduced to a set of specific rules.

One possible approach is purely conceptual. The researcher first defines the attribute theoretically, then writes questions that seem to represent it. From the hypothetical trait, love of nature, for example, one could prepare such items as, "How often do you go for walks in the woods?" "Do you enjoy sunsets?" "When did you last go on a picnic?" etc. The sophistication and rigor with which such items are derived will vary greatly, depending on how well the trait is defined theoretically.

By contrast, one might attempt a purely empirical approach to test construction by administering a large batch of haphazardly selected items to two or more samples of subjects who can be independently distinguished on some criterion attribute—say whether or not they belong to an outing club. Then responses to each item are correlated with the criterion, and those items with the best correlations are selected for inclusion in the final test for measuring love of nature. Of course, results with the empirical method are only as good as the criterion chosen; thus outing-club membership might not reflect love of nature so much as it does love of exercise or a need to be a "joiner."

Greatest success in test construction is likely to be achieved if these approaches are combined. The difficulty with the conceptual method alone is that it provides no empirical check on the researcher's judgment concerning whether the items actually measure the attribute he thinks they do. The purely empirical approach would be unduly cumbersome because of the huge number of items required to assemble a sizable group that would correlate significantly and replicably with the criterion. Preferably one would start out with a conceptual definition of the hypothetical attribute to serve as a guide for constructing items. Then these would be administered, in a pilot study, to a group of subjects on whom criterion information was available. Those items which correlated appreciably with the criterion would be retained and the others rejected. If no outside criterion for the attribute were available, one might intercorrelate the several test items, selecting those which showed fairly high average correlations, on the assumption that they constituted the purest measures of the intended trait.

We have spoken here of "correlation" among different items, with the assumption that responses to any two of them will rarely be identical. For any set of multiple operations one can usually speak only of the degree to which they represent a common concept. This is certainly true for test items, and the reasons for differing responses are various. First there is the fact, noted earlier, that any single item is almost certain to reflect more than one attribute. This follows as a logical consequence of the psychological proposition that any behavior (including a verbal response to a test item) is multiply determined. Second, one must consider the possibility of measurement error. This is a way of referring to the fact that even identical questions presented fairly close together could elicit different responses, perhaps because the subject was not paying full attention on both occasions, because he interpreted the questions differently, or for a number of other reasons. (It is difficult, in practice, to distinguish the consequences of measurement error from those of multiple determinism, discussed previously; inconsistent responses could be the result of either.)

Finally, the failure of two items measuring the same trait to correlate perfectly can often be traced to the fact that one of them demands more of the trait than the other. Though a person may reply "yes" to the question, "Do you love your country?" this does not preclude a "no" response to, "Would you die for your country?" In a sense, both questions can be said to measure the same attribute, devotion to country; only the second measures it more stringently. The failure of perfect correlation between the items may stem solely from the fact that they differ in difficulty.

CONCEPTUALIZATIONS OF PSYCHOLOGICAL ATTRIBUTES

How one conceives the trait to be measured, of course, determines to a great extent the kinds of test items he constructs for the pilot study. The conceptualization of the attribute should also affect other research procedures, such as the way the test is scored and the way one finds out if it is measuring what is intended. Unless he is careful, the researcher may thoughtlessly add up the number of "right" answers on a test and then compute reliability and validity coefficients without considering whether these procedures are at all appropriate to the concept he is trying to measure. Perhaps certain perfunctory ways of scoring and testing tests have become routine because researchers are used to thinking about psychological traits solely in terms of an additive probabilistic model. This is the most common way in which traits are conceptualized nowadays, but it is by no means universal and, when employed, may reflect the thinking habits of the psychologist more than the actual nature of the attribute in question.

An *additive* model of test behavior implies that the more responses a subject gives which indicate the attribute, the more of it he possesses.

For instance, in scoring a test of knowledge about geography, one might simply count the number of right answers and treat the sum for any subject as reflecting his level of knowledge. A *probabilistic* model further implies that any particular summative score can be achieved in a variety of ways—in other words, that a particular amount of the attribute can be manifest in many different response patterns.

These are fairly appealing assumptions in measuring knowledge, and they have been widely adopted in assessing other psychological traits as well. Many scales of motives and attitudes are scored essentially in this fashion, and classical psychometric theory assumes an additive probabilistic model of test performance. For this reason, we will devote most attention to measures of test adequacy based on this model. But in order that the reader can beware of situations in which they are inappropriate, it is worthwhile to consider briefly other ways in which attributes can be conceptualized.

An *additive deterministic* model has already been encountered in our discussion of the Guttman scale (Chapter 5). If a psychological trait is conceived in this fashion, it means that the number of "correct" responses reflects the amount of the trait but also that any given sum can be achieved by only one pattern of responses. In other words, the attribute is so structured that before a person can manifest it in one way he must have come to manifest it in a particular set of other ways as well. Psychological theories of development which postulate the cumulative acquisition of skills in some fixed order would constitute one instance in which an additive deterministic test model would be appropriate.

Additive models, of either the probabilistic or the deterministic variety, share a common feature in assuming that the more of an attribute the person possesses the more ways he will manifest it and, consequently, the more test items reflecting that attribute will he accept (or pass, or score positively on). It is conceivable, though, that various manifestations may be *alternative* rather than additive—that is, that if a person shows the attribute in one way he will not show it in others. In the logical extreme this would suggest an *alternative deterministic* model of test behavior, implying that two responses, both manifesting the same attribute, were mutually exclusive. With an *alternative probabilistic* model, one would expect that the appearance of one manifestation would make others less likely.

According to classical psychoanalytic theory, for example, libidinal energy may be variously manifest in different people, depending on the stage of psychosexual development at which fixation has occurred. The oral receptive may display excessive optimism and dependency, the anal compulsive excessive concern over orderliness, etc. But the various sorts of manifestations are, in a sense, alternative; if one appears, there is less than normal likelihood that the other will also. Thus, if one were to construct a composite measure of the "amount of libidinal energy" available to an individual by sampling a variety of possible manifestations, there is no necessary reason for expecting these various samples to correlate highly with each other; in fact, some negative intercorrelations might be expected on theoretical grounds.

These illustrations by no means exhaust the possible ways of conceptualizing psychological attributes and how they are manifest in test behavior. Coombs (1955) and Loevinger (1957) have suggested others. The fact that systematic methods of test construction and analysis have not been developed for models other than the additive probably represents only a temporary state of affairs in psychological research.

CONSEQUENCES OF AN ADDITIVE PROBABILISTIC CONCEPTION

For the remainder of this chapter we shall concentrate on tests which follow an additive probabilistic model, since these have received the greatest attention in psychometric theory and technique. Four properties characterize such tests, by definition:

1. The subject's total score on the test, measured as the number of items he accepts (or, more generally, as the sum of item scores), is taken to represent the amount of the attribute he possesses. This is at least an ordinal scale quantity; it is usually treated as an interval, and sometimes even a ratio, scale.

2. Unless special weighting procedures are used, the contribution of each item to the variance in total scores depends on the item variance. This may seem odd at first, since one might be tempted to believe that each item is weighted equally by the additive method of scoring. A moment's reflection will indicate, however, that an item accepted (or rejected) by nearly everyone cannot contribute greatly to differences in total scores, since all subjects respond about the same to it. A maximally discriminating *dichotomous* item is one that is accepted by 50% of the subjects; this proportion yields maximum item variance. Also with a multiple-category item, for example, one which represents varying degrees of acceptance, the greater the item variance, the more it contributes to intersubject variance in total scores, hence the greater its weight. (If one really wants to have all test items weighted equally—and he should think twice before deciding

this—it is necessary to construct a standard score for each item; that is, from each subject's item score the item mean is subtracted, and this difference is divided by the item standard deviation.)

3. Every test item correlates positively with every other; that is, the probability of accepting one item is contingent upon acceptance of any other. The more of the attribute a subject possesses, the more likely he is to accept both members of any random pair of test items. (This correlation between two items will almost never be perfect, since each is regarded as only a probable rather than a certain manifestation of the attribute.)

4. Every item correlates positively with the total of the other item scores. This follows naturally from the preceding property, since the total is composed of the sum of items. A shorthand way of stating these last two properties is to say that the test is *homogeneous*.

OTHER COMMONLY ASSUMED TEST CHARACTERISTICS

Besides these characteristics of a test, which follow from an additive probabilistic conception of psychological attributes, certain other properties are normally expected of it. These properties may be required even if the attribute is conceived nonadditively.

1. Test scores should agree from one administration to the next, provided the attribute has not changed in the meantime. This is the property of *stability*, sometimes referred to as test-retest reliability. Note that this is an appropriate requirement of a test only if it is intended to measure an attribute that is conceived as stable. Since most psychological traits are treated as relatively enduring properties of the organism, test stability is usually a reasonable requirement. It is conceivable, though, that one may be interested in a fluctuating attribute of a person which is nevertheless significant in that it affects some other psychological process or behavior. In such a case stability would not be an appropriate measure of the test's adequacy.

2. Different ways of measuring the same trait should yield comparable results. This characteristic has been called *convergent validity* by Campbell & Fiske (1959) and is typically demonstrated by a substantial correlation between two (or more) tests alleged to measure a single attribute. Although it is possible that some psychological traits can be conceptualized in a way that admits only one appropriate method of measurement, it is far more usual for a test to be regarded simply as a sample of behavior reflecting a particular attribute that

could legitimately be measured in other ways as well. Under such a conceptualization it is reasonable to expect that these various other ways would yield results comparable to the first. Convergent validity can obviously be demonstrated only if the researcher has at least two tests purporting to measure the same trait. Moreover, the results of the analysis depend on the adequacy of both instruments. One test cannot be shown to have high convergent validity unless the other does also.

3. A test measuring one attribute will not correlate too highly with one designed to measure a different, theoretically independent attribute. This characteristic is called *discriminant validity* by Campbell and Fiske (1959), for it implies that the trait measured by the test can be distinguished from other traits which one does not intend to measure. Just what constitutes "too high" a correlation with the allegedly distinct tests will depend on a number of considerations, including the size of the correlation representing the test's convergent validity. Two measures of the same trait should correlate better than two measures of presumably different traits. In other words, discriminant validity and convergent validity must be considered together in order to arrive at a complete evaluation of the test.

All of these characteristics are criteria for the adequacy of a test. Implicit in them is the notion of *construct validity,* which refers to the adequacy of the logic used in deriving test items from a given theoretical definition. The criteria can provide certain empirical checks on some aspects of this logic. That is, given a particular theoretical definition of an attribute, one can conclude that measurements of this attribute should display certain empirical properties. Just what these properties are will depend on the theory, so it would not do to apply mechanically any of the measures of homogeneity, stability, or validity and regard a test which does not meet these standards as inadequate. A careful consideration of the conceptual properties of the attribute will help one decide what the empirical consequences of construct validity should be in the particular case. More often than not it turns out that for the vast proportion of attributes currently employed in psychological theory most of the characteristics listed above can reasonably be expected of appropriate tests.

MEASURING TEST HOMOGENEITY

A test is homogeneous to the extent that all items in it are correlated with one another and with the total score on the remaining items.

In a perfectly homogeneous test any subject's score would be identical on all items. If the items were scored dichotomously—for example, as "pass" or "fail"—then a person who passed one of them would necessarily pass all the others; and failing one item of a perfectly homogeneous test would necessarily imply that all other items were failed. From a perfectly homogeneous test with ten dichotomous items one would obtain only two groups of subjects—those who score zero (having failed all items) and those who score 10 (all items passed). (Under these—admittedly unlikely—conditions, of course, there would be no point in using all the items, since any one of them would do the same job as the entire lot.)

In a completely heterogeneous test, on the other hand, all interitem correlations would be zero; the probability of passing one would be independent of the probability of passing all others.

When a total test score is computed from the sum of a large number of independent items, the distribution of total scores will be approximately normal. To the extent that there is positive intercorrelation among the items, however, the distribution will be flattened out, and in the extreme case of perfect interitem correlation there will be just two scores, all failed or all passed. For the usual imperfectly homogeneous test, the shape of the distribution of total scores will be somewhere between these extremes.

The variance of a maximally heterogeneous test equals the sum of the variance of its component items; when all items are perfectly correlated, the variance of total test scores equals the square of the sum of item standard deviations. So a convenient measure of the degree to which a test is homogeneous can be computed from the degree to which the obtained test variance exceeds that which would be obtained if the items were uncorrelated, in ratio to the maximum difference possible. This measure, the homogeneity ratio, or HR, is presented in detail in chapter supplement A.

The ratio has a theoretical maximum of +1.00, and it represents a kind of average intercorrelation among all pairs of items in the test. However, unless two items are of exactly equal difficulty (i.e., they are passed by the same numbers of subjects or the distributions of scores over their several categories are identical), they cannot correlate perfectly. Hence HR will generally be much closer to 0.00 than to 1.00. Moreover, it is usual practice in test construction to select items of varying difficulty so that they can better discriminate among subjects with various amounts of the attribute. Therefore, one would not necessarily aim at the maximum value for HR. Another index of test homogeneity, H_t, whose magnitude is independent of varying item difficulties, has been proposed by Loevinger (1947, 1948). Its formula is presented in chapter Supplement A with an illustrative example.

Both HR and H_t reflect the variance among total test scores, and both indices will approach their maxima to the degree that the total test variance exceeds the variance of a normal distribution which would be obtained from a composite of uncorrelated items. Thus the researcher who desires a homogeneous instrument cannot at the same time expect normally distributed total scores. If scores from a composite instrument are normally distributed, one can be fairly certain that its components are not substantially correlated.*

MEASURING TEST STABILITY

A test is, by definition, stable to the extent that it yields identical scores on two different administrations. Certain problems are encountered in measuring test stability on humans. Subjects may tend to make the same responses the second time as they did the first, not because the underlying attribute has remained constant but because they remember what they said (or did) previously and, for some reason or other, wish to be consistent. Thus the subjects' memories for specific responses can serve artificially to inflate the apparent stability of the trait being measured.

But memory can conceivably work in the opposite direction as well. Particularly on open question measures or projective instruments, the subject may say to himself, "Let's see, I told him that last time; I ought to try to say something different now." Such an orientation toward the test may serve spuriously to reduce the similarity of scores on two different administrations below what it would be if only trait stability were being measured.

Certain *ad hoc* precautions can be taken in an attempt to reduce both directions of contamination. For instance, subjects might be instructed on the re-test to "answer the questions just as you now feel (or see, or know, or think), regardless of what you said last time"; but it is never certain that they will do so. Alternatively, the second

---

* One widely used measure of "homogeneity" is the Kuder-Richardson (1937) estimate of test reliability, r_{tt}, which also depends on the total test variance in relation to the sum of item variances. However, a major determinant of r_{tt} is the length of the test; with a large number of items, this index can be very high, even though the average intercorrelation among the items is near zero. Accordingly, r_{tt} is not recommended for those cases in which one wants to measure homogeneity only. HR and H_t, both of which are independent of test length, would appear to be preferable indices for this purpose.

administration might be delayed long enough to make sure that the first responses were forgotten. That period may, however, be considerably longer than the period of relative stability assumed for the trait, hence instability of scores might just as well be the result of a variable attribute as of an inadequate measuring instrument.

In an attempt to overcome the effects of memory, without prolonging the intertest interval, the technique of measurement by parallel forms has been developed. It is impossible to offer a precise definition of parallel tests that is not circular, but the procedure essentially requires two tests that measure the same attribute, composed of items matched for difficulty and for correlation between items and total test. Thus the means and variances of two parallel tests should be equal, and, if the tests are administered simultaneously (or in immediate succession), their total scores will be very highly correlated.

One technique for constructing parallel tests (see Gulliksen, 1950) is to administer a large number of (homogeneous) items to the same group of subjects and to compute item difficulties and item-test correlations. Each item is then identified by a number and plotted on a bivariate frequency distribution, with one axis representing difficulty and the other axis the item-test correlation. Pairs of items which fall maximally close together in this array are formed, and one member of each pair is assigned to each of the parallel tests; that is, the total pool of items is divided into two stratified groups, stratification being based on item difficulty and item-test correlation. (See Chapter 9 for a discussion of stratification in subject sampling.) If the statification is successful, then the two samples of items should yield nearly identical information about the attribute being measured. That is, all subjects should score about the same on both tests.*

The concept of parallel forms is compatible with an additive probabilistic definition of the attribute to be measured. If the attribute can be assessed with one sample of test items, then it should be possible to select another—or several other—comparable samples as well. If the items for two tests are selected by simple random sampling from a population of items, then statistics computed from them, such as total scores on a given subject, means or standard deviations over a group of subjects, or average interitem correlations, should be equal within the limits of sampling error. The size of this sampling error can be reduced by stratifying the item population according to relevant characteristics like item difficulty and item-test correlation. This is what the techniques for parallel test construction aim to accomplish.

---

* This procedure can, of course, be extended to handle any number of stratified samples of items so as to yield not just two but several parallel forms of the test.

Given two tests that meet the criteria for parallel forms, they provide a method for assessing the stability of a trait, uncontaminated by recall of specific items. Whether stability is assessed with the same test administered twice or by means of parallel forms, the object is to obtain identical scores from all subjects on both administrations. The extent to which this condition occurs can be measured quantitatively by means of ρ, the *intraclass correlation coefficient* * (Haggard, 1958). The formula for ρ and an illustration of its use in measuring agreement between two sets of scores are presented in chapter supplement B.

CONVERGENT AND DISCRIMINANT VALIDITY

Empirically, a test is valid if it satisfies two criteria: it should measure the intended trait, and it should not measure some other trait that was not intended. The former aspect has received more attention in the methodology of testing than has the latter. At first glance, discriminant validity would seem not to constitute a serious problem, since one can presumably infer from the test content the traits it does not measure. Yet just as an intuitive impression of validity provides no guarantee of empirical validity (in the "convergent" sense of measuring what is intended), so the researcher should beware of using his own subjective judgment concerning what the test does not measure. Any number of occasions can be found in which an investigator thought he was measuring a particular distinct trait, only to discover that his scores correlated so highly with some other presumably irrelevant trait that there was no legitimate empirical ground for distinguishing the two.

That measures of two supposedly unrelated traits can correlate appreciably is due largely to the fact that any test necessarily taps

---

* Though the Pearson product-moment correlation coefficient is commonly used to measure test-retest reliability, this is not a direct measure of agreement between two sets of scores but rather a measure of the degree to which they are linearly related. Thus it would be possible to obtain an r of $+1.00$ between an original test and a retest, even though the scores were not identical. When the product-moment correlation is used to measure stability, it must be accompanied by additional tests (see Gulliksen, 1950) to assure that means and variances are equal on the two administrations. Often they are not (see Windle, 1954). We prefer the intraclass correlation because it measures directly the extent of agreement between scores on the two tests. The interested reader might also wish to consult the article by Robinson (1957), which provides a further discussion of the problem.

a variety of attributes in addition to the intended one. If two tests designed to measure different traits actually share a common irrelevant quality, then their scores could correlate—though the correlation would result not from similarity of the focal traits but from similarity in their irrelevant features. As an example, one might consider two tests, one intended to measure "liking for sports" and the other "liking for music," with the items of both worded in such a way that a "yes" response always indicated presence of the relevant trait. It is likely that scores on these two tests would correlate appreciably, if for no other reason than that both of them measured, in part, the tendency of subjects to say "yes" or "no." Various kinds of instrument effects or unwanted content similarity could induce correlation between *measures* of two different traits, even though the traits themselves—as conceived apart from their imperfect measures—were independent (see, for example, Couch & Keniston, 1960; Cronbach, 1955; Edwards, 1957). In the language of test theory one test includes, in addition to variance in the intended trait and random error variance, a large portion of variance caused by some irrelevant trait which is also unintentionally measured by the second test.

This kind of instrument contamination is very likely to distort measurements of convergent validity. Such measurements are usually obtained by correlating the results of two different tests intended to measure the same attribute. It is quite clear that a sizable correlation could emerge not because of commonality in the intended trait but simply because both tests shared common instrument factors or other contaminating features. In order to assess the effects due to the intended psychological trait more realistically, one must somehow partial out irrelevant instrument effects.

A method for tackling this problem has been proposed by Campbell & Fiske (1959). Essentially, it involves testing the same group of subjects on two or more traits by two or more testing methods each. Thus each trait is measured by at least two different methods, and each method is used to assess at least two different traits. Then, by intercorrelating all measures of all traits, one can compare the magnitudes of the validity correlations with the magnitudes of the unintended correlations to make certain that the former are large enough to warrant confidence in the trait's existence apart from the particular method of measuring it. Table 6-1 presents some hypothetical data derived from four different tests administered to the same group of subjects. Two psychological tendencies are represented, "dependence" and "nurturance," each measured by a projective device (say content analysis of imaginative stories) and by a direct verbal

TABLE 6-1

Correlations among Projective and Direct Verbal Measures of Dependence and Nurturance
(Hypothetical Data Showing Poor Discriminant Validity)

Trait:	Dependence		Nurturance	
Method:	Projective	Verbal	Projective	Verbal
Dependence⌉ Projective				
Verbal	.50			
Nurturance Projective	.60	.45		
Verbal	.55	.65	.40	

test of the Guttman-scale variety. The tabled results would lead one to suspect that the tests were not actually so valid as the validity correlations alone suggest.

The upper left-hand and the lower right-hand figures represent the "validity" coefficients of .50 and .40. These show the degree to which two different measures (projective and verbal) of the same traits (dependence and nurturance, respectively) are correlated. They might be regarded as large enough to justify the belief that common traits were being measured in both instances. The remaining values in the table suggest otherwise. It can be seen that dependence correlates better with nurturance when both are measured by the same method (either projective or verbal) than either trait correlates with itself when measured by two different methods. Moreover, the fact that different measures of different traits correlate as well (.55 and .45) as different measures of the same traits (.50 and .40) indicates that whatever commonality is represented by the validity coefficients reflects common methods variance, rather than common trait variance.

A more satisfactory situation is pictured in Table 6-2. There the validity correlations (.50 and .40) are considerably higher than the nonpredicted correlations between different measures of different traits (.05 and .10). Still, there are appreciable correlations (.35 and .30) between the two allegedly different traits when measured by the same method, a rather typical finding from assessment studies which have been subjected to this kind of analysis. Most of the time researchers have neglected to compute their nonpredicted correlations and have

TABLE 6-2

Correlations among Projective and Direct Verbal Measures
of Dependence and Nurturance
(Hypothetical Data Showing Satisfactory Discriminant Validity)

Trait:	Dependence		Nurturance	
Method:	Projective	Verbal	Projective	Verbal
Dependence				
Projective				
Verbal	.50			
Nurturance				
Projective	.35	.10		
Verbal	.05	.30	.40	

thus been unable to find out how the validities compared with them. It should now be apparent that convergent validity must be considered in the context of discriminant validity, for the simple fact of correlation between two tests does not constitute sufficient evidence that they measure the same trait. One must at least exclude the possibility that the correlation is entirely the result of similarity of the two instruments.

This kind of discriminant analysis is becoming more and more common in the field of psychological testing (it is implicit in factor analysis). Clearly the establishment of differential predictions—that one correlation will be higher than another or that one will be high and the other nonsignificant—constitutes more convincing evidence for the construct validity of a given test than the mere finding of a single correlation, which could conceivably be due to a number of factors other than the one intended.

OTHER EMPIRICAL TESTS OF CONSTRUCT VALIDITY

Though the criteria of homogeneity, stability, and convergent-discriminant validity are common empirical consequences of the construct validity of a psychological test, they are by no means exhaustive. Depending on the way in which a trait is conceptualized, a variety of other empirical results might be demanded before much faith can be placed in a particular test as a measure of the intended attribute. For example, it might be assumed as a fact that two definable populations of people differ appreciably on the trait, and a test purporting to measure it could thus be validated by the *known groups method*. If a test actually measures knowledge of psychology, for example, then psychology professors and sophomore students ought to perform differently on it. A test purporting to measure "religiousness" should presumably show group differences between clergymen and laymen, between Roman Catholics and atheists, between people who attend church regularly and those who never attend, etc. If such expected differences do not emerge, the investigator would have to conclude either that his test does not measure "religiousness" or that it measures a type of religiousness not reflected in memberships of these kinds. This would force him to reformulate and clarify his conceptual definition of the attribute.

Another common way of empirically validating a test is to use it as a device for predicting some other behavior with which the intended attribute is presumably related. (This is sometimes called *predictive validity;* see American Psychological Association's *Technical recommendations,* 1954.) One would expect, for example, that a satisfactory measure of intelligence would predict the level of academic success in high school. If it did not, a new test would be sought, for the usual conception of intelligence demands this result.

Again, one might explicitly conceive a psychological attribute that varies systematically with certain specific environmental conditions. A reasonable way of validating a test of the attribute could well be to create those conditions experimentally and to assess the subjects in them to see if the predicted test differences appeared. A test intended to measure loneliness, for example, might be administered to comparable samples of subjects, one of which had been deprived of human contact for some time. If they did not, on the average, score higher than the sample of normally interacting subjects, then the validity of the test might reasonably be doubted.

How does one decide what measures to use as validating criteria? This depends entirely on the properties of the attribute being assessed and on other characteristics with which it is theoretically expected to correlate. In a sense, none of these operations can serve to "validate" the test if by that term one means "prove that it measures the intended attribute." Any or all of them may be necessary conditions for adequate validity, but they are rarely sufficient conditions.

Note that in each example the meaning of any particular empirical result may be ambiguous. If, in the known-groups method, two groups do not differ in the manner expected, it could be that one's expectations were erroneous rather than that the test was invalid. Contrariwise, if the test results do turn out as predicted, this could still be because of some other reason than real differences in the intended trait. Differences in literacy, in understanding of the test items, in response sets (such as tendency to say "yes" or "no")—any of these may affect test scores in the same way as the psychological characteristic which the researcher assumes he is measuring.

The same ambiguity may hold for the other approaches to test validation. Validating a test experimentally requires that the experimental manipulations have their intended effect. In the preceding illustration, for example, if isolation of subjects did not actually produce loneliness, then the expected difference in test scores would not emerge, even with the best of tests. Finally, if a test fails in predicting another behavior to which it is supposed to relate, this could simply mean that too many other variables were operating to permit a detectable effect of the one measured by the test; or it could mean that one's reasoning concerning the likely effects of the attribute was faulty rather than that the attribute was not validly assessed. Conversely, the predicted results may appear, but for the wrong reasons, simply because contaminating factors in the test or in the research situation were not properly controlled.

Basically, the source of ambiguity lies in the fact that any validity study is necessarily an empirical investigation both of the instrument and of the theory that predicts the results—whether one uses group differences, a correlated behavior, or change in test responses due to situational influences. One must have utmost confidence in the theory to interpret negative results as reflecting lack of validity in the test; and one must have utmost confidence in his research procedures to interpret positive results as due to the intended attribute. Thus it would be hasty to say that a psychological test has been "validated" (or "invalidated") by any single set of data. Such characterizations, in the last analysis, are judgments based on accumulated evidence from a variety of relevant empirical studies. What constitutes a relevant study depends on the conceptual definition of the attribute; correspondingly, the empirical outcome of any particular validating study is likely to affect the way in which the attribute is conceptualized— by broadening or restricting or modifying the concept in the light of the data.

Perhaps more informative validating studies can be performed if they are designed to accumulate discriminant as well as convergent evidence. This suggests that a useful validation would be one that makes differential predictions—for example, that two groups will differ on one trait but not on another; that groups A and B will differ on a particular trait, but not groups A and C; that under situational manipulation trait X should change, but not trait Y; or that scores on a particular test should correlate with one behavior but not with another. All of these are examples of convergent and discriminant validation, extended beyond the particular application of correlation among tests to the broader domain of research, flexibly designed according to the theoretical requirements of a particular concept, to see if that concept is actually being measured by the test.

SUMMARY

Much psychological research involves the measurement of variables by means of verbal instruments, which confront subjects with standard questions and induce them to respond in ways that presumably reflect a common underlying attribute. The basic question in assessing the adequacy of such instruments is, "Do they indeed measure the intended attribute?" A first approach to answering this question involves a subjective examination of the question content. For more convincing answers, fairly elaborate research procedures and analyses, with multiple measures of the trait, are required.

Multiple measures are provided by a series of test items derived from a theoretical consideration of the attribute. These items are then analyzed statistically in a way that makes sense in the light of the conceptual requirements. One commonly encountered requirement is test homogeneity, or positive intercorrelation among all pairs of items. Another is stability of test scores from one administration to the next. Then there are various ways of "validating" a test by showing that scores on it vary systematically with certain other characteristics of subjects or of the testing situation. Just what is done to demonstrate that an instrument is adequate will depend on what one expects of it. Therefore, it is helpful to make one's expectations explicit fairly early in a research project so that an appropriate test can be selected on the basis of available research evidence or, alternatively, so that a new test can be constructed which more nearly fits the particular research requirements.

In a sense, any study that relates one psychological measure to another is, at the same time, investigating a research hypothesis as well as testing the adequacy of the measuring instruments. When a particular instrument has been used repeatedly and has produced successful results, then one can reasonably attribute failure of a predicted outcome to a faulty hypothesis. With a brand new instrument, one should perhaps first suspect the measure itself rather than the hypothesis. Efficient research strategy might well provide for considerable initial attention to the development and refinement of the measuring instruments before the intended "major hypotheses" are tested definitively.

SUPPLEMENT

A. Measuring Test Homogeneity

A test is homogeneous to the extent that all items are correlated with one another and with the total score on the remaining items. Of course, it would be possible to compute all correlations, but this would involve a tremendous amount of work for any test with more than a few items. Moreover, it would yield, not one index of homogeneity, but as many as there are correlation coefficients, and none of these would characterize the test as a whole. It is therefore convenient to use some measure of over-all test homogeneity that represents an average of the interitem correlations. This can be developed out of a general equation for the variance of a sum of scores (see Hansen, Hurwitz, & Madow, 1953, p. 513).

$$(1) \qquad \sigma_t^2 = \Sigma\sigma_i^2 + 2 \sum_{i \neq j} \sigma_i\sigma_j r_{ij}$$

This means that the total test variance equals the sum of variances of the individual items plus twice the sum of their covariances. (A covariance is the correlation between two items multiplied by the geometric mean of their variances. The geometric mean of σ_i^2 and σ_j^2 is $\sqrt{\sigma_i^2\sigma_j^2} = \sigma_i\sigma_j$.)

In a maximally heterogeneous test every item would be independent of every other item, and the second term on the right-hand side of (1) would be zero because r_{ij} is zero; therefore the total test variance would be

$$(2) \qquad \sigma_{\text{het}}^2 = \Sigma\sigma_i^2$$

If all items were perfectly correlated, the variance of the total test scores would be

$$(3) \qquad \sigma_{\text{hom}}^2 = (\Sigma\sigma_i)^2$$

in other words, the square of the sum of the item standard deviations.*

* With $r_{ij} = 1.00$, $\sigma_t^2 = \Sigma\sigma_i^2 + 2 \sum_{i \neq j} \sigma_i\sigma_j$. The right-hand side of this equation is simply the square of the multinomial, $\Sigma\sigma_i$:

$$(\sigma_1 + \sigma_2 + \cdots + \sigma_k)^2 = \sigma_1^2 + \sigma_2^2 + \cdots + \sigma_k^2 + 2\sigma_1\sigma_2 + 2\sigma_1\sigma_3 + \cdots + 2\sigma_{k-1}\sigma_k$$

So (3) represents the variance of a maximally homogeneous test, whereas (2) represents the variance of a maximally heterogeneous test. These two equations suggest an appropriate index of the degree of homogeneity of any test, namely the difference between the actual test variance and the variance that would be obtained from uncorrelated items in ratio to the maximum difference possible. This index is HR, the homogeneity ratio (Scott, 1960).

$$\text{(4)} \qquad \text{HR} = \frac{\sigma_t^2 - \Sigma\sigma_i^2}{(\Sigma\sigma_i)^2 - \Sigma\sigma_i^2}$$

In this formula σ_t^2 is the actual obtained total test variance, $\Sigma\sigma_i^2$ is the sum of item variances (which equals the total test variance that would be obtained if all items were independent), and $\Sigma\sigma_i$ is the sum of item standard deviations. A sample calculation is provided in Table 6-3.

If the test items are scored dichotomously (e.g., as either "pass" or "fail"), then their variances can be computed quite simply from the proportions of people accepting and rejecting them, and the formula for the homogeneity ratio becomes

$$\text{(5)} \qquad \text{(with dichotomous items) HR} = \frac{\sigma_t^2 - \Sigma p_i q_i}{(\Sigma\sqrt{p_i q_i})^2 - \Sigma p_i q_i}$$

where p_i is the proportion of subjects passing the ith item, and $q_i = 1 - p_i$. This could also be written as

$$\text{(5}a\text{)} \qquad \text{HR} = \frac{\sigma_t^2 - \Sigma p_i q_i}{2\Sigma\sqrt{p_i q_i p_j q_j}}$$

in which the term following the summation sign in the denominator represents the geometric mean of the variances of each pair of items.

This homogeneity ratio can be interpreted as a weighted average of the intercorrelations among all pairs of items; that is,

TABLE 6-3

Calculation of Homogeneity Ratio (Average Interitem Correlation)

Item	Score 0	1	2	3	4	5	6	σ_i^2	σ_i
1	186	32						.125	.354
2	72	39	62	29	16			1.613	1.270
3	151	67						.213	.461
								Σ = 1.951	2.085
Total test	51	45	52	38	15	12	5	σ_t^2 = 2.443	

$$\text{HR} = \frac{\sigma_t^2 - \Sigma\sigma_i^2}{(\Sigma\sigma_i)^2 - \Sigma\sigma_i^2} = \frac{2.443 - 1.951}{(2.085)^2 - 1.951} = .21$$

(6)
$$HR = \frac{\Sigma\sigma_i\sigma_j r_{ij}}{\Sigma\sigma_i\sigma_j}$$

In other words, one would obtain the same value if he were actually to compute the correlation between every item-pair, weight it by the geometric mean of the item variances, add all these products up, and divide by the sum of the weights. Such a computation would be unnecessarily tedious, however, since (4) and (5) permit one to calculate HR directly from the test and item variances, without knowing any of the interitem correlations.

HR will almost never approach its theoretical maximum of $+1.00$, for, unless two items are of equal difficulty (i.e., passed, or accepted, by the same number of subjects), they cannot correlate perfectly.* It is possible to take account of the ceiling imposed by varying item difficulties, provided the items are scored dichotomously. Loevinger (1947, 1948) has suggested an index of test homogeneity, H_t, which is very much like HR, except that it does correct the maximum test variance $[\sigma_{\text{hom}}^2$ in (3)] downward, in consideration of the ceiling imposed on it by the varying item difficulties.

(7)
$$H_t = \frac{\sigma_t^2 - \Sigma p_i q_i}{2\sum_{j<i} p_j q_i}$$

where $p_j < p_i$.

The numerator of H_t is the same as that of HR in (5) and (5a), but its denominator is smaller. The denominator is calculated by multiplying the proportion of subjects who passed each item by the proportion who failed each item *easier* than it,† then adding all products and multiplying by 2; H_t will always be larger than HR except for the unusual case in which all items are of equal difficulty.

The computation of both HR and H_t for a test with dichotomously scored items is illustrated in Table 6-4. The left-hand box at the top contains the components for $\Sigma p_i q_i$ and $\Sigma\sqrt{p_i q_i}$. The first of these is used in both indices, the second only in HR. The right-hand box contains the components of $\Sigma p_j q_i$, used in H_t, which are obtained as follows: (1) The items are arranged in order of difficulty, from easiest (large p_i) to hardest (small p_i). When two or more items are of equal difficulty—such as items 1 and 2 in the present example—they are placed in arbitrary order. Then the p for every item (j) is multiplied by the q for each item (i) easier than it. [Any particular item is considered, first as j for the items easier than it, then as i for the items more difficult than it; e.g., p for item 2 (.58) is multiplied by q for item 1 (.42); p for item 3 (.35) is multiplied by qs for items 2 and 1 (both .42).] There will be a total of $k(k-1)/2$ products (where k is the number of items in the test). All of these are added together to obtain $\Sigma p_j q_i$.

---

* This is generally true, even for items scored into multiple categories rather than dichotomized. Unless their response distributions are identical, the product-moment correlation between them cannot equal unity.

† If two of the items are equal in difficulty, one of them is arbitrarily designated as j, the other as i.

TABLE 6-4

Calculation of HR and H_t with Dichotomous Items

Item	p_i	q_i	p_iq_i	$\sqrt{p_iq_i}$
1	.58	.42	.244	.494
2	.58	.42	.244	.494
3	.35	.65	.228	.477
4	.28	.72	.202	.449
			$\Sigma = .918$	1.914

Item j	i	p_j	q_i	p_jq_i
2	1	.58	.42	.244
3	2	.35	.42	.147
3	1	.35	.42	.147
4	3	.28	.65	.182
4	2	.28	.42	.118
4	1	.28	.42	.118
				$\Sigma p_j q_i = .956$

Total scores	0	1	2	3	4
Frequencies	43	50	55	48	22

$\sigma_t^2 = 1.600$

$$\mathrm{HR} = \frac{\sigma_t^2 - \Sigma p_iq_i}{(\Sigma\sqrt{p_iq_i})^2 - \Sigma p_iq_i} = \frac{1.600 - .918}{(1.914)^2 - .918} = .25$$

$$H_t = \frac{\sigma_t^2 - \Sigma p_iq_i}{2\Sigma p_jq_i} = \frac{1.600 - .918}{2(.956)} = .36$$

B. Measuring Test Stability

In order to measure the extent of agreement either between two parallel forms or between two administrations of the same test, it is useful to construct an index that will measure the similarity of the paired scores in relation to the total variability of all scores. This can be done indirectly by squaring the differences between paired scores, averaging them over all subjects, and dividing the average by the total test variance, to yield a measure of the average magnitude of *disagreement* between test and retest scores, in relation to the intersubject variation in scores. To convert average disagreement into average agreement, the obtained ratio is subtracted from 1.00. Thus

$$\rho = 1 - \frac{\Sigma(X_i - Y_i)^2}{2n\sigma_{(x+y)}^2}$$

where $(X_i - Y_i)$ represents the difference between the two scores from a single subject; n is the number of subjects; and $\sigma_{(x+y)}^2$ is the total variance in test scores obtained by combining all scores from both administrations; ρ is the *intraclass correlation coefficient* (Haggard, 1958), and it has a more general use in representing the degree of similarity among several related observations. We encounter it again in our discussion of interjudge agreement (Chapter 8) and clustered sampling (Chapter 9).

An example of the use of ρ to measure test stability is presented in Table 6-5.

The difference between the original and the retest score on a single subject $(X_i - Y_i)$ is represented by the difference between the column and row scores for the cell in which that subject falls. For example, the third cell from the left in the top row indicates that four subjects had an original score of 2 and a retest score of 4; for them $(X_i - Y_i)^2 = (2 - 4)^2 = 4$. In the next cell to the right eight subjects had an original score of 3 and a retest score of 4, yielding a squared difference of 1. Multiplying each squared difference by the number of subjects who obtain it, and adding all these up, gives a $\Sigma(X_i - Y_i)^2$ of 103 for the numerator of the fraction.

The variance of the combined distribution $(X + Y)$ in the denominator is $\sigma^2_{(x+y)}$, which is obtained by superimposing both of the marginal distributions X and Y. There are 24 X-scores of 0 and 12 Y-scores of 0; added together, they make 36 scores of 0 in the combined distribution. The 36 scores of 1 in the $X + Y$ distribution are obtained by adding 20 ($X = 1$) and 16 ($Y = 1$), and so on for each pair of frequencies from corresponding X and Y scores. The variance of this combined distribution is calculated, and the result is multiplied by the number of scores on which it is based (i.e., twice the number of subjects), to yield the denominator of the fraction.

TABLE 6-5

Measuring Test Stability by the Intraclass Correlation Coefficient (ρ)

		Original test score (X)					Total
		0	1	2	3	4	
	4			4	8	12	24
Retest	3	1	2	15	18	5	41
score	2	3	12	3	4		22
(Y)	1	10	4	2			16
	0	10	2				12
Total		24	20	24	30	17	115
Combined distribution (X + Y)		36	36	46	71	41	

$$\sigma^2_{(x+y)} = 1.766$$

$$\Sigma(X_i - Y_i)^2 = 4(2)^2 + 8(1)^2 + 12(0)^2 + 1(3)^2 + 2(2)^2 + 15(1)^2 + 18(0)^2$$
$$+ 5(1)^2 + 3(2)^2 + 12(1)^2 + 3(0)^2 + 4(1)^2 + 10(1)^2$$
$$+ 4(0)^2 + 2(1)^2 + 10(0)^2 + 2(1)^2 = 103.$$

$$\rho = 1 - \frac{\Sigma(X_i - Y_i)^2}{2n\sigma^2_{(x+y)}} = 1 - \frac{103}{2(115)(1.766)} = .75$$

Subtracting this fraction from 1.00, then, yields ρ, the intraclass correlation. In general, ρ is smaller than r (the product-moment correlation) calculated from the same data, except in the special case in which all frequencies fall on the diagonal, and $r = \rho = 1.00$. (In the present example $r = .80$; this would be a deceptively high measure of agreement, for it does not reflect the fact that retest scores tend to be higher than the original scores; ρ takes this into account and therefore is somewhat smaller.)

REFERENCES

American Psychological Association. Technical recommendations for psychological tests and diagnostic techniques. *Psychol. Bull. Suppl.*, 1954, **51**, No. 2, part 2 (38 pp.).

Anastasi, Anne. *Psychological testing.* New York: Macmillan, 1954.

Buros, O. K. *The fifth mental measurements yearbook.* Highland Park, N. J.: The Mental Measurements Yearbook, 1959.

Campbell, D. T., & Fiske, D. W. Convergent and discriminant validation by the multitrait-multimethod matrix. *Psychol. Bull.*, 1959, **56**, 81–105.

Cattell, R. B. *A guide to mental testing.* (2nd Ed.) London: Univer. London Press, 1948.

Coombs, C. H. The conjunctive, disjunctive, and compensatory models for complex behavior. *Acta Psychol.*, 1955, **11**, 154–155.

Couch, A., & Keniston, K. Yeasayers and naysayers: agreeing response set as a personality variable. *J. abnorm. soc. Psychol.*, 1960, **60**, 151–174.

Cronbach, L. J. *Essentials of psychological testing.* (2nd Ed.) New York: Harper, 1960.

Cronbach, L. J. Processes affecting scores on "understanding of others" and "assumed similarity." *Psychol. Bull.*, 1955, **52**, 177–193.

Cronbach, L. J., & Meehl, P. E. Construct validity in psychological tests. *Psychol. Bull.*, 1955, **52**, 281–302.

Edwards, A. L. *The social desirability variable in personality assessment and research.* New York: Dryden, 1957.

Gulliksen, H. *Theory of mental tests.* New York: Wiley, 1950.

Haggard, E. A. *Intra-class correlation with the analysis of variance.* New York: Dryden, 1958.

Hansen, M. H., Hurwitz, W. N., & Madow, W. G. *Sample survey methods and theory.* (Vol. 1.) New York: Wiley, 1953.

Kuder, G. F., & Richardson, M. W. The theory of the estimation of test reliability. *Psychometrika*, 1937, **2**, 151–160.

Loevinger, Jane. A systematic approach to the construction and evaluation of tests of ability. *Psychol. Monogr.*, 1947, **61**, No. 4.

Loevinger, Jane. The technic of homogeneous tests compared with some aspects of "scale analysis" and factor analysis. *Psychol. Bull.*, 1948, **45**, 507–529.

Loevinger, Jane. Objective tests as instruments of psychological theory. *Psychol. Rep.*, 1957, **3**, 635–694.

Robinson, W. S. The statistical measure of agreement. *Amer. sociol. Rev.*, 1957, **22**, 17–25.

Scott, W. A. Measures of test homogeneity. *Educ. psychol. Measmt,* 1960, **20,** 751–757.

Stern, G. G., Stein, M. I., & Bloom, B. S. *Methods in personality assessment.* Glencoe, Ill.: Free Press, 1956.

Tryon, R. C. Reliability and behavior domain validity: reformulation and historical critique. *Psychol. Bull.,* 1957, **54,** 229–249.

Windle, C. Test-retest effect on personality questionnaires. *Educ. psychol Measmt,* 1954, **14,** 617–633.

CHAPTER 7

Instrumentation:
experimental equipment

Just as verbal instruments have played a major role in systematic assessment, so have complex hardware and electronic devices come to be identified with experimental research. Both of these marriages between instrument and methodology seem more fortuitous than rational. Perhaps from a distrust of introspective data that pervaded early behaviorism, many experimentalists have felt more comfortable when they could manipulate and assess variables without depending on subjects' reports. By contrast, the methodology of personality assessment grew mainly in clinical settings and interview surveys in which mechanical instrumentation and experimental manipulation either were not considered or were deemed impractical or even unethical. There are, of course, notable exceptions to these trends. Currently, a great deal of verbal instrument validation is done by experimentally manipulating the variable to be assessed, and verbal instruments are often used in experimental studies on humans, particularly to determine their subjective responses to the experimental conditions.

The basic aim of standardized instruments, whether verbal or mechanical, is to substitute objective techniques of control and measurement for subjective interpretations by a human observer. An additional aim of mechanical instrumentation is to minimize dependence on the subject's own verbal productions. Though some attributes may, in principle, be unmeasurable without the person's own self-report, whenever impersonal equipment can perform the same function as verbal stimulus material there are marked advantages to using it, since one is then less dependent on subjects' language abilities or their willingness to reveal themselves.

FUNCTIONS OF EXPERIMENTAL EQUIPMENT

The uses to which mechanical instruments have been put in psychological research may be divided roughly into three broad categories. A piece of apparatus may present a stimulus, record the stimulus, or record the response; some devices perform more than one of these general functions. Here we discuss each category only briefly and in general terms; illustrative lists of experimental equipment of each type are presented in the chapter supplement.

Stimulus-producing equipment is used for a wide variety of experimental problems in learning, motivation, and perception. A particularly high level of engineering sophistication has been achieved in the design of devices for psychophysical research by the use of the electrical relay, the vacuum tube, and, more recently, the transistor. It is now possible to maintain precise control over such characteristics of stimuli as their duration, intensity, wavelength composition, and presentation interval. Stimulus-producing equipment may also serve to hold constant or otherwise control independent variables besides the main one the experimenter is interested in; for example, audiometers, discrimination apparatus, and mazes at the same time present certain stimuli and hold constant other features of the situation (such as possible distractions) whose variation might contaminate the results.

Stimulus-recording devices include equipment for calibrating stimulus-producing apparatus, instruments for recording when a stimulus is turned on and off (often in relation to records of responses), and apparatus which records background conditions (such as temperature, time, humidity, and noise level) while the variables of central interest are being measured. Sometimes moving picture cameras or tape recorders, separately or in combination, may be used to obtain a rich and detailed record of the interplay of independent and dependent variables, of the flux of the stimulus situation in relation to the pattern of response.

Response-recording devices may provide measures of the latency, strength, duration, extent, and frequency of responses, whether they are simple muscle twitches, the speaking of words, the pressing of levers, or more complex movement patterns. Other mechanical apparatus records the position or activity level of an animal in a cage at each moment; physiological responses can be measured with such devices as electrocardiographs, muscle-tension recorders, or electroencephalographs. Response-recording apparatus is frequently combined with stimulus recording devices to provide simultaneous information about the subject and the experimental situation.

It is impossible to discuss even an adequate sample of standard experimental equipment which is now available for psychological research. Our list in the chapter supplement is only illustrative. If the student wishes to get some idea of the range of the devices, he might go on a tour of his psychology department laboratory or consult the catalogues published by various manufacturers.* (These catalogues can usually be found in the psychology department office or may be ordered direct from the manufacturer.)

ACQUIRING AND MAINTAINING EQUIPMENT

There are many ways in which experimental apparatus can be acquired: one can build it, borrow it, modify some available instrument, buy the equipment ready made, or order it constructed to specifications. Which of these avenues one chooses will depend on a number of practical and theoretical considerations. Does an available piece of equipment fit the requirements of the research problem, or must new apparatus be purchased or constructed? Can an available instrument be made adequate with minor modifications—and are there

---

* For example, Associated Research, Inc., 3758 West Belmont Ave., Chicago 18, Ill.; C & C Enterprises, 122 E. Sixth St., Williamstown, W. Va.; Cambridge Instrument Co., Inc., 3732 Grand Central Terminal, New York 17, N. Y.; Chicago Apparatus Co., 1735 North Ashland Ave., Chicago 22, Ill.; Lon R. Davis Scientific Instruments, 12137 Cantura St., Studio City, Calif.; The Esterline-Angus Co., Inc., P. O. Box 596, Indianapolis 6, Ind.; Foringer & Co., Inc., 302 Stonestreet Ave., Rockville, Md.; Garrison Co., Box 122a, Dexter, Mich.; Ralph Gerbrands Co., Scientific Instruments, 96 Ronald Road, Arlington 74, Mass.; Grason-Stadler Co., West Concord, Mass.; Grass Instrument Co., 101 Old Colony Ave., Quincy, Mass.; Hunter Mfg. Co., Inc., P. O. Box 153, Coralville Branch, Iowa City, Iowa; Iconix, Inc., 945 Industrial Ave., Palo Alto, Calif.; Lafayette Instrument Co., North 26th St. and 52 By-Pass, Lafayette, Ind.; Lehigh Valley Electronics, 215 South Third St., Allentown, Pa.; Marietta Apparatus Co., Marietta, Ohio; Phipps and Bird, Inc., 303 South Sixth St., Richmond 5, Va.; Psychological Instruments Co., Box 6113, Richmond 22, Va.; Scientific Prototype Mfg. Corp., 2032 Bath Ave., Brooklyn 14, N. Y.; C. H. Stoelting Co., 424 North Homan Ave., Chicago 24, Ill.; Toei Bussan Kaisha, Ltd., Chuseiren Building, 1-Chome, Hirakawa-Cho, Chiyoda-Ku, Tokyo, Japan; W. M. Welch Manufacturing Co., 1515 Sedgwick St., Chicago 10, Ill.; Wichita Apparatus Supply, Inc., P. O. Box 194, Lawrence, Kans.

facilities to modify it appropriately? If facilities are at hand, might it be cheaper and more convenient to start from scratch? What alternative designs would perform the required function, and which of these appears easiest to construct? If new apparatus must be built, how detailed should one make the plans and specifications? Would it be worthwhile to construct a model or mock-up before settling on the final plans?

Most departments of psychology and other institutions that engage in psychological research have many standard pieces of laboratory apparatus that can be used for a wide variety of studies, either as they are or with some modifications. The typical department includes a person responsible for equipment; consulting him and rummaging around in the storerooms may turn up a device that will do the required job.

The department budget generally provides a certain sum for equipment purchase. If the desired instrument is not already in stock, perhaps the researcher can persuade the person in charge of equipment to buy him what he needs out of the general apparatus fund. Whether or not this is reasonable will depend on the cost of the item and on the frequency with which it is likely to be used in the future. A good case can be made for stocking the laboratory with certain pieces of standard equipment widely used in the field. Normally, these instruments have been calibrated for accuracy of measurement or stimulus output, so that there is less need for concern that the device will do the intended job than would be the case if one were to construct his own apparatus. Moreover, using a standard instrument will help to make the results of one's experiments comparable to those of other investigators.

Most published reports of experiments include a description of the apparatus used. When the device is a standard one, it will generally be identified by name and manufacturer, so that all the reader need do is consult the appropriate catalogue for information on cost. Nonstandard apparatus is frequently illustrated or described in sufficient detail to make reproduction possible; one can always write to the author for additional information.

A large proportion of the experimental apparatus used in psychological research is of the "homemade" variety, usually because the requirements of the particular investigation are so specific that no standard instrument will fill them or because standard apparatus would be too expensive to purchase. Most departments have at least some kind of shop facilities for the construction or modification of research equipment. Whether the investigator himself or a trained technician does the work, it is generally desirable to draw at least crude plans and sketches of the device; the more complex the equipment, the more necessary are detailed blueprints and specifications. Especially with fairly elaborate apparatus, reduced scale balsa wood (or cardboard, etc.) models may save time in the long run, since modifications on models are usually cheaper than changes on the full-scale device itself. Construction of a complex instrument is likely to involve trying out variations in design; furthermore, a model may show unanticipated problems that would not otherwise become evident until the full-scale apparatus was built.

Under rare circumstances it may be desirable to have complex new equipment constructed to specifications by a commercial firm. Several companies * will undertake such a job and provide advance estimates or fixed bids on cost and time for construction.

Whenever equipment is purchased—and especially when it is custom made by a commercial firm—the cost is likely to be high. Even though a device may be in standard use, one cannot expect to get it at dime-store prices, for the market demand and the precision tolerances are rarely sufficient to permit mass production. So the researcher has to be realistic and foresighted about equipment costs. It is tempting, when planning an experiment, to demand the ideal in standard or custom-made precision equipment. If problems of cost and availability are not considered at the same time, then one may confront them later with such discouraging consequences that he has to give up the entire study. One way to avoid frustration is to plan from the beginning for feasible, as well as for ideal, apparatus and to consider alternative devices, including homemade ones, which might do the job adequately. It goes without saying that the simpler the apparatus, the cheaper it is likely to be, both to acquire and to maintain. If one considers the total strategy of the research project, cardboard-scissors-and-paste gadgetry is often more efficient than complex brass-instrument or electronic apparatus.

Maintenance

Any device is useless unless kept in working order. With elaborate equipment especially one must expect to spend some time and money

---

* For example, Garrison Co., Box 122a, Dexter, Mich.; Ralph Gerbrands Co., Scientific Instruments, 96 Ronald Road, Arlington 74, Mass.; Grason-Stadler Co., West Concord, Mass.; PARCO (Plastic Apparatus Research Corp.), 2622 Lee Highway, Falls Church, Va.; Wichita Apparatus Supply, Inc., P. O. Box 194, Lawrence, Kansas.

in checking and repairing it. The investigator should have sufficient knowledge of the innards of his instruments to fix them or have ready access to a technician with the requisite skills. There is no end to the details that may require attention—oiling, checking calibrations, finding short circuits, splicing wires, soldering a loose connection, cleaning lenses, re-inking recording pens, replacing a worn-out tube or a broken gear, fixing a defective cam or electrical plug, and so on. Handling equipment with care and respect, keeping it clean and in repair, pay off in avoiding breakdowns during the crucial periods of data collection.

Complex devices frequently have manuals prepared for them; it is good practice to keep the manual near the apparatus itself, where it will be available if something goes wrong; and before using the instrument, the investigator, of course, should study the manual thoroughly. It often provides information about specifications, wiring diagrams, calibration, and other facts relevant to the validity of the device as well as more routine instructions for its care, use, and maintenance.

Falling in Love with Equipment

A word of warning to the neophyte. It is natural to become attached to anything one has made with his own labor and ingenuity. The researcher is not immune to such attachments. Although justifiable pride in accomplishments is one of the more deeply satisfying aspects of the creative process, one should guard against indiscriminate "identification" with a piece of equipment he has designed. As several psychologists have pointed out, research may be either "equipment-centered" or "problem-centered." One may engage in a particular line of research because the equipment to do it happens to be available and because the instrument suggests a particular use. Or he may choose to study a problem because it is challenging, even though suitable equipment or other operational definitions have not yet been found. The reader will undoubtedly recall examples of both kinds of research, either with "brass instruments" or with verbal devices (such as the Rorschach test).

Equipment-centered research has had its successes and its failures; so has problem-centered research. It is not possible, a priori, to consider one kind superior to the other—although it might be argued that equipment-centered research is in some sense easier, less taxing than problem-centered research, and perhaps more likely to be trivial. The chief danger is that one may fall into an equipment-centered orientation without intending to, particularly when a gleaming, impressive new device has just been acquired. The investigator with a new possession should beware of becoming fixated on it; while he is thinking of all the studies he could do with his treasure, he might also stop to consider whether some other device would not be more appropriate for the problem he has in mind. It is just possible that the variables and manipulations suggested by his gadget will take him far away from his primary research aim.

TESTING THE ADEQUACY OF EQUIPMENT

Whether an instrument is to be bought, built, or borrowed, the major requirement for it is to perform the function intended. This is partly a technical problem and partly a logical one. The technical aspect concerns the accuracy of measurement or of stimulus output; this is a matter of calibration and standardization. The logical aspect concerns the relevance of the device to the theoretical variable one is aiming at; this is a question of construct validity akin to that discussed in connection with verbal tests. We shall take up in turn each of these considerations relating to whether or not the equipment is adequate to its purpose.

Accuracy

If one knows exactly what variable is to be manipulated or assessed and has already settled on the operational definition of it embodied in a particular gadget, then the only remaining question concerning the adequacy of the instrument is whether its output is accurate. If it is a GSR device intended to measure the skin's electrical resistance in ohms, then one would wish to know that the readings it gives are correct. If it is an audiometer designed to emit tones at variable frequencies and intensities, it is essential to know whether the tone at a given setting of the machine corresponds to the intended one. These questions of accuracy cannot be answered in all-or-none fashion, however.

All devices are subject to a certain amount of error; hence their accuracy is unlikely to be perfect over the entire range in which they are used. The realistic aim of instrument selection and calibration is to obtain the greatest accuracy possible for a particular range of input or output. Instrument errors are generally classified in two ways, variable and constant.

A *variable error* is represented by the fluctuation of measures or outputs around a value intended to be fixed. If, for example, resistance readings were taken repeatedly on a GSR device with some known constant input, these measures would be found to vary somewhat about a central value. A timer repeatedly set at, say, 5 seconds, will show some variability in its output. If a pure tone were generated by an oscillator and its frequency displayed on a cathode ray oscillograph, the display would show some variation around the intended frequency, even if the setting on the oscillator is repeatedly made the same. Which part of the input-output system is responsible for the variation would, of course, be indeterminate if one used only a single instrument for each. But if several GSR devices were connected, simultaneously or successively, to the same constant source, one could immediately select from among them the one which showed the smallest variable error. Similarly, if the tones from several oscillators were displayed on the same oscilloscope, their relative variations could be compared and the most consistent one selected from the group. The magnitude of the variable error is usually represented by some statistical measure of dispersion, such as the range, standard deviation, or semi-interquartile range. Other things being equal, of course, one seeks an instrument with a variable error as small as possible, for if there is sizable random error one can place little confidence in any single measurement.

The problem of variable error in mechanical instruments is comparable to that of unreliability in psychological tests. Conceptually, reliability is the degree to which two or more identical measures of the same attribute yield the same results. The difficulty in appraising the reliability of a verbal instrument stems from the fact that subjects have memories, and using the same questions twice on them is likely to yield spuriously high agreement. If the time lapse between the first and second tests is sufficient to ensure forgetting of specific responses, then the attribute itself may have changed in the meantime. Hence, for verbal tests, the test-retest measure of reliability is more appropriately regarded as a measure of stability. With mechanical measuring devices, on the other hand, one can immediately and repeatedly subject them to identical stimuli and be fairly certain that agreement in results reflects accuracy of measurement.

Given relatively little variable error in an instrument, one can afford to take a single measure or output from it as indicative of the result of repeated trials. But if the best machine one can find still shows sizable variation, then the only thing to do is to take several measures and average their results. If the error is truly random, then the various measures will, in the long run, be normally distributed about the average value. When there is large variable error, many repetitions may be required to stabilize the mean.

Just because an instrument yields low variable error does not necessarily constitute proof of its accuracy. Bathroom scales are often consistent, yet inaccurate. Mechanical research instruments are also subject to *constant error* or a discrepancy between the indicated and the true value of the phenomenon they are intended to reproduce or measure. In order to measure the magnitude of constant error, a standard measure is needed against which the instrument to be tested can be compared. If there were considerable variable error in the questionable instrument, one would compare the mean of a number of readings with the standard. This should generally be done at various points in the range of stimuli to be considered, since the size of the "constant error" may vary with the level at which it is operating. The reader may be familiar with calibration curves for such equipment as timers, in which a setting of 22.3 may be needed to produce a 20-second interval, or as earphones, whose frequency responses may change as a function of intensity and whose frequency distortions may vary in different frequency ranges. (The same condition may obtain for variable errors as well, and these, too, should be assessed at various levels.)

The concept of constant error is distantly related to that of validity as employed with reference to psychological tests. The main difference is that one rarely has an accurate standard of measurement for psychological attributes against which to compare a questionable instrument. The best one can usually do is to expect that two measures of the same attribute will be linearly related and so compute a product-moment correlation as a simultaneous test of the validity of both. In dealing with the fundamental scales of physics, however, one can do much better, for there is usually a known zero point and often an agreed-upon unit of measurement; so correlation between an alleged measure and a criterion is not in itself sufficient to establish the validity of the former. If the first inch were cut off the end of a yardstick and its measurements were correlated with those of a standard yardstick, the correlation would be perfect (within the limits of variable error); but the first yardstick would be subject to a constant error of one inch, hence invalid for a scale with a known zero point.

Correcting for constant errors is usually a fairly simple matter if the instrument can be compared with a standard over the relevant range. It is necessary only to add (or subtract) the appropriate constant at each particular level of measurement. There is no ready correction for variable errors; one simply has to take enough measures to assure a stable mean value.

A measuring instrument is said to be calibrated when the magnitudes of its constant and variable errors are known over the range that it measures or, for a stimulus-producing device, when the mean and standard deviation of stimulus values produced at each level of output are known. Crude calibrations have been performed on verbal instruments as well as mechanical. For example, the "association values" of large numbers of nonsense syllables have been ascertained by administering them to various groups of subjects, usually college students (e.g., see Hilgard 1951); similarly, researchers using TAT pictures to measure achievement motivation have calibrated many of them according to the frequency with which they elicit achievement imagery under neutral conditions of presentation (McClelland et al., 1953). The problem with such attempted calibrations is that the "stimulus value" must be judged from responses that are themselves exceedingly variable. They are, at best, averages that are applicable only to the populations included in the calibration study. An analogous condition for physical measurements might occur if a group of rocks were weighed on several different planets of varying masses (hence varying gravitational attractions) and the weights of the rocks were determined from the average measures from the several locations. Even these results would probably be more dependable than the "association values" of pictures or nonsense syllables, for at least the ordinal relation among rock weights would remain the same from planet to planet, whereas cultural differences among groups of subjects might well lead to differences even in the ordering of verbal and pictorial stimuli.

Needless to say, an instrument for which calibrations are available is generally preferable to one for which they are not; for, just as the test constructer with a new instrument needs to perform various analyses on it before taking its results seriously, so the experimentalist needs to calibrate his apparatus before he can rely on its output. This is a point in favor of using standardized experimental equipment when it is important to know just how much stimulus it emits or how to interpret the dial readings.

Standardizing Equipment Use

Calibration of a mechanical device implies certain standard conditions of use. Depending on the instrument, its effective output or accurate measurement may depend on such background factors as temperature, humidity, and electrical shielding. Whenever there is reason to suppose that the obtained measure would vary with such extraneous conditions, then instructions for using the apparatus should include specification of standard conditions.

In addition to the effects of background conditions, which are presumably the same from trial to trial for a given subject, there may be other unwanted effects which vary with repeated exposure to the instrument. Three slightly different types of nonconstant influences might be encountered, and the methods of allowing for them are somewhat different.

First is the "warm-up" or practice effect. This is recognizable as a fairly marked and systematic change in measurement during the first few trials followed by a leveling off to asymptote or by an initially high variable error that decreases rapidly and permanently. If it involves the machine, it is called warm-up; if it involves the subject's getting used to the experimental situation, it may be referred to as practice. Such effects can usually be allowed for by turning on the instrument some time before the measurements are to be taken or by discarding the first few measures on each subject. It may be worthwhile, in a pilot study, to determine the typical course of subject adjustment or warm-up so that a rational basis can be found for deciding when to turn on the machine or how many initial trials to discard.

A second kind of nonconstant effect may be caused by changes in the machine ("instrument drift") or in the subject (e.g., sensory adaptation, fatigue, or loss of motivation), occurring after prolonged contact between subject and apparatus. Such effects on the measures may occur beyond the normal warm-up period in the form of gradually changing "constant" error or of increasing variable error. In some cases these changes might be confused with the predicted experimental results, if both the experimental variable and the instrument-subject adaptation have the same effect on responses. One way to minimize these unwanted effects is to shorten the experimental period. This might require that measures on a given subject be obtained on successive days or that different subjects be exposed to different ranges of stimuli and a composite function be constructed from the pooled data. The problem with such an arrangement is that it augments the normal measurement error with errors resulting from intersubject differences or from temporal variability within each subject or the device. Thus the "average" psychophysical function obtained from such a pooling may look quite different from the function that would be obtained from any individual subject if he could be assessed in one sitting.

Finally, there may be errors which appear not as regular trends but as isolated contaminations between adjacent measures. For instance, turning a timer's dial down to 10 seconds from a longer time may produce a different output than turning it up to 10 seconds from a shorter setting. If, in the course of determining the rate of dark adaptation one uses a threshold probe that happens to be too intense, it may raise the dark adaptation level and thus distort the curve obtained from subsequent measures. In comparing the relative pleasantness of various odors, one may encounter an assimilation or contrast effect in which the subject's response to one odor modifies his evaluation of the next. One way to detect such interactions between successive stimuli is by a counterbalanced design in which some subjects, or some trials, are assigned one ordering of stimuli and other subjects or trials a different order.

It can readily be seen that such interactions between subject and instrument may influence not only the outcomes of experiments employing the instrument but also the very procedures used to calibrate the instrument. If the variable error of a mechanical measure is determined over a long period of trials, then the measured variability may be increased by some drift within the device or the calibrating standard. If the association value of a nonsense syllable is assessed only within a particular sequence of other syllables, a constant error may result from these sequence effects. So instrument calibration can, in itself, require elaborate experimental procedures. Although most researchers spend their time testing subjects, there are at least a few who devote their efforts primarily to studying tests and equipment. Their labors can be very beneficial to the investigator faced with the problem of choosing appropriate equipment and of assessing the adequacy of the devices he has chosen.

Construct Validity of Experimental Equipment

The problems of instrument validation so far considered are all concerned with the question, "Does the instrument do its job properly?" This is not the only question the researcher faces in selecting or validating an instrument. There is also the question, "Does *he* do his interpretive job properly?" Does the instrument, however accurate, measure or affect the variable that one intends? This is not likely to be a very complex problem for variables that are defined operationally by instruments with wide acceptance in the field. Electrical skin resistance is conventionally measured in ohms, and it is a fairly straightforward matter to determine whether a given GSR device measures resistance accurately. Many concepts are not so uniquely and universally defined; moreover, even the clear-cut measures are normally used as indices of more complex and vague constructs that appear in psychological theories. A GSR reading, for example, is sometimes used as an indicator of the subject's level of anxiety. But the construct "anxiety" itself is never directly assessed; only certain autonomic or behavioral concomitants of it are designated for direct measurement. Hence one must also pay attention to the logic and validity of the theory that specifies how anxiety is manifest.

Here the researcher using experimental equipment is faced with problems exactly like those to which we have devoted the bulk of Chapter 6 on verbal instruments. How does one know that the overt response reflects a particular hypothetical "underlying" attribute? Many factors other than anxiety may produce a change in the measured GSR, including such obviously irrelevant things as jarring the wires or electrodes, movement of the fingers to which the electrodes are attached, or excessive humidity in the room. Moreover, certain aspects of what one may consider anxiety may not be tapped at all by changes in skin conductivity. How, then, does one conclude that a GSR device measures anxiety rather than something else?

A variety of operations may appear reasonable to characterize a given concept, but on investigation the correlations among the measures obtained with the different operations may prove to be very poor. Which of them, if any, should then be regarded as the "true" measure of the intended attribute? Miller (1959) used several different instruments and methods as operational specifications of the concept "hunger" and found that a particular manipulation such as neural destruction or direct injection of food into the stomach may affect the various measures of hunger quite differently. Such results have led to the consideration that "hunger" is probably best thought of not as a unitary phenomenon but as composed of a number of different, perhaps only partly related, attributes.

The kind of equipment chosen to assess a complex concept is likely to have serious consequences for the conclusions drawn from an experiment. If one uses series of nonsense syllables, mazes, or pushbutton problems to study learning, he is likely to arrive at an interpretation of learning as a sequential connection of responses or of stimuli and responses; on the other hand, if subjects are presented with meaningful puzzles or readily manipulable and understandable problem boxes, detour problems, and the like, they may display insight, reorganization, and understanding as key components of the learning process. One might even suspect that the Hullian conceptions of animal learning reflect, in part, Hull's use of closed alley mazes, in which the animal is physically unable to obtain an overview of the entire situation confronting him, whereas Tolman's more cognitive interpretations of learning reflect the kind of equipment he often used—elevated mazes from which the animal could obtain at least a limited view of the entire problem. Thorndike, Guthrie, and Skinner, using puzzle boxes in which the relation between the subject's responses and the consequences of these responses were less "visible" to him, all arrived at connectionistic formulations; Köhler, Adams, and Max Wertheimer, working with detour and "insight" problems and orientations, have emphasized the Gestalt aspects of learning, thinking, and problem solving.

The kind of experimental equipment employed can thus affect the nature of the information derived from it and, consequently, one's theoretical understanding of the phenomenon being investigated. There are ways in which the researcher can try to circumvent the limitations of his instruments; he can take time deliberately to turn around and work deductively from concept to instrument. Sometime in the course of his investigations he will develop a conception of the critical attribute which is broader than the particular measure, or piece of equipment, that he is using. At that point he should try to clarify his thinking by specifying just what the complete nature of the attribute is and speculating on a variety of ways in which it might be produced or assessed. The next step is to try some of these different ways to see if they actually do yield comparable results.

This is the approach that Campbell (1956) has referred to as *methodological triangulation* and Garner et al. (1956) have called *convergent operationism.* It is formally equivalent to the procedure of convergent validation which is used to assess the adequacy of psychological tests (see Chapter 6). If only identical operations are used to produce or measure some experimental effect, then one does not know to what extent the results reflect the concept aimed at and to what extent the apparent consistency is the result of instrument factors or of situational contaminations. It requires at least two different mechanical devices to distinguish instrument effects from the effects of the variable itself. The more ways one can operationalize a concept, the more thoroughly sampled is the domain to which the concept refers, hence the better can one generalize and clarify its meaning.

Several different kinds of empirical outcomes can result from methodological triangulation. The simplest, of course, would be that in which many different procedures yield essentially identical results. Then one could be confident that he had appropriately identified the empirical referents of his concept and could afford to select any one of the operations (presumably the simplest one) as his preferred "operational definition." This is, however, a rather unusual outcome in the present stage of psychology's development.

Generally the best one can hope for are not identical but congruent or correlated results. There are, for instance, differences between sensory thresholds obtained with the serial method of limits on ascending as compared with descending sequences. Also, the differential threshold obtained with the method of adjustment or average error is generally different from that obtained by forced-choice or graphically from data collected by the method of constant stimuli (e.g., see Woodworth & Schlosberg, 1954). Yet in such cases the differences are fairly consistent and predictable, so that it is possible to translate one set of results into another. This is quite analogous to the consequences of varying difficulties of test items: the distinctions they make among subjects are correlated, though not identical. The principal difference with psychophysical measures is that the relations between various methods are relatively well known and stable enough from subject to subject that uniform allowances can be made; any particular measure may be fairly reliably converted into another. This is not so readily done with test items, since the correspondences between any pair tend to vary considerably from sample to sample.

Finally, a not at all unusual outcome of methodological triangulation is for completely different, and uncorrelated, results to emerge from different operational specifications of the "same" concept. Even this result may be illuminating, for if the researcher is sure that all his procedures were valid in the limited sense of "accuracy" discussed earlier, then he is led to conclude that they represent not one concept but several. Miller's conclusions from his experiments on "hunger" are of this nature; it is also quite likely that the concept of "learning" is too broad, in that different sets of principles may apply to different phenomena previously confused under a common label.

In order to judge the adequacy of any research operation, then, one must have available at least two different operations designed to get at the same idea. The very notion of adequacy demands a standard of comparison. When no ideal criterion is available, two less-than-ideal measures each serve as a tentative criterion for the other. The more different operations one has, the more convincingly can he determine their meaning and essential commonality (if any) and thus judge which one (or combination) is best. In the field of mental testing the typical instrument is a test item; it is relatively easy to make up test items, administer them to subjects, and intercorrelate their responses. By contrast, a tachistoscope, a maze, a device for measuring flicker fusion, or a discrimination apparatus takes time to construct and operate; such instruments are therefore less readily spawned, and often there are too few relevant to any particular idea to permit an investigator to decide whether any of them is adequate to his needs. So it is not surprising that few systematic attempts are made to investigate the construct validity of experimental apparatus in the same way that this is done for verbal instruments.

There are, unfortunately, no completely general ways of determining the adequacy of a piece of experimental equipment for one's purposes, since this is not a property totally inherent in the device; it also depends on how results of the operation are to be interpreted conceptually. In each case the researcher must examine the properties of the relevant concept and determine—logically, intuitively, or by consensus among experts—what kind of evidence is required to show that the intended attribute is actually measured or influenced by the particular instrument. The "intuitive validity" of an instrument can be supplemented by the researcher's knowledge of the literature on studies that have used it, and perhaps the results of other people's work can in part serve to validate it for him.

Thus the researcher's view of the concept he is studying will ultimately both affect and be affected by the particular equipment and research operations he uses. If he is not careful, he may end up unintentionally studying a phenomenon with an instrument or procedure that precludes certain findings that could have far-reaching consequences. No gadget is theoretically neutral. Theoretical bias is, and perhaps should be, built into one's apparatus. But let it be built in consciously and intentionally, so that the device adequately reflects the researcher's conception of the phenomenon he is studying.

SUMMARY

Problems associated with experimental equipment are conceptually very similar to those encountered with verbal devices. The basic question to ask of any instrument is whether it adequately measures or manipulates the desired attribute.

Equipment acquisition and maintenance require careful attention to the function the apparatus is intended to perform. The investigator must decide whether some available equipment will do the job adequately or whether new apparatus needs to be constructed. Whichever route he takes, he must be prepared to encounter red tape and to spend some time in seeing to it that the instrument, once in hand, continues to function properly.

Assessing the adequacy of a device involves both technical and theoretical considerations. Technical adequacy depends on the magnitude of constant and variable errors. Constant errors can often be eliminated by careful calibration, but variable errors are not so easily handled. They can be offset to some degree by repeated measures, but repetition may produce unwanted distortions.

The theoretical adequacy of an instrument depends on whether it represents a particular defined attribute. In order to find this out, one must not only establish theoretically meaningful relationships between independent and dependent variables but also relate the particular instrument's measures to measures from some other instrument designed to tap the same attribute. This kind of methodological triangulation is particularly important when there is no universally accepted standard instrument to represent the desired concept. It may result in convergent validation of the apparatus, or it may lead to a more restricted definition of the initial concept.

SUPPLEMENT

Some Standard Psychological Equipment

Considering the large number of devices available for psychological research, it is almost impossible to provide anything like an exhaustive list. In this supplement are listed only a few of the standard kinds of apparatus that have enjoyed wide use. More exhaustive lists and descriptions can be found in some of the references at the end of the chapter (e.g., Andrews, 1948a; Andrews, 1948b; Brown & Saucer, 1958; Daniel & Louttit, 1953; Grings, 1954; Townsend, 1953).

Stimulus-Producing Equipment

Many devices in this category have been manufactured to aid in the study of animal learning. There are *mazes* of many varieties; the path may be elevated or enclosed (alley), and the choice points may be of a T, Y, or U shape; some mazes are produced with interchangeable units. Among the instruments for the study of discrimination are *conditioning devices*, the Grice *discrimination box*, Lashley's *jumping stand*, and others. Munn (1950) provides a great deal of information about mazes and discrimination boxes for studying rat behavior. The *Skinner box*, in which the animal presses a bar or pushes a button in order to receive reinforcement, is widely used in rat, cat, pigeon, dog, and primate learning studies. There are also various other problem boxes, devices for *delayed reactions*, and *multiple choice apparatus*. The *Wisconsin General Test Apparatus* is a versatile instrument for presenting discrimination materials, problem-solving stimuli, etc., in individual testing; although it is adaptable to a wide range of species, it is used most frequently for testing monkeys.

The study of human learning has also led to the development of standard apparatus. For investigation of verbal learning, the *memory drum*, which presents sequences of stimuli or pairs of stimuli for controlled periods of time, has enjoyed immensely wide use. Studies of the acquisition of motor skills have made use of typewriters, *finger mazes* in which the blindfolded subject must learn to trace a raised path, and more specialized equipment such as the *pursuit rotor* or pursuit meter. One variety of pursuit rotor consists of a phonograph turntable with a small disk on it and a stylus which the subject must try to keep on the disk while the turntable rotates; when the stylus is in contact, an electric circuit is closed to provide an accurate record of the proportion of the time that the subject is "on target." *Mirror-drawing devices*, which permit the subject to see his hand in a mirror, but not directly, while drawing something or while trying to keep a pencil within the lines of a double-outlined star, have been used in the study of transfer.

A large number of devices is available for studying visual perception. Among them are the *color wheel*, which mixes colors by rotating swiftly a number of interlocked disks of colored paper, the *tachistoscope*, which makes it possible to present visual stimuli for brief periods of time, the *perimeter*, which presents visual stimuli at varying locations on the retina to permit mapping of visual functions from the fovea of the eye to the periphery, and a great variety of *adjustable illusions*, such as the well-known Müller-Lyer. Devices for the study of depth perception include the *Howard-Dolman depth apparatus*, in which the subject's task is to set a variable vertical stick so that it appears to be just as far away from him as a standard vertical stick, and the *stereoscope*, which presents slightly different images of the same object to the two eyes. *Projectors* of various kinds are also widely used, often with the amount of illumination controlled by a tachistoscopic attachment, by an electrical device which varies the amount of voltage supplied, by an optical wedge, or by an *episcotister*, which consists of a rapidly rotating disk with some sectors cut out, through which the projector's ray must pass and by means of which illumination is controlled by varying the angular size of the open sectors. *Flicker fusion apparatus*, or CFF ("critical flicker frequency") devices, which present a light stimulus which is *on* for a given proportion of time and *off* for the remainder, in a finely controlled cycle, are used in the study of some perceptual and sensory processes and in some research in physiological psychology. Other devices include the *Ishihara* or the *Dvorine plates* for detecting color blindness, the *artificial pupil*, which controls the amount of light entering the eye, and *autokinetic apparatus* for presenting a stationary pinpoint of light, which appears to move if presented in an otherwise totally dark room.

Standard equipment for the study of other senses includes the *esthesiometer* which, in spite of its complex name, is only a compass used to study the minimum separation necessary for two points of stimulation on the skin to be felt as two rather than one, the *von Frey hairs*, a graduated series of pressure-applying devices for the study of tactual sensitivity, and the *olfactometer*, a device for presenting olfactory stimuli. More recently, instrumentation in the sensory areas has turned electronic; this is especially true in audition. There are standard *beat-frequency oscillators* for the production of pure tones of variable frequency, *amplifiers* and *attenuators* for the control of intensity, and *audiometers*, which combine the functions of several separate devices to present tones of variable frequency and intensity. The vacuum tube has revolutionized apparatus in the field of sensory research; devices based on it are used not only for the control of auditory and visual stimulation but also for the controlled presentation of electrical stimuli directly to the sense organs or the sensory nerves.

Instruments for the study of motivation are not so numerous as those for controlling the stimulus in the study of sensory processes. For animal research, there are such devices as the *obstruction box*, which interposes an electrified grill between the subject and the goal, and Young's *preference apparatus*, in which one can measure the relative consumptions of various food substances or liquids. Widely used also is the *shuttle box*, in which the animal must respond to a signal stimulus by moving to a different place in order to avoid some noxious stimulus like a shock. Such devices are also frequently used in the study of learning; similarly, many of the instruments used in learning experiments have played a role in the study of animal motivation. There are only a few standardized devices for the study of human motivation, such as the *Rotter level of aspiration board*, which presents the subject with a "test of skill" in which the investigator can control the subject's score to some extent.

Other stimulus-producing devices include specialized physiological equipment like the *Horsley-Clarke stereotaxic instrument*, which permits the insertion of electrodes into specifiable parts of the nervous system of small animals, to permit stimulation with minute currents (or destruction of finely localized areas or recording of neural activity), and various electronic devices for stimulus control. *Timing devices*, from the humble stopwatch to precise electronic timers, are necessary in much research.

Stimulus-Recording Equipment

The various fields of sensory and perceptual psychology have their specialized devices for measuring and calibrating the stimulus. There are many different *illuminometers,* like the *Macbeth,* for measuring the physical stimulus characteristics of a light source; *oscilloscopes* (or oscillographs) are used for visual representation of sound and other stimuli; and *Fourier analyzers* can provide an accurate record of the wavelength and intensity of the various bands of frequencies that compose an auditory or a visual stimulus.

Tape recorders and motion picture cameras may be used to obtain a detailed record of the stimuli present in an experiment, or of the subjects' behaviors, and sometimes present the stimulus itself in perceptual studies and in studies of more complex personality or social variables. *One-way vision screens* are used in observing stimulus situations and subjects' responses. Finally, *multichannel ink-writers,* whose pens can write some eighteen different variables at once, may be used in various kinds of experiments (e.g., studies in conditioning) to record changes in stimulation as well as in the subject's behavior.

Response-Recording Equipment

Many of the devices already mentioned serve to record various aspects of subjects' responses and to present or register stimuli. Stopwatches are widely used. Multiple recording devices such as the *Esterline-Angus ink-writer* can make graphic records of many aspects of stimuli and responses simultaneously. Single-channel *cumulative recorders,* typically used with the Skinner box, can provide an immediate graphic index of the number of responses per unit time.

Motion pictures and *tape recordings* are often used, especially in studying human behavior in complex social situations or in psychotherapy; observation through one-way vision screens is another technique widely employed in these areas as well as in child psychology and in the study of psychopathology.

Devices for measuring the amount of activity displayed by animal subjects include *activity cages,* some of which have an attached cylinder in which the animal may run and in which the number of revolutions of the cylinder is automatically recorded. Others are delicately mounted on three or four points in such a way that movement of the animal tilts the floor slightly to permit measurement of the amount of movement per unit time. These devices are usually connected with *kymographs* or other apparatus which provides automatic recording.

Reaction time devices of various kinds include the *telegraph key* and the *voice key,* in which a circuit is automatically closed or opened as soon as the subject talks into a microphone.

A variety of ways to measure physiological responses is available, such as GSR (galvanic skin response) devices, which measure the electrical conductivity of the skin, the sphygmomanometer for recording breathing patterns, EKG (electrocardiograph) devices for measuring pulse and heartbeat, and EEG (electroencephalograph) apparatus for recording brainwaves.

In response recording, as in the other categories of equipment, the vacuum tube has exhibited an extraordinary versatility, and electronic devices are finding increasingly widespread use. The reader is referred especially to the book by Brown and Saucer (1958) for a detailed account of the uses and construction of electronic apparatus for psychological research.

Equipment Which Combines Various Functions

In the preceding pages we have frequently referred to apparatus that simultaneously performs several functions; no survey of the varieties of available instruments would be complete without explicit mention of such equipment. Many complex devices for psychological research fall into this category.

For purposes of illustration, we have already mentioned *motion picture cameras, tape recorders,* and *multiple-pen recorders,* which typically combine stimulus measurement and response recording; psychophysical equipment such as the usual bank of apparatus for psychoacoustic research serves both to present and to measure the stimulus. Many devices, including the *pursuit rotor,* present stimuli and record the response. All three functions are typically served by such devices as the *Skinner box* and its attachments, and the *Békésy audiometer,* which presents a stimulus tone of simultaneously varying frequency and intensity, produces a record of the stimulus, and records the subject's response of hearing or not hearing the tone; this response in turn affects the intensity of the stimulus tone so that the final automatically produced record is a fully plotted audiogram of threshold intensity as a function of frequency.

REFERENCES

Andrews, T. G. (Ed.) *Methods of psychology.* New York: Wiley, 1948a.

Andrews, T. G. Some psychological apparatus: a classified bibliography. *Psychol. Monogr.,* 1948b, **62**, 38 pp.

Brown, C. C., & Saucer, R. T. *Electronic instrumentation for the behavioral sciences.* Springfield, Ill.: Charles C Thomas, 1958.

Campbell, D. T. *Leadership and its effects upon the group.* Monogr. No. 83. Columbus: Ohio State Univer. Bur. Business Res., 1956.

Daniel, R. S., & Louttit, C. M. *Professional problems in psychology.* New York: Prentice-Hall, 1953. (See pp. 378–385.)

Garner, W. R., Hake, H. W., & Eriksen, C. W. Operationism and the concept of perception. *Psychol. Rev.,* 1956, **63**, 149–159.

Grings, W. W. *Laboratory instrumentation in psychology.* Palo Alto, Calif.: National Press, 1954.

Hilgard, E. R. Methods and procedures in the study of learning. In S. S. Stevens (Ed.), *Handbook of experimental psychology.* New York: Wiley, 1951.

McClelland, D. C., Atkinson, J., Clark, R. A., & Lowell, E. *The achievement motive.* New York: Appleton-Century-Crofts, 1953.

Miller, N. E. Liberalization of basic S-R concepts. In S. Koch (Ed.), *Psychology: a study of a science.* Study 1, Vol. 2. New York: McGraw-Hill, 1959.

Munn, N. L. *Handbook of psychological research on the rat.* Boston: Houghton Mifflin, 1950.

Townsend, J. C. *Introduction to experimental method.* New York: McGraw-Hill, 1953. (See Chapter 10.)

Woodworth, R. S., & Schlosberg, H. *Experimental psychology.* (Rev. Ed.) New York: Holt, 1954.

CHAPTER 8

Instrumentation:
human judgment

When the researcher thinks of psychological measurement, he is likely to refer exclusively to verbal or mechanical instruments of the kinds discussed in Chapters 6 and 7. Indeed, these techniques are generally aspired to because they yield precise scores relatively free from subjective bias. But someone must read and control the machines; moreover, by no means all of psychological assessment is performed with the aid of tests or mechanical equipment. Inevitably, a great deal depends on the judgment of a trained observer. It can even be argued that in the present state of the science human judgment provides the best, and the final, criterion for the more refined ways of measuring most psychological attributes. If the results of the refined procedures do not accord with the researcher's (or another expert's) own judgment of the attribute, he is likely to doubt the former rather than the latter.

Given this extreme faith that most psychologist-researchers place in their own judgments, it behooves them to build into their research procedures ways of convincing others that these judgments are sound. Though the techniques for doing this are not so highly developed and standardized as they are for some of the more precise methods of measuring psychological variables, certain preferred practices can be recommended tentatively. These practices are applicable to a variety of research situations in which judgment plays a major role in assessing either the independent or the dependent variables. In this chapter we shall consider methods of rendering objective judgments, after a brief description of some of the research situations to which they apply: observation of behavior, clinical research, and content analysis.

OBSERVATION OF BEHAVIOR

In studying the natural or experimentally induced behaviors of humans and animals, the researcher makes continual use of his own perceptions or inferences concerning what the subject did and why. That a rat turned left in a maze or displayed vicarious trial and error are data which typically depend on the observation and judgment of the experimenter. The observations that a motorist stopped at a through street or did so after noticing a patrol car at the corner represent integrated judgments involving varying amounts of perception and inference. The description of typical methods of child discipline applied by parents in some primitive tribe likewise requires the judgment either of the ethnologist himself or of some informant on whose report he relies.

Even under experimentally controlled conditions, much of a subject's behavior is not mechanically recorded but must be observed and noted by the researcher himself. Blushing and other behavioral indications of tension are sometimes assessed in stress experiments. In the experimental investigation of group interaction the contents of verbal exchanges and the gestures used by participants must usually be recorded by trained observers.

Numerous aids to observation are available which can help the researcher obtain more objective and valid records of the relevant behaviors (see Heyns & Zander, 1953; Jahoda, Deutsch, & Cook, 1951; Peak, 1953; Whyte, 1951; Zander, 1951). These aids range in technical complexity all the way from a pocket notebook through sound motion picture equipment to electrical relays and recording devices. For experimental observation of humans it is sometimes helpful to use rooms with one-way mirrors, wired for sound transmission and recording. Small portable tape recorders can sometimes be carried into naturally occurring situations in which it is important to record conversations fully.

It is in brand new research situations, in which the investigator has very little idea of the major relevant variables, that devices for obtaining complete records of behavior—such as motion picture cameras and tape recorders—are likely to be of greatest value. It may well be worth an extensive pilot study simply to decide what variables to assess and how to abstract them. Repeated listening to tapes or viewing of films may sensitize one to important features of the recorded situation which were not initially apparent. If sound-recording and photographic equipment cannot be used conveniently, it would certainly pay to take detailed notes on a small sample of behaviors, so that they may be referred to later at leisure. The purpose of such intensive records is to serve as an appropriate base from which to develop a more limited number of specific attributes which subsequently can be measured on a larger sample of subjects or situations.

Beyond the initial pilot studies, however, such complete records are seldom worth the time and expense involved in using them. Recorded conversations must be transcribed before they can be reduced to usable categories of analysis; motion pictures must be viewed repeatedly in order to abstract their essential features. The researcher who amasses a room full of tape and film records of all his data is likely to spend needless time converting them from raw to coded form, time that could have been saved had he recorded in terms of abstracted categories to begin with. Once the relevant dimensions and categories have been established, it is usually efficient to print them on sheets attached to a board, or enclosed in hard covers, so that the observer may, while watching, record essential features of subjects' behaviors directly into appropriate coding categories. Then, what serves as data is not a complete record of all that happened but a series of checks and short notes representing a very small portion of the total. Such data reduction is essential if comparable behaviors of large numbers of subjects are to be efficiently and systematically recorded.

Just what attributes and categories will appear on the final recording sheets depends largely on the purposes of the investigation. Some ready-made category systems are available (see, e.g., Heyns & Lippitt, 1954; Trent et al., 1960; and White, 1951) for certain fairly standardized situations. Before selecting any of these blindly, however, one would do well to consider their meaningfulness in the light of his own particular research aims. The considerations raised in Chapter 6 concerning the selection of tests are, of course, equally relevant in the selection of aids to behavior observation.

CLINICAL JUDGMENT

Clinical judgment constitutes a special case of observation and inference concerning human behavior. At least two phases of this judgment process come into prominence from the researcher's point of view:

diagnosis and assessment of progress in therapy. Both kinds of judgment serve to define variables that are often used in psychological research.

The detection of psychiatric illness and the application of a specific nosological category are essentially judgmental matters, though the decisions may be supported by a variety of clinical aids, informal or standardized. Projective and ordinary psychometric tests are frequently used. Always there is observation of the client's behavior, either informally or in quasi-structured interviews. It would be unusual indeed for the clinician to base his judgment exclusively on one of these aids; instead, he typically integrates cues of various sorts in a partly subjective and perhaps essentially unreproducible fashion, arriving at a diagnostic category or a combination of them. Traditionally, psychiatrists and clinical psychologists have relied heavily on a ready-made set of categories—schizophrenic, manic-depressive, neurotic, and so on, with all their subcategories (see American Psychiatric Association, 1952). This nosology has proved to be of limited usefulness, however, for it does not meet the requirements of even a nominal scale (the categories are not mutually exclusive), and placement of a patient often does little to suggest treatment procedures. Mainly for the latter reason, many contemporary clinicians prefer merely to describe symptoms or limited syndromes rather than to attempt broader classification.

Whether the diagnosis is microscopic or gross, whether the categories represent an ordinal, nominal, or quasi-nominal scale, subject placement does remain largely a judgmental matter, and use of such data for research purposes requires some information about the reliability of diagnosis. The same thing can be said for judgments about the outcome of therapy. Here one is more likely to find agreement among clinicians concerning the sort of attribute to be assessed, and there may even be fair consensus as to the categories (e.g., worse, unimproved, slightly improved, moderately improved, greatly improved). There still remains the problem of validly assigning a patient to one of these categories. Here, as in any other phase of research, validity cannot be taken for granted.

CONTENT ANALYSIS OF DOCUMENTS

Just as ongoing behavior can be analyzed according to various sets of judgmental categories, so can the products of behavior be similarly treated. The products may be various—newspapers, propaganda releases, plays, TV serials, folklore, paintings—and they may result from individual or group endeavor. Once published or otherwise placed on record, they are amenable to content analysis, and, depending on one's purpose, they may be treated as manifesting characteristics of their producers or of their audience (see Berelson, 1952, 1954; Cartwright, 1953; McGranahan, 1951; Peak, 1953; White, 1951).

One kind of product that is frequently analyzed in order to yield information about the person who produced it is the record of an open-question interview. In this instance the subject's replies to questions are usually recorded as nearly as possible verbatim, and subsequently his interview schedule is pooled with a large number of others for a systematic coding of their contents. Replies to the question, "What do you think would happen to the country if an H-bomb were dropped on Washington?" might be coded according to a set of a priori categories (e.g., "submission," "retaliation," "annihilation," "confused answer"), or a set of appropriate categories might be developed empirically from perusal of the first 40 or 50 protocols. Once established, the categories are used for coding the entire sample of interviews.

Some studies have been made of paintings by psychotic patients in an attempt to correlate characteristic styles with the nature of their disturbances or with changes in their psychiatric statuses. A popular art form, such as a movie, play, or TV drama, can be analyzed not only for characteristics of the person who wrote it but also for clues concerning the kind of audience that would appreciate such a product. This is the idea behind Freud's and Jung's interpretations of cultural myths as indicating latent concerns of the people who transmit them. Contemporary experts in psychological warfare, too, analyze an enemy's domestic propaganda in terms of what it might indicate about the state of public morale in that country.

The degree of inference involved in such judgments may range from slight to great. Sometimes it is simply a case of deciding what the subject said. At other times one may try to guess what it was that he was unable to say, either out of explicit concern for secrecy or as a psychological defense against unconscious impulses. The more inferential the decision, of course, the harder it usually is to establish agreement among independent judges as to how the material should be coded.

Since the uses of content analysis are so diverse and their purposes so specific, no general category systems have gained particularly wide acceptance. Instead, researchers are likely to rely on certain standard approaches to the development of their own appropriate coding dimensions and on a set of techniques for training coders and establishing uniform, efficient procedures. Some of these subjects are touched on in a later section.

PRINCIPLES OF RESEARCH USING HUMAN JUDGMENT

The foregoing illustrations of judgmental assessment have differed in the kinds of phenomena observed. But whether they are cultural patterns, animal behaviors, psychotic symptoms, or interview records, translating complex responses into useful scientific data poses certain common, recurring problems. Specifically, there are the problems of what to abstract, how to represent it numerically, and how to assure reliability and validity of judgment. We shall consider each of these in turn.

Abstraction of Relevant Dimensions

Confronted with complex naturally occurring behavior patterns, the researcher must abstract and simplify them in order to treat them systematically. In a sense, simplification is immediately achieved when controlled stimuli are used, for typically the stimuli focus the attention of both subject and investigator on a limited range of behavior. In a conditioning experiment the sound of a buzzer is followed by an avoidance response or it is not. In replying to a closed question a respondent says "yes" or "no." At least these are the only responses the researcher pays attention to; but in a natural situation he is confronted with *emitted*, rather than *elicited*, behavior. The subject behaves in response to exceedingly complex, largely unspecified stimuli, and it is up to the researcher to weed out irrelevant aspects of both the situation and the subject's behavior in order to concentrate on the attributes of specific interest to him.

The novice is likely to make two general sorts of mistakes in dealing with the problem of abstraction, which is central to the coding process. The first is merely expensive; the second is serious. There is a common tendency to try to code out too many attributes from the phenomena being studied. This is bound to occur particularly in abstracting from ongoing behavior which one knows cannot be brought back for a second look. So, in the observation of experimental social groups, for instance, the researcher may be tempted to assess a great many features of the conversation, group atmosphere, feelings of members, and situation, which are tangential to his main concerns. Such comprehensive assessment almost defeats the purpose of coding in the first place—namely, to end up with a manageable amount of data efficiently collected. Every time new attributes are added, they either decrease the attention that can be paid to the focal ones or necessitate hiring and training of additional observers. In judgmental observation and coding, as in other phases of the research, the guidelines should be provided by the major aims of the investigation. Matters of questionable relevance can well await more careful attention in another study.

A second common error lies in failure to specify the domain of events that is to be investigated and to sample from it appropriately. Deficiency on this score is not the exclusive property of novices. Take the problem of assessing a society's dominant values from its communication media, for example. If this were to be done on the basis of news stories and editorials only from *The New York Times,* or from that newspaper and the *Chicago Tribune,* these sources would clearly provide insufficient representation of either the main stream or the diversity of American values. The research problem is probably too grandiose to be handled adequately, but one should at least consider the vast range of media and contents in which cultural values are expressed and make an attempt to represent this range to some extent in the sample of phenomena chosen for study.

An analogous problem occurs in the clinical diagnosis of individual behavior. The intent of this coding procedure is to describe some general feature that applies to the total person—for example, he is "normal" or "neurotic" or "psychotic" or "feeble-minded." Yet often the judgment is formed on the basis of impressions gained from a very restricted sample of behavior, usually in the clinician's office, perhaps in response to a small number of specialized tests. True, the judge uses parents, teachers, acquaintances, or legal authorities as sources of information about behavior outside the clinic, but these are usually sufficient only to establish that a behavior deviation exists, rarely to diagnose it more specifically. The issue here is not the humanitarian one that a patient may have been wrongly stereotyped but the research problem of how much confidence can be placed in the diagnosis as representing one of the variables under study.

The research methods of psychology are far from arriving at even approximately satisfactory solutions to such problems, so the novice need not become immobilized for lack of a perfect definition of the behavior domain. Yet it is sometimes helpful to consider whether a broader sampling of behavior or its products might not represent the intended attribute better; failing this, one should at least restrict his conception of the attribute to match appropriately those behaviors and products that are actually sampled.

Quantitative Coding

When the relevant attributes have been decided on and the sample of responses from which they are to be inferred has been determined, the next step is to assign numbers to the various categories of each attribute so that judgments can be expressed in numerical terms. The reason for using numbers is to make analysis simpler. Much of the tabular and statistical work is done these days by IBM machines or other office equipment which works best on numbers; even if the analyses are to be done by hand rather than mechanically, numbers will provide brief and orderly ways of representing the variables.

The categories of a judged attribute might represent any of the several scale types discussed in Chapter 5, but most frequently they are intended as either an ordinal or a nominal scale. The affective component of subjects' attitudes toward world government, for example, might be represented on a five-point scale, whose categories are defined as

1. very favorable
2. moderately favorable
3. neutral; balanced opinion
4. moderately unfavorable
5. very unfavorable

In order to yield maximally reliable judgments, it is generally preferable to start out with as refined a category system as coders are capable of discriminating, then to collapse adjacent categories later in the analysis stage, as necessary; so it may be worthwhile to use a seven-, nine-, or even eleven-point scale of affective intensity. An appropriate number from this scale is selected to represent the subject's attitude as the researcher judges it.

Some responses, though, will not fit any of these categories. A subject might refuse to give an opinion or might answer in a way that leaves one in doubt about how he feels toward world government. To handle these replies, one frequently adds additional categories to the affective scale, such as

9. don't know
0. not ascertained

in order that all replies can be numerically represented. There is some advantage to keeping the meanings of numbers consistent from scale to scale—by always using 1 for the most favorable end of a continuum, 9 for "don't know," and so forth. Such standard practice will help coders learn the categories so that they will not have constant need to refer to their manuals.

Nominal scales, too, are most conveniently represented by numbers, whether or not IBM machine analyses are anticipated. Suppose one wished to distinguish the following categories of reaction to experimental frustration:

Goal-Oriented
11. Ignores experimenter; continues goal-directed activity
12. Leaves area of frustration to continue activity
13. Rebukes or attacks experimenter; then continues activity
18. Other goal-oriented response

Aggressive
21. Attacks experimenter
22. Attacks other subjects
23. Demolishes or throws objects
24. Swears or otherwise manifests anger verbally
25. Flushes but suppresses overt hostility
28. Other aggressive response

Regressive
31. Stops goal-oriented activity
32. Cries
33. Seeks aid from experimenter
38. Other regressive activity

Miscellaneous
88. Other response, not codable as goal-oriented, aggressive, or regressive
00. Response not observed

This code for judging reactions to frustration is set up for punching in two IBM card columns, the first of which stands for the major orientation (goal-oriented, aggressive, and regressive), the second for specific kinds of responses classified under the general categories. The number 8 (for example) is used consistently for "other" categories, to make it easier to learn the code (see Chapter 12 for additional suggestions concerning IBM coding and storage procedures).

Obviously the precise form of the coding aids and the nature of the category system will depend on the specific problem. But the general purpose of all these procedures is to transform selected aspects of events into numbers so that they can be analyzed efficiently and systematically. In this process the detailed richness of complex events is inevitably lost; but the loss is intentional, and what is retained is at least explicitly designated and common to all subjects (or other units of observation).

Assuring Objectivity of Judgments

When variables are recorded automatically by a mechanical device, or when scores are precisely determined by the way a subject checks a series of closed questions, there is little opportunity for subjective coding bias on the part of the researcher. He may have used the wrong apparatus or asked inappropriate questions, but at least—aside from inadvertent errors—no one can quarrel with his scoring. Every step in the assessment process is explicit and can be repeated exactly by another investigator. Not so with judgmental variables. They depend heavily on subjective interpretive work which may not be exactly duplicated from one judge to another; hence there can always be some doubts raised about coding error. This may appear in the form of bias, or systematic error, which often gives unwarranted help to the investigator's hypotheses. It may appear as random error, which merely reduces any predicted correlations or differences below what they should be. Both kinds of error are undesirable, since they lead to a distorted picture of the relations among variables.

A coding judgment may perhaps be called "objective" to the extent that it is duplicated by another trained observer who makes an independent judgment based on the same data. Objectivity can thus be represented operationally as reliability or as agreement among independent observers (see Robinson, 1957). So it is amenable to the same kinds of statistical treatment used to describe these characteristics of tests. Whenever a researcher reports results that depend on judgmental measures, he should describe the reliability of these judgments and the conditions under which reliability was measured. It will always be to his advantage to check judgmental variables, to see if they indeed represent something outside his own imagination that can be communicated to others.

Training Coders

In a large-scale investigation judgmental variables are likely to be assessed by a number of different assistants. Even if the researcher intends to make all the judgments himself, he should still get initial assistance from at least one other competent person in order to determine the objectivity of his own coding. It is good practice first to develop a conception of the attribute to be judged, then to define its categories. This may be done initially on a priori grounds alone or after looking at a sample of the events to be coded. Next the researcher will try to fit a new sample of data into the category system. If this attempt is unsuccessful, he should appropriately redefine the dimension (or its categories). Eventually he may become sufficiently satisfied with his own ability to code the attribute to try to teach his definitions to someone else. The rationale behind the dimension should be thoroughly explained to the new judge and illustrated with examples from the data at hand. After he, too, thinks he understands the coding system, both he and the original code-developer should try their hands independently on a new set of observations. "Independently" means that they must not discuss their judgments or indicate in any way how they are coding the data. This can best be done by working in separate rooms or from separate vantage points so that subtle verbal or postural cues will not contaminate the independence of ratings.

Then a measure of agreement (see below) is computed on this sample of independent judgments. If it is sufficiently high, production coding can proceed. If not, the new judge might be given further training or the dimension might be redefined to improve its clarity. As each new judge is added to the study, he should be trained and checked out in a similar fashion. (This can be done in groups if several coders are obtained at one time.) The researcher will almost always learn with surprise that definitions and judgments that appeared clear to him are ambiguous or completely uncommunicable to others. This may induce him to clarify his own thinking, to obtain "brighter," "more sensitive" coders, or, if all these fail, to conclude that the attribute is a very personal one for him, unsensed by other observers.

Besides teaching coders to make reliable judgments, the researcher must provide safeguards against errors from other sources—boredom, carelessness, and mental sets. Consistency in assigning numbers to categories will help to establish facilitative sets, help judges to learn the code faster and avoid mechanical errors of number substitution. Because coding hundreds of similar items is such a boring task, it is advisable to provide for frequent breaks and also to try to make the routine meaningful and interesting by thoroughly explaining to coders where their labors fit into the over-all research scheme. They should be encouraged to ask questions when they are really stumped but also to develop reliance on their own judgments when responses are ambiguous. Finally, accuracy may be enhanced if they are informed that their work will be checked periodically; in some situations one may wish to indicate that their future employment or pay status will be determined accordingly. (Since systematic checks on coding are needed during the entire process to ascertain the over-all reliability of content analysis, they may as well be used also to evaluate coders and to correct systematic errors in their judging.)

Measuring Coding Reliability

In order to determine the extent of agreement between two coders, one must first have a record of their independent judgments of the items they both analyzed. The kind of statistical computations performed to arrive at a measure of agreement depends on the scale type the attribute represents and on how the scores are to be utilized.

For a nominal-scale attribute an appropriate measure is π (Scott, 1955), which represents the extent to which two coders agree beyond the level that would be expected by chance alone. The formula for this index, together with a computational illustration, is presented in the chapter supplement. With a nominal scale the two judges either agree or they do not; there is no question of "degrees of disagreement." What constitutes agreement depends on the distinctions of interest for subsequent analysis. If all the subcategories in the scale are to be distinguished, then one will wish to compute the proportion of agreements *on all of them specifically*. If grosser discriminations are sufficient—for example, if one intends only to separate the first category from all others—then agreements on the gross combinations should be counted.

We know of no good measure of *agreement* for ordinal scale categories; * in practice, these are usually treated as if they were interval scales, though if one simply wanted a measure of the extent to which two judges' ratings are monotonically related, he could appropriately use τ or h (see Chapter 13, p. 344). These serve the same function for ordinal-scale data as the product-moment correlation does for interval scales.

The coding reliability of interval-scale dimensions may be represented in two different ways. The most common method is to compute a product-moment correlation between the two sets of judgments. This represents not the level of absolute agreement but the degree to which

---

* If one is interested only in the *ranking* of objects with respect to an attribute rather than in their scores on the attribute dimension itself, the Spearman rank-difference correlation coefficient (see McNemar, 1955) can provide a measure of agreement.

two sets of scores are linearly related, regardless of differences in means or standard deviations. So a high correlation between two sets of judgments could be found, even though the agreement between them was not very high. This would occur if the two coders had differing average levels, or differing variabilities, of judgment.

If one is concerned with precise agreement in scores, then the *intraclass correlation* (Chapter 6, p. 152) is the appropriate measure. Which of these measures of reliability to use, the product-moment r or the intraclass ρ, will depend on how the dimension is to be interpreted. If one simply requires a measure that is to be linearly related to some other variable, then product-moment correlation is sufficient. For example, one might hypothesize that the greater the level of students' rated adjustment the better they would perform in school. A judgmental rating scale consisting of four categories (actually ordinal) is established: "well adjusted," "moderately adjusted," "poorly adjusted," and "maladjusted." To test the hypothesis, these ratings are to be correlated with over-all grade-point average. For such use, it is not necessary for any pair of raters to agree exactly on how each student shall be placed. As long as their relative judgments are linearly related, the correlation required by the research hypothesis can be established.* So "reliability of judgment" could in this case be operationalized as the product-moment correlation between two coders' ratings.

If, on the other hand, the scale were to be used for individual diagnoses, and every person who fell in the last two categories was to be sent for psychotherapy, then it is important that all raters mean exactly the same things by their judgments. The degree to which this is true can be represented by the intraclass correlation coefficient.

There is an interesting difference here between the practical procedures of assessing attributes by judgment and assessing them by tests. On a test the attribute is measured by several items, which have been intercorrelated in a previous pilot study to ascertain their degree of homogeneity (interpreted as the degree to which they measure a common attribute). Since the items vary in difficulty (the amount of the attribute required to "pass" them), they will not yield identical distributions of subjects; but their distributions should be linearly related. Hence correlation among items is the issue. Items could be added to, or subtracted from, the total set, but this would not matter so long as the set remained homogeneous. The effects of such manipulations on the mean test score, or on the variability, are of no conse-

---

* If their means and variances differ, however, the correlation between ratings and grades for the total sample will be attenuated.

quence, since the scores are treated only in a relative fashion. There is no such thing as an absolute "high," "middle," or "low."

The variable measured judgmentally could conceivably be treated in the same manner; that is, one could use several raters and add all their scores up to arrive at a total score for each subject. Such an over-all measure would be meaningful to the extent that there was positive correlation among the judges' ratings; this would amount to saying that the population of judgments was homogeneous. They would not have to be identical to warrant such a procedure; one judge might be more "difficult" than another—that is, he might require more of the attribute in order to rate any particular subject "high" on it. One judge might be more sensitive to individual differences than another, thus yielding a greater dispersion of ratings. But as long as their judgments were linearly related, they could be legitimately pooled into one over-all rating, which would presumably constitute the best estimate of any subject's relative standing on the attribute.*

Such a procedure is clearly not feasible in the typical research project, for multiple judges are not so cheap as multiple items. The typical strategy, therefore, is to work with only one judge per subject but to try to gain maximum precision and reliability from his ratings. This is done, first, by requiring from him discriminations as fine as possible (using, for example, a seven-point rating scale rather than a dichotomous judgment of the presence or absence of the trait). Second, the researcher defines as precisely as possible the cues that are to guide the ratings, so that they can be communicated to others. Then he carefully trains himself and all other judges to be used in the project, so that they will agree as nearly as possible in their ratings of a representative sample of responses. Once fairly exact agreement is established, each judge can then work on his own, with only periodic check-coding to maintain a record of over-all coding agreement.

Validity of Judgments

As with other operations in psychological research, the meaning and measure of the "validity" of judgments are ambiguous matters. Vaguely stated, a judgment is valid to the extent that it accurately reflects the intended attribute. But the empirical methods of testing for validity are, at best, indirect and inferential. One can generally find conditions that are necessary, but they are rarely sufficient. Just

---

* A simple addition of judges' ratings would give most weight to the judge showing greatest variability. If one wanted to weight them equally, it would be necessary first to convert each judge's distribution of ratings into standard scores (see Chapter 6, pp. 136–137).

because two judges agree perfectly in their ratings of "adjustment," for example, this provides no guarantee that any meaningful attribute of subjects is being assessed; for the judges may agree simply because they hold the same erroneous theory (or prejudice or stereotype) about what constitutes maladjustment and what its signs are. One consequence of coder training is indoctrination of theories; if these theories are erroneous, all coders may be agreeing with one another, but invalidly.

Convergent Validity

There is, perhaps, a sense in which the notion of convergent validity used with reference to psychological tests (see Chapter 6, p. 142) can be applied analogously to the judgment process. Two judges might rate quite different event domains, both of which were presumed to reflect the same attribute, and the extent of agreement between their ratings could be assessed. It was urged earlier (see p. 184) that in order to have some assurance that a general attribute of a subject is being assessed it is necessary to sample relevant responses over a fairly broad range. Validity of ratings based on one population of responses might be established by the size of their correlation with ratings based on a different population. Faced, for example, with the problem of assessing the dominant values of various societies from a content analysis of their communications media, the researcher might have one judge base his ratings on newspapers while the other judge rates billboards. (The aim should be to select media which are, as far as possible, independent of one another, so that contamination among media is not substituted for contamination between judges.)

Similarly, the convergent validity of clinical diagnoses might be established by comparing judgments based on quite different kinds of behavior—such as patients' actions on the ward compared with their responses to a battery of projective tests.

Discriminant Validity

The procedure of comparing predicted with nonpredicted correlations in order to assess the discriminant validity of a test (see Chapter 6, p. 145) can be extended to judgmental variables as well. If attribute A is validly judged, then two coders' ratings of it (based on evidence from different samples of behavior) should correlate to a greater extent than the first coder's ratings of attribute A would correlate with the second coder's ratings of an allegedly different attribute, B. If the A–B correlation is approximately as high as the A–A correlation, this suggests that the two attributes are being confused, and at least one of them is not being validly judged.

Predictive Validity

Finally, if judgments concerning one variable lead to the successful prediction of different variables, in accord with theoretical requirements, this evidence can sometimes be used to bolster one's confidence that the "right" attribute is being assessed. Particular care must be taken for judgmental variables, however, to make sure that the researcher's expectations concerning the outcome do not contaminate his judgments. At least the ratings should be made "blind" (i.e., without knowing which subject is being rated or how he scored on the related variable), preferably by another judge, working independently, with no knowledge of other research results or of the hypothesis under investigation. Unless such conditions for complete independence of judgments can be maintained, the researcher must leave his mind open to the possibility that correlations found in his study represent the raters' expectations rather than significant facts about the intended variables. (This is the sort of criticism that has been leveled against much research on the effectiveness of psychotherapy: ratings of patient improvement are generally made by the very doctors who provide the treatment.)

SUMMARY

Human judgment enters into the assessment of every variable used in psychological research. Sometimes it is aided by mechanical or verbal instruments which leave little to the judge's interpretation but nevertheless require close attention for accurate measurement. At other times variables are assessed without explicit designation of the bases for judgment. Unless the discriminations required are exceedingly simple, the researcher should doubt their accuracy and objectivity sufficiently to put them to a test. Especially if other people are to assist in judging the variables, one will want to determine the adequacy of their performance before relying on the measures which they produce.

As much as practicable, judges should be trained to understand the purposes of their activity as well as the specific discriminations to be made—though, in some cases, certain aspects of the study must be concealed from them in order to avoid contaminating their judgments. After an initial training period, and then perhaps periodically throughout the observation phase, two or more independent judgments of the same sample of behaviors should be obtained and compared for agreement among the observers. This is important not only for training purposes but to obtain an estimate of the degree to which unreliability of judgments will contribute to error variance in relations involving the coded variable.

Human judgment, properly trained and used, can probably be about as precise and objective as any psychological test. On the many occasions when it is appropriate to assess psychological variables judgmentally the researcher should take special care to see that his ratings are reliable, valid, and free from contamination; for these potential defects are ones he must consider when interpreting his results, and they are also likely to be the first targets of criticism from colleagues who may question his findings.

SUPPLEMENT

π, an Index of Inter-Coder Agreement for Nominal-Scale Judgments

The proportion of judgments on which two independent coders agree out of the total number may be designated as P_o, the *observed percentage agreement*. This could be taken as a crude measure of coding reliability, but it would be deceptively high if the number of categories in the scale were small or if only a few of the categories were used with any appreciable frequency. This is because "chance" agreement with a small number of categories would be considerably above zero, and clearly the chance level must be improved upon before one can claim that the coding is reliable. If the scale consisted of two categories, both used with equal frequency, the proportion of agreements one would expect by chance—that is, if both judges coded randomly without paying attention to the attribute under study—would be .50. For any number of categories, k, all used with equal frequency, chance agreement would be $1/k$. When frequencies vary over the set of categories, *chance* or *expected agreement*, P_e, may be estimated from the following formula:

$$P_e = \sum p_i^2$$

where p_i is the proportion of cases assigned to the ith category.

The basis of this formula (see Scott, 1955) is as follows. The chance probability of both judges' placing item X in category A equals the product of the separate probabilities that each of them will place X in A. Though each judge will, in fact, use the various categories with different frequencies, the *average frequency* over all judges can perhaps be regarded as a long-run "best" estimate of the "true" population probability. So the probability that a random pair of judges will, by chance, place X in A is $(p_A)(p_A)$ or p_A^2, the square of the proportion of cases that fall in category A. Similarly, the probabilities of agreement on placements in categories B, C, $\cdots$ K can be represented as $p_B{}^2$, $p_C{}^2$, $\cdots$ $p_K{}^2$. Since the categories are mutually exclusive (by definition of a nominal scale), the probability of agreement on the total set equals the sum of probabilities of agreement on each one taken individually.

The maximum value of P_e is 1.00, which occurs when a single category contains all observations. The minimum value $1/k$ occurs when all k categories have equal frequencies (n/k). A useful index of coding reliability, then, would be the degree to which observed intercoder agreement (P_o) exceeds the level of agreement (P_e) that would be expected on the basis of chance alone, considering the marginal distribution. This index is designated π and is calculated as

$$\pi = \frac{P_o - P_e}{1 - P_e}$$

π has an upper limit of 1.00 and a lower limit of 0.00, unless the judges do worse than chance, in which case it will come out negative. P_e is estimated from the distribution of all observations over the set of categories. To determine P_o, two different judges must code independently a random sample of the observations, and P_o is the proportion of times they agree (regardless of the categories involved). An example is provided in Table 8-1.

First the proportion of cases assigned to each category of the scale is averaged for the two coders in order to yield the best estimate of p_i. These average p_is are squared and added up to give P_e, the "expected" or "chance" agreement

TABLE 8-1

Reliability of Nominal-Scale Judgments Measured by an
Index of Agreement, π

		1	2	3	4	5	6	f_{i2}
	1	40	1		13			54
	2	1	12	4			4	21
Category	3		3	11		2		16
assigned	4			8	62		1	71
by judge 2	5	3		1		12		16
	6	1	2			3	8	14
	f_{i1}	45	18	24	75	17	13	192

Category assigned by judge 1

average p_i: .258 .102 .104 .380 .086 .070

$P_e = \Sigma p_i{}^2 = (.258)^2 + (.102)^2 + (.104)^2 + (.380)^2 + (.086)^2 + (.070)^2$
$\quad\quad = .244$

$P_o = \dfrac{40 + 12 + 11 + 62 + 12 + 8}{192} = .755$

$\pi = \dfrac{P_o - P_e}{1 - P_e} = \dfrac{.755 - .244}{1 - .244} = \dfrac{.511}{.756} = .68$

percentage (.244). Then the proportion of cases on which the judges agree, P_o ($= .755$), is computed by adding up the diagonal frequencies and dividing by 192, the total number of objects judged. The difference between P_o and P_e (.755 $-$ .244) is divided by the maximum difference possible (1.000 $-$ .244 $=$ .756), to yield the ratio π.

REFERENCES

American Psychiatric Association Committee on Nomenclature and Statistics. *Diagnostic and statistical manual: mental disorders.* Washington, D. C.: American Psychiatric Association, 1952.

Berelson, B. *Content analysis in communication research.* Glencoe, Ill.: Free Press, 1952.

Berelson, B. Content analysis. In G. Lindzey (Ed.), *Handbook of social psychology.* (Vol. I.) Cambridge: Addison-Wesley, 1954.

Cartwright, D. P. Analysis of qualitative material. In L. Festinger & D. Katz (Eds.), *Research methods in the behavioral sciences.* New York: Dryden, 1953.

Heyns, R. W., & Lippitt, R. Systematic observational techniques. In G. Lindzey (Ed.), *Handbook of social psychology.* (Vol. I.) Cambridge: Addison-Wesley, 1954.

Heyns, R. W., & Zander, A. F. Observation of group behavior. In L. Festinger & D. Katz (Eds.), *Research methods in the behavioral sciences.* New York: Dryden, 1953.

Jahoda, Marie, Deutsch, M., & Cook, S. *Research methods in social relations.* New York: Dryden, 1951, Vol. I, Chap. 5, "Observational methods."

McGranahan, D. V. Content analysis of the mass media of communication. In Marie Jahoda, M. Deutsch, & S. Cook (Eds.), *Research methods in social relations.* (Vol. II.) New York: Dryden, 1951.

McNemar, Q. *Psychological statistics.* (2nd Ed.) New York: Wiley, 1955.

Peak, Helen. Problems of objective observation. In L. Festinger & D. Katz (Eds.), *Research methods in the behavioral sciences.* New York: Dryden, 1953.

Robinson, W. S. The statistical measure of agreement. *Amer. sociol. Rev.,* 1957, **22**, 17–25.

Scott, W. A. Reliability of content analysis: the case of nominal scale coding. *Pub. Op. Quart.,* 1955, **19**, 321–325.

Trent, R. D., Fernandez-Marina, R., & Maldonado-Sierra, E. D. The cross-cultural application of the adjectival check list adjustment index: a preliminary report. *J. soc. Psychol.,* 1960, **51**, 265–276.

White, R. K. *Value analysis: nature and use of the method.* Ann Arbor, Mich.: Society for the Psychological Study of Social Issues, 1951.

Whyte, W. F. Observational field-work methods. In Marie Jahoda, M. Deutsch, & S. Cook (Eds.), *Research methods in social relations.* (Vol. II.) New York: Dryden, 1951.

Zander, A. Systematic observation of small face-to-face groups. In Marie Jahoda, M. Deutsch, & S. Cook (Eds.), *Research methods in social relations.* (Vol. II.) New York: Dryden, 1951.

CHAPTER 9

Sample design: selecting subjects and estimating parameters

Pilot work eventually brings the researcher to the point where he can afford to place tentative confidence in his instruments. The next thing is to use them on a new group of subjects in order to test the hypotheses or explore the problem that impelled the investigation. It is the results of this next phase that will provide the substantive conclusions derived from the study—that a certain proportion of adults in a city intend to vote Democratic, that partially reinforced habits are more enduring than completely reinforced ones, or that there is a positive correlation between intelligence and social adjustment. Such conclusions as these are then typically intended to apply to some group of people (or other organisms) which is larger than the group actually studied. So the researcher will usually wish to generalize from his sample of subjects to some population they represent.

The inductive problem here is analogous to that encountered in the instrumentation phase. There the investigator was able to use only one or two—or ten—ways of measuring a particular attribute, but he wanted fair assurance that they would yield results similar to those that would have been obtained by some other methods he might have used. In collecting the final data he employs only a particular group of subjects, but he would like to be reasonably confident that another group would produce comparable results.

Ways of assuring the generality of psychological principles over populations of organisms have received a great deal more attention than procedures for generalizing over populations of measuring instruments. This is perhaps because populations of instruments are largely theoretical, existing only in imagination, and it is difficult to sample from an imaginary population. On the other hand, populations of people or animals can, in principle, be explicitly defined and enumerated, so it is possible to make reasonably accurate judgments about how representative any particular sample of them is.

The essence of subject sampling, as of all sampling, is adequate representation of the population to which one wishes to generalize. A small number of subjects actually studied (the *sample*) can be made to stand for a much larger number that might have been studied (the *population*), provided the former group is chosen appropriately. Even if one were able to take measures on the entire population, considerations of over-all research efficiency would usually make this inadvisable. It is generally preferable to spend extra time and money in getting ideas, refining instruments, and ensuring accuracy of the data rather than in increasing the sample size beyond the range necessary to answer the research question with the desired degree of precision. Just where that range of optimum efficiency lies will depend on certain specific considerations to be treated in this chapter.

Systematic methods of subject selection stem largely from the mathematical theory of sampling. Although the exact conditions required by the theory are rarely met in practice, one can nevertheless aim at sampling techniques that will make the theory approximately applicable. Moreover, sampling theory, for its part, has become more and more flexible, more elaborate, and better able to treat realistically the practical conditions of research. So it is quite conceivable that problems of sampling and induction—relating to subjects, instruments, or conditions—which seem intractable today will one day be adequately handled by theories and techniques that are yet to be developed. Our own treatment is likely to be outdated at its very writing, so rapid is the advance of this phase of research technology.

INFERRING POPULATION PARAMETERS

If the investigator discovers that the mean age of students in his sample is 21 years, he would like to be able to conclude that this is also the mean age of all students at the university (or other population represented). The population figure is the *parameter*, whereas the sample figure is a *statistic*. Statistics are used to estimate parameters. Many different parameters might be objects of investigation—means, proportions, modes, standard deviations, slope constants, correlation coefficients, differences between group means, and so forth. The typical research project in psychology is designed to determine relations among variables, hence the parameters of chief concern are likely to be measures of relationship, such as those discussed in Chapter 13. Frequently the research problem does not require estimation of a specific relational parameter. Instead of predicting that $Y = 4X^2 + 1.3$ or that the correlation between X and Y is .25, one will hypothesize only that X and Y are positively related. Instead of trying to find out *how much* happier men are than women, the investigator will want to know only *if* they are happier. Even with such preliminary research designs, however, one can conceive of them as aimed at estimating certain non-specific parameters (e.g., $\hat{r}_{xy} > 0.00$, $\hat{M}_1 - \hat{M}_2 > 0$ *).

Just what particular statistic is obtained, hence what estimate of the parameter is made, will depend on the particular sample of subjects that happens to be measured. One can easily see, for example, that if the mean age of an entire student body were 21 years, 4 months, 26 days, any particular sample chosen for study would not necessarily yield just that figure as a statistic; or, if all men in the country tend, on the average, to be happier than women, it would still be possible to pick a sample of each sex in which the mean happiness levels are reversed. In fact, any particular sample statistic will rarely fall exactly on the population parameter. But it is still a realistic aim to obtain statistics that do not miss their parameters by very much.

In nearly all practical sampling situations the parameter is never known. So it is impossible to tell how far away from it a particular statistic lies; sampling theory does not even attempt to estimate this discrepancy directly. Instead, the problem is translated into a somewhat different form—that is, if a number of different samples were drawn from this same population, how much variability would there be among the different statistics they yield? If 20 samples of students were studied, would the 20 different mean ages fall fairly close together or would they be widely scattered? If the former condition obtained, then the statistic (mean) computed from these samples would typically provide a more precise estimate of the population parameter than under the latter condition.

Just how much variability among the means will occur from sample to sample depends, basically, on two things: the size of the sample and

* The circumflex is used to designate a hypothetical parameter, as distinct from a sample mean (M) or correlation (r).

the variability within the population of the attribute being studied. The larger the samples, the less likely it is that the *mean* of any one of them will depart too greatly from the parameter; hence the variance among sample means will tend to be smaller for large samples. The effect of variance in the attribute itself can be readily understood from an example. A population of college students is fairly homogeneous in age compared with, say, the membership of a church (including its Sunday-school enrollment). In sampling the church population, it would not be especially unusual to encounter a mean sample age of 45 or one of 14; but in the more homogeneous student body, although an occasional member might have such an extreme age, it would be a rare thing indeed to pick randomly an entire sample of 10 or 20 persons whose *mean* was that deviant.

The variability among means from sample to sample is represented by $\sigma_M{}^2$ (the *variance of the mean*) or by its square root σ_M (the *standard error of the mean*). The dependence of $\sigma_M{}^2$ on n (the sample size) and on $\acute{\sigma}_x{}^2$ (the variance of the attribute in the population) can be expressed precisely in the equation: $\sigma_M{}^2 = \acute{\sigma}_x{}^2/n$.

The sampling variance of any statistic depends on the sample size (though the function for other statistics is not necessarily the same as it is for $\sigma_M{}^2$). Just what parameters enter into the function will depend on the particular statistic. The variance of r (the product-moment correlation coefficient) depends on the parameter $\acute{r}$ but not on $\acute{\sigma}_x{}^2$ or $\acute{\sigma}_y{}^2$. The variance of the z-statistic (see Chapter 13) depends only on n. An exact or approximate formula for the variance of any particular statistic can generally be determined, either in mathematical theory or by an empirical study (in which large numbers of samples are selected under a variety of parameter conditions and an appropriate function computed by trial and error).

In this chapter we deal only with error variances of means ($\sigma_M{}^2$) or proportions ($\sigma_p{}^2$)—a special case of the mean—and of differences between them ($\sigma_{M_1-M_2}^2$ or $\sigma_{p_1-p_2}^2$). This is mainly for simplicity of exposition at this point. Certain other sampling distributions are discussed in Chapter 13; the reader should consult statistical references (e.g., Cochran, 1953; Deming, 1950; Hansen, Hurwitz, & Madow, 1953; McNemar, 1955; Treloar, 1943) for a more thorough presentation. The formulas used for estimating the error variance of the mean will apply even to those cases in which the mean itself does not represent the scale-type of the score distribution (see Chapter 5); that is, even though the data may consist of ordinal rather than interval scale measures, one can nevertheless compute a mean of the numbers provided and expect that comparable results would be obtained on repeated random samples from the same population, within the limits of sampling error indicated by the formulas. Thus interpretation of a statistic from the standpoint of sampling error can be considered distinct from its interpretation as a measure of the underlying attribute. The considerations raised in Chapter 5 referred to the problem of selecting a descriptive statistic that represents the measuring process appropriately. Here we are merely concerned with how any computed statistic, appropriate or not, can be expected to vary from sample to sample.

Hypothesis Testing

One can easily see why the particular statistic calculated from sample data should not be taken too seriously as representing exactly the population parameter in which one is interested. A single parameter can give rise to a number of different statistics, depending on the sample that happens to be chosen. Conversely, any particular statistic could have arisen from a range of different parameters, and the researcher can never be sure exactly which one. If the correlation between X and Y computed from a sample turns out to be .50, this should not be taken as conclusive evidence that X and Y bear precisely that degree of relationship in the population from which the sample was drawn. In all probability they do not. If the proportion of intended Democratic voters among people interviewed is .40, this does not necessarily mean that the population proportion is precisely .40; it might be .38 or .46 or even .55. Thus, predicting from his sample that Democrats will lose the election, the researcher is counting on the assumption that his statistic, $p = .40$, came from a population (of all voters) in which the parameter $\hat{p}$ is less than .50. If this assumption is incorrect, his prediction will be in error.

What the researcher wants to do is guard against such an erroneous conclusion. The fact that he is inferring from a sample rather than actually measuring the entire population means that he can never eliminate the possibility altogether; for the extreme sample just might occur, regardless of how carefully it is selected. However, the probability of a false conclusion can be reduced to any desired level (other than zero) simply by taking a large enough sample.

The approach to error control afforded by the statistical theory of sampling is somewhat indirect. A *null hypothesis* is established that the population parameter is some value to be guarded against. Then a statistical significance test is constructed to see how likely it is that the obtained sample statistic could have arisen from such a parameter. In the present example, the appropriate null hypothesis would be $\hat{p} = .50$ —that is, the Democratic proportion of the two-party vote is 50%. The precise inferential question is: What is the probability that a statistic, p, as small as .40, *or smaller*, could have arisen by chance from a population in which the parameter $\hat{p}$ is actually .50? This probability can be calculated exactly because of certain things that are known about the sampling distribution of p.

The *sampling distribution* of a statistic is the set of values that might be obtained in samples from a population with a particular parameter, together with the corresponding probability of each value's occurring. For example, from the parameter $\hat{p} = .50$ a range of sample ps could arise; those in the region close to .50 would have a greater probability of occurring than those at extreme deviations from .50. (It has already been noted in the preceding discussion of means that the standard deviation of such a sampling distribution is known as the standard error of the statistic. In the case of p the error variance can be calculated as $\sigma_p{}^2 = \hat{p}\hat{q}/n$; or the standard error as $\sigma_p = \sqrt{\hat{p}\hat{q}/n}$.)

Even more importantly for the theory of statistical inference, it is also known that the various statistic ps calculated from all possible random samples of a given size, drawn from a particular population, are *normally distributed* * about the parameter $\hat{p}$. This means that the distribution of their probabilities is symmetrical and bell-shaped, and that since a precise mathematical equation for the normal curve can be written the exact probability of any particular p's occurring can be computed by means of the integral calculus. Mathematically, the probability of ps within any range arising from random samples can be translated as the area under that range of the normal curve around $\hat{p}$. In Fig. 9-1, for example, the probability of obtaining a sample p greater than p_1 from a population with parameter $\hat{p}$ equals the proportionate area to the right of p_1 under the normal curve which represents the sampling distribution of p. The probability of getting sample ps between $\hat{p}$ and p_1 from such a population equals the proportionate area under the curve between $\hat{p}$ and p_1.

Not all sample statistics are normally distributed about their population parameters, but those related to means—such as M, p, $M_1 - M_2$, ΣX, etc.—generally are (see chapter Supplement A), particularly when the sample size is fairly large.† So for all these measures it is possible to refer to a table of areas under the normal curve (see Appendix Table B)

---

* Actually the sampling distribution of p is *binomial* (see McNemar, 1955) rather than normal, but the binomial distribution approaches the normal distribution as n increases; and even with small samples (e.g., n around 30) the approximation is sufficiently close to result in very little error from treating it as normal.

† What is meant by "large" is an arbitrary matter, but as n gets up near 30 or so this is "large enough" so that the normal distribution holds to a very good approximation. See chapter Supplement B for use of the t-distribution with small samples.

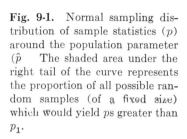

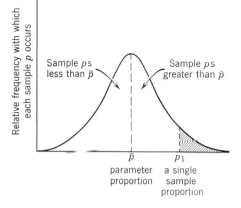

Fig. 9-1. Normal sampling distribution of sample statistics (p) around the population parameter $(\hat{p}$ The shaded area under the right tail of the curve represents the proportion of all possible random samples (of a fixed size) which would yield ps greater than p_1.

Relative frequency with which each sample p occurs

Sample ps less than $\hat{p}$

Sample ps greater than $\hat{p}$

$\hat{p}$
parameter proportion

p_1
a single sample proportion

to determine the probability of any particular range of statistics arising by chance from a hypothesized population parameter. The proportionate area under the normal curve between any two points can be calculated simply from a knowledge of the standard deviation of the normal distribution; this standard deviation is σ_p (or σ_M or $\sigma_{M_1-M_2}$, etc.), the standard error of the statistic.* So it is necessary only to estimate σ_p from the formula $\sigma_p = \sqrt{\hat{p}\hat{q}/n}$, express the obtained departure from $\hat{p}$ in units of σ_p and then read directly from the normal curve table the probability that such an extreme departure would occur in a random sample.

To illustrate, suppose that a p of 40% Democratic voters had arisen from a random sample of 65 community residents. The statistical question is, how likely is it that a proportion this size *or lower* would have resulted from a parameter of .50? Assuming that $\hat{p}$ is .50, its standard error would be

$$\sigma_p = \sqrt{\frac{(.50)(.50)}{65}} = .062$$

The next step is to express the departure of p from $\hat{p}$ in units of σ_p:

$$\mathrm{CR} = \frac{p - \hat{p}}{\sigma_p} = \frac{.40 - .50}{.062} = -1.61$$

CR stands for *critical ratio*,† or the ratio between the deviation of a particular statistic from its parameter and the standard deviation of all

* For those statistics whose sampling distributions are not normal, such as F, t, and χ^2, it is generally possible to write other equations so that appropriate probability tables can be constructed for them as well (see McNemar, 1955; Treloar, 1942).

† This statistic is frequently designated as z, the "standard normal variable" (Dixon & Massey, 1957); other sources (e.g., Wallis & Roberts, 1957) call it k.

statistics about the parameter (the latter quantity may be interpreted as the amount of departure that would be expected from sampling error). Reference to Appendix Table B shows that a negative critical ratio this large or larger would occur in slightly more than 5% of all samples (i.e., the area under the normal curve to the left of -1.61 is just over 5% of the total). Considering also the case in which the Democratic sample proportion is larger than the Republican (i.e., the area to the right of $+1.61$), a p of .60 *or larger* could arise by chance slightly more than 5% of the time from a population in which $\hat{p}$ is .50. So out of all possible samples of 65 subjects selected from a population in which $\hat{p}$ is .50, the sample p could be expected to depart from the parameter .10 *or more* (in either direction) almost 11% of the time.

Errors of Inference

If, with a sample of 65 subjects, the researcher habitually interprets ps of .40 or .60 as indicating that the parameter departs from .50 in the same direction as the obtained sample p, he will err about 11% of the time in the long run. This kind of error—rejection of a null hypothesis when it should not be rejected—is known as a *Type I error*. It might be thought of as an "error of rashness," since it usually involves concluding that a particular kind of difference occurs in the population when in fact it does not. Type I errors are always possible, given anything short of a complete sample of the total population, but the probability of their occurring—designated as α—can be set as small as one desires, simply by adhering to a given significance level for rejecting null hypotheses. In the present example the researcher might have decided in advance that he wanted α, the probability of a Type I error, to be .05. This would mean that in order to infer that the parameter $\hat{p}$ departed from .50 he would have to obtain p sufficiently far from .50 that a CR of that size or larger would occur only 5% of the time by chance. The p of .40 does not depart that far, so he would not conclude that the parameter differs from .50.*

* In this example it is assumed that either direction of departure, $p < .50$ or $p > .50$, would be of interest to the investigator, and he would be prepared to infer a corresponding parameter departure regardless of the way the sample value went. Hence the appropriate significance test is a *two-tail* test that represents the area under both "tails" of the normal curve. There are some research situations, however, in which one decides in advance to become interested only in a particular direction of obtained departure—for example, one hypothesizes a priori that $\hat{p}$ is smaller than .50, so if a sample p larger than that is obtained it will not be treated as coming from the parameter region of interest. In such a case it would seem appropriate to use a *one-tail* significance test to evaluate any obtained difference *in the predicted direction*. This will keep α at the predetermined level.

If one wants to guard very strictly against an error of rashness, this can be done quite directly by setting a stringent significance level—say .001 or .0001. But such a decision has other implications: it means that the null hypothesis will often not be rejected when it should be. This outcome is a *Type II error*—we might call it an "error of caution"—and its probability is designated as β. If, in the present example, the researcher were to conclude that the proportion of Democratic voters is not less than .50, when it actually is, this inference would be every bit as invalid as one involving an error of rashness.

The consequence of setting a very stringent significance level is to require a fairly large departure from the null parameter before the null hypothesis can be rejected. In order to conclude from 65 cases at the .0001 level of significance that the proportion of Democrats is less than .50, one would need to obtain a sample p less than .27. Such an extreme value would be quite unlikely, even if the parameter were .35 or .40; it would occur only half the time if $\hat{p}$ actually were .27! So in setting α exceptionally low to guard against errors of rashness, the researcher unduly increases β, thereby limiting his ability to detect small departures from the null parameter. The only way to compensate for this resulting insensitivity is to increase the sample size—and this may become expensive. Usually, psychologists are content with a more modest significance level, such as .05 or .01, so their conclusions are more vulnerable to Type I errors than might be desired by an absolutist looking for "certain truth." Since all inferential knowledge, however, can be only probable, never certain, the realistic approach to statistical inference would seem to be to adopt a significance level that would yield a tolerable α in the long run, and then just resign oneself to making the specified proportion of Type I errors.

Given certain previous decisions about the tolerable sizes of α and β and about the magnitude of departure from the null parameter that one wishes to detect, it is possible to determine the size of the sample that will be required in order to meet these specifications. The procedure is illustrated in chapter Supplement C.

INTERDEPENDENCE OF SELECTION AND ESTIMATION PROCEDURES

In practice, the sampling variances of most statistics can never be computed precisely; they can only be estimated from sample data. The variance of the mean, for example, depends in part on $\acute{\sigma}_x^2$, the variance of the attribute in the population from which the sample was drawn; $\acute{\sigma}_x^2$ is not known in the practical sampling situation but must itself be esti-

mated from a sample.   Moreover, the relation which $\sigma_M{}^2$ bears to $\acute{\sigma}_x{}^2$
depends on how the sample is selected.   The formulas on pp. 200 and 202
for $\sigma_M{}^2$ and $\sigma_p{}^2$ assume *simple random sampling* of population elements.
This is only one kind of *probability sample;* others (to be discussed
presently) require different formulas for estimating error variances.

The essential feature that distinguishes a probability from a nonprobability sample is that for the former type every member of the
population to be represented has a known chance (greater than zero)
of entering the sample.   It is only under such a sampling procedure
that calculated significance levels can yield precise information about
the probabilities of Type I and II errors, for use of the normal curve
to determine the likelihood that a particular range of statistics could
arise by chance assumes that every member of the population had a
chance of being observed.

The methods of selecting subjects used in most psychological research do not meet this requirement.   Hence the αs and βs calculated from the data do not really have any precise meanings.   They
can serve only to give the investigator an intuitive feeling of confidence or nonconfidence in the replicability of a particular outcome.

If such intuitive evaluations are to be replaced by precise probability statements concerning the likelihood of replication, then more
careful and explicit sampling procedures must be used.   Any formula
for estimating sampling error is implicitly associated with two prior
steps in the sample design: (1) explicit definition of the population
to which results are to be generalized and (2) a method of selecting
subjects that assures that the statistic will be distributed as the formula assumes it is.   In the next section we consider several sample
designs that meet these requirements; the estimating formulas associated with each are presented in chapter Supplements A and D.   Following this we point out certain ways in which samples used in psychological research may fail to meet these assumptions, hence detract
from the desired precision of error estimates.

DEFINING THE POPULATION

The first step in getting a representative sample of subjects consists in defining the population that is to be represented.   Often this
is done implicitly, or backward, by first picking the subjects, then
generalizing results of the study to some larger population from which
the subjects might have come.   But sampling theory is based on the
former direction of derivation, from population to sample.   Adequate

empirical definition of the population means that it is possible, in principle, to enumerate it completely, that is, to decide whether any given person, animal, or object is a part of the population. One may wish to generalize his research findings to all rats in his own laboratory colony, to all sophomores who take the introductory psychology course during the next ten years, to all current residents of London, or to all human beings. Whichever group is the object of interest, this constitutes the target population.

Just what method is used to sample from the population will depend, basically, on two sorts of considerations: (1) how its elements are distributed or arranged and (2) how maximum precision can be achieved with minimum cost. Populations of elements may be found in various forms. Starting from the simplest kind, all elements might be confined within an enclosed space and mixable. This is like the molecules of soup in a pot, like marbles in a concrete mixer, or like slips of paper in a goldfish bowl.

Another kind of population is one in which every element can be uniquely identified by a name or number, and these designations are listed. Students in a university, employees at a factory, patients in a hospital, or residents of a community which maintains a continuous census constitute such populations. In practical examples the lists of elements are likely to be outdated, so that they do not correspond exactly with the intended populations, but to the extent that they do correspond the population of names or numbers can be substituted for the intended population of elements.

A variation on the preceding population type is one in which the identifying designations are listed in some order that is related to known differences in the elements. Thus university students might be classified according to year in school, and the lists of freshmen, sophomores, etc., kept separate. Lists of factory employees might be subdivided according to occupation or pay-grade, and residents of a town could be listed by census tracts or blocks, so that neighbors appear close together on the list.

Next, one might have a population whose elements can be uniquely identified and listed but which are widely scattered geographically. Members of a professional organization would constitute such a population, as would the known paintings of a famous artist.

There also might be dispersed populations whose members are in definable locations but for whom no complete list exists. Examples of these populations would be people who have bought a major home appliance within the past six months, women who expect to have a baby within the next four weeks, or the residents of any large geographical area, such as a city, state, or nation, which does not maintain a continuous census.

Each of these kinds of populations might require a somewhat different method of probability sampling. But, no matter what the specific method, it would be aimed at assuring every element a known chance of entering the sample. Simple random sampling is appropriate for confined and mixable elements, systematic sampling for listed elements, stratified sampling for classified lists, and clustered and multistage sampling for dispersed populations. We shall describe briefly how to obtain some of the simpler types of samples; some references at the end of the chapter (e.g., Cochran, 1953; Deming, 1950; Hansen, Hurwitz, & Madow, 1953; Kish, 1953; McCarthy, 1951; Yates, 1953) provide more extensive discussions of these and other types.

SIMPLE RANDOM SAMPLING

A *simple random sample* is one that gives all members of the population *equal and independent* chances of being selected. For every pair of elements, A and B, A's chance of being selected equals B's chance, and the selection of A in no way affects B's probability of selection.* The direct way to get a simple random sample, as the soup taster well knows, is to mix up thoroughly the entire population to be represented and repeatedly draw individual or clustered elements for study. Sufficiently thorough mixing is very difficult to achieve, even with the most inert substances, and elements as vital as humans or rats are quite resistant to such treatment; so a more feasible procedure is usually substituted for random mixing of the elements themselves. The first kind of population described is converted into the second kind: that is, each member is identified with a distinct number; then n numbers are selected from a *table of random numbers*. The numbers chosen from the table represent the n elements (people or animals) that are to be selected for study.

An abbreviated sample of a table of random numbers is shown in the Appendix (Table A). (For a more complete table see RAND Corporation, 1955.) The numbers are mechanically generated, usu-

---

* This definition holds, strictly, only for *sampling with replacement* (see chapter Supplement B). For *sampling without replacement* (i.e., when a particular element, once selected for the sample, cannot be selected a second time), a more correct definition of a simple random sample would be one for which all possible combinations of n elements in the total population of N have equal probabilities of selection.

ally by a digital computer, and a variety of statistical tests is performed to assure randomness. One way to use such a table is to open it haphazardly to any page and blindly put a finger on a number. The last one or two digits of that number (depending on the size of the table) indicate the page (or column) on which to start seeking sample numbers. Turn to that page (or column) and go down the column, picking those number sets that are less than, or equal to, N. (If $N < 1000$, only the last three digits in a column need to be used; if $N < 100$, only the last two digits; etc.) For each number chosen, the corresponding element in the population falls in the sample; continue the process until n elements (the desired sample size) have been chosen.

With simple random sampling, one can apply the conventional sampling-error formulas found in most elementary statistics books. Some of these related to the distribution of the mean are presented in chapter Supplement A. Appropriate error estimates for certain other statistics, under conditions of simple random sampling, are discussed in Chapter 13.

SYSTEMATIC SAMPLING

If the numbers were randomly assigned to all members of the population in the first place, then an even simpler technique can be used. One first decides how many subjects he wants to study; call this quantity n. Since all members of the population are identified, he knows how many there are: N. Now it is necessary only to divide N by n to determine the *sampling interval* to apply to the list of potential subjects—that is, to determine every "how-manyeth" one to select; this sampling interval may be referred to as k. The table of random numbers is consulted once, to pick a single random number, r, between 1 and k. Then the rth person on the list is selected for the sample, and so is every kth person thereafter.

Say that a total population of sophomores is 2218 and one wants a sample of 50; $k = N/n = 2218/50 = 44$, approximately. One would start haphazardly in a table of two-digit random numbers (or use the last two digits only from a table with larger numbers) and pick the first number (r) encountered between 1 and 44. Say r turned out to be 29. The twenty-ninth person on the list would be selected for the sample. Then the constant sampling interval, k or 44, is added to the r, or 29, making $r + k$, or 73, and the seventy-third person falls in the sample; so does the $r + 2k$th or one hundred seventeenth.

and so on, adding the same constant, until the end of the list is reached. This method of selection is known as *systematic sampling*. It differs from simple random sampling in that the various choices are not independent. Once the first element is chosen, all subsequent members of the sample are automatically determined.

If the list were randomly constructed in the first place, this procedure would yield a sample that can be treated statistically in the same way as a simple random sample. However, it is sometimes hard to tell whether a list is random with respect to the variable under study. (Alphabetical ordering would probably be random with respect to IQ but might well not be random with respect to national origins of the subjects, if certain national groups clustered disproportionately under certain letters.) Basing estimates on a systematic sample as though it were a simple random sample might yield an error variance that was either too high or too low, depending on how the list order departs from randomness. For this reason it is good practice in systematic sampling to select not just a single sample but several independent ones and to treat the measures either as a clustered or a stratified sample of elements (see chapter Supplement D).

CLUSTERED SAMPLING

Sometimes it is convenient to study subjects in naturally occurring groups, or clusters, rather than randomly scattered in a large population. The reasons for this could be various—for example, economy, need for close supervision by a single person, or even theoretical requiredness. In studying laboratory animals, for instance, it is common practice to select as subjects a group housed together, which has undergone certain common experiences and which may even represent a common genetic strain. These subjects constitute a cluster insofar as they are alike with respect to characteristics relevant to the experimental variables. When sample interview surveys are conducted on large dispersed populations (e.g., all adult residents of a town), one often lacks a recent list of the population so that it is impossible to draw a simple random sample from it. A feasible substitute would be to select a random sample of perhaps 20 blocks from an up-to-date city map, and then interview all adult residents of these blocks only. Any single block would thus yield a cluster of respondents, alike on whatever characteristics are associated with living together. Such procedures are known as *cluster sampling*, in that the selection unit is not an individual but a group of them who were together before the researcher came along. A variation on this method is *multistage sampling* in which not the entire cluster, but just a sub-sample of it, is selected for study (see Kish, 1952).

College students are typically studied in clusters or multistage samples; that is, the professor administers a questionnaire to all members of his several classes or solicits volunteers from these classes to appear for an experiment. It is reasonable to expect that subjects so selected would tend to be more like one another in a variety of ways than would subjects selected randomly from a list of the entire student body. Even if the classes were chosen to represent faithfully a cross section of students at the university, subjects within any one class would generally be more alike than would those selected at random from the total population. (A comparable effect has been noted in clustered samples of articles from newspapers by Backman, 1956.)

The usual effect of such selection procedures is to yield sample means that vary more widely than they would from simple random samples of the same size. To the extent that cluster means vary, the variance within a cluster is smaller than the sample variance would be if the same number of subjects were randomly selected without regard to which cluster they are in. Since the simple random formula (p. 200) for the error variance of the mean is based on the sample variance, the formula yields an underestimate if the sample is clustered. The degree of underestimation depends on the degree to which elements within a cluster are more similar than randomly selected elements. This relative similarity can be measured by the *intraclass correlation coefficient* (ρ), which was encountered previously (Chapter 8) in the discussion of interjudge agreement. If the intraclass correlation is high, it means that subjects within the same cluster are relatively similar on the attribute under investigation, so that their mean has a greater chance of being deviant than the mean of independently selected subjects. This likelihood must be taken into account in estimating the sampling error of any statistic computed from a clustered sample. If all members of every cluster in the sample are selected and the clusters are of approximately equal size, the appropriate way of estimating the variance of the mean consists, essentially, in treating the entire cluster as a single element and computing the variance among the several cluster means. If there is sub-sampling within clusters (as in a multistage sample), then allowance must be made for within-cluster error variance as well as for variance between clusters. Exact formulas are presented in chapter Supplement D.

The chief procedural requirement for this method of estimating error variances from a clustered or multistage sample is that the clusters actually studied be chosen at random from an explicitly defined population of clusters. If one wanted to use this sampling and estimating procedure on an animal colony consisting of 30 cages of five animals each, he might pick a random sample of ten cages, and study all 50 animals in them or just pick every other animal within the selected cages, to yield a sample of 25 subjects.* If the clusters were not randomly selected, then the variance estimates would not hold at the assumed probability levels. More seriously, if only a single cluster of subjects were studied, there would be no way of measuring between-cluster variance at all. Hence empirical generalizations from the findings would, strictly speaking, apply only to the single cluster studied, rather than to the entire colony.

STRATIFIED SAMPLING

The effect of clustering in the sample is, essentially, to make one's significance test less sensitive to population differences. To the extent that within-cluster elements are more alike than between-cluster elements, the size of the clustered (or multistage) sample will have to be larger than that of a simple random sample in order to reject the null hypothesis at a specified level of significance.

There is a way, however, of arriving at a *more* sensitive significance test—that is, of getting greater precision of estimate from the same sample size. This is by the procedure of *stratified sampling*, which consists, essentially, in taking a random sample from each of several natural groups in the total population. Whereas clustered sampling entails picking only some groups for study out of the many in the population, with stratified sampling one studies subjects from every group. The basis for stratification (i.e., defining the groups) may be ecological, or it may involve nongeographical characteristics of the population, such as occupation, year in college, weight, nutritional history, or sex.

To get a sample of city blocks (or houses or people), stratified by quality of the dwelling area, it would be necessary first to classify all the blocks according to this attribute—for example, slum, transitional,

* When the number of clusters in the sample (10) approaches the total number of clusters in the population (30), it is worthwhile to take account of the attendant reduction in between-clusters error variance by applying the "finite multiplier" (see chapter Supplement B).

middle class, and wealthy mansion areas. Blocks of a given stratum (category) would be listed together in random order, and each would be given a unique number. Then, after determining the number of blocks desired, one would pick a random number between 1 and k and select every kth block after that for inclusion in the sample. (See the detailed description of systematic sampling above.) It would be possible to use the same sampling interval for every stratum, so that one would go on through the entire list, picking every kth block. This would yield a *proportionate stratified sample,* in which every stratum is represented in the sample in exact proportion to its frequency in the total population. Alternatively, one could use a different sampling interval for each stratum—pick a larger proportion of some strata than of others—to yield a *disproportionate stratified sample.* The reason for this procedure might be that some strata are more expensive to sample than others; or perhaps some strata are more variable than others, so that over-all precision of the sample estimate is enhanced by sampling at higher rates from the high-variance strata [see sampling error formula (9) in chapter Supplement D].

What stratified sampling accomplishes is guaranteed representation of defined population groups. Whereas in simple random sampling (or clustered sampling) it would be possible, by chance, to miss certain types of subjects, this is impossible when the population is stratified by the relevant type to begin with (and the sampling interval is small enough). In a simple random sample of a coeducational student body it is theoretically possible (though extremely unlikely) to obtain male subjects only; this outcome would not be even remotely possible if males and females had been listed separately and a systematic sample had been drawn from the total list (assuming, of course, that there were at least as many people in each stratum as k, the sampling interval).

To the extent that subjects within strata are more homogeneous than average—in other words, that the stratum means differ—on the attribute under investigation, then to that extent will stratification be worthwhile, for it permits a more accurate estimate of the population parameter than would have been possible if the strata had not been appropriately represented. Although simple random sampling makes it highly likely that all types of subjects will be represented proportionately in the sample, this condition can never be assured for any particular classification unless that classification is used in the first place as a basis for stratifying the population.

Note that stratification by any attribute requires prior knowledge of how each population member is classified on that attribute. In an animal colony one could stratify all rats according to dietary history (e.g., high protein versus low protein) if records of their feeding had been kept. This basis for stratification would be impossible in most human populations, for one could not know how to classify any person without actually questioning him to ascertain his dietary history (and even he may not know!). This fact sets a practical limitation on the effectiveness of stratification, since those characteristics which are most critical to (i.e., most highly correlated with) the attribute under study are usually not known in advance. One might want appropriate representation of income levels in a community sample; but this could hardly be achieved directly, since a list of residents and their incomes would be difficult if not impossible to obtain. The next best thing would be to stratify by an attribute presumably correlated with income and on which the population could be classified in advance. Division of the city into sections representing varying qualities of dwelling units might accomplish this objective, for presumably family income is highly correlated with quality of the dwelling area.

It can now be seen that prior classification of subjects need not be perfect; for example, it would not matter terribly whether a particular questionable block were classified in the "middle class" or in the "wealthy mansion" stratum, for stratification does not accomplish exact proportionality on the crucial attribute under investigation. It is aimed only at proportionality on a *correlated* attribute. Presumably the correlation will not be depressed disastrously by an occasional misclassification.

The increased precision of estimating a population parameter that is achieved through stratification is reflected in the error estimates from the sample. The formulas presented in chapter Supplement D show how such improved estimates can be achieved. Essentially, they include in the measures of error variance only the variance among subjects within strata; the between-strata variance is eliminated from the error term. If all stratum means turn out exactly alike, nothing will have been gained by stratification, for the variability among subjects within each stratum will be just as large as the variability among all subjects taken together, which forms the basis for the error term in estimates from simple random samples. At the other extreme, if the stratum means differed greatly, and all subjects within a given stratum were exactly alike on the attribute, then the error of estimating the population parameter would be zero. One would know exactly what the total population mean was, just as he would if all members of a (fairly large) simple random sample turned out to be exactly alike on the attribute.

In the usual assessment research, results are likely to be much closer to the former extreme than to the latter; that is, stratum means will not differ spectacularly, and there will be considerable overlap among score distributions from different strata. Hence stratification will generally afford only minor increases in efficiency, unless the per-subject cost of the research is high. In interview survey research, though, the expense of hiring and paying interviewers and of reaching the respondents is likely to bring the cost of field work alone up to something like 15 dollars per interview. So even the small saving in number of subjects afforded by a stratified sample may be welcome.

In experimental research the potential gains from stratification are often much greater. This is because the experimenter, to some extent at least, has control over certain characteristics of his subjects and can therefore create strata based on attributes that may correlate highly with the variable under investigation. In studying the effect of magnitude of reward on habit acquisition, for example, the experimenter might expect that the dependent variable (rate of learning) will also depend on the nature of the reward (e.g., whether it is a highly or moderately preferred food). He can control the influence of reward type either by holding it constant or by systematically varying it. The first choice would limit generalizability of the findings, so he might prefer to represent several kinds of reward. This can be done by an experimental design which stratifies subjects into various types of incentive (strata), offered in varying quantities (the independent variable). Some subjects will get one kind of food and other subjects another. In statistical analysis that portion of the intersubject variance associated with differences in incentive can be eliminated from the error term to permit a more powerful test of the relation between amount of reward and habit acquisition than would be possible in an experiment that simply randomized incentive type.

Such an arrangement of experimental variables comes under the heading of a *factorial design* (or a *treatment-by-levels design*), which is discussed in Chapter 10. Here we need note only that the sensitivity of statistical significance tests (i.e., their ability to detect population differences or relationships) can be increased either by stratified sampling of subjects or by experimental arrangements which have the same effect—namely to eliminate from the error term that part of the variability that can be controlled or otherwise systematically determined.

NONSYSTEMATIC DEPARTURES FROM SIMPLE RANDOM SAMPLING

The prescriptions for sampling methods so far have followed the assumptions of sampling theory. This theory is predicated on the notion of random selection of sampling units. When the sampling unit is the individual, the theory of simple random sampling assumes that all samples of individuals are equally probable—or, in other words, that every member of the total population has an equal and independent chance of falling in the sample. Application of the theory of stratified sampling for purposes of error reduction assumes random sampling within each stratum. The theory of clustered and multistage sampling involves the condition that the clusters of subjects be selected at random from a total population of clusters.

There are some research projects in which these conditions can be met exactly, and one can prove that they have been met (e.g., that all members of the population are included in the list, that their names are randomly arranged, and that all designated members of the sample were actually studied). These projects constitute remarkable exceptions rather than typical examples. By far the largest portion of empirical studies are performed on samples which do not, strictly speaking, satisfy the assumptions of the statistical theory of inference. An almost inevitable source of departure occurs in the failure of some designated subjects to be studied. Human subjects may refuse, be too sick, deaf, or psychotic to be interviewed, or may not be at home after repeated calls. Animal subjects can get sick, too, or perform so aberrantly that measures on them had best be discarded. Even in the most carefully and skillfully conducted study, subject loss through such causes may reach 10% or more of the sample.

Another common source of departure is an inadequate list of the population one intends to represent. The same person may be listed more than once (in which case he has too great a chance of entering the sample); many people may not be listed at all. If one uses a city directory for sampling community residents, or the student directory for a sample of students, he can be almost certain that the directory is out of date the day it is published, hence does not accurately represent the intended population. People who have moved away or left school do not pose a problem; they are no longer part of the intended population, so there is no need to represent them.

Rather it is the new members who cannot possibly fall in the sample because they are not listed. The seriousness of such omissions will depend on a number of considerations—the rate of population turnover, the degree to which unlisted members are like the listed ones with respect to the variables studied—and one can usually do no better than educated guessing about how these are likely to affect the results.

Finally, one may depart from theoretically adequate sampling methods through failure to define explicitly the population from which a sample is randomly selected. This is by far the most widespread defect of research designs from the point of view of sampling theory. The investigator typically obtains a "catch-as-catch-can" sample by soliciting volunteers or administering a test to those students who happen to show up for class on a certain day. If asked what population these subjects represented, he would be hard pressed to define it explicitly (so that one would know who was in it and who was not). Rather he might opine that he had a random sample of all people who were like his subjects. In the first place, it is hard to know just what that phrase means; in the second place, people "like his subjects" may not be like the population he is trying to understand, for example, all American adults or all students at his school. Volunteers behave differently from nonvolunteers in ways that are crucial to some experimental studies (e.g., submission to authority or to group sanctions), and in many respects college students are patently different, even from their parents, let alone the wider community of adults.

The consequences of nonrepresentative sampling will be more or less serious, depending on the purpose of the study and on the variables being investigated. Oftentimes it may be reasonable to assume that "any normal person" is likely to behave pretty much like any other under the particular experimental conditions. This is likely to be true, for instance, for certain perceptual functions which depend largely on physiological structures common to a species. So psychophysical experiments are frequently performed on a small number of trained subjects who, strictly speaking, have been selected haphazardly; it is assumed that nearly identical psychophysical functions would be found in all comparably trained persons with normal sensory apparatus. Other responses—for example, attitudes and personality dispositions —are much more variable. In assessing these it can reasonably be assumed in advance that all people will *not* respond similarly to the same stimulus; so a major portion of the research task consists in determining the degree of variability in the population under study.

When intersubject variability in performance is the rule, then clearly one takes a risk in generalizing from a nonrepresentative sample. If, on the other hand, a sizable number of readily available subjects performs in an essentially identical fashion with respect to the attributes one is studying, then it seems appropriate to presume, in the absence of specific reasons to the contrary, that a randomly selected sample would behave about the same.

So, in actual practice, the methods of induction are not quite so straightforward and replicable as it would appear from the mathematical theory of sampling. Typically, the investigator does not know what the probabilities of Types I and II errors are for generalizing to any known population. Rather he makes the best judgment he can on the basis of his findings and on the basis of assumptions (or perhaps information) concerning how the population of interest is likely to differ in crucial respects from the subjects he actually studied. This, then, constitutes presumptive or hypothetical knowledge, which might in the future be tested more carefully by himself or by another investigator.

The practical (as opposed to the theoretical) induction problem is often not, therefore, very different in generalizing across people than it is in generalizing across a hypothetical population of potential operational definitions or across a hypothetical population of experimental conditions. In many of these cases the researcher does not know exactly what the relevant population of subjects, operations, or conditions is. So he chooses a theoretically, or intuitively, meaningful sample that seems to represent each domain adequately. Results from this investigation are then generalized, hypothetically, to a larger population of people, operations, and conditions than were actually represented. If subsequent research on different samples corroborates the initial findings, then he tends to place more subjective confidence in the generality of the principles illustrated by them. If incompatible findings emerge from a new sample, then he is left to wonder why; and in the course of wondering, he may arrive at a new, more general, formulation which accounts for both sets of results by the introduction of new theoretical variables or the clarification of old ones. This new formulation can then provide the basis for further sampling and comparison.

The foregoing description of a typical inductive process should not be taken as an ideal model. Ideal models are provided by the mathematical theory of sampling. In practice, however, actual conditions are likely to be quite different from those assumed by the model. Perhaps the future will see an increasing correspondence between theory and practice by elaboration of theory and refinement of practice. Certainly this would result in more efficient research, for one would then know how far the findings from any one study might be generalized. For the present, though, replication of studies in which the same abstract relationships are illustrated with different subjects, different operations, and different conditions appears to be the best and safest, though perhaps not yet a very well traveled, road to knowledge.

SUMMARY

One aspect of induction consists in generalizing findings from the sample of subjects actually studied to a larger population that might have been studied. In most psychological research this is primarily an intuitive matter: the investigator either assumes, tentatively, that his results would be replicated in another sample, or he speculates concerning how the outcome might differ, depending on relevant characteristics of the subjects.

If one wishes to substitute reasonably precise probability statements for intuitive judgment, it is necessary to define the target population explicitly and sample from it in a random fashion. Then the mathematical theory of sampling can be used to estimate the likelihood that a given result would be replicated on another random sample from the same population. There are various types of random samples—among them simple random, stratified, clustered, and multistage. Each of them is associated with a different set of formulas for estimating sampling variance and the corresponding probabilities of Type I and Type II errors. Most of the commonly used significance tests are appropriate for simple random sampling, in which every element of the population has an equal and independent chance of falling in the sample. When they are employed in conjunction with other kinds of sampling procedures, they do not accurately reflect the true significance levels of the results.

Since the largest portion of psychological research is performed on samples of subjects who were not randomly selected from definable populations, the investigator should beware of attaching any magical or absolute importance to significance levels arrived at in this way. Rather he should accept them for what they are: indications of functional relations that would probably be replicated in another study of subjects like the present ones.

If one wishes to design his study in a manner that permits explicit generalization of results to a known population, then he can make use of the various sampling techniques described here to assure adequate representation. A feasible compromise between ideal representativeness and completely intuitive generalization can usually be achieved if one first translates a hypothetical population into an empirically accessible one, then samples randomly from the latter. Statements concerning significance levels can then be strictly applied to the empirical population and speculatively to the hypothetical population.

SUPPLEMENT

A. Estimating Error Variances from a Simple Random Sample

Variance of a Mean

In a simple random sample every element of the population has an equal and independent chance of entering the sample; in other words, all possible combinations of elements are equally likely to occur as samples.

If all possible samples of the same size (n) were drawn from a population with mean $= \mu$, and a sample mean (M) were computed from each, then these sample means would be found to distribute normally about the parameter μ * with a variance of

$$\sigma_M{}^2 = \frac{\acute{\sigma}_x{}^2}{n} \tag{1}$$

where $\sigma_M{}^2$ is the sampling variance (or error variance) of the mean,
   n is the sample size (constant over all samples), and
   $\acute{\sigma}_x{}^2$ is the variance of the attribute X in the total population.

One wishes to estimate $\sigma_M{}^2$ from a single sample in order to know how precise the estimate of the mean is. This can be done by substituting $s_x{}^2$ for $\acute{\sigma}_x{}^2$ in (1); $s_x{}^2$ is an unbiased estimate of $\acute{\sigma}_x{}^2$, which can be calculated from sample data as

$$s_x{}^2 = \frac{\Sigma(X - M)^2}{n - 1} \tag{2}$$

* It would be more consistent to use both $\hat{M}$ and $\hat{p}$ or both μ and π to indicate the parameter mean and proportion, respectively, but this would not accord with conventional usage, and we have tried as much as possible to adopt common symbols. However, the reader should be warned that in perusing various statistics books for elaboration of the materials presented here he is likely to encounter a bewildering variety of symbols for the same concept. One of the first things to do in using a statistics book is to become familiar with the author's notation system; otherwise needless confusion will be added to the inherent complexity.

This is just like the formula for calculating the variance of sample Xs, except that the denominator is $n - 1$ instead of n. The reason is that the sample variance σ_x^2 provides, on the average, a slight underestimate of the true population variance $\hat{\sigma}_x^2$. The smaller the sample, the greater the degree of underestimation. Multiplying the sample variance by $(n/n - 1)$ corrects it to an unbiased estimate of $\hat{\sigma}_x^2$.

$$s_x^2 = \frac{\Sigma(X - M)^2}{n - 1} = \frac{n\Sigma(X - M)^2}{(n - 1)n} = \frac{n}{n - 1}\sigma_x^2$$

Use of this formula can be illustrated in the following example: Suppose that the mean IQ of sophomore students (μ) at Griggs University were 120. A sample of 50 students is to be drawn at random from this population. What is the likelihood that the mean of this sample (M_1) will be greater than 125? This is equivalent to determining the proportion of the area under the normal curve which falls to the right of 125 (see Fig. 9-2). If one knew how far away from μ the score 125 is, in σ-units, this area could be determined directly from the normal-curve table. The appropriate σ-unit here is σ_M, which can be estimated as

(3) $$\sigma_M = \sqrt{s_x^2/n}, \quad \text{or as } \sqrt{\sigma_x^2/(n - 1)}$$

All one needs, therefore, to estimate the standard error of the mean is n, the sample size, and σ_x^2, the variance among raw-score measures in the sample. Say the latter quantity turned out to be 225. Then

$$\sigma_M = \sqrt{\tfrac{225}{49}} = 2.14, \text{ approximately.}$$

Referring to Fig. 9-2, we can see that if the population mean is 120 the value 125 would fall at $CR = (125 - 120)/2.14$, or about $2.33\sigma_M$ units above the parameter. The table of proportionate areas under various segments of the normal curve (Appendix Table B) shows that the area to the right of 2.33 σ-units is

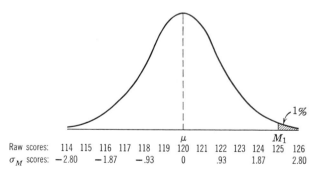

| Raw scores: | 114 | 115 | 116 | 117 | 118 | 119 | 120 | 121 | 122 | 123 | 124 | 125 | 126 |
| σ_M scores: | −2.80 | | −1.87 | | −.93 | | 0 | | .93 | | 1.87 | | 2.80 |

Fig. 9-2. Conversion of raw score units to units of the normal distribution. A sample mean of 125 or larger would occur in about 1% of all samples drawn from the population, assuming that $\mu = 120$, $\hat{\sigma}_x^2 = 230$, and $n = 50$.

about 1% of the total. This can be translated in the present example to: the probability of obtaining a mean IQ of 125 or larger in a random sample of 50 college sophomores drawn from this population (whose mean IQ is 120) is about one in a hundred.

Variance of a Proportion

Another kind of sample statistic one might compute is p, the proportion of subjects who possess attribute X. In other words, X is scored dichotomously— 1 if the subject possesses it, 0 if he does not—and p is the sample mean of an attribute scored in this fashion. The error variance of p could therefore be estimated by the same formula used for estimating $\sigma_M{}^2$, but a much shorter method is provided when appropriate substitutions are made for terms in the formula. It can be shown that the variance of a dichotomous distribution (i.e., a distribution consisting only of scores 0 and 1) is equal to $\hat{p}\hat{q}$, where $\hat{p}$ is the proportion of people possessing the attribute in the total population and $\hat{q} = 1 - \hat{p}$. From any single sample, $\hat{p}$ must be estimated; this is done directly from p. So, by applying the formula for estimating the variance of the mean from $s_x{}^2$, we have

$$(4) \qquad\qquad \sigma_p{}^2 = \frac{\hat{p}\hat{q}}{n}$$

which is estimated as pq/n. Use of this formula in hypothesis testing is illustrated in the body of the chapter (p. 203).

Variance of the Difference between Means

A null hypothesis frequently used states that the difference between the means of two independent samples is zero. Such a hypothesis might be established in the following context: the researcher draws a simple random sample from the student body and administers an adjustment inventory. On analyzing the results he finds that the 30 women in the sample had an average score of 40, whereas the 60 men averaged only 38. Accepting the inventory as an adequate operational definition of adjustment, could he conclude from these results that female students tend to be better adjusted than males? Using the null hypothesis of zero difference in the parameter means, he sets up a critical ratio

$$\mathrm{CR} = \frac{MD - \mu D}{\sigma_{MD}} = \frac{2 - 0}{\sigma_{MD}}$$

It can be shown that for two independent samples * the standard error of the difference between means is

$$(5) \qquad\qquad \sigma_{MD} = \sqrt{\sigma_{M_1}^2 + \sigma_{M_2}^2}$$

where $\sigma_{M_1}^2$ is the variance of the first sample mean and $\sigma_{M_2}^2$ is the variance of the second sample mean, both estimated from the formula

$$\sigma_M{}^2 = \frac{s_x{}^2}{n}$$

---

* In a simple random sample, since all subjects are selected independently of one another, any two groups will likewise be independent.

Let us assume that computation from the sample shows the estimates of population variance in adjustment scores to be 36 for both men and women. The critical ratio then becomes

$$CR = \frac{2}{\sqrt{\frac{36}{30} + \frac{36}{60}}} = 1.49$$

The table of areas under the normal curve (Appendix Table B) shows that a critical ratio at least this large could have arisen by chance about 14 times out of a hundred (considering both the condition in which female adjustment was superior and that in which male adjustment was superior), so that the null hypothesis could be rejected with about 14% chance of making a Type I error. (Ordinarily, one would not reject it under these circumstances; rather he would prefer to get another sample of sufficient size to permit a difference of this magnitude to turn out statistically significant if it were to occur again. See Supplement C to this chapter for a method of determining optimum sample size.)

The significance of a difference between two proportions or percentages can be determined in analogous fashion. In accordance with the null hypothesis that parameter proportions are identical, the best estimate of their error variance can be made from the total sample proportion p_t. So the appropriate critical ratio would be

$$CR = \frac{(p_1 - p_2) - 0}{\sqrt{p_t q_t / n_1 + p_t q_t / n_2}}$$

where

$$p_t = \frac{n_1 p_1 + n_2 p_2}{n_1 + n_2} \quad \text{and} \quad q_t = 1 - p_t$$

If $n_1 = 25$, $p_1 = .40$, $n_2 = 50$, and $p_2 = .20$, then

$$CR = \frac{.20}{\sqrt{[(.27)(.73)/25] + [(.27)(.73)/50]}} = 1.84$$

As reference to Appendix Table B will show, a critical ratio of this size permits rejection of the null hypothesis (against a two-directional alternative) with $\alpha = .07$, approximately.

B. Effect of Sample Size on Error Variance

It can be seen from the formulas in Supplement A that sample size plays a systematic role in determining error variance in a simple random sample. In general, the standard error of a sample mean is inversely proportional to the square root of n. In order to cut the sampling error (σ_M) in half, the sample size must be quadrupled. This is a constant effect of n for all samples. In addition, there are certain limiting conditions in which the size of the sample has other effects as well.

Small Samples

In the first of these conditions n is small. There is no absolute amount at which n suddenly becomes "small," but we are speaking generally of the range below 30 or 40. At these sizes means from successive samples are actually more variable than would be judged from the normally distributed CR. So it is necessary to refer to a different mathematical function in order to make accurate estimates of the probability of Type I errors. The general function is the t-distribution, which arises from the statistic, $t = (M - \mu)/s_M$. t is a ratio between (1) the deviation of a sample mean (M) from its parameter (μ) and (2) an unbiased estimate $(s_M = s_x{}^2/n)$ of the standard deviation of means, calculated from the sample at hand. It will be recalled that the critical ratio is quite similar $[CR = (M - \mu)/\sigma_M]$, that is, a ratio between a particular deviation and its corresponding standard deviation. But σ_M is the actual standard deviation of means about the parameter μ (which could only be determined exactly if the total population were available), whereas s_M is an estimate calculated from a particular sample. Use of s_M in place of σ_M in the formula for CR (see p. 222) introduces some distortion —which is, however, not serious when n is large. With n small, CR calculated with s_M would underestimate α, for deviant values occur more frequently than the normal distribution indicates.

The t-distribution yields a more accurate estimate of α with small samples. It refers to a family of curves (see Fig. 9-3) rather than just one, as was the case for the normal distribution. All curves of the t-family are symmetrical, but they are more peaked and their tails are higher than the normal curve—these characteristics becoming more marked as n gets smaller. Tables of areas under the t-curve, for varying n, are available (see Appendix

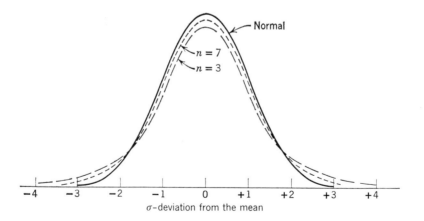

Fig. 9-3. Normal compared with t-distribution for $n = 3$ and $n = 7$. Reprinted with permission from Q. McNemar, *Psychological statistics,* copyright 1955, John Wiley & Sons, Inc.

Table C). They are generally set up differently from the normal curve tables. Instead of showing proportionate areas under the curve for varying values of t, they show the size of t that is required in order to leave 10, 5, or 1% (sometimes also 0.1%) under *both* tails of the distribution. (Since the distributions are all symmetrical, the area under one tail is always half the tabled percentage value.) The required size of t will vary, depending on n, so that the tables are usually set up for all sample sizes up to 30 or so. Also, the n that appears in the left-hand column is not the size of the sample but rather the *degrees of freedom* or the number of independent scores involved in the particular statistic. The mean, for instance, includes n - 1 independent scores, since, having selected that many, we must fix the last score in order to hold the mean constant.

Though the typical assessment research involves samples of sufficient size to warrant use of the normal curve table, most experimental studies (some systematic assessment, too) are performed on samples of less than 30 per group. In these cases the researcher should compute a t-ratio in the same way as he would estimate CR, but then refer to the t-distribution table, under the appropriate degrees of freedom, in order to determine whether his obtained t-ratio is large enough to warrant rejection of the null hypothesis at a given significance level.

Small Populations

The other limiting condition in which a new effect of sample size occurs is that in which n is large relative to N, the total population size. Here again there is no sharp dividing point at which n suddenly becomes relatively large rather than relatively small, but the effect is likely to assume practical importance when the ratio of n to N is as large, say, as $\frac{1}{10}$ or greater. In such a case one speaks of a *finite population* rather than of an *infinite population*. Of course, it is clear that all empirical populations are finite, but most of them are so large in relation to the sample size that they can be treated as infinite; this simplifies the calculation of sampling variances, since the ordinary formulas assume *sampling with replacement*. This means conceptually that once an element has been selected for the sample it is put back in the population so that it can conceivably be drawn again in the same sample. But virtually all practical sampling is done *without replacement;* that is, an element, once selected, is removed from the population so that it cannot be chosen again. When this is done, the sample has no chance of internal duplication or redundancy; each element in it adds new information. Although in sampling with replacement the smallest mean theoretically possible would be the smallest score value in the population (it might, by chance, be selected n times), in sampling without replacement the smallest possible mean would be the mean of the n smallest scores. Thus the variance among means of samples drawn without replacement is smaller than that of samples drawn with replacement.

An appropriate correction for samples drawn without replacement is provided if the estimated error variance is multiplied by the constant, $(N - n)/$

$N - 1$, which is very nearly equal to $[1 - (n/N)]$. In other words, the error variance for samples drawn without replacement is smaller than the usual estimate of σ_M^2 by an amount nearly equal to $(n/N)\sigma_M^2$. This is a trivial amount in most studies, but it can make a difference in "finite populations" —that is, those in which n is large relative to N. Hence it is sometimes called the *finite multiplier*, to indicate the condition when its use is worthwhile.

In most research using simple random samples the finite multiplier can be ignored, since it will not affect the variance estimates appreciably. With stratified and clustered samples the number of elements chosen from any subpopulation is frequently a considerable proportion of the total, hence estimates of error variance can often be substantially improved by appropriate application of the finite multiplier.

C. Determining the Required Sample Size

Perhaps the question most frequently asked by student researchers is, "How many subjects should I get?" The query is commonly answered by statements like, "Oh, take about a hundred," or "Take as many as you can get," or a pseudosophisticated, "Get at least thirty so that you can use large sample statistics." All of these answers are a bit too rough-and-ready to be really helpful, for they do not take into account the basic considerations of statistical induction as they apply to the problem at hand. Without precise definitions of the kind of sample, the null hypothesis, a critical alternative hypothesis, and the desired probabilities of Type I and II errors, the question is unanswerable within the framework of statistical theory. (Of course, sample size might be determined from other considerations, such as available time and money, but this is a different matter.)

If the researcher can say in advance how large a population difference he wants to be able to detect and the desired probability of detecting it and can obtain at least a rough estimate of the variance of the attribute in the population, then the required sample size can be estimated. Let us assume, for purposes of illustration, that simple random sampling is to be used, for that makes the error variance formulas simpler. (The problem is soluble for complex samples as well, but considerably more complicated.) Say that one wishes to test the hypothesis that the mean annual income of employees at his institution is less than the national mean for similar institutions of $10,000. The null hypothesis, then, is that the two populations do not differ in mean income; in other words, that $\mu D = 0$. This is to be rejected at the .05 level of significance, which means that 5% of the samples from this hypothetical population will lead to rejection of the null hypothesis and 95% will not.

A specific alternative hypothesis is also needed. This will be set at the minimum difference from the null value which is deemed of practical consequence. Say that the researcher wants to be able to detect a difference in the predicted direction of $300 or larger. The specific alternative hypothesis is established that $\mu D_1 = \$300$. If a difference this large does occur, he wants to have nine chances in ten of detecting it, so β is set at .10. This means that 10% of the random samples from this second hypothetical population would result in rejection of the alternative hypothesis, whereas 90% of them would not.

The problem is to select from each of the two populations a sample of such size that two particular sampling distributions of mean differences can be inferred, one around μD_0 ($0) and the other around μD_1 ($300). These sampling distributions will have the same standard deviation (since this is set by sample size), and they are to overlap each other in such a way that a common point, MD_h, can be found which cuts 5% off the right-hand tail of the first distribution and 10% off the left-hand tail of the second. (See diagram in Fig. 9-4.) This is the point at which a sample mean difference might be found that would lead to rejection of the null hypothesis (at $\alpha = .05$), since it falls at an improbable distance from μD_0, but that would not lead to a rejection of the alternative hypothesis (at $\beta = .10$), since it is within the acceptable range of random error from μD_1. This hypothetical mean difference is indicated as MD_h. Any other mean difference to the right of MD_h would accomplish the same purpose—rejection of the null hypothesis in favor of the alternative of a $300 difference (or more); any mean difference to the left of MD_h would not permit rejection of the null hypothesis at the specified significance level (or, if too far to the left, would require its rejection, but not in favor of the desired alternative).

The location of this point can be found quite directly from the designated α- and β-levels. Reference to the normal curve table (Appendix Table B) shows that for α to be .05, MD_h must be 1.64 σ-units to the right of μD_0; and, in order for β to be .10, MD_h must be 1.28 σ-units to the left of μD_1. Since both sampling distributions have the same σ, the total distance between μD_0 and μD_1 (i.e., $300) must be divided by MD_h so that the left- and right-hand portions will be in the ratio of 1.64 to 1.28. This is accomplished if MD_h is approximately $168.49. More generally, when $\mu D_0 = 0$

$$MD_h = \frac{CR_0}{CR_0 + CR_1}(\mu D_1)$$

which in this example $$= \frac{1.64}{1.64 + 1.28}(\$300) = \$168.49$$

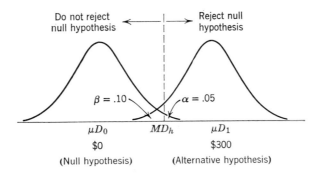

Fig. 9-4. Sampling distributions of MD around μD_0 and μD_1.

For convenience it will be assumed that the total sample n is to be divided equally between n_1 subjects randomly selected from the researcher's institution and n_2 subjects randomly selected from the remaining institutions in the country. (This equal allocation is appropriate if the variances among salaries are approximately equal in the two subpopulations.)

The required size of n_j (either n_1 or n_2) can now be determined either from the μD_0 or from the μD_1 distribution. In the first case this consists in setting n_j so that the point \$168.49 falls exactly 1.64 CR units from the mean of \$0.00. In the second distribution n_j would be set so that \$168.49 falls exactly 1.28 CR units from the mean of \$300. Either of these procedures will yield the same n_j; we shall work with the first.

The general formula for computing a critical ratio for a distribution of differences between means sampled from the same population is

$$\text{CR} = \frac{MD - \mu D}{\sigma_{MD}} = \frac{MD - \mu D}{\sqrt{\sigma_{M_1}^2 + \sigma_{M_2}^2}} = \frac{MD - \mu D}{\sqrt{\acute{\sigma}_1{}^2/n_1 + \acute{\sigma}_2{}^2/n_2}} \qquad \text{(see formula 5, p. 222)}$$

In this instance we know that CR is to equal 1.64 (since that is the value required to set α at .05). The difference, $MD - \mu D$, is \$168.49 (the difference between the null parameter and the minimal value of MD which will permit rejection of the null hypothesis at $\alpha = .05$). Since n_1 and n_2 (the sample sizes for "own" and "other" institutions, respectively) are to be set equal (to n_j), the fractions under the radical can be replaced by $\acute{\sigma}_1{}^2/n_j$ and $\acute{\sigma}_2{}^2/n_j$. This leaves us, then, with n_j, $\sigma_1{}^2$, and $\acute{\sigma}_2{}^2$ still unknown. In order to find n_j, it is therefore necessary to have values for $\acute{\sigma}_1{}^2$ and $\acute{\sigma}_2{}^2$. Ordinarily it is reasonable to assume that they are equal (though the unequal case can be handled, too); and their common value $\acute{\sigma}^2$ can generally be estimated, at least roughly, from available information. Suppose one has reason to believe that the variance in incomes for this population of employees is about \$1,000,000. (To be on the safe side, it is better to overestimate $\acute{\sigma}^2$ than to underestimate it.)

If these various required and assumed values are placed into the formula for the critical ratio, this yields

$$\text{CR} = \frac{MD - \mu D}{\sqrt{\acute{\sigma}^2/n_j + \acute{\sigma}^2/n_j}}$$

$$1.64 = \frac{168.49}{\sqrt{1,000,000/n_j + 1,000,000/n_j}}$$

Solving for n_j yields 189.5, which means that 190 subjects must be selected at random from the home institution and another 190 subjects from the remaining institutions in order to solve the problem as posed; that is, a total of 380 subjects, distributed equally between the two populations, will permit one to reject the null hypothesis of no difference in mean incomes at the .05 level of significance and to have nine chances in ten of detecting a mean difference as small as \$300, if it exists—provided, of course, that the variance in incomes which actually turns up in the selected samples does not exceed \$1,000,000.

Since both MD_h and n_j are calculated from the same data, it is possible to find n_j directly, without computing MD_h first. This can be done by means of a formula (see Cochran & Cox, 1957, p. 20) which is derived from the foregoing:

$$n_j \geq \frac{2\dot{\sigma}^2(\mathrm{CR}_0 + \mathrm{CR}_1)^2}{(\mu D_1)^2}$$

where n_j is the required sample size in each of the two populations,

$\dot{\sigma}^2$ is the true population variance of the attribute under study (usually estimated),

CR_0 is the value of the critical ratio required to reject the null hypothesis in the desired direction at the specified α,[*]

CR_1 is the value of the critical ratio required to reject the alternative hypothesis in the direction of the null parameter at the specified β.[†]

μD_1 is the value of the alternative hypothesis concerning the difference between means, that is, the difference that one wants to be able to detect.

In the present example

$$n_j \geq \frac{2(1,000,000)(1.64 + 1.28)^2}{(300)^2}$$
$$= 190$$

The researcher may find that this is a larger sample than he can afford to study. If so, then the problem is insoluble practically, even though not theoretically. With this information, however, one is also in a position to beat a hasty retreat from his initial requirements and to decide that less precise, or less certain, information would be acceptable. If he will settle for detecting a minimum difference of $500 in the predicted direction, he can get along with just 69 subjects in each group, holding α and β constant at .05 and .10, respectively.

[*] For many research problems only one direction of departure from the null parameter would be of interest. Thus in the present example the researcher wishes to find out if his institution's mean income is lower than the national average. In such cases the values of the critical ratio can be read directly from the table of normal curve functions (Appendix Table B). If, however, one wishes to detect a difference between the two populations in either direction, then he must find the CR_0 and CR_1 which would include the required α or β in both tails of the sampling distribution combined. This is accomplished by finding in the normal curve table that CR which leaves $\alpha/2$ or $\beta/2$ in the tail that is tabled. In this case, for α equal to .05 and β equal to .10, $\mathrm{CR}_0 = 1.96$, and $\mathrm{CR}_1 = 1.64$; the required n_j would then be 288.

[†] All of these estimates have been made on the basis of formulas for simple random sampling, with replacement. If stratified sampling is used, or if the population is small compared to the sample size, then the same precision of estimates can be attained with smaller n_j than indicated here. When n_j turns out to be less than 30 or so, the normal curve table no longer provides a good approximation to α and β. So one must use the table of the t-distribution (Appendix Table C) instead and pick those values of t (rather than CR) which, depending on the size of n, will yield the desired α and β. See chapter Supplements B and D.

If the requirement for β is relaxed to .50, but α and μD_1 are still left at .05 and \$300, respectively, a sample size of 60 subjects in each population would be sufficient. (This would imply, however, that the obtained sample difference in means would have to be greater than \$300 to permit rejection of the null hypothesis; such a result would have only a 50% probability of occurring, even if the parameter difference in means actually were \$300.)

Any of these compromises will seem less attractive than the original stipulations. Perhaps the researcher can accept them with greater equanimity if he realizes that no matter what specifications for α, β, and μ_1 are provided they can yield a result which has only probable rather than certain validity. The sample size estimated from this procedure is not certain to detect the required difference, no matter how small α and β are set. The unusual sample is still possible—one with too large a variance or one whose mean departs markedly from the parameter in the direction of the value assumed under the null hypothesis. If such a sample should occur, then a Type II error in inference will be made in spite of the precautions taken against it.

D. Estimating Error Variances from Complex Samples

Clustered Samples

The usual condition for clustered sampling obtains when the elements to be studied fall in natural groups and are to be selected that way. The groups may be approximately the same size or of widely varying sizes. The entire group of elements or only a subsample of them may be chosen for study. Each of these situations calls for somewhat different formulas for estimating the variances of sample statistics. In all of the examples we use the same notation:

 C = the number of clusters in the total population
 c = the number of clusters selected for the sample
 N = the number of elements (e.g., people) in the total population
 N_i = the number of elements in the ith cluster
 n_i = the number of elements from the ith cluster selected for the sample
 n = the total number of elements in the sample
 M = the mean of the entire sample
 M_i = the mean of the ith cluster (where i runs from 1 to c)

If all clusters are approximately the same size (N_i is constant, roughly) and all elements in the randomly selected clusters are studied ($n_i = N_i$), then the situation is exactly analogous to the sampling of individuals, in which a single subject's score is the mean of a number of standardly elicited responses; that is,

 c, the number of selected clusters, is analogous to n, the number of individual subjects in a simple random sample and
 M_i, the mean of a single cluster, is analogous to X_i, an individual subject's score on a test consisting of multiple items

Thus the error variance of the total sample mean can be estimated as

$$(6) \qquad \sigma^2_{M_c} = \left(\frac{C - c}{C - 1}\right) \frac{\sum\limits_{i=1}^{c} (M_i - M)^2}{c(c - 1)}$$

which is analogous to $\sigma^2_{M_r} = \left(\frac{N - n}{N - 1}\right) \frac{\sum\limits_{i=1}^{n} (X_i - M)^2}{n(n - 1)}$

used to estimate the variance of a mean from a simple random sample (see chapter Supplement A). We include the "finite multiplier" here for the sake of completeness.

The variance of a clustered sample ($\sigma^2_{M_c}$) will normally be larger than that of a simple random sample ($\sigma^2_{M_r}$) of equal n by an amount expressed in the following equation:

$$\frac{\sigma^2_{M_c}}{\sigma^2_{M_r}} = 1 + \rho(\bar{n}_i - 1)$$

where $\bar{n}_i$ is the average number of selected elements per cluster and ρ is the coefficient of intraclass correlation, representing the degree of similarity among elements in the same cluster, relative to randomly selected elements. This equation shows that to the extent ρ is large and positive $\sigma^2_{M_c}$ will be larger than $\sigma^2_{M_r}$; so use of the latter with a clustered sample would generally lead to an underestimate of the error variance of the mean.

When the cluster sizes vary considerably (but $n_i = N_i$), the appropriate formula is

$$(7) \qquad \sigma^2_{M_c} = \left(\frac{C - c}{C - 1}\right) \frac{\sum\limits_{i=1}^{c} \left(\frac{n_i}{\bar{n}_i}\right)^2 (M_i - M)^2}{c(c - 1)}$$

which is similar to (6), except that the squared deviation of each cluster mean about the total sample mean is weighted by the square of the cluster's relative size.

Multistage Samples

Both (6) and (7) take into account only the variance between clusters, not the within-cluster variance. This is because there is no error in estimating the cluster means, since all elements within the selected clusters are assessed. If subsampling were employed, however, there would be some error variance within, as well as between, clusters. This is allowed for by the second term in the following formula for estimating the error variance from a multistage sample.

$$(8) \qquad \sigma^2_{M_c} = \left(\frac{C - c}{C - 1}\right) \frac{\sum\limits_{i=1}^{c} (M_i - M)^2}{c(c - 1)} + \frac{\sum\limits_{i=1}^{c} \sigma^2_{M_i}}{Cc}$$

where $\sigma^2_{M_i}$ is the variance of the mean of the ith cluster, estimated as

$$\sigma^2_{M_i} = \left(\frac{N_i - n_i}{N_i - 1}\right) \frac{\sum\limits_{j=1}^{n_i} (X_{ij} - M_i)^2}{n_i(n_i - 1)}$$

(This is just the ordinary formula for estimating the variance of the mean from a simple random sample, with the "finite multiplier" added, and some further notation to show that this refers to the mean of a particular cluster, i, over the j elements within it.)

If the cluster sizes (n_i) vary a great deal, (8) will tend to overestimate the error variance. This condition can be corrected in either of two ways— by appropriate modification in the formula or by obtaining approximately equal clusters with the method known as "cluster sampling with probabilities proportional to size." The curious reader can explore these procedures in the chapter references (e.g., Cochran, 1953; Hansen, Hurwitz, & Madow, 1953; Kish, 1953).

Stratified Samples

Stratified sampling is worthwhile when the elements of the population can be grouped a priori into categories of an attribute that is correlated with the one under investigation. If every element is listed, then it is necessary only to arrange the list so that all members of any single category are grouped together. Then within each category a simple random sample is chosen. Sometimes strata can be established, but no complete list of all elements within them is available. So it is necessary to build up partial lists by the technique of clustered or multistage sampling within strata. Depending on the method of sampling within strata—simple random, clustered, or multistage—the formula for estimating error variance will differ somewhat; but the general effect of stratification is to eliminate from the error variance the portion that is due to differences among stratum means. The following notation is used for the formulas to be presented here:

N = the total number of elements in the population
n = the total number of elements in the sample
k = the total number of strata (in the population or in the sample)
N_h = the total number of elements in the hth stratum (where h runs from 1 to k)
n_h = the number of sample elements selected from the hth stratum
M = the mean of the entire sample
M_h = the mean of the hth stratum (estimated from the sample)

The general formula for the variance of the mean of a stratified sample is

(9) $$\sigma^2_{M_s} = \sum_{h=1}^{k} \left(\frac{N_h}{N}\right)^2 \sigma^2_{M_h}$$

which means that the total error variance equals the weighted sum of the error variances within each of the separate strata. The weight used for each stratum is the square of the proportion of the total population $(N_h/N)^2$ which that stratum includes. (In a proportionate stratified sample this will equal $(n_h/n)^2$, or the square of the proportion of the total sample yielded by that stratum.)

The relation of this estimate to that used for a simple random sample is as follows:

$$\sigma^2_{M_s} = \sigma^2_{M_r} - \sum_{h=1}^{k} \frac{N_h}{N} (M_h - M)^2$$

which says that the variance of a mean of a stratified sample $(\sigma^2_{M_s})$ is less than the corresponding variance for a simple random sample $(\sigma^2_{M_r})$ by the amount indicated in the right-hand term. This term represents the (weighted) variance of stratum means (M_h) about the total population mean (M). To the extent that the stratum means differ among themselves on the attribute under study, $\sigma^2_{M_s}$ will be smaller than $\sigma^2_{M_r}$; in other words, stratification will yield an increase in sample efficiency.

The way in which $\sigma^2_{M_h}$ is calculated will depend on the method of sampling used within strata. For simple random sampling, (1) on p. 220 is appropriate; with clustered or multistage sampling, one uses appropriate formulas like (6), (7), and (8) (p. 231). It is not even necessary that the same sampling procedure be used in all strata, so long as the samples are independently drawn and the appropriate estimation formula used for each, since then each sample yields an unbiased estimate of its own stratum variance. $\sigma^2_{M_h}$, the error variance for the total stratified sample, can be calculated from the weighted sum specified in (9).

Systematic Samples

Let us now return to the problem of estimating the sampling error from a systematic sample. This is one in which all elements of the population are listed in some order (hopefully random), and every kth element is drawn for inclusion in the sample. The problem in estimating error variance is that the listing may not be random with respect to the attribute under investigation. If there is periodicity, a clustered sample may result; if the elements are ordered in a manner that is correlated with the crucial attribute, the sample will be stratified. With only a single systematic sample, there is no way of knowing whether it is clustered or stratified. In order to find out, one needs two or more samples; that is, instead of selecting a single sample, with sampling interval k, one could select c independent systematic samples, each starting with a (different) random number and using the sampling interval ck. The variance of the total mean from all c samples is estimated from

$$(10) \qquad \sigma^2_{M(sys)} = \frac{\sum_{i=1}^{c} (M_i - M)^2}{c(c - 1)}$$

where M_i is the mean of a particular systematic sample,

M is the mean of all samples combined,

c is the number of different systematic samples chosen.

This is the between-clusters component of the error variance of a clustered sample (Equation 6, p. 231). There is no within-clusters component because each sample constitutes a complete cluster. Now, if there were indeed periodicity in the list, the means of the various samples would differ considerably, and this fact would be reflected in a larger sampling error than would have been obtained from a simple random selection. But if the list were stratified, then the means of the several systematic samples would be very close together, and this estimate would yield a smaller error variance than the formula for simple random sampling.

Hypothesis Testing with Complex Samples

The main consequence of a complex sample design, such as those treated in this supplement, is to change the formula for estimating the error variance of the mean (or other statistic). The basic principles of hypothesis testing discussed in the body of the chapter are not altered, and the form of the critical ratio for testing a null hypothesis is identical. In the first example of Supplement A, for instance, a critical ratio was established to estimate the probability of selecting a sample mean greater than 125 from a population with $\mu = 120$:

$$CR = \frac{M - \mu}{\sigma_M} = \frac{125 - 120}{\sigma_M}$$

If, instead of simple random sampling, one had used stratified, clustered, or multistage sampling, the only thing that would be changed would be the method of estimating σ_M. Instead of (1), one would use (6), (7), (8), or (9)—whichever was appropriate to the particular sampling method.

In the second example of Supplement A the significance of the difference between two sample means was tested by the critical ratio

$$CR = \frac{MD - \mu D}{\sigma_{M_1 - M_2}} = \frac{M_1 - M_2}{\sqrt{\sigma_{M_1}^2 + \sigma_{M_2}^2}}$$

The way in which $\sigma_{M_1}^2$ and $\sigma_{M_2}^2$ are estimated will depend on how the two samples were selected, but in other respects the critical ratio is handled identically with that for a simple random sample.

REFERENCES

Backman, C. W. Sampling mass media content: the use of the cluster design. *Amer. sociol. Rev.*, 1956, **21**, 729–733.

Cochran, W. G. *Sampling techniques.* New York: Wiley, 1953.

Cochran, W. G., & Cox, Gertrude M. *Experimental designs.* (2nd Ed.) New York: Wiley, 1957.

Deming, W. E. *Some theory of sampling.* New York: Wiley, 1950.

Dixon, W. J., & Massey, F. J. *Introduction to statistical analysis.* (2nd Ed.) New York: McGraw-Hill, 1957.

Hansen, M. H., Hurwitz, W. N., & Madow, W. G. *Sample survey methods and theory.* New York: Wiley, 1953. 2 vols.

Kish, L. A two-stage sample of a city. *Amer. sociol. Rev.,* 1952, **17,** 761–769.

Kish, L. Selection of the sample. In L. Festinger & D. Katz (Eds.), *Research methods in the behavioral sciences.* New York: Dryden, 1953.

McCarthy, P. J. Sample design. In Marie Jahoda, M. Deutsch, & S. W. Cook (Eds.), *Research methods in social relations.* (Vol. II.) New York: Dryden, 1951.

McNemar, Q. *Psychological statistics.* (2nd Ed.) New York: Wiley, 1955.

The RAND Corporation. *A million random digits with 100,000 normal deviates.* Glencoe, Ill.: Free Press, 1955.

Treloar, A. E. *Random sampling distributions.* Minneapolis: Burgess, 1943.

Wallis, W. A., & Roberts, H. V. *Statistics: a new approach.* Glencoe, Ill.: Free Press, 1957.

Yates, F. *Sampling methods for censuses and surveys.* (2nd Ed.) London: Griffin, 1953.

CHAPTER 10

Experimental design: assigning subjects to conditions

In observational and assessment studies one can go ahead and measure the variables as soon as the subjects have been selected. In experimental research there is an intervening step: subjects must be exposed to certain critical conditions before (or while) their scores on the dependent variable are obtained. It is this step which, for many researchers, makes an experiment a more convincing study than either naturalistic observation or systematic assessment. When the investigator himself manipulates the independent variable and standardizes other features of the experimental conditions, then he is in a better position to conclude that the manipulated variable, and not some other extraneous influence, is responsible for observed systematic differences in behavior.

"Manipulation of the independent variable" is a shorthand way of referring to the systematic assignment of subjects to the experimental conditions. This can be accomplished in a great many different ways: a single subject can be exposed to changing values of a stimulus, as is often done in psychophysical studies; or the sample of subjects can be enlarged and a number of them exposed to all values of the stimulus. Alternatively, some of the subjects might be exposed to one set of values and others to a different set. Under such an assignment procedure, the independent variable may not actually be manipulated for any particular subject; instead the several conditions to which the different subjects (or groups of subjects) are exposed constitute the values of the independent variable.

It is not even absolutely necessary that the researcher actually create the experimental conditions himself. Though in many psychological experiments the several values of the independent variable are under the investigator's direct control, it is easy to conceive of valid experiments in which this is not the case. If one wanted to assess the relative effects of rural and urban environments on the mental health of immigrants, samples from this population could be randomly assigned to various geographical areas, differing in the degree of urbanization; then some index of mental health (such as the incidence of schizophrenia) could subsequently be computed for each group to see if interpretable differences emerged. In such an experiment the researcher himself would probably have no control over the actual living experiences encountered by the immigrants; yet he could afford to be fairly certain that any systematic differences in rates of mental illness were attributable to these experiences rather than to pre-existing characteristics of the subjects, since these latter attributes had presumably been equated by the random assignment procedure.

The essential feature of an experiment, we would suggest, is controlled assignment of subjects to conditions. The independent variable which is necessarily under the experimenter's control is exposure of subjects to the conditions; the actual conditions themselves need not be. This contrasts with a naturalistic or systematic assessment study in which one must take subjects as he finds them—exposed to whatever conditions they happen to have encountered in the absence of experimental intervention. One might argue that somewhere between these two lie ex post facto experiments in which one studies the consequences of an experience among people who have been exposed to it, in comparison with a group who were not exposed. Such a designation is likely to be misleading if the word "experiment" is interpreted to imply that the independent variable can readily be identified as the presence or absence of the critical experience. If the researcher had no control over who was exposed to the experience and who was not, then it is quite possible that something else about the people or their environment determined exposure in the first place, hence that the "something else" rather than the experience itself may have constituted the critical independent variable. An ex post facto "experiment" is therefore not different from a systematic assessment study.

A kind of research in which psychologists frequently participate is the study of educational methods. One class of students may be taught by an experimental technique and another class by a traditional technique. This can properly be called an experiment if students are randomly assigned to the two classes. If they know in advance which method is to be used and are permitted to volunteer for one class or the other, then any subsequent difference between the classes cannot legitimately be attributed to the teaching method; for pre-existing characteristics of the subjects may have disposed them to volunteer for a particular method of instruction, and it might have been these pre-existing characteristics that accounted for their response to the method or even for their postcourse achievement regardless of teaching method. The kind of data yielded by an "experiment" in which subjects assign themselves to the conditions is actually no different from that yielded by an assessment study. In this research strategy one can inquire about what sorts of experiences subjects have already had, or are undergoing at present, to see if these relate to contemporary psychological characteristics. In the study of teaching methods with self-assigned subjects the fact that the researcher watches them as they undergo the presumably critical experience does not mean that he can identify the efficient independent variable any better than he could have from interviewing the subjects afterward.

For these reasons we shall restrict our use of the term "experiment" to those research designs in which the investigator himself determines who shall be assigned to what conditions when, and the subjects have no say in the matter. Also, for economy of illustration, we limit our discussion here to preliminary experimental designs. In Chapter 4 these designs were distinguished from systematic designs in that they provided for just two or three conditions of the independent variable rather than for a fairly large number. The familiar experimental-versus-control group study is an example of a preliminary design in that only two values of the independent variable are represented—presence and absence. Even the two-condition design can be complicated considerably by the simultaneous use of two or more independent variables; such multivariate arrangements are discussed after an initial presentation of two-condition designs involving just one independent variable. Systematic designs require multiple categories of the independent variables; this kind of design is used far more frequently in contemporary psychological research than is implied by our restriction to two-category illustrations.

In the body of the chapter several methods of subject assignment are treated in some detail. Just as in sample design (Chapter 9), each method is associated with a different statistical procedure for testing the significance of the experimental effect. How the error variance is estimated will depend, in part, on how subjects are assigned to conditions. Appropriate formulas for each design are presented in the chapter supplement, with computational illustrations. Although other comparisons are also frequently of interest, all our illustrations involve differences between means, which are descriptively appropriate for interval scales. However, these formulas are also correct for other scale types as well, since the estimates of sampling variance are indifferent to the scale type which the data represent. If the investigator is concerned with *describing* noninterval-scale data appropriately, he may wish to use some nonparametric statistics and their associated significance tests. These can be found in Mosteller & Bush (1954), Siegel (1956), and Smith (1953).

The general principles of subject assignment can be readily applied to more than two conditions of a single, or of several, independent variables. However, in such systematic designs one is usually interested in describing more precise functional relations among the variables than is provided by a simple comparison of means. Therefore, a regression equation or some other descriptive statistic, such as r, h, or η, would be used, together with the significance tests appropriate to them. Some of these methods of statistical analysis are presented in Chapter 13; others can be found in the references listed at the end of this chapter (e.g., Cochran & Cox, 1957; Cox, 1958; Edwards, 1960; Finney, 1955; Fisher, 1942; Kempthorne, 1952; Lindquist, 1953; Maxwell, 1958).

The classification of preliminary experimental designs presented here is at best an arbitrary one which has gained some currency in the field. Every study raises its own peculiar design problems, and the arrangement of experimental conditions must, of course, fulfill the requirements of the particular problem being investigated. So the reader should be warned against trying to "learn the designs" in cookbook fashion, memorizing the recipes of each and applying them uncritically. One is more likely to develop a design suitable for his particular study if he forgets about names and considers instead just what arrangement of conditions would best meet the needs of his own experimental problem.

SOME VARIETIES OF TWO-CONDITION DESIGNS WITH A SINGLE INDEPENDENT VARIABLE

Simple Randomized Subjects Design

The simplest possible experimental arrangement requires two groups of subjects, each assigned to a different condition; the two conditions represent different values of a single independent variable. In the ideal form of this design two different simple random samples are selected from the desired population and then randomly assigned to the two conditions (see Chapter 9, pp. 208 f. for a description of simple random sampling). This can be accomplished in at least two ways: subjects may be drawn individually at random and assigned alternatingly to the conditions or two different simple random samples may be selected first and their group assignment determined subsequently by a flip of a coin. Whatever the technique, its essential feature is that all subjects be independently selected: no particular quotas are established, and the compositions of the two groups are not made to correspond, except as this may occur naturally in the process of random assignment.

One group is exposed to condition 1, the other to condition 2. In all other respects the two groups are treated alike. Members of both are then measured on the dependent variable. If the average measure in one group turns out to be different from that in the other, this is presumably the result of two things: chance differences between the two groups of subjects and the intended differences between the two conditions. It is, of course, the intended differences in which the experimenter is interested, so he computes a critical ratio to see if the obtained difference between means is sufficiently larger than would be expected on the basis of individual subject differences alone (see chapter supplement).* If it is, then he can be reasonably confident that the experimental conditions were indeed responsible for it.

In such a design the conditions are often called "experimental" and "control" if one group receives a particular treatment while the other does not. Thus one could assess the distracting effect of a loud noise on problem solving by using two groups, both of which must solve a set of problems, one in a noisy environment ("experimental") and the other in a quiet one ("control"). Sometimes such a designation is not appropriate, since each condition provides a basis of comparison or a

---

* Occasionally the results may be so clear-cut that no significance test is required—for example, if the two distributions of scores are nonoverlapping.

"control" for the other; for example, the legibility of writing could be compared under two degrees of magnification or the speed of rats' running on two maze floors of different slope.

Randomized Matched Subjects Design

One trouble with the simple randomized subjects design is that it depends completely upon random selection to obtain equivalent groups. By chance alone it is, of course, possible for the groups to start out different on the attribute the experiment is intended to affect, and the design provides no assurance that the groups are really comparable before the treatments are applied. At first sight, one might think that matching the groups on a pretest of the dependent variable would permit unequivocal interpretation of any posttest difference as due to the effect of the experimental manipulation. Some investigators, after randomly assigning subjects to one group or another and subsequently checking group means and dispersions on a pretest of the dependent variable, discard a few subjects to make the groups more similar before the experimental treatment is applied.

This procedure has disadvantages so severe that we recommend against it strongly. For one thing, if the sample of subjects had been randomly selected in the first place, the truncated sample no longer could be considered representative, hence results could not easily be generalized. Also, since it is the relatively deviant subjects who are most likely to be discarded, the dispersion of posttest scores is usually decreased, producing a reduced denominator in the significance test, hence an inflated estimate of the statistical significance of any obtained postexperimental difference. Finally, when subjects are discarded to make means more similar, typically one extreme (high scores) is lopped off from one group while the other extreme (low scores) is removed from the second. Regression effects are therefore not symmetrical, and any postexperimental difference may be either contaminated or offset by the upward regression of the group lacking high scores and the downward regression of the group lacking low scores. (See Campbell & Stanley, 1962, for a description of regression effects and the dangers of matching groups nonrandomly by discarding subjects.)

Although it is usually not possible by any method of random assignment to make absolutely sure that two experimental groups will start out exactly equal, the size of the pre-experimental difference can be controlled somewhat by a subject-matching technique which, nevertheless, does not bias the results, since assignment to the groups is random. Pretest measures on the dependent variable are obtained from

all potential subjects. These measures are paired so that cohorts'
scores are as close together as possible; one member of each cohort pair
is randomly assigned to one treatment and the other to the second
treatment. (A flip of the coin will result in appropriately random
assignment.)

To find out whether the experimental treatment was significantly
more effective than chance, each control subject's posttest score is subtracted from his experimental cohort's score, and these differences are
averaged over all pairs (keeping track of signs). The average difference between pairs will always be numerically equal to the difference
between the means of the experimental and control groups. With this
design, the error term against which the mean difference is compared
is based, not on the variability of subjects' scores, but on the variability of the pair *differences*. This variability is usually much smaller
than that of the subjects' scores, hence any particular size difference
between group means typically yields a larger critical ratio than in a
simple randomized subjects design; the randomized matched subjects
design thus tends to be more sensitive to the experimental effect.

The degree to which variability among difference scores is less than
the variability among the original scores will depend on how well the
posttest scores of the matched pairs correlate. The intent of subject
matching on the pretest is to pair experimental with control subjects
in a way that will produce a high correlation between the groups on
posttest scores; this correlation decreases the standard error of the
difference between group means below what it would be if the two
samples were independently selected (see chapter supplement).

The randomized matched subjects design is thus more powerful
than the simple randomized subjects design; it reduces the probability
of a Type II error, so that a smaller experimental-control group difference can be detected with the same number of subjects; or, alternatively, a smaller number of subjects can be used to detect the same
size difference. However, it is necessary to exercise care in subject
assignment in order to avoid a loss in generalizability of the results.
Ideally, the entire population would be pretested and a sample of experimental cohorts selected randomly from the population of matched
pairs, in order that one may know to what population the results
could be generalized. Ordinarily this is not feasible, but at least the
matching of all potential subjects must be complete, and the assignment of the members of each pair to the conditions must be determined randomly. If one or more subjects should be excluded because
an appropriate cohort could not be found, this would bias the sample
in an unknown fashion. It is essential to match every subject (even

though the matching is only approximate) and then assign randomly to the two conditions.

Matching Subjects on an Attribute Correlated with the Dependent Variable

Often it is impractical or impossible to match groups on a pretest of the dependent variable. Perhaps the attribute is not yet manifest; perhaps the researcher has not yet developed a measure of it at the time subjects must be selected; or perhaps he does not want them to find out what the experiment is all about by testing them first. It may still be possible to match them on some other related characteristics that *can* be measured conveniently. Thus, in an experiment designed to increase IQ, if subjects were too young to yield stable measures of IQ at the time they were selected, perhaps they could be matched on family income level or on parents' education—variables that are known to be somewhat related to children's intelligence—before assignment to the two experimental conditions. Matching experimental subjects on a correlated attribute has the effect of reducing at least to some degree the differences between cohort pairs on the dependent variable that the experiment is designed to affect. Thus, even following exposure to the experimental conditions, there should be less variability in difference-scores (i.e., differences between cohorts) than in the raw scores themselves, hence a smaller error term. To the extent that this turns out to be the case, the experiment is more efficient than it would have been with only a randomized subjects design.

Exact matching of cohorts, although desirable, is not absolutely necessary. An approximate matching (either by a pretest of the dependent variable or by one or more presumably correlated variables) will generally be better than no matching at all, since some degree of correlation between scores on the dependent variable can be achieved even if the pre-experimental matching is not perfect. The error term against which the difference between groups is assessed decreases as the correlation induced by matching increases.

Using Subjects as Their Own Controls

One effect of the matched subjects design is to reduce the extent to which experimental differences can be accounted for by initial differences between the groups. With ideal matching, each pair of cohorts would be exactly alike to begin with and therefore a consistent experimental effect, no matter how small, would be detected by such a procedure. In actual practice, of course, matching is never this good. Even if subjects' pretest scores on the dependent variable happened to be identical, other differences between the cohorts might make them differentially susceptible to the experimental conditions. Even if pairs of identical twins or littermates are used as cohorts, the differences between them on a wide variety of attributes are likely to be great enough to produce a relatively sizable error term. One of the best ways to reduce this error term, hence to obtain a large critical ratio with a particular size of group difference, is to have subjects serve as their own controls. If the same subjects could be measured simultaneously under both conditions, then maximal control over individual differences would have been exercised and the experimental design would be maximally powerful.

Though it is almost always impossible to achieve the required simultaneity of measurement, the same subjects can be measured successively, first under one experimental treatment and then under the other. This is sometimes called a treatment-by-subjects design because every subject gets both (or all) experimental treatments. For instance, the same people might be required to memorize two different sets of nonsense syllables, one set with high and the other with low association value. The difference in learning time between the two sets is found for each person, and the average difference over all of them can be tested for significance against an error term derived from the variability of all difference scores.* The analysis is thus formally similar to that used in a matched subjects design, but the error term will in all probability be considerably smaller.

A variation on this arrangement is the *pre- and posttest design,* in which subjects are measured on the dependent variable, once before exposure to the experimental conditions and once after (or during) exposure. Such a design is frequently employed in studies of attitude change or of teaching effectiveness. Pretest scores are subtracted from posttest scores, and the pre to post difference for the entire group is tested for significance against an error term based on the set of difference scores.

Counterbalancing

Whenever the same subjects are exposed to two or more conditions, there is a possibility that *order effects* will influence the results; that is, the impact of a particular condition may depend on whether it is administered first or second. For example, in the experiment designed

---

* This procedure has serious defects as sketched here; we return to this illustration presently.

to measure the relative ease of learning high- and low-association non-sense syllables, there could be a secondary effect of "learning to learn" or of getting used to the task, so that whichever list appeared second would have an advantage over the first. Conversely, fatigue or inter-ference effects might result in poorer memorization of the second list. Therefore, it would be undesirable to give all subjects the same order of treatment, for the order effect could *confound* the treatment effect, thereby either masking or exaggerating it. Instead, one would typi-cally give a random half of the subjects one order and the remaining subjects the other order. (With more than two conditions, this prin-ciple could be extended to the point at which all possible orderings were administered, each to a different subsample of subjects; or, if the total number of permutations were too great, a *Latin-square design,* which selects a representative set, could be used; see, for example, Cochran & Cox, 1957; Kempthorne, 1952; Lindquist, 1953.)

Such a counterbalancing procedure yields certain additional infor-mation from the data. First, one can determine the *main effect* of each treatment for the two (or more) orders combined. Second, one can see if a simple order effect did occur, by comparing the average score for the first treatment in sequence with the average score for the second, etc. Finally, it is possible to test for the significance of an *interaction between treatment and order effects,* such that, for example, performance on *B* is better when it is presented first, but *A* exhibits no such effect. In the experiment on nonsense-syllable learning a counter-balanced design might show that low-association syllables are suscep-tible to order effects but high are not. If this difference proves to be statistically significant (see chapter supplement), then the interpreta-tion of the results must be modified accordingly—for example, that in-experienced subjects find high-association syllables easier to learn at first, but once they have practiced on a single list they can handle either high- or low-association syllables about equally well.

Pre- and Posttest Design with Control Group

It is, of course, impossible to use a counterbalanced design if one condition must always follow the other, as in a pre- and posttest ar-rangement. Then one cannot be sure whether any difference between the two conditions is caused by the intended experimental variable or by other factors, such as an order effect or the mere passage of time. In a study of the efficacy of psychotherapy, for instance, a comparison between patients' pre- and post-therapy levels of adjustment may well demonstrate an average difference in favor of the latter. One cannot readily attribute such a difference to the specific treatment being used unless he can show that spontaneous remission, or the same amount of "cure" without that particular kind of therapy, could not account for it.

Such a conclusion would require a control group which also received a pre- and posttest but without the presumably critical intervening experience. This does not necessarily mean that control subjects receive no experience at all; sometimes it is desirable to do something specific with them in order to avoid the possibility that their poorer performance on the posttest can simply be attributed to their feelings of being neglected. It is common practice in certain learning experiments to give the control group some kind of irrelevant interpolated activity between pre- and posttests, while the experimental group is receiving specific training for the task. In an experiment on the effects of a particular drug, one would wish to administer a placebo (such as aspirin, a sugar pill, or a saline injection) to the control group without letting them know that they were being treated differently from the experimental group. The "placebo effect" is well known in medical research: sometimes patients feel improved when they think they are being treated but actually are not. So whenever the effectiveness of a new drug is tested, injected patients must be compared, not with their preinjected selves or even with an uninjected group, but with members of a *placebo control* group who think that they too are being medicated but actually are not. (If neither the doctor nor the patient knows who receives the drug and who the placebo, this is known as a *double-blind* experiment. It is sometimes used to keep the doctor from permitting his impression of the case to be affected by his opinion of the drug and from transmitting his expectations to the patient by means of subtle cues during the injection contact.)

This kind of design is diagrammed in Table 10-1. Subjects are assigned randomly to the two conditions. The appropriate comparison

TABLE 10-1

Pre- and Posttest Design, with Control Group, for Evaluating the Effect of Psychotherapy

Group of Ss	Pretest	Experimental Treatment	Posttest
Experimental	x	Therapy	x
Control	x	Placebo	x

lies between the changes in experimental subjects' scores and the corresponding changes in control subjects' scores. This is handled by subtracting the average control group change from the average change for the experimental group and determining whether this difference in average changes is significantly greater than zero (see chapter supplement).

If the control group is matched subject for subject with the experimental group (and assignment of cohorts to the two conditions is random), a further gain in efficiency is achieved. One can then compare the pre to post change for each experimental subject with that of his cohort. To the extent that matching is successful, the variability of these differences between changes will be less than the variability of the changes themselves. The former quantity forms the basis for the error term in such a *matched-subjects-pre-posttest* design, so that a smaller experimental-control group difference can be detected statistically. The reasoning is comparable to that in the simple matched subjects design discussed above.

It may, of course, be desirable to use *several* control groups or conditions in such a design. Thus for studying the therapeutic effectiveness of a particular drug, one may want to use both a placebo control and a control group which receives no medication at all. In an experiment on latent learning, in which the experimental animals first run a maze without reward for a number of trials and are then given rewarded trials, one may want one control group that never finds a reward and another that is always rewarded.

Pre-Post Combined with Post-Only Design

The main purpose of using subjects as their own controls is to increase the efficiency of the experimental design by reducing the variability of the scores one analyzes, hence the error variance against which the experimental effect is compared. Such procedures may, however, lead to a loss in the generality of conclusions that can be drawn from a pre-post design. Strictly speaking, the effect of a pre-post experiment is demonstrated only on a pretested group of subjects, not on subjects who have not been pretested. In a study of the effects of a new teaching method, for example, one might like to be able to conclude that the method is superior to others now in use. This conclusion should apply whether or not students are given the particular pretest used in the experiment. But if a pre-post design is used alone, all of the subjects have been pretested, and one cannot tell whether the effect of the new teaching method would have been the same on an unpretested group.

Furthermore, it is possible that the pretest has different kinds of effects under different experimental conditions. For example, suppose that one criterion for the success of a new teaching program in political science is the proportion of students who get their political news from a "sophisticated" source like *The New York Times*. During the course itself no special emphasis is placed on this particular source; but it, along with several others of somewhat lower repute, is made available to students. If this is a pre-posttest design, the pretest questionnaire might include an item like, "Do you read *The New York Times* for political news?" This question alone may be enough to sensitize the experimental students to that newspaper, so that when it becomes available during the course they will be more likely to pick it out from the others. But the control group is not intentionally exposed to the various news sources, hence the pretest question never has an opportunity to exert its "sensitizing effect" on them. What might happen in such a study, then, is that the experimental group shows greater attentiveness to *The New York Times* on the posttest than the control group, not owing just to the course content but to the combined effect of course content and pretest. A new class taught by the same method, but not pretested, hence not "sensitized," may show no greater attentiveness to the *Times* than the control group.

Such an effect represents an *interaction* between the pretest and the experimental variable. The effect of the pretest is not similar for both groups; rather it affects the experimental and control groups in different ways. Whenever the effect of the pretest might be interactive, it is useful to add two new groups to the study—an experimental and a control group, neither of which is pretested. The arrangement is schematized in Table 10-2. It involves combining the pre-post-experimental-control design (Table 10-1) with the simple randomized

TABLE 10-2

Pre- and Posttest Design Combined with Posttest-Only Design, for Assessing a New Teaching Method

Group of Ss	Pretest	Teaching Method	Posttest
Experimental (E_1)		New	x
Experimental (E_2)	x	New	x
Control (C_1)		Traditional	x
Control (C_2)	x	Traditional	x

subjects design. Such a combination takes advantage of the increased precision afforded by the pre-post procedure and at the same time shows how the experimental condition affects an unpretested group of subjects.

The influence of the experimental conditions on a pretested group can be determined by comparing the posttests of E_2 and C_2 or the pre-post changes of E_2 and C_2; the effect of the experiment on an unpretested group is found by comparing E_1 and C_1. If the average differences between posttest scores E_1-C_1 and E_2-C_2 are about the same, then the experiment must have had a comparable effect on pretested and unpretested groups. One could also find out the same thing directly by comparing the E_2 posttest with E_1 and the C_2 posttest with C_1. Such comparisons serve to clarify the meaning of any differences found between the pre- to posttest changes of E_2 and C_2. (See the chapter supplement for significance tests appropriate to such analyses.)

TWO OR MORE INDEPENDENT VARIABLES

All of the designs discussed so far provide for systematic manipulation of one independent variable to produce an effect on the dependent variable. Perhaps it has occurred to the reader that in the process of counterbalancing the order of treatments in a treatment-by-subjects design (see p. 244) a second independent variable is actually being manipulated—that is, order of presentation; similarly, presence or absence of a pretest represents a second independent variable in the design just considered. The effect of order itself or of the pretest is usually not of major theoretical concern. These variables serve merely as controls to assure that the main effect of the treatments is properly interpreted. There is no reason why some theoretically meaningful variable might not be used in a formally similar fashion. Its main effect and interaction with the principal independent variable could be determined in the same way as in a treatment-by-subjects or a pre-post combined with post-only design. The information yield of an experiment can be increased markedly by assessing the simultaneous effects of two or more independent variables. Two different varieties of multivariate design are commonly distinguished: a *treatment-by-levels* experiment, in which the effect of a single independent variable (treatment conditions) is of primary concern and one or more subsidiary independent variables are used for statistical control (i.e., to increase the power of the significance test), and a *factorial* experiment, in which several independent variables are of equal interest and one wishes to assess their separate and combined effects. Though their purposes differ to some extent, the two design structures are formally similar.

Treatment-by-Levels Design

In this design the effect on the dependent variable of the main experimental treatment is assessed at each of several "levels" of one or more secondary independent variables. The different levels typically represent naturally occurring selected groups of subjects, although one might also conceive of a treatment-by-levels study with the "levels" groups created by the investigator in the course of performing his experimental manipulations. An example of natural levels would be a study performed on two groups of children—say bright ones and dull ones—to see how the amount of incentive affects the likelihood that they will transpose a newly learned concept. Another example would be an experiment to determine how the degree of food deprivation affects incidental learning, in which different groups of rats are separated on the basis of maze-running ability.

The circumstance in which a treatment-by-levels design is appropriate is when there is some reason to believe that the value of the dependent variable will be affected, not only by the principal independent variable, but also by certain subsidiary independent variables which can be assessed in advance. If all subjects were combined, regardless of their positions on the subsidiary variables, there would be marked individual differences on the dependent variables within treatment groups. Since the magnitude of individual differences contributes to the error term against which the treatment effect is compared, heterogeneity of subjects with respect to the subsidiary independent variables may increase the error variance unduly. If, on the other hand, various levels of subjects are distinguished on the basis of these subsidiary variables, then only the individual differences remaining within each level contribute to the error variance. The function of the different levels is thus mainly statistical rather than stemming from theoretical interest in the "levels" variables themselves. A treatment-by-levels design permits a more powerful significance test for the main effects of treatment. In addition, it enables one to determine whether the treatment has comparable effects over all levels, and thereby enhances the generalizability of experimental results.

Consider the example in Table 10-3. The main purpose of the research design is to test the effect of a particular method of psychotherapy on patients' level of adjustment. But the investigator antici-

TABLE 10-3

Treatment-by-Levels Design for Evaluating a Method of Psychotherapy with Three Diagnostic Groups

Level	Treatment	Posttest
1. Hysterical neuroses	a. Experimental therapy	x
	b. Control therapy	x
2. Anxiety neuroses	a. Experimental therapy	x
	b. Control therapy	x
3. Obsessive-compulsive neuroses	a. Experimental therapy	x
	b. Control therapy	x

pates that the therapy may be differentially effective, depending on the nature of the psychiatric disturbance. Therefore, three categories of patients are distinguished, hysterical, anxiety, and obsessive-compulsive neurotics. (More diagnostic categories and additional attributes, such as age, sex, etc., might, of course, be used to create a larger number of levels.) Patients within each level are randomly assigned to the experimental or the control treatment. Following the prescribed period of therapy, adjustment measures are taken and the scores recorded for every subject. (If a pretest is used, the scores will represent not the final adjustment ratings but the changes in adjustment from pre- to posttest. Such change scores will probably be less variable than the posttest scores themselves, so that interindividual variability, hence error variance, is further reduced.)

From this set of scores one could compute several different means. First of all, the average adjustment (or change in adjustment) of each group can be obtained. Next, one can compute an average for each level, that is, for each diagnostic category of the experimental and control groups combined. Finally, the experimental groups from all three levels can yield a combined average and so can the combined control groups.

If the therapeutic technique was uniformly more effective than the control, then within each diagnostic category the experimental group should have a higher average score than the controls. The investigator can assess the statistical significance of the over-all average experimental-control difference by comparing it with an error term based on individual differences. These individual differences are determined not from the total group of subjects combined but from the six subgroups distinguished in the experiment. If, indeed, the mean scores for the three levels are different, this will necessarily imply that the average intersubject variance within levels is less than the total intersubject variance from the three levels combined. So the error variance in a treatment-by-levels design is reduced below that in a randomized subjects design to the extent that the levels variable is correlated with the dependent variable. A detailed calculation for the present illustration is presented in the chapter supplement. The reader will note that this analysis is formally identical with the comparison of means from two stratified samples, discussed in Chapter 9 (p. 232). A treatment-by-levels design in experimental research is structurally the same as a stratified sample design in systematic assessment research.

Factorial Design

In a treatment-by-levels design one is primarily interested in the effect of a single major independent variable and uses others simply to increase the generality or precision of the experiment. In a factorial design one is interested in the separate and interactive effects of two (or more) independent variables; both may be experimentally manipulated or one of them may depend on subject selection (as in the preceding illustration). If two dichotomous independent variables are cross-classified, this will yield four experimental conditions, as schematized in Table 10-4. This hypothetical experiment represents an attempt to determine the relative effectiveness of two propaganda appeals, "emotional" and "rational," on attitudes of two

TABLE 10-4

Factorial Design for Testing the Effects of Two Propaganda Methods on "Important" and "Unimportant" Attitudes

Subject Group	Independent Variable X_1 Centrality of Attitude	Independent Variable X_2 Propaganda Method	Posttest
1	Important	Emotional	x
2	Important	Rational	x
3	Unimportant	Emotional	x
4	Unimportant	Rational	x

different degrees of "centrality." The centrality of attitudes toward a particular issue might be assessed by asking people how important the issue is to them. Two categories of replies could be distinguished, "important" and "unimportant," and from each category subjects are then randomly assigned to the two different communications, thus yielding four independent groups of subjects. (Different methods of assignment might have been used, such as matching subjects on some presumably relevant characteristics or exposing the same subjects in counterbalanced order to both types of propaganda. These methods would increase the power of the significance test but would pose practical problems.)

Following their exposure to the propaganda appeal, the attitudes of subjects toward the same issue are assessed to determine the direction and amount of change. Three different sets of average posttest or pre-to-post change scores could be computed: the mean for each group separately (M_1, M_2, M_3, M_4), the mean for the "important" against the "unimportant" attitudes (M_{12}, M_{34}), and the mean for the emotional against the rational appeal (M_{13}, M_{24}).

To find out if the two propaganda methods differ in average effectiveness, one compares the difference between M_{13} and M_{24} with the difference that would be expected on the basis of intersubject variance. This "error variance" is now computed from the average variability among *subjects within groups* (see chapter supplement). Similarly, the relative susceptibility to change of important and unimportant attitudes is assessed by comparing the difference between M_{12} and M_{34} with the amount of difference between these means that would be expected on the basis of *within-groups intersubject variance*. In each of these tests for the *main effects* of propaganda technique and of centrality one variable serves as a levels control for the other, thereby reducing the error variance against which the particular difference in means is compared. Thus a factorial design accomplishes in one experiment what otherwise might require two separate studies; one set of subjects is made to do the work of two.

Additionally, a factorial design permits one to assess the *interaction* between the two independent variables—that is, the differential effects of one of them at different levels of the other. (This can, of course, also be accomplished in a treatment-by-levels design, but there an analysis of interaction is usually of less interest than an analysis of the main effect of the major independent variable.) In the present illustration, for example, it might be discovered that the emotional appeal was relatively more effective when applied on important attitudes but relatively less effective on unimportant ones. A conclusion of this kind could not have been reached without both variables being simultaneously represented in the experiment.

Elaborations

Such principles of multivariate design can be extended to more complex experiments, involving a large number of independent variables simultaneously manipulated (or assessed). In a treatment-by-levels design one would be interested in the effects of only one of them, and the others would be used simply for experimental control and consequent reduction in error variance. In a factorial design one is concerned with the main effects of several independent variables and also with their interactive effects. The investigator should realize that if too many factors are manipulated or controlled simultaneously the experiment and analysis become unwieldy and certain of the combinations of conditions may be highly artificial.

Another way of elaborating a multivariate design is to use not just two but several values of each independent variable. Thus the experiment becomes a systematic (rather than preliminary) design for several variables treated simultaneously. The variety of relational forms which may emerge from such a study is almost endless. One of the simplest would occur if the effect of each independent variable on the dependent variable were linear and all of their separate effects were additive. This result would yield a multivariate equation of the form

$$Y = aX_1 + bX_2 + cX_3 + \cdots + k$$

Of course, any of the component relations might be nonlinear, so that a more complex equation would be required to represent the total multivariate relationship. Further, if there were interactions among any of the independent variables, no single equation would apply to the entire set of results; for each different level of X_1 the functional relation between Y and X_2 would be different, and so on for all interactive combinations.

The mere contemplation of such complexities will perhaps help the reader to understand why most psychological research is designed more simply than that. Most studies nowadays are performed either with just one independent variable at a time or with a few variables that have been dichotomized. This is probably not a permanent state of affairs, for, with the development of electronic computers, one of the major obstacles to complex multivariate analysis—the tedium of calculation—has been removed. Of course, it will still be necessary to run large numbers of subjects under large numbers of conditions in order to represent all combinations of several values of multiple independent variables. Clearly, these are expensive designs, generally profitable only after preliminary work has indicated that the variables are important. So for some time in the future, we suspect, the sorts of simple experimental designs discussed in this chapter will continue to predominate in the bulk of psychological research.

SUMMARY

The aim of experimental research is to demonstrate convincingly the effect of one or more independent variables by assigning subjects to experimental conditions in such a way that contaminating influences are either controlled or randomized. One pattern of assignment might be for each subject to be exposed to every different experimental condition (representing selected values of the independent variables). This design is a very efficient one, since it permits one to detect even small effects with relatively few subjects. However, it generally requires counterbalancing the order of presentation, and there are some circumstances in which this cannot be done because exposure to one experimental condition would ruin the subject for others.

So a statistically less efficient design is frequently employed, in which different subjects are exposed to the various experimental conditions. Even here it is possible to achieve greater economy than simple random assignment affords if one can match subjects, either individually (with a "matched subjects design") or in subgroups (with a "treatment-by-levels" or "factorial" design).

Which of these—or other—experimental arrangements to use will depend on the purposes of the study and on the practical limitations of the research situation. Sometimes a matched subjects or treatment-by-levels design is not feasible because one has little idea of the variables to match on. Also, it could be that the most efficient design statistically would be inefficient from an over-all point of view because obtaining the necessary measures and maintaining control over subject assignment would be excessively time consuming. For some experimental problems, the per-subject cost of research increases considerably as the design becomes more complex. So one must always try to balance out the advantage of the extra information against the disadvantages of the extra cost to obtain it. In some situations a systematic multivariate design will seem well worth the effort; for other problems a simple randomized-subjects, two condition design will be quite adequate.

SUPPLEMENT

Statistical Analysis of Some Experimental Designs

The designs presented in the body of the chapter provide data that can be analyzed in a variety of ways. Occasionally the results will be so clear-cut that statistical analysis is an unnecessary, pedantic exercise. One can simply present graphs or equations showing how subjects performed under the experimental conditions. Usually, though, there will be sizable individual differences in performances, such that score distributions for the various experimental groups will overlap considerably. It will then be necessary to determine the probability of a Type I error in generalizing results to a larger population. This is the function of significance tests.

Out of the numerous available significance tests we have selected only a few for illustrative purposes. They are all variations on the critical ratio or t-test for differences between means. Thus they are easy to comprehend conceptually without elaboration beyond the materials presented in Chapter 9.* For two-category independent variables, of the kind represented in the illustrative designs of this chapter, differences between group means can be tested directly by appropriate critical ratios, providing either one-tail or two-tail significance levels. If more than two categories are represented in the independent variables, the direct comparison of means via CR or t-test is cumbersome, and some other analysis technique (e.g., analysis of variance, correlation, or regression equations) would be preferable.

Simple Randomized Subjects Design

If posttest measures are taken on two groups of subjects which have been independently selected, one would simply compute the mean score of each group, M_1 and M_2, and test the difference between them with a critical ratio (CR) or t-test:

$$(1) \qquad \text{CR} = \frac{M_1 - M_2}{\sigma_{M_1 - M_2}} = \frac{M_1 - M_2}{\sqrt{\sigma^2_{M_1} + \sigma^2_{M_2}}}$$

---

* A very general approach to significance testing is provided by the analysis of variance (see Cochran & Cox, 1957; Edwards, 1960; Lindquist, 1953). It is particularly useful for designs involving several independent variables, since interaction among them can be calculated quite efficiently. However, when the independent variables are represented by multiple, ordered categories, analysis of variance provides a weak, or even inappropriate, test against specific alternatives to the null hypothesis (see Chapter 13, p. 332).

A detailed illustration of this critical ratio can be found in Supplement A to Chapter 9. In order to use the t-test (for small samples), both $s_{M_1}^2$ and $s_{M_2}^2$ must be computed from a single estimate, s_x^2, of their common population variance, that is,

$$\sigma_{M_1}^2 = \frac{s_x^2}{n_1} \quad \text{and} \quad \sigma_{M_2}^2 = \frac{s_x^2}{n_2}$$

where

$$s_x^2 = \frac{\Sigma(X_1 - M_1)^2 + \Sigma(X_2 - M_2)^2}{n_1 + n_2 - 2}$$

See the bottom of Table 10-5 (Independent Subjects) for illustrative calculations.

Randomized Matched Subjects Design

Matching two experimental groups subject for subject is intended to introduce a correlation between the two sets of scores. This has the effect of reducing the standard error of the difference between means by an amount equal to twice the covariance of the means:

$$(2) \qquad \sigma_{M_1-M_2} = \sqrt{\sigma_{M_1}^2 + \sigma_{M_2}^2 - 2\sigma_{M_1}\sigma_{M_2}r_{12}}$$

To the extent that scores on the dependent variable are correlated over the subject pairs, the standard error of the difference between means will thus be smaller than for independent (randomized) groups. Therefore, a smaller difference is required to yield a particular value of the critical ratio.

Ordinarily in such a design one does not actually compute the correlation coefficient between the two sets of scores, but instead can use a less laborious analysis procedure which accomplishes the same thing. When scores are paired (e.g., on the basis of subject matching), a simpler formula for the standard error of the difference between means may be used:

$$(3) \qquad \sigma_{M_1-M_2} = \sigma_{MD} = \sqrt{\dot{\sigma}_D^2/n}$$

σ_{MD} represents the standard error of the mean difference between paired scores (which difference is mathematically equal to the difference between group means), and $\dot{\sigma}_D^2$ represents the variance of difference scores in the population from which the two samples were drawn. This quantity can be estimated from the data at hand by means of s_D^2, defined as

$$(4) \qquad s_D^2 = \frac{\sum\limits_{i=1}^{n} (D_i - MD)^2}{n - 1}$$

where D_i is the algebraic difference (with sign) between scores from a matched pair of subjects,

MD is the mean algebraic difference between paired scores, and

n is the number of subject-pairs.

A computational formula for the standard error of the mean difference between correlated scores can be derived from the above:

$$(5) \qquad \sigma_{MD} = \sqrt{\frac{n\Sigma D_i^2 - (\Sigma D_i)^2}{n^2(n-1)}}$$

This "error term" can be incorporated in a critical ratio or in a t-ratio to test the statistical significance of the difference between the two experimental group means. An example appears in Table 10-5. It presents hypothetical data from a study of the effect of glutamic acid on measured intelligence. Let us say that ten children had fortified diets for six years, and another ten children, matched subject-for-subject on family income and mother's education level, had a normal diet. At the end of that period, their IQs were measured by the Wechsler Intelligence Scale for Children. A mean difference of 12.5 points in favor of the special diet group reaches the .05 level of significance when the appropriate formula for matched subjects is used. Note that the same difference, analyzed by the formula for randomized subjects, would not reach an acceptable level of statistical significance ($t = 1.39$), even with the increased degrees of freedom (18) that result from independent selection of subjects. The fact that the pairs of scores are correlated appreciably ($r = .76$) yields a sizable reduction in the error variance (σ_{MD}^2).

Treatment-by-Subjects Design

When subjects are used as their own controls in a pre- and posttest design or when the same subjects are studied under two different experimental conditions, the analysis of differences between the two conditions can be handled in the same way as in a matched subjects experiment. Scores under one condition are subtracted from those under the other, to yield a set of difference scores. The mean difference can then be compared, by CR or t-ratio, with its standard error, estimated from (5).

If the two conditions are counterbalanced so that one half of the subjects receive them in order A–B and the other half in the order B–A, this is just like running two separate but complementary experiments, with $n/2$ subjects each. Their results can be combined to show the average effect of the experimental treatments, regardless of order. They could also be combined to show the average effect of the order in which a treatment appears, regardless of the treatment. Finally, one could compare the two separate experimental orders to see if the relative effectiveness of a treatment depends on whether it appears first or second. Usually the experimenter is primarily interested in the first of these analyses—concerning the average effect of treatment—but by counterbalancing order of presentation he has, in effect, introduced a second independent variable, so that the statistical analysis is somewhat changed.

One way of testing the influence of the principal independent variable in such a design would be to treat each order of presentation as a different level or stratum and compute the standard error of the mean difference between treatments by the formula for a stratified sample (see Chapter 9, p. 234). But if the variability of difference scores is roughly the same within both orders, then one might wish to pool them both for a single "best" estimate of the average within-strata variability. s_D^2, the estimate of variance among

TABLE 10-5

IQ's of Children Fed a Normal Diet and a Diet Fortified with Glutamic Acid (Matched-Subjects Design)

Subject Pair	Diet		Difference
	Glutamic Acid	Normal	
1	105	105	0
2	125	120	5
3	115	120	−5
4	85	65	20
5	100	65	35
6	65	75	−10
7	105	85	20
8	120	100	20
9	125	105	20
10	95	75	20
Mean	104.0	91.5	12.5
ΣX	1,040	915	125
ΣX^2	111,400	87,775	3375

Matched Subjects

$$s_{MD} = \sqrt{\frac{n\Sigma D_i^2 - (\Sigma D_i)^2}{n^2(n-1)}} = \sqrt{\frac{10(3375) - (125)^2}{100(9)}} = 4.49$$

$$t = \frac{MD}{s_{MD}} = \frac{12.5}{4.49} = 2.78 \quad df = n - 1 = 9; \quad p < .05$$

Independent Subjects

$$s_x^2 = \frac{\Sigma(X_1 - M_1)^2 + \Sigma(X_2 - M_2)^2}{n_1 + n_2 - 2}$$

$$= \frac{\dfrac{n_1\Sigma X_1^2 - (\Sigma X_1)^2}{n_1} + \dfrac{n_2\Sigma X_2^2 - (\Sigma X_2)^2}{n_2}}{n_1 + n_2 - 2}$$

$$= \frac{\dfrac{10(111,400) - (1,040)^2}{10} + \dfrac{10(87,775) - (915)^2}{10}}{10 + 10 - 2} = 405.14$$

$$s_{M_1 - M_2} = \sqrt{s_{M_1}^2 + s_{M_2}^2} = \sqrt{\frac{s_x^2}{n_1} + \frac{s_x^2}{n_2}} = \sqrt{\frac{405.14}{10} + \frac{405.14}{10}} = 9.00$$

$$t = \frac{M_1 - M_2}{s_{M_1 - M_2}} = \frac{104.0 - 91.5}{9.00} = 1.39; \quad df = n_1 + n_2 - 2 = 18; \quad \text{N.S.}$$

difference scores in the population from which the samples were drawn, is then based on the weighted average variance of the two samples, which can be calculated as

(6)
$$s_D{}^2 = \frac{\Sigma(D_1 - MD_1)^2 + \Sigma(D_2 - MD_2)^2}{n_1 + n_2 - 2}$$

In comparing this formula with (4) on p. 257 for calculating $s_D{}^2$ from a single group, the reader will note that the numerator now consists of two sums of squared differences—one from each subgroup. Likewise, the denominator consists of two $(n - 1)$ terms added together. Here n_1 and n_2 represent the numbers of subjects exposed to each of the two treatment orders. Formula (6) can be algebraically manipulated into a form that permits calculation directly from the difference scores:

(7)
$$s_D{}^2 = \frac{\dfrac{n_1 \Sigma D_1{}^2 - (\Sigma D_1)^2}{n_1} + \dfrac{n_2 \Sigma D_2{}^2 - (\Sigma D_2)^2}{n_2}}{n_1 + n_2 - 2}$$

This average within-groups variance estimate can then be used in the formula for the standard error of the mean difference:

(3)
$$\sigma_{MD} = \sqrt{s_D{}^2/n}$$

When comparing the effects of treatments, a CR or t-ratio is computed in the usual way (1), and now MD refers to the mean of differences between treatments for all subjects. (This is algebraically equal to the difference between the two over-all treatment means.)

If one wishes to test the significance of the order effect itself, the same kind of ratio is again constructed, but this time MD represents the mean of differences between the first and second presentation for all subjects. (This is algebraically equal to the difference between the mean of the first-presented and the mean of the second-presented treatment.)

Finally, one might wish to know whether the difference between the A and B treatments depends on which is presented first. The mean A–B difference under one order is subtracted from the mean A–B difference under the other order, and this difference between mean differences is tested against its standard error:

(8)
$$\sigma_{MD_1 - MD_2} = \sqrt{\sigma^2_{MD_1} + \sigma^2_{MD_2}}$$

Each of the terms under the radical is estimated as

(9)
$$\sigma^2_{MD} = \frac{s_D{}^2}{n}$$

$s_D{}^2$ is the same estimate of population variance in difference-scores used to test the main effects of treatment and the main effects of order; but n, in this case, is the number of subjects who received that particular order of treatments rather than the total number of subjects in the experiment.

Examples of these calculations are presented in Table 10-6. Suppose that

TABLE 10-6

Number of Trials Required to Learn Nonsense Syllables
with High and Low Association Value
(Counterbalanced Treatment-by-Subjects Design)

Subject	Order	Association Value Low (list A)	High (list B)	Differences Association Value (A–B)	Order (second– first)
1	1. Low–	12	8	4	−4
2	high	10	7	3	−3
3		8	10	−2	2
4		8	4	4	−4
5		13	9	4	−4
6		12	9	3	−3
	Mean₁	10.50	7.83	2.67	−2.67
	ΣD_1			16	−16
	$\Sigma D_1{}^2$			70	70
7	2. High–	8	6	2	2
8	low	7	7	0	0
9		12	11	1	1
10		7	10	−3	−3
11		9	8	1	1
12		9	6	3	3
	Mean₂	8.67	8.00	0.67	0.67
	ΣD_2			4	4
	$\Sigma D_2{}^2$			24	24
	Grand mean	9.58	7.91	1.67	−1.00

$$s_D^2 = \frac{\dfrac{n_1 \Sigma D_1{}^2 - (\Sigma D_1)^2}{n_1} + \dfrac{n_2 \Sigma D_2{}^2 - (\Sigma D_2)^2}{n_2}}{n_1 + n_2 - 2} = \frac{\dfrac{6(70) - (16)^2}{6} + \dfrac{6(24) - (4)^2}{6}}{6 + 6 - 2}$$

$$= 4.87$$

Effect of Association Value

$$t_1 = \frac{MD}{s_{MD}} = \frac{MD}{\sqrt{s_D^2/n}} = \frac{1.67}{\sqrt{4.87/12}} = 2.62; \qquad df = 10; \qquad p < .05$$

Effect of Order

$$t_2 = \frac{MD}{\sqrt{s_D^2/n}} = \frac{-1.00}{\sqrt{4.87/12}} = -1.57; \qquad df = 10; \qquad \text{N.S.}$$

Interaction between Association Value and Order

$$t_3 = \frac{MD_1 - MD_2}{\sqrt{\sigma_{MD_1}^2 + \sigma_{MD_2}^2}} = \frac{2.67 - 0.67}{\sqrt{4.87/6 + 4.87/6}} = 1.57; \qquad df = 10; \qquad \text{N.S.}$$

the experimenter is trying to check whether nonsense syllables with high association value are easier to learn than those with low association value. He uses two lists, one of them (list A) of low, and the other (list B) of high association value. Half the subjects learn first list A, then list B; the other half learns them in reverse order.

The number of trials required by each subject to learn each list is recorded in the first two data columns of Table 10-6. The difference due to association value is found by subtracting the list B score from the list A score for each subject. Under both orders the mean difference is in the same direction; but it is greater ($MD_1 = 2.67$) when the high association list appears second in order than when it appears first ($MD_2 = 0.67$). Thus it appears that association value may interact with order of presentation in affecting the rate of learning.

To determine whether any of these apparent effects might reasonably have occurred by chance sampling from a population of conditions that did not differ, they can be compared against their appropriate error terms; t_1 in Table 10-6 presents the mean difference due to association value, in ratio to the estimate of its standard error. It permits one to reject the null hypothesis of no difference between lists at the .05 level of significance; t_2, testing the effect of order of exposure to the lists, does not reach an acceptable level of significance, and there is no basis for inferring that the second list is more readily learned than the first. Finally, the apparent dependence of the association value effect on the order of presentation is not large enough, with this size sample, to warrant any conclusions about population differences ($t_3 = 1.57$). The general conclusion from the experiment would be that nonsense syllables with high association value are learned more readily (i.e., with fewer trials) than those with low association value. (The hint of an order effect and of an interaction between order of presentation and association value might be further explored with a larger number of subjects, but these effects could well disappear rather than be confirmed in a second study; so no positive conclusions are justified on the basis of these data alone.)

Pre-Post Change with Control Group

In one of the commonest instances of a treatment-by-subjects design subjects are measured both before and after (or during) exposure to a single experimental condition. Since the order of treatments ("before" and "after") cannot be counterbalanced, one cannot be certain whether a difference in scores from pre- to posttest is due to the experimental stimulus or to the temporal ordering of measures. (The subjects might have changed scores systematically even without the intervening experience because of practice on the pretest or some other uncontrolled influence.)

In order to exclude any such temporal effects from the change scores, it is desirable to use a control group that is tested at the same times as the experimental group but is not exposed to the experimental treatment. The changes of the control group can then be subtracted from those of the experimental group and the mean difference between group changes compared, by means of CR or t-ratio, with its standard error. If the experimental and control groups are independently selected (i.e., each is a simple random sample from the same population), (8) can be used or a computational form can be derived from it:

$$(10) \qquad \sigma_{MD_1-MD_2} = \sqrt{\frac{n_1\Sigma D_1^2 - (\Sigma D_1)^2}{n_1^2(n_1-1)} + \frac{n_2\Sigma D_2^2 - (\Sigma D_2)^2}{n_2^2(n_2-1)}}$$

In this formula n_1 and n_2 are the numbers of subjects in the experimental and control groups (which are, of course, not necessarily equal).

If the experimental and control groups are matched subject for subject on their pretest scores or on some other measure that is correlated with the dependent variable, this will introduce a correlation between the two sets of change scores so that the formula for the standard error of the difference in changes becomes

$$(11) \qquad \sigma_{MD_1-MD_2} = \sqrt{\sigma_{MD_1}^2 + \sigma_{MD_2}^2 - 2\sigma_{MD_1}\sigma_{MD_2}r_{D_1D_2}}$$

This is structurally identical with (2) on p. 257; but, in place of M (standing for a group mean), we find MD (standing for a mean difference or a change in group mean). As before, the correlation between the change scores of paired subjects in the experimental and control groups need not actually be computed. It is more convenient to determine the algebraic difference between the changes of each cohort pair and from this distribution of "difference in change" scores compute the estimate of population variance for insertion in (12), which is parallel to (9) on p. 260:

$$(12) \qquad \sigma_{MD_1-MD_2} = \sigma_{MD_{ch}} = \sqrt{s_{D_{ch}}^2/n}$$

A calculational formula can be derived by substituting $s_{D_{ch}}^2$ with its equivalent (cf. (5), p. 258).

$$(13) \qquad \sigma_{MD_{ch}} = \sqrt{\frac{n\Sigma D_{ch}^2 - (\Sigma D_{ch})^2}{n^2(n-1)}}$$

where D_{ch} is the difference between the changes from pre- to posttest of any particular cohort pair and n is the number of pairs of matched subjects.

Hypothetical data from a pre-post study to test the effect of psychotherapy are presented in Table 10-7. They are analyzed in two ways, first assuming that experimental and control subjects were independently selected and then assuming that they were matched on the basis of pretest scores. (Note that matching was not perfect, since the pretest scores of cohorts were not identical; but it was good enough to introduce the desired correlation in their change scores, and the pretest means are quite close together.) It can be seen from the first three columns of the table that psychotherapy had a general effect of raising the level of adjustment, though this was more pronounced among patients who scored lower to begin with. (Perhaps there

TABLE 10-7

Adjustment Scores before and after Psychotherapy for an Experimental Group and a Control (Placebo) Group

Subject Pair	Psychotherapy Group Pre-test	Post-test	Change	Placebo Group Pre-test	Post-test	Change	Difference in Changes
1	32	30	−2	35	33	−2	0
2	28	30	+2	28	28	0	+2
3	25	29	+4	25	23	−2	+6
4	25	25	0	24	23	−1	+1
5	22	21	−1	20	22	+2	−3
6	20	26	+6	20	20	0	+6
7	20	26	+6	18	20	+2	+4
8	15	20	+5	16	18	+2	+3
9	10	21	+11	12	17	+5	+6
10	7	15	+8	5	8	+3	+5
Mean	20.4	24.3	+3.9	20.3	21.2	+0.9	+3.0
ΣX			39			9	30
ΣX^2			307			55	172

Independent Groups

$$s_D{}^2 = \frac{\Sigma(D_1 - MD_1)^2 + \Sigma(D_2 - MD_2)^2}{n_1 + n_2 - 2}$$

$$= 11.21 \text{ (cf. bottom of Table 10-5)}$$

$$s_{MD_1 - MD_2} = \sqrt{\frac{s_D{}^2}{n_1} + \frac{s_D{}^2}{n_2}} = 1.50$$

$$t = \frac{MD_1 - MD_2}{s_{MD_1 - MD_2}} = \frac{3.9 - 0.9}{1.50} = 2.00$$

$$df = 18; \quad p < .10 \text{ (two-tail)}$$

Matched Groups

$$s_{MDch} = \sqrt{\frac{s_{D_{ch}}^2}{n}} = \sqrt{\frac{n\Sigma D_{ch}^2 - (\Sigma D_{ch})^2}{n^2(n-1)}} = \sqrt{\frac{10(172) - (30)^2}{100(9)}} = .955$$

$$t = \frac{MD_{ch}}{s_{MDch}} = \frac{3.0}{.955} = 3.14; \quad df = 9; \quad p < .02 \text{ (two-tail)}$$

was a ceiling effect, such that those who started out fairly well adjusted could not go much higher.) The change scores for patients in the placebo-control group show a similar pattern, except that both ends of the distribution tend to converge toward the mean on the posttest.

When the groups are treated as independent—that is, when no account is taken in the statistical analysis of the fact that they were matched on the pretest—the difference in their mean increases is only twice as large as the estimate of its standard error; but when the changes in matched subjects are compared directly, it is seen that in eight out of ten cases the patient receiving psychotherapy improved more than his cohort. When the variance of this distribution of differences in change scores is used to compute the standard error of the difference in mean increases, a t-ratio of 3.14 is obtained. Even with the reduced degrees of freedom, which result from matching (9 versus 18 in the independent groups analysis), the difference now turns out statistically significant ($p < .02$).

Pre-Post Change Combined with Post-Only Comparison

In order to find out if the pretest interacts with the experimental manipulation in its effect on the dependent variable, two new groups, neither of which is pretested, are added to the design. This yields a combination of the simple randomized subjects design and the pre-post change with control group design and thus permits two separate tests of the experimental effect —one by a comparison of mean change scores in the experimental and control groups which were pretested, the other by a comparison of posttest scores in the two unpretested groups, only one of which received the experimental treatment. If the first comparison shows an apparent experimental effect, but the second does not, then the researcher can conclude only that the manipulation is effective for a pretested population, not for people in general. More precisely, the statistical analysis permits one to test the significance of interaction between pretest and experimental treatment to see if conclusions concerning the main effect of the experimental treatment need to be restricted.

Table 10-8 presents hypothetical data from a study of the effectiveness of a new teaching method. The two experimental and the two control groups have the same designations used in Table 10-2. Instead of presenting all the raw scores, we show only the group means, with their ΣXs and ΣX^2s, for these are the essential components of the t-tests. One way of assessing the effect of the teaching method would be to compare the posttest means of groups E_1 and C_1 in the manner of a simple randomized subjects design (see p. 256). Another way would be to compare the changes in means of the E_2 and C_2 groups from the pre- to the posttest (see analysis of *independent group* change scores in Table 10-7); this would usually provide a more powerful significance test. Since these two comparisons represent independent tests of the effectiveness of the teaching method, their significance levels could be combined by the logarithmic formula presented in Chapter 13 (p. 369).

TABLE 10-8

Examination Scores of Students Exposed to Traditional (C) and to Experimental (E) Methods of Teaching History

Group of Ss		Pretest			Posttest			Change		
	n	M	ΣX	ΣX^2	M	ΣX	ΣX^2	M	ΣX	ΣX^2
1. (E_1)	10				29	290	8,574			
2. (E_2)	8	24	192	4720	33	264	8,788	+9	72	836
3. (C_1)	12				28	336	9,476			
4. (C_2)	15	25	375	9557	27	405	11,147	+2	30	140

Estimate of Population Variance on Posttest

$$s_x^2 = \frac{\left[\dfrac{n_1\Sigma X_1^2 - (\Sigma X_1)^2}{n_1} + \dfrac{n_2\Sigma X_2^2 - (\Sigma X_2)^2}{n_2} + \dfrac{n_3\Sigma X_3^2 - (\Sigma X_3)^2}{n_3} + \dfrac{n_4\Sigma X_4^2 - (\Sigma X_4)^2}{n_4} \right]}{n_1 + n_2 + n_3 + n_4 - 4}$$

$$= \frac{\left[\dfrac{10(8574) - (290)^2}{10} + \dfrac{8(8788) - (264)^2}{8} + \dfrac{12(9476) - (336)^2}{12} + \dfrac{15(11\ 147) - (405)^2}{15} \right]}{10 + 8 + 12 + 15 - 4}$$

$$= 12.68$$

Interaction between Pretest and Treatment

$$t = \frac{(M_1 - M_3) - (M_2 - M_4)}{\sqrt{s^2/n_1 + s^2/n_2 + s^2/n_3 + s^2/n_4}} = \frac{(29 - 28) - (33 - 27)}{\sqrt{12.68 \left(\frac{1}{10} + \frac{1}{8} + \frac{1}{12} + \frac{1}{15} \right)}} = \frac{-5}{2.18}$$

$$= -2.29; \qquad df = n_1 + n_2 + n_3 + n_4 - 4 = 41; \qquad p < .05 \text{ (two-tail)}$$

But before looking at the main effect of the new method, it is well to make sure that this effect is the same regardless of whether students are pretested. A glance at the posttest means shown in Table 10-8 suggests that it is not. For pretested subjects (E_2 and C_2), the difference in posttest means is six points $(33 - 27)$; whereas for unpretested subjects (E_1 and C_1) the difference is only one point $(29 - 28)$. There apparently is an interaction between pretest and teaching method, which had best be tested for statistical significance before proceeding with the analysis of main effects. One way of doing this is to compare the difference between differences of means with an estimate of its standard error. Since all of these groups were independently selected, an appropriate estimate would be

$$(14) \qquad s_{(M_1-M_3)-(M_2-M_4)} = \sqrt{s_1^2/n_1 + s_2^2/n_2 + s_3^2/n_3 + s_4^2/n_4}$$

Each of the s^2s in (14) represents an estimate of the variance among posttest scores in the population from which the particular group was drawn. If it can be assumed that these population variances are all equal, then the several s^2s can simply be treated as different estimates of the same variance. So a single best estimate could be obtained by pooling them all in the manner shown in the middle of Table 10-8. This pooled s_x^2 is then used as the numerator for each of the terms representing the variance of a particular group mean. The standard error of the difference between differences in means thus turns out to be 2.18—less than half as large as the obtained difference of five points.

The significance level of this result leads one to believe that the effect of the new teaching method on pretested students is greater than it is on unpretested students. It might therefore be misleading to go on and talk about an over-all effect of the teaching method. Instead, one could test the significance of the difference between changes in the pretested groups (E_2 and C_2) and report that as one result; then the significance of posttest differences in the E_1 and C_1 groups could be tested and treated as a separate finding. In the present example the former difference is reliable, but the latter is not, and the appropriate conclusion from this experiment alone would be that the teaching method is effective only on pretested students.

Treatment-by-Levels Design

In a treatment-by-levels experiment results can be analyzed in several ways that take into account the increased precision it affords. One would be to treat the difference from each level (class of subjects) separately—computing, say, a t-ratio and its corresponding significance level for the class, then combining them all into a single test of the main experimental effect by the procedure described in Chapter 13 (p. 369). Another way would be to pool the intragroups variance into a single estimate of population variance, using this in the error term against which the over-all difference between experimental and control group means is compared. (See the illustrations in Tables 10-6 and 10-8.) A third method is illustrated here in order to demonstrate the parallel between this experimental arrangement and the stratified sampling procedure discussed in Chapter 9 (see pp. 212 and 232).

In Table 10-9 are hypothetical data from a study of the relative effectiveness of two therapeutic procedures on three classes of neurotic patients— "hysterics," "anxious," and "obsessive-compulsives." Following the prescribed period of "experimental" or "control" therapy, each patient is rated as "improved" or "not improved." (In a careful study this rating would be made

TABLE 10-9

Proportions of Patients Improved Following Experimental and Placebo Therapy in Three Diagnostic Groups (Treatment-by-Levels Design)

Levels (h)		Treatment	
		Experimental	Control
Hysterical neuroses	p_1	32%	16%
	n_1	25	25
Anxiety neuroses	p_2	80%	60%
	n_2	15	15
Obsessive-compulsive neuroses	p_3	50%	30%
	n_3	10	10
Total	p	50%	32%
	n	50	50

$$CR = \frac{p_e - p_c}{\sqrt{\sigma^2_{p_e} + \sigma^2_{p_c}}}$$

Stratified Samples

$$\sigma^2_{p_e} = \sum_{h=1}^{k} \left(\frac{n_k}{n}\right)^2 \sigma^2_{p_{e_h}} = \left(\frac{25}{50}\right)^2 \frac{(.32)(.68)}{25} + \left(\frac{15}{50}\right)^2 \frac{(.80)(.20)}{15} + \left(\frac{10}{50}\right)^2 \frac{(.50)(.50)}{10}$$

$$= .00414$$

$$\sigma^2_{p_c} = \left(\frac{25}{50}\right)^2 \frac{(.16)(.84)}{25} + \left(\frac{15}{50}\right)^2 \frac{(.60)(.40)}{15} + \left(\frac{10}{50}\right)^2 \frac{(.30)(.70)}{10} = .00362$$

$$CR = \frac{.50 - .32}{\sqrt{.00414 + .00362}} = 2.05; \quad p < .05 \text{ (two-tail)}$$

Simple Random Samples

$$\sigma^2_{p_e} = \frac{p_e q_e}{n_e} = \frac{(.50)(.50)}{50} = .00500; \quad \sigma^2_{p_c} = \frac{(.32)(.68)}{50} = .00435$$

$$CR = \frac{.50 - .32}{\sqrt{.00500 + .00435}} = 1.861; \quad p < .10 \text{ (two-tail)}$$

by someone who did not know to which therapy any given subject had been assigned.) The table shows the proportion (p) of patients in each subgroup who were rated "improved," together with the size (n) of the subgroup.

The experimental and the control subjects consist essentially of two stratified samples of a population of neurotics. Within each stratum patients were randomly assigned to one treatment or the other, and it is assumed that each subgroup constitutes a simple random sample of the larger population designated by the class name. An estimate of error variance $(\sigma_{p_e}^2)$ for the proportion improved (50%) of the total group which received experimental therapy is provided by the following formula:

$$(15) \qquad \sigma_{p_e}^2 = \sum_{h=1}^{k} \left(\frac{n_h}{n}\right)^2 \sigma_{p_h}^2 \quad \text{[cf. (5) p. 222 of Chapter 9]}$$

where k is the number of strata,

n_h is the number of subjects in the hth stratum,

n is the total number of subjects, and

$\sigma_{p_h}^2$ is the variance of p (per cent improved) in the hth stratum.

The same formula can be used to estimate the variance of the proportion improved (32%) in the total control group $(\sigma_{p_c}^2)$.

Since the experimental and control groups are independent (i.e., not matched), the standard error of the difference between proportions is provided by a term like the denominator of (1) (p. 256):

$$(16) \qquad \sigma_{p_e - p_c} = \sqrt{\sigma_{p_e}^2 + \sigma_{p_c}^2}$$

To obtain the error term, $\sigma_{p_h}^2$ is estimated for each of the subgroups; these are then weighted by the square of the proportion of the groups they constitute $(n_h/n)^2$, and these weighted variance estimates within the experimental and control treatments are added up separately to yield $\sigma_{p_e}^2$ and $\sigma_{p_c}^2$; the square root of their sum yields $\sigma_{p_e - p_c}$, the standard error of the difference between proportions computed from two stratified samples. By estimating the standard error in this way, the null hypothesis of no difference between the two therapies can be rejected at the .05 level of significance (see Table 10-9). If the increased efficiency afforded by stratification into three classes of patients had not been taken into account, the significance level would have been somewhat poorer (.10). The reason that this treatment-by-levels design increases the precision of the significance test is that the experimental and the control therapies are differentially effective in the three subpopulations, and this variance due to levels (strata) has been eliminated by use of an appropriate formula for error variance.

Factorial Design

Hypothetical data from the study schematized in Table 10-4 are presented in Table 10-10. Here we have recorded the mean attitude changes under an "emotional" and a "rational" propaganda appeal for the two kinds of attitudes, "important" and "unimportant." Also shown are ΣXs and ΣX^2s for each group, since these sums are needed to compute the three t-tests. It will be noted that in these data the important attitudes appear somewhat more resistant to change, on the average, than the unimportant ones but that their relative susceptibility seems to depend strongly on the type of propaganda used. Over-all, the emotional and rational appeals do not differ in effectiveness. (The mean change score of -0.10 in the lower left-hand group means that the attitudes of these subjects tended to move away from the direction of the propaganda.)

To test the statistical significance of the apparent differences among means, one needs an estimate of population variance in attitude change scores to use in the appropriate error terms. This can be obtained by pooling the within-groups variances, to obtain an average s_x^2 of .974 (cf. formula at middle of Table 10-8). Since subjects with important and unimportant attitudes are not matched, the standard error of the difference between their means is

$$(17) \qquad s_{MI-MU} = \sqrt{s_x^2/n_I + s_x^2/n_U}$$

The degrees of freedom for this t-ratio are 76 (the total number of subjects minus the number of different groups from which the within-groups variance estimate was computed). The main effect of attitude centrality fails to reach an acceptable significance level.

The effect of interaction between centrality and propaganda type may be tested by comparing the size of the difference between important and unimportant attitudes obtained under the emotional appeal with the size of the difference obtained under the rational appeal. This difference between differences is used in the numerator of a t-ratio (keeping track of signs). The denominator represents an estimate of the standard error of the difference between differences; since all four groups are independent this equals

$$(18) \qquad s_{(M_1-M_2)-(M_3-M_4)} = \sqrt{s_x^2/n_1 + s_x^2/n_2 + s_x^2/n_3 + s_x^2/n_4}$$

The interaction turns out to be significant (see Table 10-10), though neither of the main effects is. Therefore, the appropriate conclusion from the experiment would be that the relative effectiveness of the two propaganda types depends on the centrality of the attitude involved; an emotional appeal affects "important" more than "unimportant" attitudes, whereas a rational appeal affects "unimportant" more than "important" ones. Stating the same thing in another way, the relative resistance to change of important and unimportant attitudes depends on the kind of propaganda to which they are subjected. (Since the "centrality" variable was assessed rather than experimentally created, it might be prudent to undertake further analyses to make sure that centrality rather than some other attribute—such as attitude extremity, for example—was responsible for the result.)

TABLE 10-10

Changes in "Important" and "Unimportant" Attitudes Induced by Two Types of Propaganda
(Factorial Design with Four Independent Groups, $n = 20$ Each)

Kind of Propaganda		Centrality of Attitudes		Total M
		"Important"	"Unimportant"	
"Emotional" appeal	M	+ 0.80	+ 0.20	+.50
	ΣX	+16	+ 4	
	ΣX^2	32	24	
"Rational" appeal	M	− 0.10	+ 1.10	+.50
	ΣX	− 2	+22	
	ΣX^2	10	46	
Total	M	+ 0.35	+ 0.65	

Estimate of Variance from Within-Groups

$$s_x^2 = \frac{\left[\dfrac{n_1\Sigma X_1^2 - (\Sigma X_1)^2}{n_1} + \dfrac{n_2\Sigma X_2^2 - (\Sigma X_2)^2}{n_2} + \dfrac{n_3\Sigma X_3^2 - (\Sigma X_3)^2}{n_3} + \dfrac{n_4\Sigma X_4^2 - (\Sigma X_4)^2}{n_4}\right]}{n_1 + n_2 + n_3 + n_4 - 4}$$

$$= \frac{\dfrac{20(32) - (16)^2}{20} + \dfrac{20(24) - (4)^2}{20} + \dfrac{20(10) - (-2)^2}{20} + \dfrac{20(46) - (22)^2}{20}}{20 + 20 + 20 + 20 - 4}$$

$$= .974$$

Main Effect of Centrality

$$t = \frac{M_I - M_U}{\sqrt{s_x^2/n_I + s_x^2/n_U}} = \frac{.35 - .65}{\sqrt{.974/40 + .974/40}} = -1.36; \quad df = 76; \quad \text{N.S.}$$

Main Effect of Propaganda Type (N.S.)

Interaction between Centrality and Propaganda Type

$$t = \frac{(M_1 - M_2) - (M_3 - M_4)}{\sqrt{s_x^2/n_1 + s_x^2/n_2 + s_x^2/n_3 + s_x^2/n_4}} = \frac{(.80 - .20) - (-.10 - 1.10)}{\sqrt{4(.974)/20}}$$

$$= 4.08; \quad df = 76; \quad p < .001$$

REFERENCES

Campbell, D. T., & Stanley, J. C. Experimental and quasi-experimental designs for research in teaching. In N. L. Gage (Ed.), *Handbook of research on teaching.* Chicago: Rand-McNally, 1962.

Cochran, W. G., & Cox, Gertrude M. *Experimental designs.* (2nd Ed.) New York: Wiley, 1957.

Cox, D. R. *Planning of experiments.* New York: Wiley, 1958.

Edwards, A. L. *Experimental design in psychological research.* (Rev. Ed.) New York: Rinehart, 1960.

Finney, D. J. *Experimental design and its statistical basis.* Chicago: Univer. Chicago Press, 1955.

Fisher, R. A. *The design of experiments.* (3rd Ed.) Edinburgh: Oliver & Boyd, 1942.

Kempthorne, O. *The design and analysis of experiments.* New York: Wiley, 1952.

Lindquist, E. F. *Design and analysis of experiments in psychology and education.* Boston: Houghton Mifflin, 1953.

Maxwell, A. E. *Experimental design in psychology and the medical sciences.* New York: Wiley, 1958.

Mosteller, F., & Bush, R. R. Selected quantitative techniques. In G. Lindzey (Ed.), *Handbook of social psychology.* (Vol. 1.) Cambridge: Addison-Wesley, 1954.

Siegel, S. *Non-parametric statistics.* New York: McGraw-Hill, 1956.

Smith, J. E. K. Distribution-free statistical methods and the concept of power efficiency. In L. Festinger & D. Katz (Eds.), *Research methods in the behavioral sciences.* New York: Dryden, 1953.

CHAPTER 11

Obtaining and dealing with subjects

It is one thing to think theoretically about subject sampling and assignment, but another to deal with subjects in the flesh. Making contact, securing cooperation, and maintaining rapport while measures are taken entail a host of practical problems. The ability to look ahead realistically and skill in interacting tactfully with people will often make the difference between obtaining all the information on all the subjects and obtaining only some or, indeed, none at all.

MAKING CONTACT AND OBTAINING COOPERATION

In considering his sample design, the researcher has determined the population that is to be studied and either picked a probability sample from it or decided to make do with a catch-as-catch-can sample. The next step is to see to it that the appropriate subjects become available for measurement and that they will cooperate in the research procedures. The particular techniques for making contact and assuring cooperation will differ, depending on the kind of subjects— whether they are animals, college sophomores, neurotics, or people from a different culture—and depending on how the sample is comprised—whether of volunteers, coerced groups, or subjects specifically designated by probability sampling. The basic problem of ensuring cooperation remains the same for all. The researcher may use praise, flattery, money, candy, cigarettes, bananas, wet mash, or release from an unpleasant situation as inducements, but in this phase of the project he is a salesman—and usually one who asks the subject to give him something for very little in return. If he keeps this fact in mind, that *it is the subject who is doing him a favor rather than vice versa*, he is more likely to promote reasonable public relations and obtain subjects' cooperation, whether they are human or animal.

Obtaining Designated Human Subjects

If one is using a probability sample design, intended to assure adequate representation of a defined population, then he will know at this stage exactly which individuals are to be studied. The only thing to do is to get them. No substitutions can be permitted, and each lost subject impairs the representativeness of the sample. So the researcher will have to plan an approach calculated to assure the cooperation of each person. No single tactic will be uniformly successful, but a general strategy which is perhaps most likely to be effective with the largest number is to try to convince them that they will be doing you a favor, that you are competent to make intelligent use of the data they provide, and that participating in the study will be an interesting experience.

Sometimes the potential subject is approached personally in his home or at work, and measures can be obtained from him on the spot. This is true, for example, in most interview survey work. The first thing the investigator does in such a case is to introduce himself, and explain the purpose of the study and how the respondent happened to be selected. It is best not to misrepresent the purpose in this introduction, for the subject will only be antagonized later when he finds out from the nature of the questions that he was misled in the beginning. If certain aims of the study must be disguised in order to avoid contamination of responses, then the introductory explanation should merely omit these aspects and describe other (valid) purposes which are interesting but not damagingly revealing.

If the introduction is tactful and appealing, most respondents will be prepared to admit the investigator immediately or to make an appointment for a more convenient time. For those who hesitate or refuse, one must be prepared to continue with a new appeal designed to the respondent's own individual requirements. This will often require all the perceptiveness, tact, patience, and perseverance the researcher can muster in order to overcome the barriers and gain acceptance. Some people will suspect a sales ploy (a not unreasonable suspicion, considering how the "I'm doing a survey" line has been exploited recently). Others will be concerned with the "personal" nature of the questions or with the possibility that their neighbors will find out about their private lives. It may even happen that some shady respondent will see the interviewer as a detective in disguise, come to get the goods on him. And there are people who just do not like to be bothered.

It is up to the investigator in each case to try to figure out what it is that concerns the person and to improvise an appeal that will allay his anxieties and put him in a cooperative frame of mind. Certainly anonymity should be assured (and maintained); the respondent can be told that his answers will be treated confidentially, that he will become just a number along with 200 other people, that the person who is to analyze the data will not know which protocols came from whom, etc. Sometimes interest can be aroused by reference to a new personality test, to the importance of psychology in public affairs, to recent studies of ESP—whatever allusion is reasonably close to the content of the study. Other subjects will respond to prestige and authority references—"The University is conducting research on . . . ," "The Air Force is supporting a study of . . . ," "X Bureau of the government wants to find out. . . ." Occasionally flattery or appeals to the respondent's sympathy may work (e.g., "I'm a graduate student at X University, and I need some data from you in order to complete the research for my thesis"), but these should probably be used only as a last resort, since strangers in our culture are not ordinarily moved by such personal touches. One should also beware the promise of monetary incentive; this may alienate more people than it motivates, and the researcher ought to be pretty sure that the respondent wants to be paid for his time before offering to do so.

Often entry will be facilitated by advance notice that an interviewer is to call. Individual letters, typed on letterhead stationary, can be addressed to each designated subject a few days before the visit. (If the respondent's name is not known, this letter can be addressed simply to "Head of Household," which places additional emphasis on anonymity.)

If the research is to be performed in a laboratory or some other central place, one must be prepared to encounter further difficulties in persuading people to come to the designated location. Perhaps the most efficient thing to do is to start off with a general letter to all prospective subjects, explaining in some detail the purpose of the study, its sponsorship, how the person was selected, why it is important that he participate, and how the results will be used. Then indicate that the research procedures will be interesting but a little complex and that it will be necessary to perform them in the laboratory. (Perhaps offer a guided tour through the lab as an additional inducement.) Try to anticipate what times will be convenient for the addressee and give him a range of choices; ask him to call you for a special appointment if none of the suggested times is suitable.

The purpose of such a letter is to get in as many willing subjects as possible without further ado. Clear directions for finding the lab must be given and possible questions or objections anticipated in the letter. Even with the most seductive appeal, though, it would be unusual for as many as three quarters of the designated persons to show up. So one proceeds to the next phase of subject solicitation. This can be a second, shorter, letter referring to the previous communication and requesting that the addressee either come at one of several new times or call a specified telephone number for an individual appointment.

It is possible that such a follow-up will yield a few more subjects— those who did not receive the first letter or were out of town at the time or those who needed just a little more prodding. If this still does not work, a different mode of communication is required. The researcher may wish to telephone or visit the delinquent personally, using whatever appeal seems appropriate. Perhaps a questionnaire could be delivered or mailed with sufficiently detailed instructions to ensure its proper completion. Maybe the researcher will have a mobile laboratory which could be taken to the subject's home sometime at his convenience.

If all reasonable suggestions fail, then there may be nothing left to do but chalk this potential subject up in the "refusal" column. At least such a tally lets the researcher know what proportion of the initially representative sample did not get studied so that he can make appropriate allowances in generalizing his findings. This would not have been possible if only volunteers or easily available people had been approached in the first place.

Whenever subjects are asked to appear for testing, it is, of course, essential that the investigator see that they are met. Novice researchers sometimes get themselves into unfortunate situations which, with foresight, could easily have been avoided. On occasion, for instance, a subject has been known to show up at a time and place specified by the investigator, although the investigator himself failed to appear. This produces irate subjects. One way to prevent such a mishap is to keep a running appointment schedule and to check it each time a new subject is added. The least one can do, if he is unable to keep

an appointment, is to let the person know ahead of time or to leave
a message for him which he will receive at the appointed place. Again,
a subject may be asked to "come to the psychology laboratory" at
such-and-such a time on such-and-such a date without being informed
of the researcher's name, the nature of the study, or the room number.
If this occurs in a department in which many studies are going on concurrently, the subject may find himself drifting around an unknown
building, asking unfamiliar people where some uncertain kind of experiment is going on, until he leaves in disgust. Any procedure that
guards against this kind of misunderstanding is to be highly recommended—to put it mildly.

Soliciting Volunteers

A relatively small proportion of current psychological research is
performed on subjects designated by probability sampling procedures.
Although such procedures should probably be used more frequently
than they are at present, there are numerous practical reasons for studying nonprobability samples. In the early years of work on a problem
the investigator is often not prepared to invest the time and money required for adequate sampling until he obtains some preliminary indications that the particular line of inquiry is likely to pay off. Even in
advanced stages, ready availability of subjects is always an important
consideration, and it is evident that a randomly designated sample will
take more time to study than a nearby captive group. Some research
procedures are quite tedious, or even insulting or painful, so that
one may not wish to risk the bad public relations that might result
from imposing them on groups of unwilling subjects. If, on the other
hand, people can be induced to volunteer for an admittedly unpleasant
task in the first place, they are generally prepared to see it through
to completion, so that subject attribution in mid-experiment should not
be great. Another practical occasion for preferring nonprobability
samples is when one does not know how to define empirically a particular population so that it can be sampled representatively. A probability sample of all alcoholics, or all homosexuals, might be very
desirable, but it is unlikely that such a population could be designated
empirically. So the researcher makes whatever contacts he can through
available channels and studies those people who are willing to expose
themselves. In all such cases the adequacy of the sample depends on
personal judgment (subject perhaps to checking in future studies)
rather than on "objective," easily replicable procedures; but it may
well be deemed better than no sample at all.

Soliciting through Groups

One of the most efficient ways to secure large numbers of subjects quickly is to approach groups whose membership includes the right kinds of people. College students obtained in classes undoubtedly provide the bulk of present psychological data on humans, but other groups may be more appropriate for a given purpose (and they are perhaps also less likely to be "test-wise" or "over-studied"): church groups, women's clubs, firemen, chambers of commerce, hospital patients, people waiting for trains at a railroad station—any of these may provide appropriate subjects, either en masse or as individual volunteers. Often there are channels which must be gone through before the group can be approached—"gatekeepers" whose assent or active support should be obtained to make direct solicitation profitable (or ethical). In approaching both the gatekeeper and the members themselves, the researcher should be prepared to offer an appeal tuned to his target's interest. Most frequently this will simply consist of a description of the problem he is studying and the reasons why this particular group would make appropriate subjects. But as in convincing individually designated subjects, one often has to use a variety of inducements and assurances to overcome initial resistance. The leaders of the particular group (teachers, officers, etc.) can often suggest appeals that are likely to be effective—provided the question is put to them diplomatically (e.g., "What things about this study do you suppose the group members would be especially interested in?").

Generally, it is appropriate to assure anonymity of the group as well as of the individual subjects. This is particularly important in sensitive areas of inquiry. For instance, if a fraternity or sorority were to submit to a study of their attitudes toward minority groups and discrimination clauses, they would be entitled to the promise that their organization would never be named in reports of the results— especially if these results might be damaging.

Often one is able to promise feedback of results to the group or to individual members, although it is well not to over-promise, for one could easily find himself spending all his time telling subjects how they did or advising an organization on what it should do about some of its problems that became apparent in the inquiry. Whenever feedback is promised, the researcher must be sure to hold up his end of the bargain—and to do so within a reasonable time, so that the subjects will remember what it was all about and feel rewarded for their participation. If the source of subjects was a class, one must be prepared to tell them something about the outcome before the end of the term—even if this means that only preliminary results can be reported at that time. The subjects in many studies are not particularly interested in the same aspects of the data as the researcher; rather than a complete analysis of relationships among theoretical variables, they will generally want just a simple description of what was going on and how many people did what.

Depending upon the circumstances, the investigator may have two different immediate objectives in approaching the group. He may want to get all the members to participate, or he may want to solicit individual volunteers to be studied at another time. The first aim is likely to yield more subjects, particularly if the instruments can be administered immediately after group assent has been obtained. The social pressures on group members to remain for testing will probably be sufficient to keep too many of them from leaving the room. On the other hand, motivation to participate may not be particularly high among those who feel they have been coerced. Moreover, this tactic raises some ethical problems related to "captive audiences." Introductory psychology classes have been exploited as subjects so frequently that the American Psychological Association felt compelled to question the propriety of such practices in its recommendations regarding ethical standards for psychologists (APA, 1953, 1959). Students take psychology classes to learn about psychology (or to meet some college requirement), not to donate their services as subjects, and so have a right to be outraged if this proves to be a major portion of their class activity.

A potentially annoying and irrelevant situation can generally be turned into one of increased interest and of pedagogic value if the researcher will take the trouble to make class-time data collection a learning experience for the subjects. Immediately following the administration of a questionnaire, for instance, he can enlist the help of the class in performing some simple analyses illustrating what he expects to do with the data.

For nonuniversity groups, which are to be tested en masse, one should generally provide an opportunity for unwilling members to escape if they do not like the sound of the task. A sufficiently interesting appeal, combined with implicit pressure from those who do remain, will probably help to limit the exodus.

Often an instructor is unwilling to devote class time to testing, or the research procedures are such that subjects must be run individually in a laboratory. In such cases individual volunteers may have to be asked to make appointments for a later time. It is often useful to call for a show of hands from those who are willing to cooperate. If a sufficiently large number volunteers, this can provide social facilitation for some of the rest. Indeed, stooges have been successfully used with large groups to help create a "volunteering mood."

When the group setting is used only for soliciting volunteers, a "sign-up sheet" may be passed around, listing dates and times with blanks for the subjects to insert their names (and perhaps telephone numbers so that they can be called for a reminder). It is good practice to head the sheet with the title of the project, the researcher's name, and the exact location to which the person is to come and to ask each one to record them so that he will not forget them. The researcher also may wish to distribute cards indicating his name, title of the project, location of the experimental room, and the exact time of the appointment. The potential subject retains the card after inserting his name in the appropriate place on the sign-up sheet.

Such a procedure is preferable to asking all volunteers to come to the front of the room at the end of the meeting or to see the researcher outside the door. Asking people to come to an office to sign up for the study is not advisable, since the extra effort required may be enough to discourage many of them from participating.

Follow-up

Whenever the research procedures cannot be initiated immediately upon contact with the subject, a follow-up technique may be desirable before the appointment. Verbal agreements or signatures on a sign-up sheet serve as sufficient notification for most subjects but are likely not to be enough if the researcher wishes to keep drop-outs to a minimum. Sometimes reminders can be read out loud during a class hour or on the job, announcing name, place, and time of appointment for each subject a day or so ahead of time. Postcards are useful, if they include the necessary information and are mailed at an appropriate time. They should contain some statement to the effect that the addressee had agreed to appear for the study, the name of the investigator, the title of the study, and the time and place at which the subject is expected. It is also desirable to include the researcher's address and telephone number, so that the subject can notify him if he is unable to come. A courteous and tactful telephone call on the day or evening before the subject is due may add greatly to the likelihood that he will appear. Such procedures help to convince the subject of the researcher's interest in him, hence are likely to improve his motivation.

Approaching Authorities

Procedures of the kind suggested so far can be modified to fit groups other than students—for example, children, workers in a plant, inmates of a prison, or patients at a mental institution. But whenever a captive group is to be used, the investigator must, of course, work through appropriate channels before approaching the potential subjects. If kindergarten pupils are to be subjects, one should first obtain permission from the teacher and the parents; probably the principal of the school and possibly the school superintendent should also be consulted first. In studies of institutionalized persons, such as mental defectives, psychotics, convicts, and so on, the investigator must first solicit the aid of the official who has the highest level of responsibility and then work down through the hierarchy until the potential subjects themselves are approached. Thus one might first seek out the superintendent of a mental hospital, then the clinical director, then the psychiatrist responsible for a given ward, then the nurses and attendants, and only when the cooperation of all of these people has been assured would the patients themselves be asked.

The beginning investigator may not recognize the need for such complex procedures until some irate gatekeeper who was not properly informed stops data collection at the last moment and thereby scuttles the study. Administrators and others responsible for the welfare of the potential subject group by no means automically grant permission for others to meddle with their charges. In each case, and especially with institutionalized subjects, a great deal of preliminary groundwork is often required before cooperation is achieved. This may involve seemingly unnecessary red tape and endless frustrations. Yet the very fact of institutionalization may have its advantages once the channels are opened; it generally makes the subjects easier to get than if no organized channel were available.

Problems with Deviant Groups

Special problems may arise in attempts to study subjects who, for one reason or another, are considered socially deviant—such as alcoholics, psychotics, Communists, dope addicts, professional thieves, and so forth. Even if the behavior pattern that characterizes these people is not an illegal one, they have undoubtedly had the unpleasant experience of being singled out in some way or other and are ashamed of their condition; they may be unwilling to cooperate with the researcher or even to reveal themselves. It is in an attempt to gain access to such subjects that the researcher may encounter particular difficulties in translating a theoretical population into an operational one. The "ideal" operational definition may well be one that simply will not work in practice; the feelings of the subjects, legal sanctions, and other practical matters may have to play a major role in the way that attributes such as homosexuality, mental deficiency, juvenile delinquency, and prostitution are defined for purposes of the study. It is often useful in such cases to explore alternative ways of operationalizing the critical subject characteristics in terms of the group's accessibility as well as of the validity of the selection criterion.

Consider, for example, an investigator interested in studying alcoholics. He might visit a nearby chapter of Alcoholics Anonymous, go to a state hospital to try to interview some alcoholics, check with a court for names of people repeatedly in trouble with the law over their inebriety, or hang around Skid Row and use local bartenders as the judges of who is and who is not an appropriate person for study. There may be difficulty in obtaining cooperation from the officers of Alcoholics Anonymous. The director of the state hospital may be reluctant to permit access to the confidential hospital records; also alcoholics may not stay there long enough to be reached through the proper channels. Court records may not be up-to-date and, in any case, will include only those alcoholics in trouble with the law. Bartenders may not agree on who is alcoholic. The likelihood of obtaining cooperation from a person chosen in any of these ways will differ, and the researcher may prefer willing subjects to coerced ones. Faced with such alternatives, the investigator will have to choose one that yields the operational definition of alcoholism most appropriate to his interest and yet is most likely to assure the cooperation of appropriate subjects.

Consider the researcher interested in homosexuality. There are several ways in which he might go about obtaining subjects, each of them imperfect and with its success dependent to a large extent on his skill in public relations and the degree of unselfconscious tolerance he can display. He might try to solicit the cooperation of the Mattachine Society, whose officers are generally willing to aid research on homosexuality if it seems likely to further public understanding of the problem. Of course, such a voluntary group might be quite unlike "typical" homosexuals. Certainly they would provide an operational definition of homosexuality different from that achieved by the researcher's hanging around a "gay bar" and meeting subjects there and different from the definition implied if people imprisoned as a result of conviction for homosexual practices are studied.

If an institutionalized group is used, incidentally, the fact of institutionalization provides no automatic justification for using them as subjects in research. The investigator should display this understanding in all contacts with institutional authorities. Moreover, he should not treat the supervisor's permission as a substitute for that of the subjects themselves. Although there is generally little difficulty in obtaining most inmates' acquiescence—especially if the research procedures provide a welcome relief from dull institutional routine—one should always show them the courtesy of requesting their consent rather than taking it for granted.

Obtaining Animal Subjects

Although some animal studies are done strictly because of interest in the particular species, such a research objective is relatively rare in contemporary psychology. Most of the time the investigator wishes, explicitly or implicitly, to discover principles that will hopefully be applicable to humans, but, for one reason or another, he chooses not to work directly on *homo sapiens*. The reasons for studying animal subjects are various. The scientist's own habitude, his repertory of research skills, and the ready availability of animals in his laboratory are probably the main ones, though perhaps not often offered explicitly. Many important psychological problems could not be studied in people, since they require procedures of manipulation and control that would be intolerable for human subjects. The faster reproduction and maturation rates in certain infrahuman species and the possibility of controlling them to some extent make animals superior subjects for studies that span a considerable portion of the life cycle.

Though the possibilities—and limitations—of generalization to human populations may be a matter of deep concern to some comparative psychologists, these problems cannot be treated statistically in the manner that we have discussed in Chapter 9. There is nowhere available a significance test that will tell a researcher how likely it is that a relationship found in a rat study will be replicated on human subjects. This must be a matter of judgment—informed by considerations of structural similarities between the species, of results from comparable studies on other animals, and of phylogenetic continuities (and discontinuities) in functioning. Generalizing from animals to humans is always risky. One can do so only insofar as he can reasonably assume that the two species operate under a common principle. Usually it is necessary to check whether the principle found to characterize the animal actually holds as well in humans.

For that matter, caution should be exercised in generalizing from one infrahuman species to another or even among different strains of the same species. Hooded rats and albinos behave quite differently in many tasks; and it has been suggested that certain strains, such as the Sprague-Dawley or the Wistar, may perform atypically in, for example, incidental learning tasks. The experimenter may also wish to consider whether a particular batch of animals sent him may not be scrawnier, less pigmented, etc., than other members of the strain. Such questions as these can be treated objectively and quantitatively if subjects are selected as probability samples. But the way animals are ordinarily obtained—by buying a batch from a supplier or taking available young rats from the local colony—there is no way of assessing probabilistically the representativeness of a particular sample. One can only judge on the basis of prior experience with "normal" members of the species.

Suitability to the Problem

In deciding what species to study, the researcher will wish to take a number of things into account—considerations both practical and theoretical. Perhaps the most important concern should be with how well the species is suited to the problem to be studied. Certain animals have particular characteristics that make them especially desirable for certain kinds of investigations. Thus, if the study requires feeding through an esophageal fistula (a tube inserted through the neck which connects the esophagus to the outside of the animal), dogs are superior to rats because the esophagus of the rat is small and hard to work with; chickens are cheaper than dogs and reasonably good for this purpose because they have a large esophagus. The squid has giant axons, conveniently large for certain kinds of neurophysiological work. Pigeons have a pecking response that is easy to hook into recording equipment and a reaction time that is usefully rapid. The life span of rats is conveniently short, which makes them suitable for developmental and genetic studies. For physiological work on the brain, monkeys—or better yet, chimpanzees—are superior to lower animals not only because of the brain's greater size but because of its greater similarity to the human brain, which the investigator usually wants to know about in the long run. The cat skull is surgically easier to penetrate than that of the chimpanzee, so this may make the cat a preferable species for some brain studies.

Often litter-mate controls are used in animal studies; that is, siblings from the same litter are divided so that they become parts of different groups undergoing different experimental treatments. This can provide an approximate control on hereditary factors and increase the precision of an experiment by means of the matched subjects design it affords. Such litter-mate matching obviously requires a species with multiple births.

Examples of this kind could be multiplied indefinitely. The point is that selecting animals appropriate to the problem requires a great deal of knowledge about many different species. Some sources of relevant information will be indicated shortly.

Availability

Equally important as the "right-species-for-the-problem" consideration is the matter of where one is going to get the animals. If the researcher is employed at an institution that maintains a rat colony and a monkey lab, it will, of course, be easier for him to work with these animals than to purchase and house guinea pigs, dogs, or chimpanzees. Usually he can gain access to local animals by negotiating with the caretaker of the colony, but this may also require getting permission from several other people beforehand and going through appropriate channels.

If one has the option of purchasing his own subjects, he should consider not only the initial price of each animal but also the cost of maintenance. At the present writing, chimpanzees can be bought for about $1500 each, some kinds of monkeys for $40, rats around $1.25, and chicks for about 7 cents each; animals such as fruit flies are free. Certain species may profitably be bred in the laboratory, whereas for others it is more economical to purchase young adults directly from a commercial house. Many animal suppliers advertise in journals like *Science*. If the researcher is adept and can get to the right place, he may be able to trap some species for himself.

Often it is impractical or uneconomical to purchase new animals and house them in a local laboratory. Instead, one may wish to explore the possibility of going to another laboratory where the species is normally available. For certain kinds of animals, it may be best to follow them in the field, whether in wild open country or a farmyard; before doing this, however, one must, of course, check with the farmer, ranger, or whoever else is responsible for the welfare of the animals. Arrangements can sometimes be made with zoos to study wapiti, kangaroos, elephants, and so forth, which may be inconvenient or impossible to house in a laboratory or to get to in their natural habitats.

Maintenance

Human subjects usually do not have to be fed and housed by the investigator, but animals are generally not ready to be used for research until maintenance problems are solved. Maintenance costs ordinarily increase with the complexity and size of the animal. Fruit flies can be kept quite easily in bottles on a desk top, and cages for animals such as pigeons, cats, guinea pigs, rats, mice, and chicks can be purchased at reasonably low cost from a variety of laboratory suppliers. Monkeys, dogs, chimpanzees, and other larger animals may require specially constructed housing. Food for standard laboratory animals can also be obtained from suppliers, but exotic species are likely to have special dietary requirements. The time of maintenance that will be required before the animal becomes a useful experimental subject is an important consideration in selecting a species. Some mature more rapidly, and this makes them less costly in the long run.

In order to select and maintain animals properly, one must know a good deal about their habits. Some species have seen enough experimental use to supply a considerable amount of information. Handbooks are available (e.g., Farris & Griffiths, 1949; Munn, 1950; Spector, 1956) which provide a wealth of data concerning housing, feeding, disease control, cleaning, and the like. Articles in journals publishing animal research may be helpful, and animal suppliers often put out free handbooks or periodicals dealing with animal maintenance (e.g., the Carworth Farms *Quarterly Newsletter* or the Purina Company's *Care and feeding of laboratory animals*). Animal psychologists, pharmacologists, biologists, and other specialists who know the peculiarities of certain species can be consulted for advice. It is useful to pick up as much lore as possible, from any source, about the animal to be used. Better knowledge is likely to lead to fewer errors in feeding, maintenance, and experimental procedures and thus to fewer losses by illness or death. For that matter, certain species are subject to diseases that can afflict man, and the investigator's own health may be endangered if he lacks sufficient knowledge.

Disposal

When one is obtaining animals in the first place, he should also give thought to the question of what to do with them when the study has been completed. Disposing of animals often raises unpleasant problems, especially if the researcher has become somewhat attached to them. In the zoo, at the farm, or in the field there are no difficulties in getting rid of the animals at the end of the study. You just leave. But if you are maintaining them yourself, things are not that simple. Sometimes they can be given away as pets—or to other researchers, preferably in pharmacology, in which the previous training and experience of the animal is less likely to affect the new research. If the animal must be sacrificed, a quick, painless method such as chloroform is easiest for all concerned. Most laboratories have their own techniques; sometimes a local humane society can help.

Subject Loss

However conscientious the investigator may be, it is almost inevitable that some human subjects will refuse or fail to show up at the appointed time and place. Animals, if housed in the laboratory, are much more dependable than humans in keeping appointments, but they may get sick, escape, or die. What can one do under such conditions, which are at best very frustrating?

The first and natural reaction of the researcher, especially if the missing subject is human, is resentment and anger. For obvious public relations reasons he cannot afford to let his feelings show. There is very little he can do, other than trying to find the errant subject directly or by telephone and persuading him to come to the laboratory immediately or, if the design and the requirements of the study permit, making a second appointment. Although the researcher, in his frustration, may wish to probe for the reason behind the delinquent's absence, such probing is likely to antagonize, and quite often the offender may have a reason that seems, to him at least, quite legitimate.

The seriousness of subject loss varies greatly from one investigation to another. If volunteers are run singly through the research procedures, all that is lost is a bit of the investigator's time. If the subjects are run in groups and the design requires the simultaneous presence of a specific number, the inconvenience may be multiplied. (For such studies, the investigator may wish to schedule one more subject than he needs; but this practice has its drawbacks if all of them show up or if it becomes known among future subjects that not all of them will be able to participate.) If subjects are specifically designated by probability sampling, losses constitute a serious threat to the representativeness of the sample; and in some factorial designs a single subject missed may reduce the sample size for a particular subcondition by 50 per cent. If an animal dies, quite aside from the problem of diminished sample size, the generality of the findings may become restricted, since the sample could thereby have become biased toward "stronger" organisms. In human studies those subjects who do not show up may differ in some critical way from those who do, thus yielding a nonrepresentative sample.

There are no easy general answers to the question of what to do under such conditions; the researcher is well advised to expect that whatever he does some subjects will still be lost and to consider ahead of time the best way of handling the situation in light of the design requirements of the particular study. It is perhaps wisest to aim at prevention; strive to make the subject procurement procedure foolproof, maintain good public relations, and keep animals as clean, comfortable, and disease-free as possible.

MAINTAINING COOPERATION

Once the subject has been obtained, there is still no assurance that his cooperation, even if initially bestowed, will continue throughout the research procedures. The investigator must therefore see to it that appropriate techniques are used to keep the subject involved until the session has been completed. For most human adults, little besides occasional encouragement may be called for, but with children, psychotics, animals, and so forth, additional devices may be necessary.

Dealing with Humans

Use of mature interpersonal relations practices is the best way to ensure cooperation from administrators and from the subjects themselves. Respect for and interest in the person can go a long way toward keeping him motivated. In doorstep interviewing and other techniques in which the research procedures follow immediately on the initial contact with the subject, the investigator can use various methods designed to maintain rapport. Keeping the questions and procedures interesting and encouraging the subject repeatedly serve to maintain continued cooperation. If one is trying to find out things that are not easily divulged or if the subject matter might alienate the respondent, the investigator must take pains to minimize barriers to free communication. These barriers include the respondent's concern whether the interviewer would approve of his attitude, what his friends might think if they knew, or whether he knows enough about the issue to express an opinion.

In an attempt to overcome some of these barriers, one may repeatedly assure the respondent of complete anonymity and use a nondirective approach. This not only helps to maintain cooperation but is also intended to increase the validity of the subject's replies. It serves to convince the respondent of the researcher's interest in, and acceptance of, what he is saying, without seeming to adopt his position. Since implied agreement may encourage him to go further than he really meant to, it is perferable to use a supportive response that implies understanding ("Uh-huh" or "I see") rather than agreement ("That's what I say too" or "Ain't it the truth!"). Comparably, nondirective probes such as "Could you tell me a little more about that?" or "I'm not sure I followed" imply interest and desire for further information, without forcing the respondent into a position that may not be his own, as in "Are you trying to say that . . . ?" or "You mean that you don't think war is likely?" The interviewer, in other words, should aim at encouraging the subject as much as possible, without at the same time damaging the validity of the data (cf. Hyman, 1954; Kahn & Cannell, 1957).

This principle holds as well, of course, for procedures other than survey interviewing. Encouragement, showing respect for the subject and interest in what he does, keeping procedures as direct as possible, and avoiding monotony, boredom, and fatigue help to assure continued cooperation. Behavioral evidence of the researcher's competence also enhances the subject's interest and conviction that the investigator knows what he is doing, hence can make good use of the data. Behavioral evidence includes remaining calm and unflustered, asking and recording questions in a straightforward, efficient manner, using memorized instructions rather than having to read them, avoiding long intervals in which he is doing something mysterious while the subject stands or sits there waiting for what is to come next.

In general, rapport is perhaps best maintained if the researcher is empathic and can, in effect, get inside the skin of the subject to see how the research procedures look to him.

Children as Subjects

This holds particularly if children are to be tested; youngsters pose special research problems of their own (see, e.g., Mussen, 1960). Many children will cooperate readily with any change in routine, especially if the researcher has previously broken the ice by talking briefly to the group as a whole, by showing them the experimental equipment, or by just being around them for a short time. Some children will at first refuse to "play games," but often further cajoling will do the trick; others may remain adamant and nothing can be done to persuade them to cooperate. Such obstinacy will probably be rare if the experimenter can enlist the aid of other children, the teacher, or a parent, in helping to influence recalcitrant subjects. There are children who will refuse to wait their turns, insisting that they want to be first; judicious and mature handling of such a situation will usually minimize problems of refusal or emotional upset.

Both in the original persuasion and during the data collection itself, the researcher must be careful to gauge his communications as best he can to the level of the child; it may be important for maintaining cooperation that he aim his language neither too high *nor too low*. Many children are alienated if they feel they are being "treated like babies"; this may be especially true in a school setting, with its highly structured social hierarchy, in which successive grades often are, in effect, castes.

Motivation is hard enough to sustain in an adult; in a child it may be even more difficult. If procedures are brief, changing, and intrinsically interesting to the child, his attention may be retained for relatively long periods; but in any case, a half hour for any child under 10 or 12 can stand as a rule-of-thumb maximum for the entire session. Although children are likely to be enthusiastic about any new activity, this enthusiasm, especially in the very young, tends to wane rapidly. At a critical period in the middle of the experimental session the subject may lose interest, act silly, start saying "I don't know," stare out the window, pop his thumb into his mouth and withdraw, or just walk out of the room. A bright toy, crayons, and encouragement are useful for counteracting such behavior and regaining the child's cooperation; in the initial stages of the session they can also help to cement the relationship, hence to minimize the likelihood of subsequent uncooperativeness.

Special Groups

Unique difficulties may arise with particular groups of human subjects—amputees, psychotics, quadriplegics, criminals, blind subjects, aphasics, people with very low IQs, etc. Problems of rapport, communication, and motivation are likely to be greatly enhanced. Some may be particularly unwilling to cooperate with the researcher; others, although willing enough, may be unable to do so for lack of communicative or intellectual abilities.

Work with special groups can thus raise problems which are at the same time fascinating and frustrating. Establishing communication and rapport and initiating and maintaining motivation may require great ingenuity; the techniques required will be different from group to group and from subject to subject. With any kind of population, the more the researcher can find out about them, the better; advance information may not only serve as forewarning about specific problems but may also suggest ways of overcoming them. Often the officials responsible for a group can help the researcher anticipate difficulties and devise appropriate countermeasures.

Dealing with Animals

In many laboratory animals it is easier to sustain motivation and assure continued cooperation with the experimenter than it is in human subjects, for one has ready recourse to deprivation techniques as incentives. For example, food or water can be withheld for a specified time and feeding or drinking made contingent upon the animal's performing a designated task; escape from shock can be provided only if the animal exhibits some particular behavior. Although there may be some question about the comparability of results obtained in human and animal studies because of the different levels of motivation involved, the more intense motivation typically used with animals at least assures their cooperation to a greater extent than is possible in the usual study with human subjects.

It is also worth keeping in mind that if motivation is made too intense performance may become disorganized. An ideal would be some level of drive that is strong enough to produce an alert, cooperative animal but not strong enough to cause distress and disruption of functionally organized, goal-oriented behavior. Rather than employing deprivation incentives, many studies can be designed to make use of the less stressful exploratory, curiosity, or manipulatory motives.

Part of the technique of maintaining cooperation in animals consists of eliminating distracting conditions. A highly controlled, quiet, separate chamber such as the Skinner box minimizes the possible influence of unwanted distractions. Also, the practice of "gentling" or "taming" the animal before the regular research procedures are undertaken reduces the disruptive effect of the researcher's presence. It is now customary to handle rats for a few minutes daily, simply to get them used to humans. Indeed, with some monkeys and chimpanzees the presence of a familiar person during the research procedures will reassure the animal so that he is more eager to manipulate the apparatus and more capable of undisturbed attention to the task.

It is wise not to require tasks that are inappropriate, very difficult, or monotonous for the animal if its interest and attention are to be held. Incessant repetition of a single activity or forced contact with an inordinately difficult discrimination problem may lead to disruption of performance or even "neurotic" behavior.

In general, just as with humans, patient, gentle, humane, friendly dealings with animal subjects are advisable. Quite aside from the ethics of subject treatment, such an approach is more likely to ensure cooperative subjects than is harsh, irresponsible, inconsiderate handling.

SOME ETHICAL CONSIDERATIONS

Throughout this chapter and others we have occasionally emphasized the need for integrity, good public relations, and considerate dealings with others. Such mature and ethical behavior is to be recommended not only on the ground that it is a mode of behavior demanded by the society in which we live, it will also make it much easier for the researcher to achieve his own ends. Considerations of ethics are relevant in every phase of the researcher's life for both social and practical reasons.

Specifically, the investigator must be conscientious in holding up his end of any bargain he makes with subjects. He should consider ahead of time the implications and consequences of reporting individual performances. If he promises to report either individual or group results, he must see to it that these obligations are fulfilled. When doing so, he must try to refrain from oversimplifying or "cleaning up" his report to such an extent that results will be falsified or made to appear more earthshaking than is warranted.

If the subject is assured of anonymity, this commitment to him is, of course, never broken; and even if no explicit promise of anonymity is made each person's performance is nevertheless kept in strict confidence. Any other course can only lead to embarrassment, or to worse consequences, for the subject, the researcher, and possibly the researcher's institution and his discipline.

Exploitation of groups is unethical. Members must be given a reasonable choice about their own participation, and the right to their own privacy should be respected. It is not acceptable practice to force all students in a class to take part in a study against their will. Comparably, if institutionalized subjects are involved, the supervisor's approval is not enough to justify the researcher's using them without their own consent.

In concrete cases the investigator may feel that the study necessitates certain practices that come close to the fringe of acceptable conduct on his part; he must then search his conscience to decide as best he can whether the questionable aspect of treatment is warranted and unavoidable. Whenever the design includes procedures that are likely to be unpleasant to the subject, ethical issues become particularly trenchant. The best principle is to avoid these procedures if at all possible, even though it may require a major reorganization of one's research plan. If induction of pain, dissembling, stress, and so forth, are definitely necessary to the study, the researcher must handle the situation in such a way that the trauma is minimized. Forewarning may help, if pain is to be used; if dissimulation is a necessary part of the procedure, the investigator must consider how to set things right again when the research procedures are completed. It is best if this can be done immediately at the end of the session. Though "giving away" the procedure may permit subjects who have taken part to broadcast it to future participants, thus making them useless, such leakage can usually be fairly well controlled if the subjects' confidence has been won and they understand the reason for maintaining strict silence until the study is completed.

Some necessary procedures may be so unpleasant that it is advisable to provide an opportunity for subject catharsis after the session. This may range from a semitherapeutic interview to letting the person observe future victims or actually helping the researcher conduct the study. (This device can be used readily, for example, in studies that require only a single member of a group as the true subject, while the remainder, who bring strong social pressure to bear on him, are confederates of the investigator.) In general, any effort expended to make the research experience a reasonably pleasant one is likely to pay off in increased cooperativeness from present and future subjects. An investigator planning to use an unpleasant or stressful procedure should think twice before actually doing so and thrice before using it on children or institutionalized subjects. Permission and cooperation will not be easy to come by. Perhaps he would be wiser to study an entirely different problem or to use animals.

But animals, too, cannot be manhandled. Treatment of animal subjects before, during, and after the study must be humane. The investigator should make every effort to avoid pain to the subjects; anaesthesia is used for all operations; operated preparations are treated with special care; the animals, when sacrificed, must be disposed of humanely. The American Psychological Association has a detailed code of appropriate practices in the use of animals; cruelty in the treatment of animal subjects is both inhumane and against the law (see the APA's *Rules regarding animals*, 1949).

The ethics of relations with subjects (as well as ethical principles concerning other aspects of the psychologist's conduct) are treated in great detail in the American Psychological Association's *Ethical stand-ards of psychologists* (1953). We strongly recommend that the reader become thoroughly familiar with this APA code of ethics before engaging in subject contacts.

SUMMARY

Captivation and care of subjects involve many practical details which are best handled with thorough knowledge of the subjects' characteristics and with tact, decency, and patience. The process of approaching them, obtaining cooperation, and maintaining motivation is typically not just a simple routine chore. Procedures for subject procurement depend upon the nature of the sample to be obtained. Solicitation of specifically designated subjects is likely to be more difficult and expensive than the use of captive groups or volunteers.

In approaching subjects through groups, however, one must be prepared for some reluctance to grant permission by authorities responsible for the subjects' welfare. The best sequence typically is to consult the person highest in the hierarchy and then to work down through it step by step, meeting the subjects themselves only after the cooperation of all the higher echelons has been assured. Once the subject himself has been persuaded to participate, various devices may be necessary to maintain his continued cooperation throughout the course of data collection. Subject loss may cause serious damage to the representativeness of a sample; it is best avoided by setting up the details of the procurement procedure and of the research tasks in such a way that the likelihood of drop-out is minimized.

Treatment of subjects must be ethical. This means that the researcher fulfills his obligations to them and maintains the individual's anonymity. He is careful not to exploit his subjects or to make unwarranted intrusions on their privacy. Procedures that may jeopardize their welfare in any way are preferably not used at all; but if they must be employed every attempt is made to limit the unpleasantness of the situation and to remove any undesirable after-effects that may have been generated.

REFERENCES

American Psychological Association, Committee on Precautions in Animal Experimentation. *Rules regarding animals.* Washington, D. C.: American Psychological Association, 1949.

American Psychological Association. *Ethical standards of psychologists.* Washington, D. C.: American Psychological Association, 1953. (See also, same author, same title, *Amer. Psychologist,* 1959, **14,** 279–282.)

Farris, E. J., & Griffiths, J. Q. (Eds.) *The rat in laboratory investigation.* (Rev. Ed.) Philadelphia: Lippincott, 1949.

Hyman, H. H. *Interviewing in social research.* Chicago: Univer. Chicago Press, 1954.

Kahn, R. L., & Cannell, C. F. *The dynamics of interviewing.* New York: Wiley, 1957.

Munn, N. L. *Handbook of psychological research on the rat.* Boston: Houghton Mifflin, 1950.

Mussen, P. H. (Ed.) *Handbook of research methods in child development.* New York: Wiley, 1960.

Spector, W. S, *Handbook of biological data.* Philadelphia: Saunders, 1956.

CHAPTER 12

Arrangements for
data collection

Once the research instruments are ready and subjects have been obtained, some studies can be run without further ado. It is only a matter of keeping records on each subject's performance so that they can be analyzed to answer the question at hand. The beginning researcher is well advised to keep his study within such simple bounds that it will not require further preparation. However, the time may come—perhaps even on the first research project—when attention to a wider range of concerns is demanded. Perhaps the study requires special space arrangements or assistants to help run subjects. If so, then one cannot avoid at least this degree of administrative involvement. Perhaps the research procedures themselves are sufficiently complex to make a last-minute dress-rehearsal advisable so that the investigator gets himself trained and the instruments get a final checkout. In any study with more than 50 subjects and as many as half a dozen variables the problem of efficient record keeping is likely to become important enough to merit attention. This is not only to assure that data do not get lost, but also to see that they are collected and maintained in such a way that their analysis is facilitated.

Sooner than he would prefer, no doubt, the new researcher will encounter problems such as these. We shall try to anticipate some of them in this chapter dealing, essentially, with housekeeping details. The chronology of their occurrence does not necessarily correspond to the present chapter location. Many of them will have been faced well in advance of the actual data collection stage. In fact, if one is not to be overwhelmed with a myriad of details at this time, he would be wise to consider such administrative problems early in the evolution of his study design.

HOUSEKEEPING

Even the simplest piece of research involves some administrative chores, and the study can be seriously hampered if they are handled inadequately or haphazardly. In preceding chapters we discussed such matters as finances, equipment, and subjects, so we shall not consider them again here except to point out once more that they must be approached with foresight and with the recognition that they will require an appreciable amount of time. Other details which need attention but which we have not yet covered include arranging for adequate research space, obtaining the help of others whose services may be necessary, and maintaining optimal public relations during the process of data collection.

Space

Securing suitable research space may involve nothing more than a brief talk with an administrative officer or it may require long hours of planning and consultation. Some studies need no more than a desk and a chair or two; others call for a number of specialized rooms, elaborately set up. Sometimes space is necessary for such things as assistants' quarters, subjects' waiting room, equipment, and data storage or processing as well as data collection. In addition to the amount of space required, and when and how long it will be used, the investigator must also think about the specifications the space must meet. Is a dark room essential? Should the room be relatively soundproof? Are several rooms needed, interconnecting in a particular way? Is there some minimum dimension required for the size of the room? Must water be available? How many and what kind of electrical outlets are necessary? Early attention to such details will avoid the frustration of arranging for space which may later prove to be unsuitable.

In most places where research is conducted some member of the staff is responsible for the assignment of research space. One should, of course, present him with detailed specifications of the space needs and be prepared to offer reasons for them. A clear request, with a defense, can save both the staff member and the investigator a considerable amount of time and annoyance.

More often than not, the investigator will be unable to obtain ideal accommodations. Because there frequently is a shortage of available research space, he may have to share a room with someone else; careful scheduling of room use will help to avoid unpleasantness in such an arrangement. When forced to make do with less than optimal space, one will have to consider the advantages and disadvantages of putting off his study until a time when the overcrowding becomes less severe (if such a time can ever be anticipated) against making do with what is available here and now—perhaps changing some details of the research plan to fit the facilities. The latter is usually by far the more realistic alternative.

Some space requirements are so specialized that nothing satisfactory is readily available. If the researcher needs an anechoic chamber or a room which is electrically shielded, there may be no alternative to waiting until he is in a location in which such facilities are available. However, it is often possible to convert some space to make it usable. Almost any room can be made into a temporary dark room by covering the windows and door cracks or by waiting until an appropriate time of day to do one's research; hanging heavy draperies or putting acoustic tile on the walls and ceiling and a rug on the floor may deaden sound reflections enough for certain purposes. On occasion, it may also be possible to obtain financial aid for converting a room; sometimes substantial grants are made to construct certain kinds of research space or even a whole building.

In any event, it is worthwhile to check the research room at the time of day and under the general conditions in which it is eventually to be used. Problems of temperature, lighting, potential sources of unwanted noise or other distractions, adequacy of electrical and water supply, etc., may not become apparent until such a check has been made.

Personnel

Although many projects can be undertaken by the investigator alone, others require the help of additional personnel. They may be needed in designing and formulating the problem, in the process of data collection, in data tabulation and analysis, and in interpreting the results. Some designs require two or more experimenters, working simultaneously; group studies may call for proctors to answer subjects' questions, hand out forms, and so forth.

The decision to use assistants is not always easy. How much is gained by having them and how hard is it to obtain their help? Will they add a source of uncontrolled error or variability to the research procedures? How many assistants are to be employed, and for how long? Just what will each one have to do? Are they to be recompensed for their time? If so, at what rate and how easy would it be to obtain the necessary funds? Is the time required to train other personnel likely to be so excessive that the investigator would do better to change his design so that he could do the job alone?

Colleagues, both local and distant, are often quite willing to help in formulating a research project. Students, teachers, researchers with whom one corresponds—any of these people may be consulted on the design. Presenting the problem to those who do not know the field may also help to clarify one's own conception of the project and may make one aware of the kinds of issues likely to arise in administering the research. Approached tactfully, most people are willing to give advice, especially if they are permitted to take their time about it.

Sometimes it is possible to obtain help in other aspects of the study in the same way, especially if the assistance is required for only a short time. Other people may become interested enough in your project to be willing to donate their services for nothing. Colleagues, undergraduate students, graduate students, professors, and other professionals are all possible sources of free assistance. Graduate students can often persuade undergraduates to contribute time to their research, with benefit to both. Staff members at a college or university can obtain help from undergraduate or graduate students, often through research assistantships which not only get the research done but also offer excellent apprenticeship training and make it financially possible for the student to pursue his studies.

Although the beginning researcher is unlikely to be in the position of paying others to assist him, perhaps he should be aware of the personnel issues associated with larger projects involving the services of many people. If a great deal of time is required of an assistant, he should probably be paid (or made a collaborator—or both). For some projects it may be advisable to obtain research assistants or research associates. The great majority of research assistantships are filled with students at one's own institution. The typical procedure for hiring research associates is to obtain applications from several well-qualified people and to assemble as much relevant information as possible about each one before deciding whom to hire. Several routes are useful for advertising major openings. The APA's *Em-*

ployment Bulletin lists job descriptions and availability notices every month; openings are published without cost to the employer. More informally, word of mouth, notices on bulletin boards, letters, and contacts at professional meetings can serve to bring researcher and potential employee together.

Careful assessment of the skills required will help in the recruiting process and also make it more likely that the assistant's time, once he is hired, will be used optimally. An informal job analysis will help avoid the problem of asking him to perform duties he is not equipped to handle or to do routine tasks that do not require the special skills for which he was hired. Many clerical, statistical, secretarial, and technician functions can be served by nonprofessional help or by machines. It is cheaper, and better for the research assistant's morale, not to saddle him with too much tedious activity which does not employ his talents to good advantage.

Public Relations

Maintaining appropriate public relations is partly a matter of ethics; but it is also true that tactfulness, decency, and maturity in relations with others pay high dividends in furthering one's own research aims, both short and long term. If a person's or a public group's first encounter with research yields a satisfying experience, cooperation is all the more likely in the future; but if the initial experience is unpleasant a source of subjects or of other aid may become inaccessible to future researchers or to the investigator himself in later projects. Reports of pleasant relationships tend to circulate and to make future research that much easier. Reports of irritating experiences may well circulate even faster, and irreparable harm can be done by a well-meaning but inconsiderate investigator. Every researcher, in his professional contacts, is not only an individual, he is also seen as a representative of his discipline, and his behavior will reflect upon the other members of his field as well as upon himself.

Proper public relations means more than a recognition that one should consider the feelings of the people involved; tact must be coupled with honesty and a willingness to contribute time. One must, of course, take care not to promise more than will actually be delivered, whether to a contractor or to a subject. One should be prepared to give detailed nontechnical descriptions of his problem, technique, and findings to appropriate individuals and groups. If the researcher realizes in advance that he may have to spend a great deal of time talking with subjects, administrators, and others, he will not become unduly irritated when unanticipated demands are made on him.

Many detailed principles and codes of conduct are to be recommended for professional relations with subjects, administrators, public groups, newspapers, etc.; the American Psychological Association's code of ethics (1959)—especially the longer version (1953)—and *Public information guide* (1954) include many of them, explicitly and implicitly. Basically, all of the principles reduce to common sense and to tactful and responsible maturity. In almost all public contacts, the researcher is getting something out of the relationship; even when he is giving information to a representative of the mass media, he is getting free publicity, if nothing else. Especially when contacting organizations or individuals in an attempt to obtain space, funds, data, or subjects, recognition that it is the researcher who is receiving a favor rather than vice versa may help him view his conduct and role appropriately.

FINAL PREPARATIONS

Before formal data collection begins, it is worthwhile to re-examine the entire plan to ascertain whether the design and operations are really likely to yield the desired information. This check on the adequacy of the operations includes reviewing the conceptual background, reexamining the procedures, and conducting pilot studies. A careful review may make the difference between answering the specific research questions of interest and obtaining irrelevant information. At stake is the validity of the results, hence the convincingness of the entire research venture. Do the operations really tap what is desired? Do they do so with sufficient reliability so that random error will not obliterate the relations of interest? Can alternative explanations of the anticipated outcome be eliminated reasonably easily, or are further controls needed before the data are likely to produce the conviction that the independent variable you think is responsible for changes in the dependent variable actually is? Is the subject sample going to be adequate to its purpose? Is the over-all strategy of the plan an efficient one? Reconsidering the design from these points of view before formal data collection begins is, of course, better than doing it afterwards when it may be too late.

Frequently it will be hard to tell, as the project develops, where the "pilot phase" ends and "formal data collection" has begun; these stages typically merge into each other. Yet it is often useful, at some fairly advanced stage of the project's development, to attempt a final check, a kind of dry run or dress rehearsal of the data-collection procedures. If nothing else, the dress rehearsal will provide a final jelling of the procedures.

By no means do all projects progress smoothly through the pilot phases into a dress rehearsal and formal data collection. It is much more common to encounter difficulties which at first appear insurmountable and which yield only with prolonged effort.

Some operational definitions turn out to be unsatisfactory for any of a large number of reasons; a control may seem absolutely necessary yet appear impossible to institute; a piece of apparatus proves to be particularly recalcitrant; adequate sampling of subjects or conditions may be impossible within the realistic time and money limitations; a preliminary finding makes no sense. At every new encounter of a snag the researcher may feel discouraged or even like dropping the whole thing. The need for patience, persistence, and a high frustration tolerance becomes particularly great when a difficult obstacle is encountered.

Obviously, the basic decision to be made at such a juncture is whether to give up or to go on, whether the study is worth conducting even if some aspects of it appear inadequate. In the early stages of planning it is usually easier to consider dropping the problem entirely than it is after a lot of time has been devoted to it; but one probably should not let initial discouragement permit him to leave the field prematurely. Some difficulties, some adverse criticisms, some imperfections are to be expected in every project, and in each case one must judge, to the best of his ability, whether the problems encountered in the study are sufficiently great to warrant the relatively drastic step of quitting entirely. The newcomer to research would probably do better to lean over backwards and continue his tenacious hold on the project until he simply cannot stand it any more—and even to continue working on it past this point. The impression that another problem will prove less difficult is likely to be illusory. On the other hand, every investigator will encounter his share of intractable problems, so one might as well be prepared for failure in a sizable proportion of his research endeavors.

The Dress Rehearsal

If the project seems worth following through, then sometime the design and all the details of procedure have to become set and firm. Once formal data collection is begun, no further modifications can be made, for this would make data collected at one time incomparable with those obtained at another. It is often difficult to decide whether to settle on a particular research design or to mull it over a bit more. In the early phases it is probably wise to remain open-minded about alternative ways of attacking the problem; one should try not to rigidify prematurely but, on the other hand, not remain open-minded so indefinitely that the empirical study is never performed.

After an apparently satisfactory procedure is developed, the final dress rehearsal is, at least ideally, conducted exactly like the "real thing" and on subjects like those to be included in the final study. If anything is to go wrong, it is better to have it happen here than later when it could prove costly. A dress rehearsal serves other functions as well. It gives the investigator initial practice in running subjects, so that early ones in the regular study will be treated just like later ones. It lets him see if his data sheet is efficiently designed (see below) and may even yield some preliminary hint of the study's outcome. It permits final specification of the research proposal, down to the last details of subject handling. Ideally, the proposal is complete if it could be handed to a technician and he could use it as a manual to run the study exactly as the researcher had intended.

The dress rehearsal also tells how long various parts of the procedure will take, hence provides a basis for scheduling data collection realistically. It is generally advisable to prepare at least a rough schedule of all aspects of the data-collection phase at this point: when each subject is to appear or to be approached; where the subject will be met and by whom; who else has to be met when and about what; when holidays, examinations, or other events might interfere with subjects' availability; when equipment will be turned on to let it warm up; when it will be serviced; who cleans what cages when; when the researcher (or his assistants) will have "dead time" to catch up after unanticipated delays; and so on. Even though subsequent events may force one to deviate from this schedule, it will at least encourage consideration of all the details that will have to be attended to.

COLLECTING THE DATA

The data-collection phase of research consists of following instructions one has set for himself in the research proposal and keeping records of what happens. If the study design is sufficiently explicit and has been thoroughly pretested in pilot studies, ideally the researcher can function in this stage like an automaton, simply doing what he has previously told himself to do or seeing to it that other people do it. The kinds of records, too, and the forms in which they are to be kept, will ideally have been so thoroughly anticipated that no new decisions on them are necessary at this point. But it is the rare researcher who is so foresighted and compulsive. Even if such a paragon existed, he would probably have trouble running the study because all of the people, animals, and things he worked with would not have been consulted in the design of his plan, hence might be expected to object or to go wrong in some way at the last minute.

Unanticipated Snags

Any part of the research design can cause trouble in the data-collection phase. One never knows how or what to troubleshoot until something appears to shoot at. If the apparatus breaks down, fix it. If the tests are illegible, reproduce them. If the subjects do not show up, turn back to Chapter 11. All one can try to do is anticipate as best one can and be prepared to overcome a variety of unforeseen difficulties. Obviously the best way to decrease the number and severity of unforeseen problems is to try to foresee them. In spite of all reasonable precautions, though, certain snags will arise, and some of them may be crucial to the validity of the research results. If the apparatus is more complex than pencil and paper (and even pencil points may break), it is likely that some part will go wrong. Or the power may go off. A thunderstorm may come directly overhead during an auditory experiment. The experimenter may sneeze at an inopportune moment. An apparatus breakdown may not be detected until too late and some essential data are lost. The experimental procedure may have to be changed in minor ways because something is not working as it should. A subject may see through a deception before he is supposed to and thus respond in a manner incomparable with the others. During the course of the measurements, what was initially a reasonably valid and reliable operation may, through wear or carelessness, slip from standard.

The decision about what to do with data obtained when something was not operating quite correctly must, of course, take into account how these data would affect the validity of the study as a whole. Some investigators feel that the decision is most likely to be fair if one does not know what data the deviant procedure yielded—whether they would support or contradict his hunches or hypotheses. Partly for this reason and partly to keep himself from inadvertently influencing the results, it is a useful precaution for the researcher to try during formal data collection to keep from finding out how individual subjects are performing. But if he cannot help knowing the effect on the outcome, he might decide to err on the side of caution by discarding those data that support his hypotheses and retaining those that contradict them. Such a course, however, implies a commitment to the position that "errors of rashness" are more serious than "errors of caution" (see Chapter 9), a position that may or may not be appropriate in any particular circumstances.

An idealist might say that under such conditions one must throw all the results out and start again from scratch. This may be the only course of action possible in some rare instance, but usually the impurity constitutes such a minor part of the total study that it is far preferable to go ahead with what one has. Besides, it is most likely that next time the study is run something else will go wrong to invalidate some of the data.

Whatever the researcher decides to do with the deviant data, he should present in his final report a description of the nature of the difficulty and how he handled it. This is scientifically—and ethically—proper practice, and it may help the reader to get additional knowledge or hunches from the report that he would not otherwise have obtained.

Keeping Records

Researchers do not have computer memories. Hence it is necessary to keep reasonably detailed records of procedures, observations, and data manipulations. Such records not only eliminate the need for reliance on memory, but make it possible for anyone who doubts the conclusions to search into their bases as far as he wishes for an alternative explanation. If necessary, he can repeat the study himself. An essential part of the data-collection process, therefore, is the production and storage of adequate records. This will help satisfy others concerning the validity of the research; it will also permit the researcher to know, himself, at a much later date, just what it was he did and observed that made him think a particular conclusion was justified. Further, with complete and orderly records, he or others can reanalyze the original data in ways not anticipated at the time they were collected.

Raw Data

The records kept in a typical study may be considered under three classifications—raw data, coded data, and the research diary. The *raw data* are those measures of variables that are taken and recorded directly at the time the behavior occurred. These can be questionnaires, test protocols, tape recordings, movies, kymograph tapes, tallies made or pointer readings recorded by the researcher, etc. *Coded data* are secondary records constructed out of categorizations and transformations of the raw data. Such a distinction is, of course, not hard and fast; one might argue that, strictly speaking, "raw data" do not exist apart from the observer's perceptual coding of them. At a practical level, one researcher may record as coded data what another would consider raw. In studying group interaction processes, for example, some researchers prefer to tape-record an entire discussion and analyze its content at leisure according to some subsequently developed coding system. Others prefer to code the interaction as they observe it, tallying various aspects of the discussion into sets of predetermined categories.

Which approach to use—precoding or postcoding of data—will depend on two things: how sure one is of what he is looking for and how accurately he can code it on the spot. It is generally inefficient to have large masses of raw data lying around, in the form of movies, tapes, or verbatim transcripts, for the researcher has then to go through them all again. Besides consuming an inordinate amount of time, such playbacks are never so satisfactory as the events from which they were made. Some of the discussion may be inaudible; part of the interaction that depends on visual cues or events that occur "off camera" may be missed, etc. So, to avoid being faced with a mountain of raw data that will take him months or years to transform and analyze, the researcher would do well to decide in advance what aspects of the occurrences he is interested in, then practice coding them on the spot rather than attempting to record "everything" (actually, of course, he cannot do it) and just putting off the decisions until later.

There are some circumstances in which an attempt at a "complete" recording of "all" relevant occurrences may be worthwhile. In the exploratory stages of a study the researcher may have little idea of the significant dimensions of the problem and so may want to have the opportunity to review a full record of events over and over until some essential features become salient for him. Usually the purposes of such explorations are adequately served by just a few "full" records. There are also occasions (e.g., performance in an automatic Skinner box or the close-up study of wild animals) when all the raw data have to be recorded in the researcher's absence by some mechanical device (such as a cumulative response recorder or a motion picture camera) and subsequently studied from the record. In such cases there is no alternative to amassing large quantities of data, and all the researcher can do to simplify subsequent stages of his study is devise some efficient means of extracting the attributes he is interested in from the complete record.

Coded Data

Coding, or *content analysis* (see Chapter 8), involves, essentially, classifying aspects of events into categories. The aspects selected vary with the intent of the research. They may be such indisputably "objective" attributes as a pointer reading, how often a rat enters a blind alley, or the number of trials to criterion in a learning experiment or they may be more subtle, evanescent qualities such as group cohesiveness, subject cooperativeness, or pleasantness-unpleasantness. Whatever its position on this "objective-subjective" dimension, it is well for the researcher to maintain sufficient doubt concerning his judgments to test the reliability with which they can be made. Generally, the most appropriate reliability check is provided by having two or more independent coders classify the same data into the predetermined categories and then computing a relational statistic to represent the magnitude of their agreement (see Chapter 8, p. 189).

The particular data sheet form and data categories to be used should, of course, be designed with a view to their eventual analysis. Thus, if the numbers representing, say, a subject's position on several attributes, are later to be punched into IBM cards, it is wise to anticipate this operation by designing the observation sheet, interview schedule, clinical checklist, or other record form for direct punching. For instance, the study, card, and subject numbers might be punched into the first several columns, and a space for them should be left at the top of the data sheet; responses could be coded, as suggested in Chapter 8, in the direct numerical form in which they are eventually to be punched into the analysis cards.

Usually the data sheet is most efficient if it is set up so that all the investigator needs to do when collecting information is fill numbers and other material into appropriately labeled blanks; the resulting uniformity later allows for ease of transcription or analysis. Sometimes it is also desirable to leave specifically labeled spaces for transformations (such as percentages and totals) on the data sheet.

A well-planned *summary* sheet, in addition to the individual forms, facilitates analysis. This usually consists of a large piece of paper on which columns may refer to the various measures; a separate row is allotted to each subject. All the data from the study are then conveniently displayed in one place. In designing this sheet, one should, of course, anticipate the eventual analysis and leave some blank columns for computations. Sometimes, the original observations can be recorded directly on the summary form, dispensing with individual forms for each subject or each trial.

If data sheets have been adequately designed, there should be little trouble in recording observed measures, whether "raw" or "coded." The practice gained in the dress rehearsal should bring the researcher to a stage in which recording is essentially an automatic process; he has in effect made himself into a measuring machine which, at appropriate occasions, produces certain numbers in specified places on a prepared sheet.

The Research Diary

The data of the study, in raw or coded form, provide records of the variables which the researcher intends to interrelate in the analysis. In addition to these, many things are likely to occur in the course of data collection which were not initially planned or which cannot properly be regarded as variables of the study. Any of the mishaps alluded to earlier—from power failure to an intoxicated subject—may have a bearing on the outcome, and it is essential to keep a record of the event. Several months afterward, when the researcher is trying to make sense out of his data, he will have a hard time recalling just what the circumstances were that might account for peculiar results in a given period.

The research diary, which is so useful in the earlier stages of getting ideas and making them concrete, can also come in handy at this point. If the experimenter records these relevant events which have not been explicitly provided for in the data records, it will give him something to refer to in case the results of analysis lead him to suspect that something distorted the outcome of the study. Occasionally, the initially unplanned diary entries can be used to add a new variable to the study by indicating another way in which subjects or experimental conditions differ, besides the ways provided for in the original design.

PREPARING DATA FOR ANALYSIS

If the data are initially obtained and recorded with an eye to later analysis, much clerical time will be saved. The data summary sheet should typically have extra columns for anticipated transformed or derived scores, such as ratios, percentages, reversed scores, means, difference scores, or logarithms; and the original data sheets should be set up to make computations or transformations from them reasonably easy.

Punch-Card Storage

One of the more convenient ways to process and analyze research data is with IBM punch cards; these cards also permit compact, durable, readily accessible storage. Hence in many research projects direct transformation of the raw data into punch-card form is the preferable procedure. In addition to the storage advantages, punch cards can be run through machines that will prepare tables, perform calculations, and operate on information in almost any manner that one can specify (see chapter supplement). All this is done at such high speeds that the savings in time will generally more than offset the extra expense of planning and processing—at least when identical operations are repeated perhaps fifty or more times.

Though IBM (International Business Machines, Inc.) is the best known among producers of data-processing and calculating equipment, there are other brands of computers (such as Remington, Bendix, and Royal McBee) which will do some kinds of work just as well, often at much less cost. Some universities have their own homemade computers (the Illiac at the University of Illinois or the Midac at the University of Michigan) or have access to IBM computers at some other institution (see chapter supplement). There are also several older mechanical devices for data processing, such as Keysort or McBee cards, which, though limited in speed and flexibility, may nevertheless be more efficient than electronic computers for relatively small jobs. The great variety of mechanical aids to data storage and processing precludes anything like adequate coverage; we shall touch only on the IBM devices, which are by far the most widely used at the time of this writing. Details on these and other methods can be found in some of the references at the end of this chapter (Gruenberger, 1952; Hartkemeier, 1942; IBM, 1950, 1957; Mace & Alsop, 1957).

The basic element in IBM analysis is the Hollerith punch card, on which the data are recorded and stored. The card has 12 rows and 80 columns, so that a hole could be punched in any of the 960 cells formed by their intersections (see Fig. 12-1). Actually, it is usual to make only one punch per column and to use only 10 of the 12 rows for that purpose. In one kind of card layout each column (or sequence of columns) stands for an attribute or item of information and each row in that column for a category in the dimension. Thus column 26

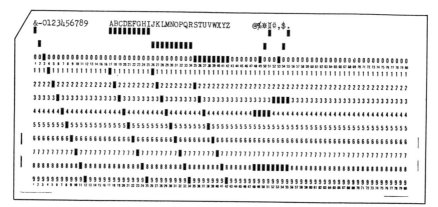

Fig. 12-1. Facsimile of a Hollerith Punch Card.

might be designated "political party affiliation" and rows 1 to 4 of that column used to represent "Democrat," "Republican," "Other," and "Unaffiliated." If more than 10 (or, as a maximum, 12) categories of response are distinguished, one can use two columns, thus increasing the total number of available categories to 100 (or to a maximum of 144, if all 12 rows are used). So chronological age, for example, might be represented in columns 15 and 16 together.

The holes are punched into the appropriate space in each column by means of a key punch. This machine automatically feeds cards into punching position, and the operator strikes a keyboard something like that of a typewriter. If the data to be recorded were the responses of subjects to 60 items in a test, the first two columns might identify the subject number, and the next 60, the test items, with the different rows representing alternative responses. When a "1" is punched on the keyboard, a hole is made in the "1" row of the column, and the carriage moves the card to the next column, ready for punching. Thus the entire record of a single subject's test behavior could be punched on one card; each subject would have a different card and each test item a different column or pair of columns; responses could be coded in any of a variety of ways. Chapter 8, p. 186, gives an example of a set of coding categories that could be readily transferred to an IBM card.

Sometimes it is convenient to punch cards directly from an interview schedule, tally sheet, or other form on which the data were recorded. Occasionally, especially if insufficient foresight was used in planning the recording sheets, the data will be scattered on numerous pieces of paper that are inconvenient to leaf through during key punching. In such cases a summary data sheet is particularly helpful so that all code numbers can be recorded in orderly fashion in a single place before attempting to punch them. For IBM work, one kind of convenient coding sheet would consist of square-ruled paper with 80 columns and an appropriate number of rows (say between 25 and 40). Each row is used for a different IBM card (i.e., a different subject), and each cell contains the number that is to be punched into the corresponding column on the card. Although the total procedure, since it consists of two successive stages, is undoubtedly more time consuming and error producing than punching directly from precoded material, it is the only feasible practice for some kinds of data.

Clerical Control of Records

No matter how careful the researcher is and whether or not he uses machine analysis techniques, some errors are bound to creep in. A number may be transferred incorrectly from a data sheet to a summary sheet, it may be misread in calculation, or an entire set of figures may be read from the wrong column. For these reasons, it is always essential to double-check every step in copying and computing. This is time consuming but necessary for accurate results.

Complete labeling of the raw data, transformations, analysis sheets, and results is necessary too. If a reasonably thorough job is done in squeezing everything one can from the data, a sizable pile of tables, charts, and graphs will accumulate. The typical forgetful researcher may return to a scatterplot he made a month ago only to find that he did not label the axes, and he has no way of knowing what it represents. If the variables and their component categories are compulsively recorded at the time they are related, this may save needless reanalyses of the same results. It may also be helpful to write down on each table a brief summary of what it means, so that sometime later when the specific analysis is forgotten the researcher can still find out quickly why he did it.

It is a good idea to save all the data and all the analysis sheets, instructions, etc., from every study. Discard nothing, because at a later time you may want to return for a check on some inconsistent result or for a reanalysis stemming from some new hunch that occurs only as an afterthought. If the data are adequately stored, a new hypothesis formulated at a later date might be tested directly on available data rather than requiring a whole new study.

Making records in the first place implies that one is ready to keep them around. If provisions for data storage have not been made, the records are bound to be scattered over desk tops and floors until they become lost or disordered beyond repair. Storage facilities may be nothing more complicated than a manila folder, a box, or a desk drawer; they may also be as elaborate as a roomful of files of IBM cards or microfilms.

Whatever the scope of storage, it is essential to have its system explicitly recorded. Items of data and records of analysis should be clearly labeled to indicate their contents, and batches of records that are alike in some important respect should be stored together (or at least cross-indexed together). The record items might include almost anything—questionnaires, test papers, data sheets, kymograph records, tape recordings, or films; some types of records—such as long continuous sheets or tapes—may be quite difficult to label in a way that will permit immediate access to any desired portion of them. Early attention to an adequate storage system and to adequate labeling will avoid at least some of the problems of finding what one wants later.

Problems of identification must therefore be anticipated in the planning of data storage. It will do little good to amass huge quantities of records that the researcher cannot interpret—or even wade through—a year later when he is finally ready to. Moreover, it is generally not sufficient that the researcher himself understand his storage and classification system thoroughly. It should be so explicit that someone else could find his way around in the data pretty readily with a minimum of instruction. This is not only to permit continuation of the research should the principal investigator leave in the second act; it is to make the routine analyses easier for the investigator himself or for an assistant. It often happens that by the time the detailed analysis phase rolls around, the researcher is off thinking about another project and may no longer be sufficiently immersed in the old one to remember quickly what various notations mean. If assistants are employed, they may constantly have to keep coming to him to clear up problems stemming from inadequate data labeling which could better have been attended to earlier. There is enough tedium and concern with minutiae which form a necessary part of any research project to make one doubly anxious to avoid the unnecessary. Neat storage of records and explicit detailed labeling, performed as soon as possible after the data are collected, will help keep tedium to a minimum.

SUMMARY

The researcher's administrative duties include taking care of requirements for financial support, space, assistance, equipment, and subjects. Maintenance of good public relations is essential if these requirements are to be met. Space needs can usually be filled by consulting the appropriate staff member of the institution with which one is associated; sometimes extensive remodeling may be necessary, and often one will have to make do with less than optimal space arrangements. Assistance in conducting the research can be obtained through colleagues, undergraduate and graduate students, secretarial and clerical personnel, and sometimes professional psychologists, depending upon the work required of the assistant.

The basic function of pilot work is to assess and improve the adequacy of all operations that constitute the research project. The early crude pilot studies give some indication whether the problem can be attacked empirically at all; later pilot work serves to develop the project; the dress rehearsal affords a final check, preliminary data, a basis for the final revised proposal, and training for the experimenter.

The data-collection phase of the study, of course, is the culmination of all the previous stages. If these stages have been thoroughly attended to, then data collection can be almost automatic. The investigator may only need to keep records and attend, as necessary, to any problems not handled in the original design and in the pilot work. It will frequently require ingenuity and patience to meet the various unanticipated difficulties that crop up if the actual project is to bear a close resemblance to that laid out in the final design.

Careful recording procedures decrease the likelihood of frustration and uninterpretable figures later on. As data accumulate, they should be recorded in readily accessible, clearly labeled form. A well-planned data summary sheet may provide an efficient form for analysis and storage. Often it is worthwhile to store data on IBM cards in anticipation of future analyses. Whatever the form, if some thought is given early to the kinds of analyses likely to be performed on the data, optimal recording and storage procedures can be devised.

SUPPLEMENT

Aids to Computation

Many analyses can be done quite satisfactorily at one's desk, with pencil and paper and perhaps some graph paper. Even some statistical computations are fairly easy to do with nothing but an inexpensive hand adding machine (like the VePoAd) and a slide rule. It takes only a few minutes to learn how to use them; and this small amount of time is well spent if one is going to add large numbers, multiply, divide, or take square roots.

Computation of most formal statistics is fairly laborious, and with large quantities of data manual calculation becomes prohibitive. For this reason, the researcher should at least have access to a desk calculator of the automatic type (such as the Monroe, Fridén, or Marchant). These machines permit accumulation of frequencies and products, which are required for most statistics. Even mechanical aids of this kind are insufficient for massive research projects that require hundreds of calculations. It may take 15 or 20 minutes to compute and verify a single product-moment correlation on an automatic calculator. With anything like a hundred correlations, this method becomes very inefficient. The researcher would be wise, in such circumstances, to arrange for access to data-processing and computing machines of the IBM type, which permit simultaneous calculation of large numbers of correlation coefficients (and other statistics) in a matter of minutes. Many other steps in data processing can be performed on them with a comparable increase in efficiency.

The basic bivariate and multivariate frequency distributions themselves can be produced with the aid of an IBM counter-sorter or a tabulating sorter. The counter-sorter has a dial for each row in the card; when a column indicator is set for a particular column and the cards are run through the feed hopper (at a rate as high as 1000 a minute), the number of cards with punches in each row of that column is automatically counted. The tabulating sorter will perform the same function (though more slowly), except that frequencies are automatically printed rather than displayed on dials. Either of these machines will also sort the cards into 12 different pockets; this way a bivariate or multivariate frequency distribution can be prepared rapidly, giving numerical data from which any needed statistic can be calculated.

At this point the researcher can look at the distribution and decide what statistics, if any, to compute on the desk calculator. If the same computing operations are to be performed hundreds of times, it is probably better to have them done by an electronic computer. Most of these computers are basically fast adding machines, but an amazing number of complex operations can be built up out of the simple one of addition. An accomplished computer can multiply, divide, take square roots, factor-analyze intercorrelation matrices, write polynomial equations, and play an end game of chess. All that is necessary is to break the desired operation down into simple elements that the machine can understand and feed this set of instructions into it as a program.

A program for an IBM computer is typically a set of IBM cards into which are punched, not data, but instructions to the machine. These instructions are read, stored, and utilized by the machine at appropriate stages of the calculating process. First the program is fed into the computer and then the data to be analyzed. When all computations called for have been completed, the results are automatically punched out in new cards or printed on rolls of paper attached to the machine.

Writing a program and checking it out to see if it works is likely to be the most time-consuming part of the procedure. This can be done by the investigator himself, after reading a programmer's manual (e.g., IBM, 1957) or taking a short course in computer programming, or he can have it done by hiring a programming technician; this is likely to be quite expensive—perhaps costing as much as several hundred dollars (including machine rental time for "debugging"). One would not want to write a new program if it were to be used for just a small number of calculations that could be done cheaply and accurately by other means.

Gradually, as these machines are used for psychological research, a library of *canned programs* is being built up so that it is no longer necessary for each investigator to write his own. He can simply get in touch with the library (at IBM's central office or at any installation that has its own computer) to see what appropriate programs—for example, correlation, curve-fitting, and significance tests—are available and to find out what specifications his data have to meet in order to use them.

Getting Access to Machines

Almost any data-processing or calculating machine can be bought from the manufacturer. Purchase by an institution such as a university may be economical in the long run, but often only if a sizable academic discount is negotiated with the IBM corporation or a different machine is bought from one of that company's competitors (whose prices are generally lower, but whose lines are less complete). If the machine is purchased, however, it must be maintained by the owner, and this is likely to be unduly expensive, unless enough machines are owned to warrant employing a full-time electronic and machine technician. If only a few machines are needed, it is frequently better to rent them from the IBM corporation on a monthly basis. Some sample rental costs, as of 1962, are shown in the list on p. 316. These costs include maintenance and servicing as needed.

An additional advantage of rental, of course, is that old machines can be replaced as they become obsolete. Obsolescence is likely to be a chronic problem in this young industry, and the researcher-utilizer may wish to avoid getting caught owning a roomful of out-of-date machines. Given the cultural lag in most institutions, however, it is likely that plenty of good use will be found for any of these machines long after they are outmoded. In fact, the 075 counter-sorter still had not been introduced to most psychologists many years after IBM stopped producing it commercially. The relative advantage of machine rental and purchase, then, will depend on the complexity of the operation required and on the extent to which the ultimate in speed of computation is essential to the research.

Purchase or rental, though, the lone psychologist or the typical impecunious department can rarely afford prices like these. In order to be economical, full-time possession usually demands near-full-time machine utilization.

IBM Machine	Approximate Monthly Rental in 1962 (including service) *
026 Printing key punch (for punching data onto cards)	$ 60
519 Reproducer (for copying cards and transferring data from several cards into one)	110
548 Interpreter (for printing the punched holes on the card)	100
082 Sorter (for separating cards into piles, at the rate of 450 cards per minute)	40
083 Sorter (for separating cards into piles, at the rate of 1000 cards per minute)	110
083 Sorter with bank of counters (for counting numbers of cards in piles)	140
101 Electronic statistical machine (for sorting, counting, and printing the results)	245
1620 Data-processing system †	1,600
1401 Data-processing system †	2,425
650 Data-processing system †	3,750
704 Data-processing system †	28,750
709 Data-processing system †	33,100

* Academic institutions can frequently obtain sizable discounts from these rates if the machines are to be used for instruction or for nonprofit research.

† For a variety of algebraic and statistical calculations; the more expensive the computer, the faster and more versatile it is.

More likely one will have just a few hours' work to perform each month (or year). There are several ways of meeting such intermittent needs. The most direct, perhaps, would be to hire the machine work, either by a nearby IBM office or by some other computing service (these sometimes advertise in the *American Psychologist*). Though requiring a minimum of attention on the researcher's part, such channels are likely to be expensive. Fortunately, many universities which do not own their own machines are nowadays able to share in cooperative installations such as the Western Data Processing Center (University of California, Los Angeles) and the MIT Computation Center (Cambridge, Mass.). These centers provide canned programs, machine time, operators' services, and program consultation at no cost to the individual researcher. He can get convenient access to them simply by calling his local campus representative or writing directly to the center.

The main drawback of such facilities is that they are usually a long way off, and all contacts and instructions must be accomplished by mail. If one knows fairly well what he wants done, this will work fine, but it is not too satisfactory for simply "playing around" with analyses until something meaningful appears. For such purposes, one wants machines close by. Sometimes these can be found in local organizations—such as university business offices, insurance companies, or federal bureaus—agencies which own or rent their equipment but do not use it 24 hours a day. They are often quite cooperative—and may even go out of their way to help—in arranging machine time and the necessary access to their building during off-hours. Usually they cannot provide an operator, and they must be assured that the person running their machines is competent and trustworthy (it may be the researcher himself or a trained operator whom he hires). The rental rate they charge to an outside user will vary widely. Some agencies figure that an hourly rate of ¹⁄₁₇₀ of their monthly rental will cover costs, hence is a fair price. Others will point out that their machines cannot be used full-time even during working hours, hence their hourly rate must be high enough to compensate for their dead time. Then there are some charitable institutions which may permit after-hours use at a nominal price.

Whatever the arrangements, they almost always involve a favor to the researcher, for, unless renting machines is their business, these organizations would rather not be bothered by casual users who might damage their equipment. The investigator should understand this and not treat people's courtesy as a purchasable commodity. The best approach is usually to estimate how many hours' time will be required on each type of machine, mention this to the agency at the time you make your request, and then tell them how much money you have to spend for that purpose. They will tell you whether it seems reasonable to them. If not, you can try somewhere else— or go back to the desk calculator and the slide rule.

Learning to estimate machine costs realistically takes much personal experience. The researcher can usually get some help in this by calling on one of his colleagues who has worked with data-processing machines before, describing his analysis problem in detail, and working out a joint time and cost estimate with him. (If no such colleague is available, the commercial computing service agencies will generally provide time and cost estimates—at *their* prices.) Whatever the avenue to processing and computer service, it is generally a sizable budget item. The researcher should allow for it amply and be ready to shop around and consider alternatives to make the best use of the available funds. IBM or other forms of mechanical data processing are efficient mainly because they permit accurate performance of gigantic routine tasks in a hurry. If one does not have gigantic routine tasks or if money is more precious than time, then machine computation may cost more than it is worth.

REFERENCES

American Psychological Association. *Ethical standards of psychologists.* Washington, D. C.: American Psychological Association, 1953.

American Psychological Association. Ethical standards of psychologists. *Amer. Psychologist,* 1959, **14,** 279–282.

American Psychological Association. *Public information guide.* Washington, D. C.: American Psychological Association, 1954.

Gruenberger, F. *Computing manual.* (3rd Ed.) Madison, Wisconsin: Univer. Wisconsin Press, 1952.

Hartkemeier, H. P. *Principles of punch card machine operation.* New York: Crowell, 1942.

International Business Machines, Inc. *Bibliography on the use of IBM machines in science, statistics, and education.* New York: Author, 1950.

International Business Machines, Inc. *Programmer's primer for FORTRAN.* New York: Author, 1957.

Mace, D., & Alsop, Joyce. *A simplified system for the use of an automatic calculator.* New York: International Business Machines Corp., 1957.

CHAPTER 13

Analyzing the results

The research finally reaches the stage toward which all the preceding discussion has been aimed: discovering and interpreting the outcome. In a sense, of course, any result is latent in the research procedures that led up to it. But by no means all the important findings of a study are necessarily anticipated from the beginning; so the investigator may be in for some surprises at this stage.

The clean and neat approach to research consists of knowing in advance exactly what hypotheses are to be examined, designing instruments or experimental procedures which can test them, collecting data on the optimal number of subjects, then performing, if necessary, statistical computations to assess how likely it is that the relations or differences found are due only to chance. This is the ideal way that should perhaps be recommended to novices: anticipate your analyses from the beginning so that all phases of the research can be designed to permit clear, unambiguous interpretation of the outcome. If the potential analyses are not constantly kept in mind as the goal of the entire process, then one may reach this stage only to discover that the hoped-for results cannot possibly be demonstrated by the research methods chosen. An early statement of specific hypotheses will presumably help guard against such a disappointing conclusion; it can also make the analysis phase a fairly routine affair, in which one looks for the anticipated relations only; if they are not found, the researcher revises his theory, and new data are collected to test it.

We know of very little psychological research that is performed in this manner.

319

What more frequently happens at the analysis stage is that the researcher tests the original, specific hypotheses (if he had any); most of them do not come out in the anticipated way—or, at best, the results are murky—so he then looks for ways to account for the failure or tries to discover what conclusions, if any, his data do suggest. Some new, unanticipated result may lead him to a different interpretation of the critical variables in his study. Perhaps this interpretation can be checked by independent analysis in the same data; perhaps it will require a completely new study in which measures and manipulations are formulated specifically around the new hypotheses. Such a diffuse approach to data analysis might suggest that the researcher does not quite know what he is doing and never did; on the other hand, it might reflect an underlying belief that thorough exploration of available data will make it possible for nature to tell him something that would have remained hidden with a more rigid approach.

Without seeming to endorse either of these approaches to analysis, the clean or the messy, we can simply note that both kinds occur in research enterprises—depending perhaps on the individual researcher or on the phase of the research program in which he finds himself. Common to both approaches is a search for relationships among variables. The eventual aim is to make these relationships, whether formulated a priori or a posteriori, understandable on the basis of theory, of other known facts, or of common sense. It is perhaps the last kind of meaning (derived from the wider culture) that tends to dominate both our psychological theories and our interpretations of facts, and we shall try in this chapter to look at analysis within the framework of common-sense views of relationships.

SOME KINDS OF RELATIONSHIPS SOUGHT

It is characteristic of common-sense thinking that simple explanations are preferred to complex ones. Psychologists generally share this preference—some because they believe the world really is simple if understood at a fundamental level, others perhaps because they modestly believe their own minds incapable of very complex formulations. One way to simplify relationships is to consider only two variables at a time. Another is to conceive of the relationship deterministically rather than probabilistically. A large portion of psychological research is formulated from a bivariate deterministic model.

Some Simple Bivariate Relationships

The simplest kind of bivariate determinism is expressed in the statement, "X causes Y" or "X is a necessary and sufficient condition for Y." Here both X and Y may be thought of as dichotomous variables, which are either present or absent. The statements imply that whenever X occurs, Y will be found with it; whenever X does not occur, Y will not be found either; there will be no cases in which one phenomenon appears without the other. The kind of data that one might ideally expect from such a formulation may be represented in a four-cell table:

Y	X	
	Absent	Present
Present		𝍸 𝍸 |||
Absent	𝍸 𝍸		

A slightly more complicated expression of bivariate determinism would be, "Different forms of X will be associated with different forms of Y." This relational statement differs from the preceding in that it anticipates more than two categories within X and/or Y. The different categories are not ordered with respect to one another but simply constitute a nominal scale. An example might be, "The kind of car a person buys will depend on where he lives: people at River Rouge will own Fords; those at Kenosha, Ramblers; residents of Florida will have Renaults; and people in California will buy Toyopets." The data in this table are perfectly consistent with such an assertion:

Automobile	Location			
	California	Kenosha	Florida	River Rouge
Ford				𝍸 𝍸 ||
Rambler		𝍸		
Renault			𝍸 𝍸	
Toyopet	𝍸 |||			

Another variation on this simple model consists in treating each of the attributes, X and Y, as a continuous variable, divided into categories which can be uniquely ordered according to the amount of the attribute they represent. (This is an ordinal scale.) The relational statement then asserts that, "The more of X a person has, the greater (or less) will be his Y." This is a monotonic relationship, illustrated in the following idealized table, where X and Y are taken to mean ambition and income, respectively:

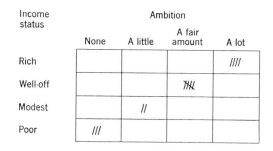

Income status	Ambition			
	None	A little	A fair amount	A lot
Rich				////
Well-off			⑪	
Modest		//		
Poor	///			

Becoming somewhat more precise, one might believe that he could predict exactly how much Y a person had from a knowledge of his X, according to a linear equation of the form, $Y = aX + b$. An artificially simplified example is: "Each gram of food ingested by a laboratory animal will yield a half-gram increase in its weight." The expected relationship would look like this, with all measures falling exactly on the line, $Y = \frac{1}{2}X + 100$, where 100 is the animal's initial weight, X is the amount of food in grams, and Y the resulting weight.

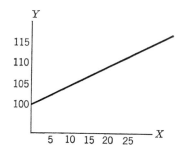

A linear equation is not, of course, the only method for predicting Y exactly from X. Logarithmic or quadratic or other nonlinear functions might be used as well. Also, these functions need not be single-valued; any X-score might be associated with two or more Y-scores and vice versa. But such multivalued functions tend to surpass the realm of simple common-sense relationships ordinarily entertained in the analysis of psychological data.

One way of complicating these bivariate models (and, incidentally, making them somewhat more realistic) without stretching our theoretical and analytic capacities too far is to consider them in probabilistic, rather than deterministic, terms. A probabilistic relationship is one in which a given value of Y is more likely to be associated with a particular X than are other values of Y. So, with dichotomous variables, one might say, "When X is present, Y is more likely to be present (or absent) than when X is not present." The following data would be consistent with such a model.

		X
Y	Absent	Present
Present	//	////
Absent	ⅢⅩ //	/

A probabilistic monotonic relationship would be stated something like, "The more of X a person possesses, the more of Y he is likely to possess," and so on; each of the deterministic relations mentioned above could be translated into appropriate probabilistic language.

Regardless of how psychological relationships are formulated theoretically, deterministically or otherwise, they almost invariably show up probabilistically in the data brought to bear upon them. This result might be attributed to errors of measurement or to the belief that Y depends also on other variables besides X, which were not assessed (in other words, an admission that the bivariate model is insufficient). It might also be interpreted as reflecting a more fundamental fact about real-world relationships—that they are essentially probabilistic and indeterminate. Whatever the assumed reason for the departure of empirical results from the deterministic models, the very fact of departure confronts the researcher with a two-fold task: first to state the simple deterministic relation that best fits his data and second to tell how good that fit is. Both of these kinds of conclusions are arrived at probabilistically.

Some Simple Multivariate Relationships

Given that bivariate formulations can usually provide, at best, a very inexact fit with empirical data, most research psychologists confronted with a real-world problem immediately start thinking of multivariate relationships. They see Y, the dependent variable, as a function of a number of independent variables, combined in various ways. One kind of simple combination is *additive*. This means that Y is associated with several different independent variables, all in essentially the same way. The more that any one of them occurs, the more will Y occur. Stated in deterministic fashion, with all variables dichotomous, such a relationship would sound like: "If either X_1 or X_2 occurs, Y will also; if neither X_1 nor X_2 appears, Y will not appear." Ideal data would look like this table:

Y	X_1:	Absent		Present	
	X_2:	Absent	Present	Absent	Present
Present			////	卌 /	///
Absent		卌			

A probabilistic formulation would state: "If either X_1 or X_2 occurs, Y is also more likely to occur than otherwise; if both X_1 and X_2 appear, Y is more likely to appear than with either X_1 or X_2 alone." The following data would be consistent with such a model:

Y	X_1:	Absent		Present	
	X_2:	Absent	Present	Absent	Present
Present		//	卌	卌	卌/
Absent		卌	////	///	/

If all three variables were treated as continuous interval scales, then a deterministic linear formulation might be phrased as follows: $Y = aX_1 + bX_2 + c$. There would be some correspondence between Y and either X_1 or X_2 taken alone, but accurate prediction could be made only from the specified combination. Stated probabilistically, this three-variable linear relationship might be expressed as: "A constant increment in Y tends to go with a constant increment in either X_1 or X_2; a better prediction of Y can be made by adding the contributions of both independent variables in the specified manner." This is equivalent to saying that Y can be more accurately predicted from $aX_1 + bX_2$ than from either aX_1 or bX_2 alone (adding an appropriate constant, c, in each case).

Additive multivariate relationships can be extended to include as many independent variables as desired. Extended models of this type imply that each new X_i considered will improve the prediction of Y beyond what was possible from the previous set of independent variables. Moreover, the way in which any new X affects Y is uniform over all values of the old Xs; that is, it does not matter how much of X_1 is present, since X_2 will still have the specified increment of effect on Y.

Although perhaps closer to fact than the simple bivariate models, multivariate formulations that are simply additive will also be found deficient when applied to many psychological problems. This is because independent variables typically are found to combine in nonadditive ways. So simple models of *interactive* effects are frequently proposed. One of these might be called a *conditional relationship*. Stated in all-or-none fashion, this implies that in the absence of X_1, X_2 will not lead to Y, but X_1 and X_2 together will produce Y. An example of a conditional formulation of psychological variables would be: "Severe punishment of children (X_2) will produce hostility (Y) *if, and only if*, the parents display a generally rejecting attitude (X_1)." Ideal data might appear as follows:

Y	X_1: X_2:	Absent		Present	
		Absent	Present	Absent	Present
Present					𝖳𝖧𝖫 /
Absent		𝖳𝖧𝖫	///	////	

A somewhat different form of interactive relationship among independent variables may be referred to as a *suppressor relationship*. An all-or-none way of describing such a combination would be: "Either X_1 or X_2 alone will produce Y, but both together will not." To make this example concrete, think of Y as representing unhappiness (present or absent), X_1 as a married state (present or absent), and X_2 as the rearing of children (present or absent). One might expect an American woman in her middle years (35–45) not to be unhappy, either if she were married and had children or if she had neither husband nor children; but social strains, and consequent unhappiness, might be predicted if the woman were faced with either of these conditions, marriage or children, alone. In other words, this theory suggests that unhappiness (or its obverse) cannot be predicted either from the presence of children alone or from the married state alone without knowing the condition of the other independent variable.

The feature common to both of these interactive relationships can be stated in general terms as follows: the relationship between X_1 and Y is not uniform but depends on the level of X_2. Quite often X_2 refers to a difference between populations of people, so that one might pre-

dict one X_1–Y-relationship in one population, and a different X_1–Y-re-
lationship in another population of subjects. The form in which such
multivariate interactive relations are most frequently found is not a
deterministic but a probabilistic one; that is, the probability that X_1
will lead to Y is greater (or less) if X_2 is present than if it is absent.

Just as additive combinations of independent variables can be complicated by including more of them, so can interactive combinations
become increasingly complex the more independent variables one considers. At some stage in thinking about the problem, the typical psychologist stops adding variables—either because his limited mind cannot interpret more complex combinations or because the few he already
has account for enough variation in Y to suit him for the moment.
We have deliberately dwelt here on only the simplest sorts of bivariate and multivariate relationships, since these are the ones most frequently encountered in psychological research. But it is easy to think
of elaborations and variations. For instance, one might conceive of
a case in which the dispersion of Y (e.g., $\sigma_y{}^2$) varies systematically
either with X or with $\sigma_x{}^2$. When confronted with data that suggest
such complex relationships, most psychologists would probably try to
account for them by adding new variables that would reduce the complexity to a simpler state of additive or interactive relations such as
those described above. In fact, as one reviews the vast amount of research and theory in psychology, he is impressed with the fact that by
far the largest portion deal with simple bivariate linear relationships
or simple additive and interactive relationships involving, at most,
three dichotomous variables.

VISUAL REPRESENTATION OF RELATIONSHIPS

So far we have discussed some basic relationships that a researcher
might wish to consider. The analysis problem is to see which of them,
if any, is best approximated by the data. The direct way to find this
out is to plot the data in an appropriate fashion and look at them.
Scores can be displayed in a *bivariate frequency distribution* (or
scatter plot), such as Table 13-1, in which X-scores are shown along
the horizontal axis and Y-scores along the vertical; each subject is
represented by a tally at the intersection of his X and Y scores. Alternatively, a graphical plot of group means may be constructed (see
Fig. 13-1, which is based on the data of Table 13-1). The shape of
the relational function can often be seen at a glance in such a plot.
If the means seem to fall, roughly, on a sloping straight line, then this

TABLE 13-1

Tabular Bivariate Frequency Distribution Showing (Probabilistic) Linear Relation between X and Y

						X	
Y		0	1	2	3	4	5
5		3	1				
4		2	2	3			
3			3	4	1		
2				1	3	2	
1					2	3	2
0						1	4

constitutes excellent evidence that X and Y tend to be linearly related. If some curvilinear relationship is displayed, the researcher
can often guess at the general form of an equation which would approximate the observed function. This is among the most effective
methods for teasing out a hidden trend from the camouflage of variability and measurement error characteristic of most data.

These techniques can also provide lucid displays of the way in
which X_1 and X_2 interact in their effect on Y. A multivariate frequency distribution could be formed, as in Table 13-2, which shows
two dichotomous independent variables tabulated simultaneously
against a continuous dependent variable. The same data are displayed

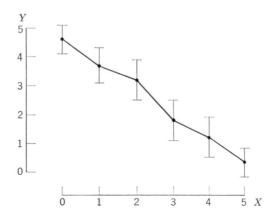

Fig. 13-1. Graph of data in Table 13-1. The dots represent means and the
vertical lines, standard deviations.

TABLE 13-2

Frequency Distribution with Two Dichotomous Independent Variables and an Interval-Scale Dependent Variable, Showing Interaction between X_1 and X_2

	X_1:	Low		High	
Y	X_2:	Low	High	Low	High
8		3	2		4
7		5		1	4
6		6	2		8
5		4	4	2	2
4		2	7	4	1
3		1	5	8	
2			3	7	2
1		1		3	
0			1	4	
M_y		5.8	4.0	2.6	6.0

in the graph of Fig. 13-2. Just which display is preferred, tabular or graphic, will depend partly on the complexity of the relationship and partly on the researcher's experience in "reading" relationships from data. To the practiced eye, Table 13-2 strongly suggests an interaction between X_1 and X_2, since both the first and last columns tend to have higher Y scores than the middle two: whether high X_2s go with low or high Ys depends on whether X_1 is high or low. Figure 13-2

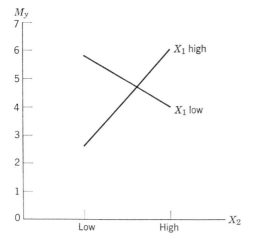

Fig. 13-2. Graph of means in Table 13-2 showing interaction between X_1 and X_2.

provides an even clearer indication of interaction: the linear function relating X_2 to Y has a different slope when X_1 is high than when it is low.

When the numbers of categories of X_1 and X_2 exceed two or three, a frequency distribution is likely to be hard for anyone to interpret at a glance, so it may be well worth the extra effort required to plot out the results in a graph or other visual display (see any elementary statistics text), in order to help clarify the essential relationships. An additional advantage of graphical displays is that they can often be included in the report of research findings (see Chapter 14) to aid in communicating results to the reader. The researcher himself may understand all his tables thoroughly, but they make rather rough reading for someone who is only casually interested in the study.

Even though construction of tables and graphs is laborious, it is generally well worthwhile both for the novice who does not know what a relationship "looks like" and for anyone else, novice or seasoned researcher, who is trying to explore his data thoroughly. New insights may emerge concerning peculiar patterns that might otherwise have been overlooked; the researcher may be alerted to the fact that a particular statistical measure (such as a correlation coefficient or a specified curvilinear function, for example) would be misleading. It is a rare project which does not have built into it the possibility for many analyses that were not specifically anticipated from the beginning. Whether or not the predicted results emerge, the investigator will virtually always find it profitable to "milk the data" in a search for additional relationships, to suggest new interpretations and problems for future studies.

STATISTICAL REPRESENTATION OF RELATIONSHIPS

Visual displays—particularly graphs—can serve important functions both in discovering relationships and in communicating them to others. But they generally are inadequate as end-products of the analysis. In the first place, they take up a great deal of space in publications and are expensive to print; more efficient ways of reporting the results are usually required. More importantly, interpretation of a visual display is too subjective. Different people looking at the same set of data might draw different conclusions from them, especially concerning inferences about the population which the sample is intended to represent. Some consensual way of choosing among alternative interpretations is required, and this is provided by the statistics of inference

(Chapter 9). Therefore, in writing up his results for publication—and even in clarifying their meaning to himself—the researcher typically has to include appropriate statistical analyses to substantiate his interpretations. This means that graphs must usually be accompanied by descriptive statistics and significance tests. Descriptive statistics provide concise summaries of relationships found in the data, whereas significance tests provide a way of deciding whether comparable relations are likely to appear in a new sample from the population.

A step on the way to computing most statistics is the construction of a frequency distribution, either bivariate or multivariate. (This step is often omitted in the use of electronic computers and even in some routines with desk calculators; but we do not recommend omission to the novice until he is in a position to judge from the summary statistics how his data *would* look in a frequency distribution.) Therefore, for each statistic discussed in the remainder of this chapter we shall present (sometimes in the chapter supplement) an appropriate frequency distribution together with an illustrative calculation. The reader should not infer from this, however, that such tables are appropriate substance for journal articles and other research reports. Only on rare occasions will the actual distribution from which a statistic was calculated be included in an article. Such detailed presentation would be too costly and too hard to read. As a rule, the frequency table should be regarded merely as a step on the way to computing a statistic or drawing a graph.

The choice of appropriate statistics is quite a complex matter. Ideally, one might like to have a competent statistician constantly standing by during the analysis phase to advise on what measure to use for what purpose. A typical comment that might be heard from him, though, would be something to the effect: "The way you collected your data and measured your variables, no statistical manipulation can solve your problem now." Freely translated, this means that the researcher should have consulted the statistician at the time he was designing his study rather than after the data were all collected. This is good advice but sometimes impractical. It may be that the researcher did not anticipate all his analyses, so he would not have known what statistical questions to ask; or, if he had, perhaps no willing and communicative expert could have been found. (Statisticians have their own ways of saying things and their own foci of concern; unless they are used to talking with psychological researchers about the latter's kind of problem, the contact may prove less than optimally rewarding.)

Though situations will often arise in which statistical consultation will be useful (and perhaps even madatory), there is really no way in which most researchers can avoid at least a passing familiarity with a few statistical procedures. Without a basic knowledge, one is not likely to know when he needs help or how to convey his problem in a way that the statistician can understand. So the typical researcher's development consists in gradually acquiring a fair comprehension of some fundamentals; this will decrease his dependency on outside expertise and at least help him decide what sorts of interpretations lie beyond the bounds of the techniques he knows. But sometime, in all honest ignorance, he will report data analyzed in a seemingly appropriate way, only to have the journal editor return his manuscript pointing out statistical defects. Perhaps these can be repaired easily with a different analysis technique. If not, then at least the investigator is better equipped for his next venture. The main thing to realize is that most statistical conventions exist for a reason. If data arc improperly analyzed, one may draw unjustified conclusions from them. This is a case in which a technical error may promote a substantive error. So any proficiency one can acquire in statistical comprehension is likely to be well worth it to assure valid interpretations of data.

Choosing the Right Statistics

With the large number of descriptive measures and significance tests available, any one researcher is likely to be familiar with only a few of them. Yet a relatively limited number, creatively used, will satisfy a surprisingly large proportion of the average investigator's requirements. The main thing is to avoid getting fixated on a particular statistic simply because one is used to it. Some people may compute means, correlation coefficients, chi-squares, or analyses of variance habitually, whether or not they fit the problem at hand. A better approach is to try to understand just what it is about any given set of data that requires statistical representation, then from one's memory store select the descriptive measure or significance test that will meet the need best.

A great many different considerations might be brought to bear in deciding what statistic is "best" for any given purpose. We shall review briefly some of the principles that guided our selection of those to be presented in this chapter; the reader may well develop his own set of different criteria.

In choosing a descriptive statistic—such as a mean, median, mode, standard deviation, interquartile range, correlation coefficient, or index of order association—the basic consideration is that it represent the data properly. For us this means the following:

(a) All the relevant data are used in computing it.

(b) The statistic is not misleading regarding the general form of the distributions it represents; if misinterpretation is likely, then appropriate qualifications should be made explicit.

(c) The descriptive statistic is appropriate for the scale type that the data are assumed to fit. This consideration forms the basis for our major classification of relational statistics in this chapter.

(d) A relational statistic is invariant under scalar transformations. Certain operations on the scale are permitted without affecting the way in which it represents the attribute being measured (see Chapter 5). Any such permissible operations should leave the descriptive measure of relationship unaltered so that the reader can interpret the magnitude of association, regardless of arbitrary transformations.

In choosing a significance test—such as CR, t, F, chi-square, a one-tail versus a two-tail test, and so forth—one should make sure that it is appropriate to the particular null hypothesis and alternative hypothesis (or the ranges of hypotheses) actually considered. Specifically, this means:

(e) The inferential statistic is sensitive only to the kinds of departures from the null hypothesis that are in the direction of the particular alternative(s) of interest. If the relationship to be inferred is a specific one, the significance test should be sensitive only to data patterns that reflect that relationship.

(f) When no specific relational alternative is entertained, a priori, then the significance test should represent the likelihood of various patterns of departure from a random association between the variables. Only if a general significance test permits confident rejection of the null hypothesis can one then test the significance of particular departures that become apparent after the data are plotted.

These points are more fully elaborated in the discussion of specific statistics.

Three other considerations have been explicitly rejected as bases for choosing descriptive or inferential statistics:

(g) It does not matter what the general strategy of data collection was—naturalistic observation, systematic assessment, or experiment. Present-day experimentalists are prone to use analyses of variance and F-tests. Systematic assessors (such as personality testers) tend to use correlational statistics. Naturalistic observers may use no statistics at all or very primitive tests like the chi-square. Such unnatural bases for selection have perhaps been reinforced by frequent references to the strategy of systematic assessment as "correlational research," in contrast to "experimental research" (e.g., Cronbach, 1957). Correlations can be computed from experimental data, just as F-tests can be performed on data from psychological tests. The relevant question in selecting a relational statistic is not "Were the variables manipulated or assessed?" but "What kind of relationship appears between them?"

(h) The distribution of an inferential statistic from sample to sample does not depend on the nature of the scale type from which it was computed. Hence a significance test can be computed to assess the probability that an obtained statistic departs from a hypothetical parameter, even though neither the statistic nor the parameter provides a meaningful description of the data. As an extreme example, a mean could be computed on the numbers assigned to a sample of nominal-scale objects (such as brands or model numbers of automobiles); even though that mean does not represent any interpretable characteristic of the automobile population, one can nevertheless be confident that if a second random sample were drawn and a mean similarly computed any difference between the two would be attributable to sampling error.

(i) Choice of inferential statistics does not depend on whether subjects (or other units of observation) were randomly selected from a defined population; in order to use the statistics of inference to generalize sample results precisely to known populations with known probabilities of Type I and Type II errors, the samples *must* have been chosen by probability methods. This is true whether the inferential statistic is a CR, a chi-square, a sign test, or any other significance test. If the sample is not random, the actual α and β cannot be determined. The significance test can serve only to give the researcher a subjective feeling of confidence that his results could (or could not) be replicated. Such a feeling can be acquired with a variety of statistical media.

In the remainder of this chapter we present certain common analysis problems, with descriptive and inferential statistics appropriate to them. These are generally not the only statistics that could legitimately be used, but they usually appear best to us, as judged by the foregoing criteria. First we discuss statistics for representing bivariate relations between various combinations of scale types. Then we treat, briefly, certain forms of multivariate analysis. More detailed illustrations of the measures and significance tests are presented in the chapter supplements. Generally the emphasis here is on significance tests more than on estimation of parameters because the largest portion of contemporary psychological research is simply concerned with rejecting null hypotheses. Indeed, this is a necessary stage in studying a phenomenon—to single out those variables that seem at all related and therefore worth further study. But as the science matures—for example, as in much of sensory psychology—researchers become increasingly concerned with the question, "What is the exact form of relation between X and Y at various specified ranges of both?" Hence the current stress on hypothesis testing should not obscure the ultimate relevance of more precise research questions.

Some Statistics of Bivariate Relationships

Difference between Group Means

One of the simplest statistical analyses is the measurement and testing of the difference between group means. The dependent variable Y is assumed to represent an interval scale, so that M_y and σ_y may legitimately be calculated. The independent variable X may be of any scale type, since it is dichotomized in any case. An example of such a relationship is provided in the first two columns of Table 13-2. The magnitude of relationship might be represented crudely by $M_1 - M_2$, the difference between group means on the Y-variable, but clearly a linear transformation of the Y-scale would change this numerical value, even though the essential form of the relationship remained the same. So a preferable measure of relationship, invariant under linear transformations, would be provided by the *point-biserial correlation*, defined as

$$r_{pb} = \frac{(M_2 - M_1)\sqrt{pq}}{\sigma_y}$$

where p is the proportion of the total sample which falls in the "positive" or "high" category of the independent variable (if X is a nominal scale, choice of the "positive" category is arbitrary),

q is $1 - p$,

M_2 is the mean of the Y-scores in the p group,

M_1 is the mean of the Y-scores in the q group,

σ_y is the standard deviation of the total distribution of Y-scores (p and q groups combined).

If there is no difference between the groups means, r_{pb} will equal zero. It has theoretical limits of $+1.00$ and -1.00, representing the maximum differences possible between two groups, given the total σ_y. These theoretical limits can be reached only if the Y-scores are dichotomized in proportions corresponding exactly to the X-dichotomy. So, in the normal case in which Y is a continuous variable, r_{pb} must always be less than 1.00.

One null hypothesis that is typically of interest is that $r_{pb} = 0$, or, in other words, that the obtained difference between the two group means $(M_1 - M_2)$ is within the bounds of chance fluctuation that would be expected when two such samples are randomly selected from a population in which the difference in means $(\mu_1 - \mu_2)$ is zero. The appropriate significance test against this null hypothesis (or against any other specific null hypothesis about $\mu_1 - \mu_2$) is provided by the critical ratio of the difference between the means (see Chapter 9, p. 222). The only additional point is to make sure that the significance test is sensitive only to those differences which are of a priori interest. If the alternative to the null hypothesis is the very general assertion that there will be a difference between group means (direction unspecified), then, of course, either direction of observed departure should be considered as leading to rejection of the null hypothesis in favor of the alternative. If, on the other hand, the only alternative of interest is the case in which M_1 is greater than M_2, then only differences in the specified direction will be tested for statistical significance. (A sample difference in the opposite direction could, of course, arise by chance from a population in which μ_1 is really greater than μ_2; this would be possible no matter how large the population difference or how large the sample. Such a deviant outcome would simply be treated, for purposes of testing this particular hypothesis, like any other nonsignificant difference.)

Linear Relationship between X and Y

An extension of the preceding relationship occurs when both X and Y are continuous interval-scale variables and one wants to find out if their relationship can be represented by a linear equation. This would mean that a constant increment in X is associated with a constant increment (or decrement) in Y, and vice versa. If one knows in advance just what linear equation to specify (e.g., $Y = 0.5X + 100$), then the first research question is, "How well do the data fit this equation?" The *goodness-of-fit* is inversely related to the average variability of observed Y-scores about their predicted values on the specified line. To obtain this measure one computes, for every X-score, the average squared deviation of actual Ys about the Y predicted for that X. (This is different from the usual method of computing the variance of Y-scores about their own mean, for it is not their own mean that is at issue here but rather the mean value predicted from X.) Then this average squared deviation is averaged over all X-categories to represent the goodness-of-fit (actually, poorness-of-fit) for the entire range of X.

The main thing to watch for here is that the average discrepancy between actual and predicted Y-values be roughly the same throughout the entire range of X. If this were not true, then the average squared deviation would be a misleading measure of the over-all goodness-of-fit, since the specified linear function would hold better in some parts of the X-range than in others.

A General Linear Hypothesis

Sometimes one is interested in determining whether there is a linear relationship between X and Y but not enough is known about them to decide in advance just what particular equation would be of interest. That is to say, the a and b in $Y = aX + b$ are not specified, but one is willing to hazard the guess that some standard increment (a) in X is associated with a standard increment in Y and that, therefore, Y could be predicted from X if only a and the additive constant b could be found. The reason for such ambiguities in prediction lies in the fact that the choice of interval size for psychological variables is generally arbitrary and the natural zero-point is often not known either. The same thing happens with physical measures; if one were to represent temperature by the Fahrenheit scale, this would yield a different linear function relating temperature to beer consumption than would measurement on the Centigrade scale.

Given psychological data measured without an absolute scale unit or zero point, one can only make the general assertion that X and Y are linearly related. The analysis task consists in finding the *line of best fit*, or the linear equation that most closely represents the relation between X and Y. The closest representation is assumed to be that around which the sum of squared deviation scores is minimized. This is known as the *least-squares criterion*. The problem is to find the a and b in the equation $Y = aX + b$ that will satisfy this criterion. Then the goodness-of-fit of the data to this line can be determined in the same way as before.

From a particular sample of data at hand, a and b can be calculated as

$$a = \frac{n\Sigma XY - \Sigma X\Sigma Y}{n\Sigma X^2 - (\Sigma X)^2}$$

$$b = M_y - aM_x$$

where n is the total number of subjects in the sample,

ΣXY is the product of X- and Y-scores for each individual, summed over all individuals,

ΣX is the sum of X-scores over all individuals,

ΣY is the sum of Y-scores over all individuals,

ΣX^2 is the square of each X-score summed over all individuals,

M_y is the mean of the Y-scores (computed as $\Sigma Y/n$),

M_x is the mean of the X-scores ($= \Sigma X/n$).

(This may look like a formidable amount of calculation, but it is no more than is required to obtain the product-moment correlation, and one can readily find various aids to computational efficiency; some of these are discussed in the supplement to Chapter 12.)

Thus, starting out with a general linear hypothesis, one can compute from the data the constants for an equation of the form $Y = aX + b$, which will represent the results as well as possible in the sense that the average squared deviation of actual Y-scores about the line (representing predicted Ys) is minimized. Such a line of best fit is sometimes called a *regression line*, and the equation for it, a *regression equation*.

If one wished to turn the problem around and predict X from Y, the same general approach would be followed; only this time the object would be to minimize the average squared deviation of actual Xs about predicted Xs, and the regression coefficients would be computed differently—that is, for the equation $X = aY + b$, a and b would be calculated as

$$a = \frac{n\Sigma XY - \Sigma X\Sigma Y}{n\Sigma Y^2 - (\Sigma Y)^2}$$

$$b = M_x - aM_y$$

The degree to which these regression equations represent the observed relationship can be calculated from the average squared deviation of observed Ys about the first regression line or, alternatively, from the average squared deviation of observed Xs about the second regression line. Either of these measures can be seen as reflecting, in a sense, the strength or size of the X–Y-relationship. When the average squared deviation is small, the magnitude of relationship is great—that is, Y can be accurately predicted from X or vice versa; the actual values fall very close to those predicted from the regression equation. If the average squared deviation about the regression line is large, then there is much error in prediction; accordingly, there cannot be a very close linear relation between X and Y.

What constitutes "large" and "small" average squared deviations about the regression line will depend on how much spread there is in the total scatter plot representing the X- and Y-scores together. The ratio of the variability about the regression line to the total variability of Y-scores about their own mean can be considered as one good measure of *relative absence of relationship*. One need only subtract this measure from 1.00 to get the converse—a measure of the relative presence of relationship between X and Y. In fact, the most widely used measure of the magnitude of linear relationship r, the *Pearson product-moment correlation coefficient*, can be defined as

$$r = \sqrt{1 - (\sigma^2_{y \cdot x}/\sigma_y{}^2)}$$

where $\sigma^2_{y \cdot x}$ is the variance of actual Y-scores (in the vertical direction) about the regression line and
$\sigma_y{}^2$ is the variance of Y-scores about M_y.

$\sigma_y{}^2$ can be thought of as the total variance in Y-scores, r^2 as that proportion of the total Y-variance which can be predicted from a knowledge of X, and $\sigma^2_{y \cdot x}/\sigma_y{}^2$ as the proportion of Y-variance which cannot be predicted from X.

The product-moment correlation coefficient can be calculated directly from the raw data as

$$r = \frac{N\Sigma XY - (\Sigma X)(\Sigma Y)}{\sqrt{[N\Sigma X^2 - (\Sigma X)^2][N\Sigma Y^2 - (\Sigma Y)^2]}}$$

where the meanings of the terms are the same as in the formula for the regression coefficient a.

When there is no linear relation between X and Y—that is, when the regression coefficient a equals zero—r will equal zero; and it will range between zero and 1.00 ($+1.00$ or -1.00), depending on the magnitude of the X–Y relationship (or on the goodness-of-fit of the regression lines).* r is also invariant under linear transformations of

---

* These theoretical maximum and minimum values can be reached only in practice when the marginal frequencies of the X- and Y-variables are identical; that is, when the corresponding categories include equal numbers of subjects. Otherwise, the upper and lower limits for r will be less than 1.00.

X and Y, so it satisfies one of our major criteria for choosing among alternative measures of relationship.

Whenever a linear relation of either a specific or general kind is sought in the data, the researcher is first concerned with rejecting the null hypothesis that a, the slope of the regression line, is zero. This null hypothesis would imply that the average value of Y is constant for all values of X, hence that X is of no help in predicting Y. Whenever a is zero, the product-moment correlation must be zero also, for the "regression line" will be horizontal, crossing the Y-axis at b, which in this case is the mean of the Ys; therefore, the variance of Y scores about this regression line is identical with their variance about the Y-mean, and r is zero. A significance test for evaluating this null hypothesis is presented in chapter Supplement A.

Given an a priori linear equation for predicting Y from X, it may be of interest to show that the data do not fit some other specific equation better. Such a situation could arise, for example, in a test between two competing theories from which two different linear equations could be deduced.* The sample size and distribution of X-scores could be chosen to permit rejection of a null hypothesis representing the competing prediction, with a specified probability, α, and to detect a slope within reasonable sampling variation (given a specified β) of the favored prediction. (See Chapter 9 for a discussion of α and β in the context of testing hypotheses concerning population means. The situation here is analogous: one is testing hypotheses concerning the line of best fit in the population from which the sample was drawn.)

Regardless of which linear equation emerges as the line of best fit, one may sometimes wish to test the null hypothesis that scores are scattered about this regression line to yield a specified nonzero value of the correlation coefficient. One might, for example, test the hypothesis that the present sample was drawn from a population in which the parameter $\hat{r}$ equaled .60. A related problem arises when one is trying to find out if the correlations between the same pair of variables in two independent samples are significantly different: could sample rs of .50 and .70 both have come, by chance, from a common population with a given (perhaps intermediate) parameter $\hat{r}$? Null hypotheses appropriate for such cases are best tested not directly with r, but with the statistic z, which is a normalized transformation of r (see Appendix Table D). The reason for the transformation to z is that sample rs are distributed normally about

---

* Usually, the choice between alternative psychological theories is not this simple, for precise functions can rarely be derived for comparison; if they can, they are generally linear functions.

the parameter $\hat{r}$ only when that parameter is zero. For any other value of $\hat{r}$ the distribution of sample rs around it is skewed. The higher the $\hat{r}$, the greater the skew; it becomes distinctly noticeable with rs of $\pm.40$ or greater because of the upper limit of 1.00 imposed on the statistic r. With a parameter $\hat{r}$ of .99 it would be theoretically possible, by chance, to draw samples with r much lower than that, but it would be impossible to get a sample r more than .01 above the parameter. This extreme example illustrates that sampling distributions of rs around nonzero $\hat{r}$s are necessarily skewed—and quite badly so at relatively high values—so that the normal curve tables do not adequately represent the probabilities of Type I errors. The z-statistic, into which r can be transformed, was specifically constructed to have a nearly normal sampling distribution in its entire range, so the significance of differences between nonzero rs can be tested indirectly by their corresponding zs. The reader is referred to chapter Supplements A and F for specific examples.

Nonlinear Relations between X and Y

A linear equation rarely provides a very good description of actually observed relationships. The very fact that r is less than 1.00 usually demonstrates the insufficiency of a general linear hypothesis. The relevant question at this point, however, is, "Will any other specific equation fit the data better?" It could be that the reason for the poor linear fit lies wholly in "random" variation of scores about the ideal predicted values. If this is the case, then no other equation will improve the prediction, and the investigator may as well be tentatively satisfied with the best linear approximation.

Sometimes careful study of the scatter plot will suggest that there is a definite pattern of relationship, even though it is nonlinear. Perhaps the investigator undertook the study in the first place expecting a nonlinear relationship between X and Y. The theory that guided his research may predict a specific functional relationship; but, if not, the practiced investigator who knows his nonlinear curves can often discern a tendency that roughly follows a simple theoretical function, such as $Y = aX^2 + bX + c$, $Y = \sqrt{X}$, $Y = \log X$, or $Y = \sin X$. There are curve-fitting procedures for finding the function of a particular type—say, a general polynomial of second or third order— that fits the data as well as possible. For example, the analysis of orthogonal components (or orthogonal polynomials; see Grant, 1956) is designed to test the statistical significance of higher order polynomial functions by an analysis of variance model. Procedures such as these accomplish the same thing for certain nonlinear functions as the method described above for finding the best fitting linear equation and testing it against the null hypothesis that $a = 0$. It is necessary only to enter the analysis with some general form in mind and let the appropriate constants emerge from the data. The tedium of the operation is greatly reduced by the use of electronic computers which can be programmed to try a variety of different general or specific functions to see which of them fits the data best. The goodness-of-fit may be described, as before, by a measure of the average variance of actual Y-scores about the Ys predicted from the equation.

One would, of course, want to know whether each more complicated function represented the data significantly better than some less complex equation. This is because one aim in scientific description is to select from among equally accurate, and equally general, functional relations the one that is simplest.* The very simplest relationship is often conceived to be linear, and one would at least want to reject that. Depending on what other function is to be rejected, then, a specific null hypothesis is established and treated in a manner comparable to that already mentioned for linear hypotheses.

A General Curvilinear Hypothesis

Just as a bivariate distribution of X and Y can be approached with a general hypothesis no more specific than that they are linearly related and analyzed to see if the best fitting line has a slope significantly different from zero, so it is possible to set out on a general curvilinear analysis without a specific form of relationship in mind, to see whether X and Y are related in any way at all. Perhaps Y increases with X first slowly and then rapidly; it might first increase then decrease or the mean Y-score might go up and down irregularly with an increase in X. The researcher may be interested in detecting any kind of systematic departure. (A systematic departure in this context simply implies that the mean Y-scores in the several columns —representing categories of the X-variable—differ more than would be expected by chance.)

This general curvilinear hypothesis is not, of course, very useful, since it does not suggest any particular form of relationship between X and Y. It is fairly widely used in psychological research, nevertheless, under the cloak of simple *analysis of variance*, and it may have some value for initial exploration.

The best fitting curvilinear function is taken to be the line which goes through all the column means (see Table 13-3).† The best pre-

---

* What is simplest for one person or for one stage of theoretical comprehension may not necessarily be so for another, but we will side-step this problem for now.

† This could, of course, in the limiting case be a straight line, whereupon the best fitting linear and curvilinear functions would coincide. The linear function is a special case of a curvilinear function.

TABLE 13-3

Curvilinear Relation between X and Y with Relational Function Unspecified

Y	0	1	2	3	4	5	6
5	7	2	1	1	5	4	2
4	12	4	1	3	7	6	5
3	9	8	7	8	2	6	9
2	3	5	7	3	1	3	5
1		2	6	2		1	2
0	1		1				1
M_y	3.6	3.0	2.2	2.9	4.1	3.5	2.9

diction of Y that can be made from knowing a subject's X-score is the mean Y of all people who have the same X as he has. This method of prediction will minimize the average squared deviation about the predicted values and so provides a "curve of best fit" in the same sense that the linear regression equation provides a line of best fit. Again, analogously, the goodness-of-fit, as measured by the variance in Y-scores about the column means, can be converted into a relative measure of the "magnitude" of the curvilinear relationship. This measure is *eta*, the *correlation ratio*.

$$\eta = \sqrt{1 - (\sigma_{y \cdot x}^2 / \sigma_y^2)}$$

where η is the measure of general curvilinear relationship,

$\sigma_{y \cdot x}^2$ is the average variance of actual Y-scores about the column means and

σ_y^2 is the total variance of Y-scores about M_y.

The value of η is always positive, between 0.00 and $+1.00$, and it is invariant under linear transformations of X and Y. In fact, the independent variable X can even be a nominal scale, for the columns can be reordered in any conceivable way, and the same η would still result. If one were to reverse the problem (assuming that X is an interval scale) and attempt to predict X from Y, the procedure would be identical, except that the mean X-scores from the several Y-rows would constitute the predicted values. Usually, the average variance of X-scores about the row means would be different from the average variance of Y-scores about the column means, and a different η would result from this analysis. Accordingly, it is customary to designate by appropriate subscripts the variable being predicted; η_{yx} means that Y is predicted from X, and η_{xy} means the reverse.

There are usually only two null hypotheses that one wishes to examine in this kind of general curvilinear analysis. The first one states that the column means do not differ significantly from one another—in other words, that η is zero. The second relevant null hypothesis is that the best fitting curvilinear function is not significantly different from the best fitting linear function—in other words, that the average variance of Y-scores about a linear regression line is not significantly greater than their average variance about the column means. If the first null hypothesis can be confidently rejected, but not the second, then the researcher might just as well represent the form of the X–Y-relationship by a linear equation and its magnitude by the product-moment correlation coefficient. Significance tests against these two null hypotheses are usually performed by means of the F-statistic (see chapter Supplement B).

The only time when η (and the corresponding F-tests of significance) would appear appropriate is when the researcher has no particular curvilinear relationship in mind but merely wants to see if the column means differ systematically in some way yet to be discovered. Since η reflects all kinds of departures from the null hypotheses, of whatever form, a significant η does not immediately tell one what sort of relationship obtains. Moreover, the likelihood of detecting a specific kind of departure with η is not so great as it is with a statistic that reflects only the specific departure of interest. Therefore, the probability of Type II errors ("errors of caution") for any specific alternative hypothesis is larger than it should be.

On the other hand, if the researcher really entertains no particular a priori alternative to the null hypothesis (even as general an alternative as, "The Y-means will first go up, then down"), he might well plot a graph or scan the data until he sees some particular difference between columns. But it would be highly misleading to test it alone for statistical significance. Such a procedure would take undue advantage of chance fluctuations in column means, thereby increasing the probability of Type I errors ("errors of rashness") far beyond the stated level of statistical significance. The thing to do in the absence of any particular notions about what sort of relationship to expect is first to perform an F-test for the over-all significance of differences among column means before taking any particular a posteriori difference seriously. Sometimes, even though the F-test is not significant (perhaps because the number of X-categories is very large), a particular apparent difference between certain column means can be rationalized after the fact. If so, and if the rationalization seems compelling, then the most prudent course of action, before leaping to an opportunistic conclusion, is to collect new data on the same variables and determine whether the difference can be replicated or whether it was just due to chance.

Monotonic Relationship between X and Y

Any specific linear (or curvilinear) equation relating X and Y implies that both variables have been measured on interval scales. This is because the constant a in the equation is intended to represent equal units of difference between scores in the entire ranges of X and Y. If this appears to be an improbable assumption, one can still talk about a *monotonic* relationship: an increase in X tends to be accompanied by an increase (or decrease) in Y. One does not specify how much increase, or even that it will be the same over the entire range of X, but just that Y will always tend to increase as X increases. A linear relationship is a special case of the monotonic; so are typical growth functions and learning curves. Of interest here, though, is the most general case, in which the shape of the monotonic function cannot be specified because there is no unit of measurement.

For instance, when a number of objects are to be rank-ordered according to the amount of some attribute they possess, no unit of measure is specified. One need not know how far apart the first and second ranked objects are or how this distance compares with that between ranks five and six. All that is intended is that each higher ranked object represent more of the attribute than those below it. If two different people rank the same set of objects, one may wish to determine from these results the degree to which they view the attribute similarly. Hypothetical data are presented in Table 13-4 to show how two different subjects ranked the relative "pleasantness" of ten musical compositions. It looks as if they disagree considerably, suggesting somewhat opposite standards for "pleasantness."

One good way of measuring the degree of similarity (or dissimilarity) is to count the number of pairs of objects on which their orderings agree $(S+)$ and the number on which they disagree $(S-)$, subtract the second sum from the first and express the difference in ratio to the total number of pairs involved in the ranked series. (In this case the total number of pairs is 45; more generally, the total number would be $k(k-1)/2$, where k is the number of objects to be ranked.) Such a ratio is known as *tau* (τ), or Kendall's *coefficient of rank association*, defined as

$$\tau = \frac{(S+) - (S-)}{k(k-1)/2}$$

TABLE 13-4

Relationship between Two Subjects' Rankings of the "Pleasantness" of Ten Objects

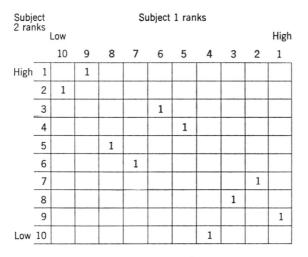

Subject 2 ranks	Subject 1 ranks									
	Low									High
	10	9	8	7	6	5	4	3	2	1
High 1		1								
2	1									
3					1					
4						1				
5			1							
6				1						
7									1	
8								1		
9										1
Low 10							1			

$S+$ (sum of frequencies to right and above each entry, starting with left-hand column)

$$= 1(1) + 1(2) + 1(2) + 1(3) + 1(1) = 9$$

$S-$ (sum of frequencies to right and below each entry, starting with left-hand column)

$$= 1(8) + 1(8) + 1(5) + 1(4) + 1(5) + 1(4) + 1(1) + 1(1) = 36$$

$$\tau = \frac{(S+) - (S-)}{k(k-1)/2} = \frac{9 - 36}{10(9)/2} = \frac{-27}{45} = -.60$$

Computation of τ for this example (see Table 13-4) shows it as $-.60$.[*]
When there are no ties in rank, τ can vary between $+1.00$ and -1.00, 0.00 representing random similarity. It is invariant under any ordinal transformation of either X or Y; that is, the specific numbers assigned to the ranked categories do not matter so long as their order is preserved. Furthermore, minor modifications in the calculation of τ will make it applicable to the more general case of mono-

[*] The Spearman rank-difference correlation (ρ), derived from the Pearson product-moment correlation (r), is still used by some to represent the extent of association between ranks. We prefer τ, since it is of more general use and is invariant under order-preserving transformations of the data, whereas ρ is not (see Kendall, 1955).

tonic relation in which any number of objects can be assigned to each X- or Y-category. This is equivalent to permitting ties in the ranking of objects; such a condition almost always occurs when k is large, for most objects are not susceptible to indefinitely fine discrimination. An example is illustrated in Table 13-5; say that it shows how a sample of 100 people were rated on two ordinal scales representing, respectively, helpfulness and dominance. Evidently the investigator does not want to assume that the categories of either scale are equidistant but only that they fall in the order implied by their names.

The analysis problem is to determine the degree of monotonic relationship between attributes X and Y. The similarity in rankings of individual subjects is not the focus of interest here (there are too many tied ranks to say anything very definite about it); rather it is the magnitude of relationship between the two sets of ranked categories.

$S+$ (the number of times that pairs of subjects are ordered in the same direction on both attributes) is determined in a way similar to that used in the ranking example (see Table 13-4), and so is $S-$, the number of times that pairs of subjects are oppositely ordered.

TABLE 13-5

Relation between Two Ordinal Scales—Ratings of 100 Subjects on "Helpfulness" and "Dominance"

Dominance	Helpfulness				
	Very low	Low	Moderate	High	Very high
Very high	3	2	1	0	1
High	4	2	1	3	0
Moderate	1	12	7	8	2
Low	2	6	20	8	2
Very low	0	3	11	1	0

$$S+ = 4(4) + 1(10) + 2(39) + 2(2) + 12(6) + 6(23) + 3(53) + 1(1) + 7(4)$$
$$+ 20(14) + 11(24) + 3(1) + 8(1) + 8(3) + 1(5) = 1090$$
$$S- = 3(86) + 4(80) + 1(51) + 2(15) + 2(63) + 2(59) + 12(42) + 6(12)$$
$$+ 1(24) + 1(21) + 7(11) + 20(1) + 3(4) + 8(2) + 8(0) = 1649$$
$$h = \frac{(S+) - (S-)}{(S+) + (S-)} = \frac{1090 - 1649}{1090 + 1649} = -.20$$

The difference between $S+$ and $S-$ provides the numerator of the ratio, as before. The denominator is altered to take account of the fact that not all of the $k(k-1)/2$ pairs are considered. Subjects scored identically on either variable (i.e., those within the same row or the same column) cannot be compared because they represent, in effect, instances of tied ranks. The total number of possible comparisons is $(S+) + (S-)$. So h, the index of order association used here (Senders, 1958; Wallis & Roberts, 1957), is simply

$$h = \frac{(S+) - (S-)}{(S+) + (S-)}$$

h is thus a variation on τ and represents the proportion of similarly ordered pairs to the maximum number that could be similarly ordered, given the particular marginal distributions of X and Y.* It can also range between $+1.00$ and -1.00, regardless of the form of the bivariate distribution, and a value of 0.00 represents an intuitively meaningful absence of ordinal relationship, since in this case the number of opposite orderings would equal the number of identical orderings.

To determine whether the degree of order-association (measured by either τ or h) is significantly different from zero, one can establish the null hypothesis that the numerator of the ratio, $(S+) - (S-)$, has a parameter value of zero in the population from which the sample was drawn. Since this sample statistic is normally distributed around its parameter when the latter quantity is zero, the table of areas under the normal curve can be used to estimate the probability of Type I errors. A formula for the standard deviation of the sampling distribution and an illustrative calculation of the appropriate critical ratio are presented in chapter Supplement C.

Reduction of Uncertainty in Predicting Y from X

All of the relational statistics discussed so far refer to a particular class of probabilistic relationships between X and Y, namely those in which the central tendency of Y varies systematically with X. A linear correlation describes, in effect, the relative degree to which the Y-means fall on a single sloping line when plotted against X. Nonlinear measures of relationship also reflect only differences in column means. (This is true for specific equations, in which the pattern of

---

*Kendall (1955) proposes another variation on τ, which also corrects for tied ranks, but it has a maximum value less than 1.00 unless the same numbers of ties occur in exactly the same places on both variables—that is, unless their marginal distributions are identical.

means takes a specified form, as well as for the general curvilinear relationship measured by η.) The index of order association, h, is sensitive only to a general progression in the median Y-values associated with an increasing X. None of these measures of relationship is designed to detect systematic departures which do not include variations in central tendency. Yet there are times when the researcher might be interested in such differences.

Consider the case illustrated in Table 13-6. Though the Y-means of the two columns (categories of X) do not differ at all, there is clearly a sizable difference in their variabilities. The import of this observation for the research problem is clear: though a knowledge of X would not affect the mean value of predicted Ys, it would affect the degree of certainty with which the prediction could be made. Without knowing X, one would expect that the "average error" in predicting Y (i.e., the standard error of estimate) would be reflected by the standard deviation of the total Y-distribution, which is 1.04. But knowing that $X = 0$ would permit one to place more confidence in the predicted Y, since on the average it would be wrong by a smaller amount, as indicated by the σ_y (0.77) within the first column only. (Knowing that $X = 1$, one would either constantly predict Y as 3, which would minimize the average error, or distribute his predictions over categories 2 and/or 4 to maximize the number of correct estimates; with either strategy, one would not place much confidence in the predicted value.)

This example, then, illustrates a kind of relation between X and Y, not in the sense of increasing one's knowledge of *what* Y to predict from X but rather in the sense of letting one know *when* to predict

TABLE 13-6

Reduction in Uncertainty by Predicting Y from X

		X	Total
Y	0	1	
5	2	5	7
4	5	20	25
3	30	4	34
2	5	20	25
1	2	5	7
M_y	3.0	3.0	3.0
σ_y	0.77	1.22	1.04

and when not to, or more generally, in permitting one to place varying degrees of confidence in the predicted Ys depending on the value of X. This is, therefore, a relationship involving dispersions rather than central tendencies. The magnitude of the relationship can be represented by the degree to which the certainty of predicting Y is increased by a knowledge of X.*

Some general indices of uncertainty reduction are provided by Attneave (1959), Kullback (1959), and Senders (1958), using concepts from information theory. One of these, D, is based on the amount of dispersion of frequencies over the cells in a bivariate distribution, relative to the amount of dispersion that would be expected "by chance," from a combination of the X- and Y-distributions considered as independent. (See chapter Supplement D for definitions and computational illustrations.) The obtained dispersion can never be larger than the chance dispersion; to the extent that it is smaller, X and Y may be said to be related in this general sense.

It is indeed a very general sense, for this quantitative measure of relationship does not reflect any particular pattern of dispersion. It may result from relatively increased frequencies in any of the cells of the table. In the example of Table 13-6, for instance, the same increase in certainty of prediction could have resulted from a number of different arrangements of the cell frequencies. This ambiguity in interpreting the indices of uncertainty reduction stems from the fact that they are applicable very generally to all types of scales, including nominal. They are invariant over any kind of scale transformation, which means that the categories could be renumbered and reordered without affecting D in the slightest.

D is therefore an appropriate measure of relationship between two nominal-scale variables. It is sensitive to all kinds of departures from a random bivariate distribution and, consequently, to no one specific form of departure in particular. When D is used as an index of relationship for more powerful scales—such as ordinal or interval —it cannot be regarded as indicating any particular pattern, such as variation in central tendencies or variation in particular row frequencies, which seems apparent from a visual inspection of the table. Separate measures must be derived to represent specific patterns of relationship.

The problem of determining whether an obtained D is significantly

---

* Of course, a difference between the column means (or medians or modes) would produce a relationship in the present sense, too, but it is not the only way to reduce the uncertainty of the prediction.

different from zero can be approached through the chi-square test (see chapter Supplement D), based on the sum of the squared deviations of all cell frequencies from the values that would be expected for them if X and Y were independent. This test, too, is sensitive to all kinds of departures of whatever pattern and so is not especially suited to detecting any particular kind that may be of interest.

If the researcher is seeking a particular kind of relationship in his data—for example, that the proportion of cases in a certain row will increase (or decrease or simply vary) with X—then he should select a descriptive measure and a significance test that will reflect that relationship only. Computation of D and χ^2 will only confuse the interpretation by permitting too many different kinds of differences to show up and perhaps failing to detect one of particular interest. On the other hand, if the first time one suspects a specific relationship is after he has studied the bivariate distribution and mentally discarded all kinds of possible patterns, then it would not do to make too much of the isolated "finding" that turned out significant on the basis of a specific test for it. Such a strategy would take undue advantage of chance departures in a generally random array. The thing to do first, before jumping to any a posteriori conclusions, is to compute a chi-square significance test for the entire bivariate table and then decide whether to pursue the specific analysis that looks promising.

Summary of Bivariate Relational Statistics

Up to this point we have reviewed a small sample of relational statistics and significance tests which may be helpful in clarifying certain commonly encountered patterns of relationship between two variables. If one wants to know the degree to which two interval scales are linearly related, he can compute a product-moment correlation coefficient. The approximate form of the relationship may be represented by two regression equations, one for predicting Y from X, the other for the reverse prediction. Even if the form of the relationship is not precisely linear, one may wish to know the degree to which it is so and therefore compute r as a measure of linearity. Specific nonlinear relationships involving variation in central tendency can be represented by a variety of equations, simple and complex.

For relating two variables that constitute ordinal rather than interval scales, one may use h as an index of monotonic order association. With nominal-scale variables, whose categories cannot even be uniquely ordered, the only meaningful measures of size of relationship are those that represent reduction in uncertainty or changes in the dispersion of Y associated with changes in X. If a nominal-scale X is to be related to an interval-scale Y, an appropriate measure of relationship is provided by η.

Any of the correlational statistics can be interpreted in a limited sense only as representing the magnitude of association between X and Y in the particular sample from which they were computed. For purposes of inference, they may be treated as sample statistics that might have arisen by chance from a population with a different parameter relationship. In order to guard against inferring a general or particular kind of relationship that does not, in fact, exist, one can set up an appropriate null hypothesis to test whether the obtained statistic (or a derivative of it) departs sufficiently from the null parameter (usually zero) to warrant rejection of the hypothesis. Sometimes there is a known sampling distribution around parameters other than zero, so that a number of different null hypotheses can be rejected, leading to a confidence interval within which the parameter relationship can be fairly assumed to lie. By such use of statistical inference, the researcher can do more than merely describe the extent of relationship in the data at hand; he can also make some rather good guesses about how strongly X and Y will be related in future samples from the same population.

Not all research is performed with particular kinds of relations in mind. One may simply decide, after the data are collected, to plot X against Y and see how they turn out. Here a variety of relational patterns may come to view. Some of them will look like linear or specific curvilinear functions; others will suggest systematic, though unordered, differences among group means; and still others may show patterns involving differences in dispersions, with or without varying central tendencies. It is certainly worthwhile to make the utmost use of such unanticipated outcomes. Only the researcher should be careful lest a chance relationship be interpreted as meaningful. Using the .05 significance level as a basis for rejecting null hypotheses, one can expect to reject them erroneously (making a Type I error) about one time in 20. A good practice to keep from getting caught too often within the 5% pile (or whatever other α is utilized) would be to perform some over-all significance test (such as F or χ^2) sensitive to all departures of a given kind, before treating any one departure seriously. The use of these tests is to be recommended, however, only in those cases in which the researcher does not know precisely what he is looking for until he sees it. Whenever the search process can be narrowed down a priori to particular patterns of relationship, then the probability of a Type I error is more accurately represented by the specific significance test than by a general one.

Some Statistics of Multivariate Relationships

When two or more independent variables are simultaneously related to a third (dependent) variable, the number of different relational patterns that could be found is increased vastly over the two-variable case. This sort of analysis therefore typically permits a richer—and presumably more accurate—description of psychological phenomena than would be possible with any of the bivariate techniques discussed so far. Up to this point we have merely asked, "Is there a systematic relation between X and Y?" and "If so, how much?" and "What does it look like?" With two independent variables, X_1 and X_2, we may complicate the matter considerably by asking such additional questions as: "Is there a relationship between X_2 and Y which is additional to (independent of) the X_1–Y-relationship?" "Is the X_2–Y-relationship the same regardless of X_1 or does the level of X_1 have to be taken into account in order to describe how X_2 and Y are related?" For each new independent variable added to the analysis, the questions concerning additive and interactive relations become more complex; so for the sake of simplicity we shall direct attention here mainly to the three-variable situation.

Additive Relations among Independent Variables

The relation between X_1 and X_2 is additive if the relation of each of them to Y is the same, regardless of the other. Suppose one found the following two sets of bivariate relations among measures, in which each of the variables is simply dichotomized as "high" and "low."

Y	X_1 Low	X_1 High		Y	X_2 Low	X_2 High
High	55	70		High	45	80
Low	75	48		Low	83	40
Total	130	118		Total	128	120

These two bivariate frequency distributions suggest that both X_1 and X_2 are similarly related to Y. The next question to be asked is, "Are the two relationships independent?" In other words, "Does the X_2–Y-association hold within both levels of X_1?" and "Does the X_1–Y-association hold within both levels of X_2?" The answer is provided by a table that combines all three variables:

X_1		Low		High	
Y	X_2	Low	High	Low	High
High		35	20	10	60
Low		65	10	18	30
	Total	100	30	28	90

Since the ratio of high to low Y-scores is larger in the second and fourth columns than it is in the first and third, this analysis suggests that X_2 is uniformly related to Y, regardless of X_1. But the X_1–Y-relationship disappears when X_2 is controlled, as a reordering of the independent variables shows:

X_2		Low		High	
Y	X_1	Low	High	Low	High
High		35	10	20	60
Low		65	18	10	30
	Total	100	28	30	90

The ratio of high to low Y-scores is about the same in the first column as it is in the second, and the ratios in the third and fourth columns are identical. The relationship between X_1 and X_2 is nevertheless additive rather than interactive, even though only one of them is an independent correlate of Y.

Such a result may have important implications for the interpretation of X_1 and X_2. Suppose the researcher had designed the study to test the hypothesis that students who have taken psychology are better adjusted than those who have not. X_1 is a dichotomous variable representing the presence or absence of psychology courses in the students' past curricula, and Y is a crude measure of adjustment that merely distinguishes "well adjusted" subjects from "poorly adjusted." In discussing his research design with friendly colleagues, someone had suggested that the researcher also assess the class status (year in school) of his subjects as a second independent variable, X_2, that might be related to adjustment. If the outcome of the analysis approximated the hypothetical results above, the investigator might well conclude that taking or not taking psychology courses has very little to do with adjustment. It is simply the fact of getting older, taking all kinds of courses, or being able to stay in school past the sophomore year that is related to adjustment; and the only reason for the first apparent relationship is that students who have taken psychology courses have also been in school longer.

This example shows how statistical control can sometimes be substituted for experimental control in clarifying relationships among variables. In the ideal experimental design, all kinds of subjects— old and young, freshmen and seniors, well and poorly adjusted—would be assigned in balanced fashion to the two conditions of X_1. One group would be exposed to psychology courses and the other would not. If any group differences emerged, these could be fairly safely attributed to X_1 because all other factors that might account for the difference had been either controlled or randomized by the assignment procedure. Such an ideal experiment would be very difficult to perform in practice because complete control over subject assignment would be contrary to university policies. So it is up to the researcher to exercise the best statistical control he can by "partialing out" extraneous effects in his data analysis.

There are some specific statistical techniques for doing this, such as partial correlation and analysis of covariance (see Du Bois, 1958; Lindquist, 1953; McNemar, 1955), but they are beyond the scope of this presentation. Instead, we shall just describe one very general approach that may be used in a variety of research situations in which one wants to see if X_1 and Y are significantly related when a number of other variables (X_2, X_3, X_4, etc.) are "held constant" (or, better, controlled statistically). The control variables can be anything— interval, ordinal, or nominal scales—just so each of them can be divided into two or more categories to yield groups of subjects with similar scores. If X_2 had three categories, X_3 had five, and X_4 had two categories, combining all three control variables would yield $3 \times 5 \times 2 = 30$ groups of subjects. (Unless the total sample size is large, such a division may make some of the subgroups too small for reliable measurement; in this case one must either reduce the number of control variables or just dichotomize each one, yielding eight groups instead of 30. Neither of these constitutes an ideal solution, since it reduces the effectiveness of the control procedure, but it is still better than not controlling at all.)

The next step is to plot the X_1–Y-relationship within each of the groups. The present example would yield 30 such bivariate distributions. The researcher would study the entire set to see if the same general form appeared consistently throughout. If it did, then he could be fairly confident that the relationship was independent of those variables that had been controlled by the grouping procedure. For many such analyses, however, the results would be far from clear-cut. Relations within some of the groups might be very slight or even reversed from the general trend. Under these circumstances, one needs some way of deciding whether to conclude that there is a consistent *partial relationship* between X_1 and Y. An aid to this decision is provided by a chi-square test of the over-all significance of any seemingly consistent trend (Fisher, 1941; Jones & Fiske, 1953). It is constructed by combining significance levels of all the separate relationships. Illustrations of its use are provided in chapter Supplement E.

The same kind of analysis could be carried out to test the consistency of relation between another independent variable, X_2, and Y when the remaining variables, including X_1, are controlled statistically. Through an extended multivariate analysis of this type, it is possible to assess the partial relation of the dependent variable to each of the independent variables when all the remaining relationships are statistically controlled. Thus, from assessed variables, one can arrive at interpretations that are similar to those concerning "main effects" in experimental designs of the factorial or treatment-by-levels variety (see Chapter 10).

Interactive Relations among Independent Variables

X_1 and X_2 bear an interactive relationship if the manner in which one of them relates to Y depends upon the other (see, for example, Fig. 13-2). An interaction between X_1 and X_2 in their relationship to Y can be illustrated by a slight modification of the table on p. 353:

Class:		Lower division		Upper division	
Adjustment	Psychology:	No	Yes	No	Yes
High		35	20	60	10
Low		65	10	30	18
	Total	100	30	90	28

These results might mean that, among freshmen and sophomores, students who have taken psychology tend to be better adjusted than those who have not, whereas among juniors and seniors the trend is reversed. (Perhaps only bright students are admitted early to psychology classes and at that level intelligence is associated with good adjustment; but later on in school, when more people have been exposed to psychology, the main concomitant of good adjustment might be the anticipation of a highly paid job—a trait perhaps found more frequently among those kinds of students, such as engineers, who tend not to take psychology courses.)

It can readily be seen that interactive relationships require considerably more complex interpretation than simple additive ones. Quite often the researcher will have had such complex expectations in mind when he designed his project. If so, the search for interactions can be very straightforward: one simply compares the magnitude of the X_1–Y-association at one level of X_2 with the corresponding magnitude at another level of X_2 and constructs an appropriate statistical test to see if the two magnitudes are significantly different.

If, for example, the X_1–Y-relationship can be measured by a correlation coefficient, one would just compute a different r for each level of X_2 and test to see if they differ more than would be expected by chance; or, if X_1 and X_2 were dichotomous and Y continuous, one could compute four different M_ys and test to see if the difference between the first two is significantly greater (or less) than the difference between the second two. (See chapter Supplement F for detailed illustrations.)

Often, however, interactions appear without being specifically sought. The investigator who is looking for a uniform effect of an experimental variable may find on detailed analysis that the effect is not constant but seems to depend on the type of subject or on other conditions that have been manipulated in the experiment. Again, in comparing a number of X_1–Y-relationships within several groups established by statistical control, it may become apparent that the magnitude (or even direction) of the relationship seems to vary, with different combinations of the control variables. Such interactive effects as these will, of course, serve to reduce the over-all significance of the main relationship the researcher was looking for. Before coming to any definite conclusions about whether a particular interactive combination accounts for differences in the main effect, he should consider carefully just what the chance probability of this interaction is. With more than two independent variables, or with more than two categories per variable, the number of potential sources of interaction increases tremendously; and, by chance, any one of them might turn up in the sample of data at hand without necessarily signifying the same interaction in the parent population.

Careful practice in such instances would be to resort to some general significance test, sensitive to all related types of interaction that might be found under these circumstances. Such general tests are provided by analysis-of-variance models discussed, among others, by Lindquist (1953) and McNemar (1955). After determining the results of an over-all significance test, the researcher could then decide whether to take seriously the particular form of interaction that was apparent in his data. If any doubt remained, the thing to do would be to run the same study again on a new sample of subjects and see if a comparable effect appeared. Thus the general strategy for the analysis of interactive relationships is similar to that suggested for bivariate relationships; if the researcher knows what to look for (on the basis of theory, hunch, previous findings, or practical considerations), then he can devise a specific test sensitive only to the critical types of interaction. But if a variety of patterns would be of interest, and he is not going to choose among them until after he has seen the data, then he should try to avoid interpreting one chance result out of many as if it were a significant finding.

SUMMARY

Analysis of the data typically involves looking for relations among variables. The relationships sought differ in kind and precision from study to study. The search is facilitated by plotting the data in tabular or graphical form; trends otherwise hidden in the data may emerge clearly in appropriately constructed visual displays. These are also useful in helping to communicate the results readily to others.

However, interpretations based on visual methods alone are often too subjective; they generally do not permit selection among alternative inferences about the population from which the sample was drawn. Statistical analyses can serve this purpose. By means of the statistics of inference one can examine alternative hypotheses, to see how likely it is that any relational (or other) statistic arose from a population with a particular parameter. In most recent psychological research the parameters of chief interest have been those specified by a null hypothesis that there is no relation between the variables.

Besides their use for purposes of inference, statistics provide precise and concise ways of describing relationships found in the sample. Choice of statistics for describing sample relationships will depend not only on the obtained patterns of association but also on the researcher's judgment concerning what relations are of interest and perhaps on consideration for the scale type which the measures represent. For example, r measures the degree of linear relationship between interval scales, whereas η can be used to represent the goodness-of-fit of a nonspecific nonlinear function. Monotonic relationships in ordinal-scale data are appropriately measured by τ or h. D can be used to represent the magnitude of association between two nominal scales or, in general, as an index of the reduction in uncertainty by predicting one variable from another.

Multivariate statistical techniques permit the simultaneous assessment of relations among several variables in combination. Two kinds of combinations, additive and interactive, have been treated here. They both pertain to the general question whether the relation between two variables is independent of a third.

SUPPLEMENT

A. Significance Tests for Product-Moment Correlation

If it is expected that increase in one variable will be accompanied by a constant rate of increase (or decrease) in another, then one is hypothesizing a linear relationship between the two. The Pearson product-moment correlation coefficient (r) provides a descriptive measure of the magnitude of linear relationship in the sample. However, its sampling distribution around the parameter $\hat{r}$ is not normal, so significance tests are rarely performed directly with r. Instead, Fisher's (1941) transformation to the normally distributed z-statistic is used:

$$z = \log_e \sqrt{(1 + r)/(1 - r)}$$

From Appendix Table D one can read directly the value of z corresponding to any obtained r. Then a critical ratio is constructed:

$$CR = \frac{z - \hat{z}}{\sigma_z} = \frac{z - \hat{z}}{\sqrt{1/(n - 3)}}$$

If the r obtained from a sample of 15 subjects were $+.40$, this would correspond (see Appendix Table D) to a z of $+.424$. To test the null hypothesis that $\hat{r} = 0$ (hence that $\hat{z} = 0$) against the alternative that $\hat{r}$ is positive, one would form the critical ratio

$$CR = \frac{.424 - 0}{\sqrt{1/12}} = 1.62$$

yielding an α just over .05. If the investigator were intending to work at the .05 level of significance, he would not reject the null hypothesis with these data.

To test the null hypothesis that $\hat{} = .80$ (hence that $\hat{} = 1.099$) against the alternative that $\hat{r}$ is less than .80, one would form the critical ratio

$$CR = \frac{.424 - 1.099}{\sqrt{1/12}} = -2.59$$

which yields an α less than .005. The investigator can therefore be quite confident that the parameter $\hat{r}$ in the population from which this sample was drawn is less than .80.

Note that the standard deviation of the sampling distribution of z (σ_z) depends only on n, and also that z is normally distributed even when n is quite small; hence the size of α can be determined from the normal curve table (Appendix Table B) in nearly all practical cases.

The significance of a difference between two rs from independent samples is tested by transforming them both to zs, then computing the standard error of a difference between zs

$$\sigma_{z_1 - z_2} = \sqrt{\frac{1}{n_1 - 3} + \frac{1}{n_2 - 3}}$$

to fit into the appropriate critical ratio. Calculation for some illustrative results follows:

$$n_1 = 100 \qquad r_1 = .30 \qquad (z_1 = .309)$$

$$n_2 = 70 \qquad r_2 = .50 \qquad (z_2 = .549)$$

$$CR = \frac{z_1 - z_2}{\sigma_{z_1 - z_2}} = \frac{z_1 - z_2}{\sqrt{1/(n_1 - 3) + 1/(n_2 - 3)}} = \frac{.309 - .549}{\sqrt{\frac{1}{97} + \frac{1}{67}}} = -1.51$$

$\alpha = .07$, approximately, if only sample differences where $r_2 > r_1$ were to be considered,

$\alpha = .13$, approximately, if either direction of sample difference were acceptable.

B. Calculating η and Testing Two Relevant Null Hypotheses

η_{yx} is a measure of the degree of relationship between (at least) a nominal-scale variable, X, and (at least) an interval-scale variable, Y. It represents the degree to which the mean Y-score varies systematically with X. If X is measured on an interval scale, η can be interpreted as an index of curvilinear relationship between X and Y, with the precise function specified not by an equation but by the mean Y-scores in each column of X. In definitional form

$$\eta = \sqrt{1 - \frac{\sigma_{y \cdot x}^2}{\sigma_y^2}}$$

where $\sigma_{y \cdot x}^2$ is the variance of Y-scores about their column means and σ_y^2 is the total Y-variance.

A convenient calculating form can be derived:

$$\eta = \sqrt{1 - \frac{\sum\limits^{c} \sum\limits^{r} Y^2 - \sum\limits^{c} [(\sum\limits^{r} Y)^2 / n_c]}{\sum\limits^{c} \sum\limits^{r} Y^2 - (\sum\limits^{c} \sum\limits^{r} Y)^2 / n}}$$

The superscripts over the summation signs indicate that the Y-scores are summed first over the r rows within each column and then over the c columns. Thus $\sum\limits^{c}\sum\limits^{r} Y^2$ is the total sum of all squared Y-scores.

$\sum\limits^{c} [(\sum\limits^{r} Y)^2/n_c]$ means that the Y-scores within a given column are first added up over the rows; this sum is squared and divided by the number of scores (n_c) in that column. The same thing is done in every column and the results added over all of them. $(\sum\limits^{c}\sum\limits^{r} Y)^2$ is the square of the total sum of all Y-scores.

A computational example is presented in Table 13-7, which shows a bivariate frequency distribution, with the components of η required for the calculational formula. The sums 1720 and 1538 appear at the bottom right of the table; the value 1491 is obtained by squaring 476 and dividing by 152.

In order to test the null hypothesis that the column means are identical (and, therefore, that $\eta = 0$), one constructs an F-statistic, which is a ratio between two estimates of population variance. This is known as simple (one-way) *analysis of variance* (see, e.g., Lindquist, 1953; McNemar, 1955). The numerator estimate is derived from the variability among column means, the denominator estimate from the average variability of Y-scores within columns. To the extent that the first estimate exceeds the second, the F-ratio will be greater than 1.00, and the null hypothesis can be rejected at the level of significance indicated in a table of the F-distribution (see Appendix Table F). This F-ratio can be computed directly from η:

$$F = \frac{(n - c)\eta^2}{(c - 1)(1 - \eta^2)}$$

where n is the total number of subjects and
     c is the total number of columns (categories of the X-variable).

Calculation of this statistic is shown as F_1 in Table 13-7. To find out if the obtained value is large enough to reject the null hypothesis at the .05, the .01, or the .001 level of significance, one enters the F-table (Appendix Table F) with two different degrees of freedom. Along the top of the table one selects the degrees of freedom appropriate for the numerator ($c - 1$), and along the left-hand side of the table, the degrees of freedom appropriate for the denominator ($n - c$). If the obtained F exceeds the tabled values, then the null hypothesis can be rejected with α as indicated.

The other null hypothesis of interest is that the column means fall in a sloping straight line (and therefore that $\eta = r$). An appropriate F-ratio is computed directly from these two statistics (see calculation of F_2 in Table 13-7). It reflects the degree to which η exceeds r:

$$F = \frac{(n - c)(\eta^2 - r^2)}{(c - 2)(1 - \eta^2)}$$

where the symbols mean the same things as before. This time, however, the appropriate number of degrees of freedom for the numerator is ($c - 2$) and for the denominator, ($n - c$).

TABLE 13-7

Calculation of η and Fs from Data of Table 13-3

	X							Total
Y	0	1	2	3	4	5	6	
5	7	2	1	1	5	4	2	
4	12	4	1	3	7	6	5	
3	9	8	7	8	2	6	9	
2	3	5	7	3	1	3	5	
1		2	6	2		1	2	
0	1		1				1	
n_c	32	21	23	17	15	20	24	152
$\sum^r Y$	116	62	50	49	61	69	69	476
$\frac{(\sum^r Y)^2}{n_c}$	420.5	183.0	108.7	141.2	248.1	238.1	198.4	1538
$\sum^r Y^2$	460	208	138	159	259	263	233	1720

$$\eta = \sqrt{1 - \frac{\sum^c \sum^r Y^2 - \sum^c [(\sum^r Y)^2/n_c]}{\sum^c \sum^r Y^2 - (\sum^c \sum^r Y)^2/n}} = \sqrt{1 - \frac{1720 - 1538}{1720 - 1491}} = .453$$

$$r = \frac{n\Sigma XY - (\Sigma X)(\Sigma Y)}{\sqrt{[n\Sigma X^2 - (\Sigma X)^2][n\Sigma Y^2 - (\Sigma Y)^2]}} = .00$$

$$F_1 = \frac{(n - c)\eta^2}{(c - 1)(1 - \eta^2)} = \frac{(152 - 7)(.205)}{(7 - 1)(.795)}$$

$$= \frac{29.7}{4.77} = 6.23; \quad df = 6, 145; \quad \alpha < .001$$

$$F_2 = \frac{(n - c)(\eta^2 - r^2)}{(c - 2)(1 - \eta^2)} = \frac{(152 - 7)(.205)}{(7 - 2)(.795)}$$

$$= \frac{29.7}{3.98} = 7.46; \quad df = 5, 145; \quad \alpha < .001$$

It can be seen that the fairly large η in Table 13-7 permits confident rejection of both null hypotheses.

C. Testing the Significance of a Monotonic Relationship

The size of a monotonic relationship between two ordinal-scale variables can be represented by τ or h. Both of these statistics have the same numerator,

$(S+) - (S-)$, which we may designate for convenience simply as S. Testing the null hypothesis that either τ or h is zero amounts, therefore, to a test that $\hat{S} = 0$ in the population from which the sample was drawn. When the sample size is 10 or larger, the sampling distribution of S around the parameter zero is very nearly normal. Thus, given the standard deviation of this sampling distribution, it is possible to construct a critical ratio

$$CR = \frac{S}{\sigma_S}$$

and test the significance of S by reference to the normal curve table (Appendix Table B).

If there are no ties in ranks on either variable, the variance of the sampling distribution of S may be calculated from the formula

$$\sigma_S{}^2 = \frac{n(n-1)(2n+5)}{18}$$

Thus, in the illustration from Table 13-4 (p. 345), we have

$$\sigma_S{}^2 = \frac{10(9)(25)}{18} = 125; \qquad \sigma_S = 11.2$$

$$CR = \frac{S}{\sigma_S} = \frac{-27}{11.2} = -2.41$$

Therefore, one can reject, at the .02 level of significance (see Appendix Table B), the null hypothesis that there is no monotonic relationship between X and Y. (It is assumed here that either a positive or negative τ was of interest, hence a two-tail significance test is employed.)

When there are ties in rank on either variable, the formula for the variance of S becomes somewhat more complicated.* Assuming fixed marginal totals, it is

$$\sigma_S{}^2 = \frac{S_{2R}S_{2C}}{n-1} - \frac{S_{2R}S_{3C} + S_{2C}S_{3R}}{n(n-1)} + \frac{S_{3C}S_{3R}}{n(n-1)(n-2)}$$

where S_{2R} is the sum of products of row totals taken two at a time,
    S_{2C} is the sum of products of column totals taken two at a time,
    S_{3R} is the sum of products of row totals taken three at a time,
    S_{3C} is the sum of products of column totals taken three at a time, and
    n is the size of the sample.

Table 13-8 shows the calculation of σ_S from the data of Table 13-5 (p. 346). S_{2R} is computed from the row totals, shown in the extreme right-hand column. The products of all pairs can be obtained conveniently by multiplying the first (7) by each of the others (10, 30, 38, and 15) in succession; then multiplying the second (10) by each of those following it (30, 38, and 15); and so on. S_{2C} is obtained in the same way from the column totals (10, 25, 40, 20, and 5). To get

---

* This general formula for the variance of S was developed by Smith (1956).

TABLE 13-8

Calculating σ_S with Tied Ranks

			X			Total
Y	1	2	3	4	5	
1	3	2	1		1	7
2	4	2	1	3		10
3	1	12	7	8	2	30
4	2	6	20	8	2	38
5		3	11	1		15
Total	10	25	40	20	5	100

$$h = \frac{-559}{2739} = -.20 \qquad \text{(see Table 13-5)}$$

$$S_{2R} = 7(10) + 7(30) + 7(38) + 7(15) + 10(30) + 10(38) + 10(15) + 30(38)$$
$$+ 30(15) + 38(15) = 3641$$

$$S_{2C} = 10(25) + 10(40) + 10(20) + 10(5) + 25(40) + 25(20) + 25(5) + 40(20)$$
$$+ 40(5) + 20(5) = 3625$$

$$S_{3R} = 7(10)30 + 7(10)38 + 7(10)15 + 7(30)38 + 7(30)15 + 7(38)15$$
$$+ 10(30)38 + 10(30)15 + 10(38)15 + 30(38)15 = 59{,}630$$

$$S_{3C} = 10(25)40 + 10(25)20 + 10(25)5 + 10(40)20 + 10(40)5 + 10(20)5$$
$$+ 25(40)20 + 25(40)5 + 25(20)5 + 40(20)5 = 58{,}750$$

$$\sigma_S{}^2 = \frac{S_{2R}S_{2C}}{n-1} - \frac{S_{2R}S_{3C} + S_{2C}S_{3R}}{n(n-1)} + \frac{S_{3C}S_{3R}}{n(n-1)(n-2)}$$

$$= \frac{3641(3625)}{99} - \frac{3641(58{,}750) + 3625(59{,}630)}{100(99)} + \frac{58{,}750(59{,}630)}{100(99)(98)}$$

$$= 93{,}489; \qquad \sigma_S = 305.8$$

$$\text{CR} = \frac{S}{\sigma_S} = \frac{-559}{305.8} = -1.83; \qquad \begin{array}{l} \alpha < .04 \text{ (with one-directional alternative)} \\ \alpha < .07 \text{ (with two-directional alternative)} \end{array}$$

S_{3R}, one takes the products of all triplets of row totals—(7) (10) (30), (7) (10) (38), (7) (10) (15), then (7) (30) (38), (7) (30) (15), and so on; S_{3C} is calculated comparably from the triplets of column totals.

These components are then entered into the formula for $\sigma_S{}^2$ as indicated, yielding 93,489. The square root of this number (305.8) is the σ_S which is used as the denominator of the critical ratio, $\text{CR} = S/\sigma_S$.

D. Measuring Uncertainty Reduction

The basic notion of a relationship between two variables, X and Y, is that, given knowledge of a subject's score on X, one can predict Y with greater certainty than he could without such knowledge. Such a conception of relationship applies to multivalued as well as to single-valued functions (i.e., those in which two or more values of Y may be associated with a particular value of X); and it is appropriate for any scale type the data may represent.

Accordingly, we shall present the measure of relative uncertainty reduction, D, in its most general application to the case in which both X and Y are nominal-scale variables.

If X and Y were completely unrelated, a scatter plot (see Table 13-9) would show the same proportionate distribution of frequencies within each column that obtains for the total Y-distribution and also the same proportionate distribution of frequencies within each row as obtains for the total X-distribution. In other words, prediction of Y could not be improved from a knowledge of X and vice versa. The original uncertainty in prediction of X can be represented by H (see Attneave, 1959), the measure of dispersion for nominal-scale data presented in Chapter 5 (Table 5-1):

$$H = \Sigma p_i \log_2 \frac{1}{p_i}$$

where p_i is the proportion of cases that fall in the ith category of X and the logarithm of the fraction is to the base 2. This measure serves the same function for a nominal scale that σ^2 does for an interval scale. An equivalent formula for computing H directly from the raw frequencies is

$$H = \log_2 n - \frac{1}{n} \Sigma n_i \log_2 n_i$$

where n is the total sample size and n_i is the number of cases in the ith category. Manual computation is facilitated by the use of Appendix Table G, which gives $\log n$ for all values of n up to 1000, and Appendix Table H, which gives $n_i \log n_i$ for all values of n_i up to 500.

H_x and H_y (the uncertainty measures associated with the X and Y variables, respectively) are calculated from the marginals of the bivariate distribution, as shown in Table 13-9. Similarly, one can calculate a measure of dispersion from the individual cells of the scatter plot, indicating the joint uncertainty of X and Y together. This measure we may designate H_{xy}; it is computed from the same formula, except in this case n_i refers to the number of scores in a particular cell of the table rather than to a particular marginal frequency.

When X and Y are completely independent, as in the present example, H_{xy} (4.40257) is exactly equal to the sum, H_x (2.28064) $+ H_y$ (2.12193). In other words, the joint uncertainty of the bivariate distribution equals the sum of the uncertainties associated with each of the variables separately. This is the maximum uncertainty that a bivariate distribution can have.

TABLE 13-9

Random Association between X and Y (Maximum Uncertainty)

Y (a nominal-scale variable)	X (a nominal-scale variable) 1	2	3	4	5	Total
1	4	6	8	8	6	32
2	8	12	16	16	12	64
3	2	3	4	4	3	16
4	2	3	4	4	3	16
5	4	6	8	8	6	32
Total	20	30	40	40	30	160

$$H_x = \log_2 n - \frac{1}{n} \Sigma n_i \log_2 n_i$$

$$= \log 160 - \tfrac{1}{160} (20 \log 20 + 30 \log 30 + 40 \log 40 + 40 \log 40$$

$$+ 30 \log 30)$$

$$= 7.32193 - \tfrac{1}{160} (86.43856 + 147.20672 + 212.87712 + 212.87712$$

$$+ 147.20672) = 2.28064$$

$$H_y = 7.32193 - \tfrac{1}{160} (160.00000 + 384.00000 + 64.00000 + 64.00000$$

$$+ 160.00000) = 2.12193$$

$$H_{xy} = 7.32193 - \tfrac{1}{160} (4 \log 4 + 8 \log 8 + 2 \log 2 + 2 \log 2 + 4 \log 4$$

$$+ 6 \log 6 + 12 \log 12 + 3 \log 3 + 3 \log 3 + 6 \log 6 + 8 \log 8$$

$$+ 16 \log 16 + 4 \log 4 + 4 \log 4 + 8 \log 8 + 8 \log 8 + 16 \log 16$$

$$+ 4 \log 4 + 4 \log 4 + 8 \log 8 + 6 \log 6 + 12 \log 12 + 3 \log 3$$

$$+ 3 \log 3 + 6 \log 6) = 4.40257$$

Quite a different situation obtains in Table 13-10. There X and Y are perfectly related, in the sense that knowledge of one permits exact prediction of the other. Their joint uncertainty is exactly equal to the uncertainty of either variable alone; this is the minimum value that H_{xy} can have.

It is evident, then, that H_{xy}, the joint uncertainty of a bivariate matrix, must vary between H_x (or H_y) as a minimum and $H_x + H_y$ as a maximum. With these limits in mind, we may construct a measure of relationship, D, between X and Y:

$$D = \frac{H_{max} - H_{xy}}{H_{max} - H_{min}} = \frac{H_x + H_y - H_{xy}}{H_x + H_y - H_x} = \frac{H_x + H_y - H_{xy}}{H_y}$$

The numerator of D represents the degree to which the obtained joint uncertainty falls short of its maximum—in other words, the degree to which X and Y

TABLE 13-10

Perfect Association between X and Y (Minimum Uncertainty)

Y (a nominal-scale variable)	1	2	3	4	5	Total
			X (a nominal-scale variable)			
1			40			40
2		30				30
3					30	30
4	20					20
5				40		40
Total	20	30	40	40	30	160

$$H_x = H_y = H_{xy} = 7.32193 - \tfrac{1}{160}\,(20 \log 20 + 30 \log 30 + 40 \log 40$$
$$+ 40 \log 40 + 30 \log 30) = 2.28064$$

are related beyond mere random association. In order to obtain a measure that will vary between 0.00 and +1.00, we express this difference in ratio to the maximum difference possible $(H_{max} - H_{min})$, given the obtained marginals.

In the present example H_x and H_y are equal, and either of them can be inserted in place of H_{min}, leaving either H_x or H_y in the denominator of the right-hand fraction. In the general case H_x and H_y will not be equal, and the denominator of the ratio will differ, depending on one's purpose. An exact value of H_{min} could be obtained by fiddling with the cell entries until they were as concentrated as possible without altering the marginals. It is much more convenient to use as an approximation to H_{min} either H_x or H_y, whichever is the larger. This is a conservative approximation in the sense that it is always equal to, or smaller than, the actual minimum value given these particular marginal distributions; hence D calculated in this manner will usually not be quite so large as it would be if the exact value for H_{min} were used. The approximate measure of association between two nominal-scale variables with different marginal distributions is therefore

$$D = \frac{H_x + H_y - H_{xy}}{H_s}$$

where H_s is the uncertainty of the variable with the smaller dispersion. D in this case represents the amount of uncertainty reduction accomplished by the joint distribution in ratio to the maximum amount of reduction possible, which is H_s.

When H_x and H_y are unequal, one might use the larger value in the denominator of D, instead of the smaller value. Such an index would represent the amount of uncertainty reduction in ratio to the original uncertainty in Y, given no knowledge of X. Thus two different indices can be distinguished by subscripts, D_{yx} and D_{xy} (see Attneave, 1959). In the terminology of information theory

D_{yx} represents the amount of information about X that is contained in Y, whereas D_{xy} represents the amount of information about Y that is contained in X. Ordinarily these indices will differ unless the initial uncertainties of the two variables are the same. Calculations are illustrated in Table 13-11, which is based on the data of Table 13-6.

TABLE 13-11

Calculation of D and χ^2 (Data of Table 13-6)

Obtained frequencies

Y	0	1	Total
5	2	5	7
4	5	20	25
3	30	4	34
2	5	20	25
1	2	5	7
Total	44	54	98

X

Expected frequencies

3.1	3.9	7
11.2	13.8	25
15.3	18.7	34
11.2	13.8	25
3.1	3.9	7
43.9	54.1	98

$$H_x = 6.61471 - \tfrac{1}{98}\,(240.21499 + 310.76393) = 0.99248$$

$$H_y = 6.61471 - \tfrac{1}{98}\,(19.65148 + 116.09640 + 172.97374 + 116.09640$$

$$+\ 19.65148) = 2.07931$$

$$H_{xy} = 6.61471 - \tfrac{1}{98}\,(2.00000 + 11.60964 + 147.20672 + 11.60964$$

$$+\ 2.00000 + 11.60964 + 86.43856 + 8.00000 + 86.43856 + 11.60964)$$

$$=\ 2.75224$$

$$D_{yx} = \frac{H_x + H_y - H_{xy}}{H_x} = \frac{0.99248 + 2.07931 - 2.75224}{0.99248} = .32$$

$$D_{xy} = \frac{H_x + H_y - H_{xy}}{H_y} = \frac{0.99248 + 2.07931 - 2.75224}{2.07931} = .15$$

$$\chi^2 = \Sigma\,\frac{(O-E)^2}{E} = \frac{(2-3.1)^2}{3.1} + \frac{(5-11.2)^2}{11.2} + \frac{(30-15.3)^2}{15.3} + \frac{(5-11.2)^2}{11.2}$$

$$+\ \frac{(2-3.1)^2}{3.1} + \frac{(5-3.9)^2}{3.9} + \frac{(20-13.8)^2}{13.8} + \frac{(4-18.7)^2}{18.7}$$

$$+\ \frac{(20-13.8)^2}{13.8} + \frac{(5-3.9)^2}{3.9}$$

$$=\ 39.52; \quad df = (C_x - 1)(C_y - 1) = (1)(4) = 4; \quad \alpha < .0001$$

Testing the Statistical Significance of Nominal-Scale Relationships

Ordinarily the null hypothesis of major interest in this kind of bivariate uncertainty analysis is that $D = 0.00$. This is not tested directly because the sampling distribution of D is too complicated. Instead, one computes the statistic chi-square (χ^2), which is not algebraically related to D, though it accomplishes the desired purpose.

$$\chi^2 = \Sigma \frac{(O - E)^2}{E}$$

where O is the frequency obtained in any particular cell of the table, and E is the "expected" frequency corresponding to it, under the assumption that X and Y are independent. When every O in the table is very close to its corresponding E, both χ^2 and D will be small. To the extent that the Os depart from their Es, both statistics will be increased, indicating some magnitude of relationship— some degree of uncertainty reduction.

In order to calculate the expected frequencies for all cells, one in effect creates a frequency distribution for each column with numbers proportional to the marginal distribution of the Y-variable. (This amounts to the same thing as making all the row frequencies proportional to the X-marginals.) Such a distribution of expected frequencies is shown in the upper-right corner of Table 13-11. Concretely, this can be accomplished for any cell by multiplying the total frequency of the row in which it falls by the total frequency of its column and dividing this product by n, the total sample size. For example, the expected frequency for the upper left-hand cell in Table 13-11 is calculated as $(7)(44)/98 = 3.1$.

As a check on one's computations, the sum of the expected frequencies in any column (or row) should equal the corresponding marginal frequency in the obtained distribution. (In the present example this is true within rounding errors.) Once the expected frequencies for all cells are obtained, they are subtracted from their corresponding observed frequencies and the difference is squared and divided by the particular expected value. These quantities are then summed over all cells in the bivariate distribution, to yield a number which is looked up in a table of the chi-square distribution (Appendix Table E). This table tells the probability of obtaining a χ^2 as large as, or larger than, the one obtained, given the particular number of independent components, that is, the *degrees of freedom*. For a bivariate distribution whose marginal frequencies are considered fixed, the degrees of freedom is $(C_x - 1)(C_y - 1)$, where C_x and C_y are the numbers of categories in the X- and Y-variables, respectively. This product is the number of cell frequencies that can be independently set and still keep the marginal frequencies constant.

In the present example χ^2 turns out to be 39.52, which with four degrees of freedom is well beyond the most stringent significance level. Thus one can be very confident that variables X and Y are not independent. However, the nature of their relationship is not ascertainable from either D or χ^2. The latter statistic simply tells one that Y can be better predicted from a knowledge of X than without such knowledge; and D just shows how well the best fitting multivalued function—whatever that may be—fits the data. The specific predictions to be made must be determined by first looking at the table to see what departures from expected values appear to account for the obtained result, then testing each one of them by a specific significance test—such as the CR for a difference between percentages—to see if the apparent sources of departure are reliable.

E. Combining Independent Significance Tests of Partial Relations

A partial relation between X_1 and Y is one that remains after controlling for possible contaminating effects of other independent variables, X_2, X_3, etc. One general approach to discovering a partial relation is to divide the sample into several groups on the basis of their scores on the independent variables which are to be statistically controlled, then look for a consistent X_1–Y-relationship within each of these groups. To tell whether the entire set of groups tends to display the same partial relation, one tests, within each group, the same null hypothesis—that the parameter relationship is zero—against the same alternative hypothesis—that the parameter relationship is in a particular direction (determined a priori or after inspection) for all groups. Each test yields a different α, or probability of Type I error; and they are all independent, since the tests are performed on different subsamples.

It has been shown by Fisher (1941, pp. 97–98; see also Hald, 1952, p. 407; Jones & Fiske, 1953) that the product of several independent αs can be transformed into a function which has a χ^2 distribution by the following formula:

$$\chi^2 = -2 \log_e \prod_{i=1}^{k} \alpha_i$$

$$\chi^2 = -2 \log_e (\alpha_1)(\alpha_2)(\alpha_3) \cdots (\alpha_k),$$

where k is the number of independent tests of significance.

Since all of the αs are less than 1.00, their product will be too. The logarithm of a number less than 1.00 is negative; multiplying by -2 will yield a positive product, which is looked up in a chi-square table (see Appendix Table E), under $2k$ degrees of freedom. If the obtained χ^2 is larger than the tabled value for, say, the .05 significance level, then one can be reasonably confident that the same partial relationship would be replicated in another sample from the same population.

The foregoing formula is based on natural logarithms. If only a table of common logarithms is available, a different multiplicative constant must be used:

$$\chi^2 = -4.60517 \log_{10} \prod_{i=1}^{k} \alpha_i$$

Table 13-12 illustrates a combined significance test from three different X_1–Y-relationships, all in the same direction, but none of them significant by itself at the .05 level. Within each group a chi-square significance test is used, since no a priori direction of relationship was sought. The χ_t^2 resulting from the product of the three αs is 14.1835. With six degrees of freedom ($2k$, or twice the number

TABLE 13-12

Partial Relation between Two Nominal-Scale Variables, X_1 and Y, with a Third Nominal-Scale Variable, X_2, Held Constant

X_2:		1		2		3	
Y	X_1:	1	2	1	2	1	2
1		5 7.5	10 7.5	10 14.1	20 15.9	20 25	30 25
2		20 17.5	15 17.5	30 25.9	25 29.1	50 45	40 45
		$\chi_1^2 = 2.381; df = 1$		$\chi_2^2 = 3.476; df = 1$		$\chi_3^2 = 3.111; df = 1$	
		$\alpha_1 = .13$		$\alpha_2 = .08$		$\alpha_3 = .08$	

In the above table boldface figures are observed frequencies (Os); italicized figures are expected frequencies (Es). The three individual chi-squares are calculated from the formula

$$\chi^2 = \Sigma \frac{(O - E)^2}{E} \qquad \text{(see Table 13-11)}$$

$$
\begin{aligned}
\chi_t^2 &= -4.60517 \log_{10} \alpha_1 \alpha_2 \alpha_3 = -4.60517 \log_{10} (.13)(.08)(.08) \\
&= -4.60517 \log_{10} (.000832) = -4.60517 (6.9201 - 10) \\
&= 14.1835; \qquad df = 2k = 6; \qquad \alpha_t < .05
\end{aligned}
$$

of independent tests that are combined), this value is significant beyond the .05 level.

Table 13-13 presents a different situation. The investigator had expected a uniform positive linear relationship between X_1 and Y, but in controlling on X_2 (a four-category variable) he found one reversal. The question to be asked is, "Is the apparent general trend a dependable one?" The significance level of each r is computed, this time against a one-directional alternative, so that α for the reversed group is greater than .50.

F. Testing the Significance of Specific Interactions

X_1 and X_2 interact in their relationship to Y if the direction, or magnitude, of the X_1–Y-relation depends on X_2. If one enters the analysis expecting a specific form of interaction, it is fairly easy to devise a specific straightforward test for it.

For example, from the data of Table 13-2, p. 328 (repeated in Table 13-14), if one wished to determine whether the first two columns have a difference in means larger than (or in the opposite direction from) the difference in means of the last two columns, he would establish a null hypothesis that the difference between the two sets of differences equals zero:

$$(\mu_1 - \mu_2) - (\mu_3 - \mu_4) = 0$$

The obtained difference is:

TABLE 13-13

Partial Relation between Two Interval-Scale Variables, X_1 and Y, with a Third Variable, X_2, Held Constant

X_2		1						2				
X_1	0	1	2	3	4		0	1	2	3	4
Y 4				1	1	4					2
3		2	2	4		3			2	1	2
2		3	2		2	2	3	1	2	3	
1	2					1	2	2		1	2
0	1	1				0		1	2		

$r_1 = .63;$ $\alpha_1 = .001$ $\qquad$ $r_2 = .40;$ $\alpha_2 = .02$

X_2		3						4				
X_1	0	1	2	3	4		0	1	2	3	4
Y 4	1					4					
3		3	1	2		3			2	1	
2	2	1	1		3	2		1	2	3	1
1	1		3	2	2	1	2	2	1	1	2
0		2				0					

$r_3 = -.15;$ $\alpha_3 = .76$ $\qquad$ $r_4 = .19;$ $\alpha_4 = .23$

$$\chi_t^2 = -4.60517 \log_{10} (.001)(.02)(.76)(.23)$$

$$= -4.60517 \log_{10} (.000003496)$$

$$= -4.60517 (4.5435 - 10)$$

$$= 25.13; \quad df = 8; \quad \alpha_t < .005$$

$$(M_1 - M_2) - (M_3 - M_4) = (5.8 - 4.0) - (2.6 - 6.0) = 5.2$$

(It is necessary to keep track of signs, since the direction of differences is not the same in the two comparisons.)

A critical ratio can be established as follows:

$$\text{CR} = \frac{[(M_1 - M_2) - (M_3 - M_4)] - [(\mu_1 - \mu_2) - (\mu_3 - \mu_4)]}{\sigma_{(M_1 - M_2) - (M_3 - M_4)}}$$

When all the means are based on independent observations (i.e., they come from different subjects), the standard error of the difference between differences in means is

TABLE 13-14

Testing the Significance of the Difference between Differences in Means
(Data of Table 13-2)

	X_1:	Low		High	
Y	X_2:	Low	High	Low	High
8		3	2		4
7		5		1	4
6		6	2		8
5		4	4	2	2
4		2	7	4	1
3		1	5	8	
2			3	7	2
1		1		3	
0			1	4	
M_y		5.8	4.0	2.6	6.0

$$\sigma_{(M_1-M_2)-(M_3-M_4)} = \sqrt{\sigma^2_{M_1} + \sigma^2_{M_2} + \sigma^2_{M_3} + \sigma^2_{M_4}}$$

$$= \sqrt{\frac{\sigma_1^2}{n_1 - 1} + \frac{\sigma_2^2}{n_2 - 1} + \frac{\sigma_3^2}{n_3 - 1} + \frac{\sigma_4^2}{n_4 - 1}} \quad *$$

These four variances are calculated from Table 13-14 as

$$\sigma_1^2 = 2.81; \qquad \sigma_2^2 = 3.21; \qquad \sigma_3^2 = 2.66; \qquad \sigma_4^2 = 2.76$$

* Alternatively, a single estimate of population variance, s^2, could be made from the sums of squared deviations around the column means:

$$s^2 = \frac{\sum\limits_{c=1}^{k} \sum\limits_{i=1}^{n_c} (Y_{ic} - M_c)^2}{n - k}$$

where Y_{ic} is a particular score in column c,
   M_c is the mean of column c,
   n_c is the number of cases in column c,
   k is the total number of columns and
   n is the total sample size $\left(= \sum\limits_{c=1}^{k} n_c\right)$.

A common s^2 is then used in the estimate of the standard error of the difference between differences in means:

$$s_{(M_1 - M_2) - (M_3 - M_4)} = \sqrt{\frac{s^2}{n_1} + \frac{s^2}{n_2} + \frac{s^2}{n_3} + \frac{s^2}{n_4}}$$

(See (18) in Chapter 10, p. 270.)

The critical ratio in this case is

$$CR = \frac{5.2 - 0}{\sqrt{(2.81/21) + (3.21/23) + (2.66/28) + (2.76/20)}} = 10.27$$

and the null hypothesis can be very confidently rejected.

Another illustration of a possible interaction is provided in Table 13-13 (p. 371). Even though a positive partial relation between X_1 and Y has been found, this relation appears higher in the first two groups than in the second two. One simple way of testing the significance of this apparent difference is to combine the first two groups into one table and compute an r for them; then do the same for the remaining two groups. This would yield rs of .48 and $-.04$. The significance of the difference between these two rs can be tested by means of z-transformations:

$$CR = \frac{z_1 - z_2}{\sqrt{1/(n_1 - 3) + 1/(n_2 - 3)}} = \frac{.523 - (-.040)}{\sqrt{\frac{1}{44} + \frac{1}{39}}} = 2.56$$

A critical ratio of this size permits rejection of the null hypothesis at the .01 significance level, and it is reasonable to conclude that X_1 and X_2 do interact in their relationship to Y: when X_2 is "high," the X_1-Y-relationship is less than when X_2 is "low." (Note that the division on X_2 into "high" and "low" was arbitrarily made so that the two resulting groups were as nearly equal in size as possible. This is an appropriate way of dividing the data for this kind of analysis, unless some more logical cutting point had been established before the results were known.)

From these two illustrations the reader may see the general approach to testing the significance of specific interactions which are anticipated beforehand. If, however, one does not entertain the possibility of interactive relationships before perusing the data, then he had better be careful about picking out for test only the one interaction, out of many possible, that becomes apparent on inspection. Such a procedure would create an unrealistic picture of the probability of Type I errors, leading one to infer a particular pattern of interaction which was merely a chance occurrence in the sample. In the first illustration provided here (Table 13-14) there were only two different patterns of interaction possible. (In addition to the one observed, M_1 and M_4 could have been lower than M_2 and M_3.) Underestimation of α would not have been serious in this case; but in the second example, with four different correlations to look at, 24 different orderings of their magnitudes might have been found. So if there were no a priori reason to expect any particular one of them, it would not be appropriate just to pick out the highest r, for example, and test it against the other three combined. This procedure would greatly underestimate the probability of a Type I error.

There are general significance tests for nonspecific interactive relationships, just as there are for nonspecific bivariate relations. These can be found in sources listed in the chapter references (e.g., Lindquist, 1953; McNemar, 1955; Schaie, 1958; Wilk & Kempthorne, 1955).

REFERENCES

Attneave, F. *Applications of information theory to psychology.* New York: Holt, 1959.

Cronbach, L. J. The two disciplines of scientific psychology. *Amer. Psychologist,* 1957, **12**, 671–684.

Du Bois, P. H. *Multivariate correlational analysis.* New York: Harper, 1957.

Fisher, R. A. *Statistical methods for research workers.* (8th ed., rev.) Edinburgh: Oliver & Boyd, 1941.

Grant, D. A. Analysis-of-variance tests in the analysis and comparison of curves. *Psychol. Bull.,* 1956, **53**, 141–154.

Hald, A. *Statistical theory with engineering applications.* New York: Wiley, 1952.

Jones, L. V., & Fiske, D. W. Models for testing the significance of combined results. *Psychol. Bull.,* 1953, **50**, 375–382.

Kendall, M. G. *Rank correlation methods.* (2nd Ed.) London: Griffin, 1955.

Kullback, S. *Information theory and statistics.* New York: Wiley, 1959.

Lindquist, E. F. *Design and analysis of experiments in psychology and education.* Boston: Houghton Mifflin, 1953.

McNemar, Q. *Psychological statistics.* (2nd Ed.) New York: Wiley, 1955.

Schaie, K. W. Tests of hypotheses about differences between two intercorrelation matrices. *J. exper. Educ.,* 1958, **26**, 241–245.

Senders, Virginia. *Measurement and statistics.* New York: Oxford, 1958.

Smith, J. E. K. On the analysis of contingency tables with ordered classifications. *Amer. Psychologist,* 1956, **11**, 398 (Abstract). (Dittoed copy of paper available from author.)

Wallis, W. A., & Roberts, H. V. *Statistics: a new approach.* Glencoe, Ill.: Free Press, 1957.

Wilk, M. B., & Kempthorne, O. Fixed, mixed, and random models. *J. Amer. Stat. Assn.,* 1955, **50**, 1144–1167.

CHAPTER 14

Interpreting and reporting the results

After a period spent in computation and detailed analysis, it is time to come up for air, get an overview of the findings, and try to decide what they mean. If a thorough job was done in anticipating various possible outcomes in the research proposal, this process may not be too difficult. Typically, one will find, when faced with actual results, that his thinking was insufficient. Although the earlier considerations can be very helpful, the particular pattern of results is likely to raise a whole series of new ideas. To bring some order into the speculations, it is useful to review the findings from several points of view: their significance for the original theory or problem, alternative interpretations that might be entertained, and the kind of research that needs to be done next. Once a fairly complete overview has been obtained, if things seem to make sufficient sense and to fit together reasonably well, the next step is to organize the material in such a way that it will be comprehensible to someone else, write it up, and get it into the public domain where it will be accessible to anyone interested.

INTERPRETATION

Implications for the Original Problem

It is customary to speak of "positive" and "negative" findings from research. The first kind are those that confirm the initial expectations; the second kind either fail to confirm or actually contradict the predictions. Of course, the distinction is meaningful only if one had clear expectations to begin with. In exploratory research one would simply distinguish between "clear" and "ambiguous" findings.

To decide whether a predicted outcome was confirmed or not, one should consider the total pattern of results relevant to the prediction. A single null hypothesis tested and rejected at the .001 level of significance constitutes convincing evidence. But so may a series of independent tests with significance levels consistently between .25 and .10. The size of the relationship demanded will depend on the ambitiousness of one's expectations, on the reliability of measures, and on how many variables, besides those included in the present study, affect the phenomenon of interest. The researcher need not be discouraged if his relationships are not crystal clear. A correlation of .20 might be just as exciting in some circumstances as an r of .90 would be in others. There is no magical number that can, by itself, transform a hypothesis into an empirical generalization. Such a transformation can only be accomplished subjectively by the investigator himself—and, eventually, by the scientific community, if it comes to share his conclusions.

One should, of course, distinguish between statistical significance and practical (or theoretical) importance. A particular independent variable may account for only a trivial proportion of the variance in the dependent variable, but any proportion can turn out to be statistically significant with a large enough sample. So, in interpreting positive results, the investigator must be careful not to create the impression that his independent variables have a preponderant effect when they have not.

If the results are consistent with the initial expectations, then they help increase one's confidence in many different processes on which they depend—the assumptions and derivations of the theory, the measurement of relevant variables, and the operations by which variables were manipulated. Negative results are more ambiguous: one cannot tell which of these (or other) steps are at fault, so it is not exactly clear what the conclusions should be. Presumably one would like to interpret negative results to mean clearly that the variables are not related in the specified manner; but before such a conclusion is warranted other possible explanations of the outcome must be reasonably discarded. There is never any sure way of doing this, but certain checks built into the research can help reduce the plausibility of some interpretations. If one designs each new study to include some measures and manipulations that have worked before, then it is possible to replicate a known result before seeking an uncertain one. The replication serves to increase the researcher's confidence in at least some of the components—e.g., the particular measures involved and the sample of subjects—so that negative results could not so readily be attributed to deficiencies here.

Once their sources are clearly identified, negative results may have a significance equal to that of positive results. This is particularly true when they lead to revision or extension of a theory to which they are relevant.

Far more frequent than clear-cut positive or negative results are muddy findings. Some expected trends appear, others do not, some are reversed; differences do not fall into a clearly meaningful pattern, and they permit rejection of the null hypotheses at the .07 or .15 rather than the magical .05 or .01 level of significance. Perhaps there are barely more results significant at a given level than would be expected by chance from that number of tests. Under these conditions —which perhaps represent the usual case in most contemporary psychological research—one must simply do the best he can in trying to make sense of the data. One helpful approach to this problem may consist in trying, mentally, to "pull apart" the results in various ways. Those involving one measure or manipulation may be tentatively separated from others; findings on female subjects may be examined separately from those on males, subjects early in the experiment might be distinguished from those later on, and so forth. Such hunch-impelled analyses may uncover interactions that have obscured the main effects or permit identification of the one good measure among the several poor ones. Usually, confused results require a rethinking of the problem as well; and, to be convincing, any new interpretations discovered in this haphazard search process will probably require replication of relevant parts of the study.

Alternative Interpretations

When a researcher claims that his results support a particular theory or suggest one solution to a particular problem, he is either explicitly or implicitly rejecting alternative interpretations of the findings. Since interpretations, as well as specific findings, constitute the output of the study, this is a serious choice. Of course, it is unrealistic to demand explicit consideration of all reasonable competing interpretations before choosing the most likely one. Yet if the investigator himself does not take some small steps in this direction, he is likely to find his critics doing it for him—and sometimes not in a very constructive way. The least he can do is consider certain trivial interpretations of a methodological rather than a substantive sort.

The first of these is the sampling error interpretation—that his results are chance and would not be replicated in another study. Enough has already been said about statistical procedures for guarding against this interpretation; if the researcher chooses appropriate significance tests and consistently respects the meaning of a significance level, he can assess the probability of such unwanted results. It often happens that a strong desire to interpret one's findings in a particular manner leads to an incautious conclusion without an adequate significance test. Thus, if three different correlation coefficients all turn out to be significantly different from zero, this finding may lead the eager researcher to talk about differences among them—for example, that their magnitudes are ordered in a way that his theory would predict. This is a different conclusion from the statement that none of them equals zero; it requires testing another null hypothesis (that this particular order occurred by chance). The only way to avoid careless overinterpretations is to examine carefully each statement about the findings and make sure that it can be supported by a specific significance test in which the probability of a Type I error is made explicit.

Another trivial interpretation is that of contamination between independent and dependent variables. If scores for both are derived from the same measures or from measures that are somehow not independent, then the most straightforward explanation for the finding that X and Y are related is simply that X and Y are not distinct variables but just two different measures of the same thing. There are many ways that nonindependence of measures can come about. One of the commonest is for the same person (the subject himself or an outside observer) to make judgments about both the independent and the dependent variables. If he has a built-in expectation about their relationship, this may contaminate the outcome. Any apparent correlation between the two may reflect only the judge's belief that they are related rather than a real relationship. Contaminating circumstances can be much subtler and more difficult to detect than this. One general strategy for avoiding them is to try always to measure different variables with different sets of data. When this has not been done, the researcher should at least explicitly recognize the contamination interpretation as an alternative to his own.

Aside from methodological interpretations that are substantively trivial, there will always be competing theories to account for a particular outcome on the basis of other variables. An experimenter may have intended to manipulate X_1 in his experimental conditions, but another theorist might come along and say that the experimental operations also resulted in the manipulation of X_2 and that the latter variable "really" accounted for the result. A correlation between X and Y is reported from an assessment study, but a critic contends that this is "really" due to the fact that both are correlated with W. The number of different interpretations that merit consideration will depend on how much is already known about correlates of the dependent variable and on how many well accepted theories have something definite —and different—to predict. Quite often it will be found that allegedly different theories and known correlates come down to meaning essentially the same thing; or perhaps the researcher does not care whether his interpretation is distinguishable from a particular set of alternatives. But there may be certain other theoretically or empirically meaningful interpretations that he definitely wants to avoid because he is trying to say something different from, or additional to, them. In this case his research design should include variables relevant to the competing interpretations, as well as to his own, and these should be taken into account in the analysis and presentation of his results. Two general techniques for doing this are provided by factorial designs (Chapter 10) and the statistical analysis of partial relations (Chapter 13). If the findings do not permit definite rejection of the alternative interpretation, then it is foolish to claim exclusive validity for one's own.

It is the rare study that accounts for so much of the variance in a phenomenon that nothing is left over to be accounted for by other independent variables that did not happen to be represented. Distributions typically overlap, rs are less than 1.00, etc. Multiple causation is the rule for most psychological attributes, so it would be surprising if the one or two independent variables chosen for study were to account entirely for differences in the dependent variable. The mere demonstration that one particular interpretation is supported by the results should not be taken as presumptive evidence that an alternative interpretation is therefore invalid—unless that alternative, too, was specifically tested. Although this may be an obvious, common-sense observation, it is surprising how many investigators write up their results as if they demonstrated conclusively that their own theory was correct and every one else's wrong. These are really two separate contentions, each of which requires its own relevant evidence. Even if two theories appear logically contradictory, the researcher should be sufficiently modest to put his logic to empirical test.

After seriously considering a variety of competing explanations, the researcher is ready to ask himself some critical questions. Are these results, and their meaning, clear enough to merit formal reporting? Or are some of the plausible interpretations so trivial that the findings have no clear substantive meaning? Do they lend themselves as well to an interpretation which was to be excluded as they do to the preferred interpretation? These will not always be easy questions to answer unequivocally, for what is a trivial interpretation, or what is a competing one, depends greatly on the point of view. The main value of asking these questions is to help the researcher arrive at a point of view that permits the closest fit between his results and the meaning he attributes to them. If an intended broad meaning gets converted into an undesirably narrow one or an intended single meaning is transformed into a multiple, inconclusive one, then the researcher may well decide that it is better to withhold publication until he has collected new data, or performed new analyses, that will clarify his results.

Implications for Further Research

Regardless of whether the outcome is clear or ambiguous with respect to the initial problem, it will inevitably leave many relevant questions unanswered. For that matter, the value of a research project might be judged, in part, by the number of new, specific questions that it raises. Such questions can provide the framework within which new research is designed.

One whole set of questions relates to a clarification and elaboration of the present findings. These will be particularly pertinent with an ambiguous, inconclusive outcome, but they may stem from clear, positive results as well. If an experiment demonstrates that animals with a portion of the brain removed show a marked change in food preference, accepting a greater variety of substances than unoperated controls, then one may immediately wonder why this should be so. Is it because they can no longer taste (or smell) differences, because their desire for new experience has been heightened, or because they just don't care? Each of these interpretations is pretty vague as it stands, but a bit of imaginative consideration may lead to precise operations and to an experimental design that will permit one to choose among them. Thus an initially clear finding concerning behavioral differences is converted into a question concerning mechanisms that might have mediated the behavior.

Suppose that, in attempting to replicate this result in another species, one found no consistent effect of surgery on food preferences. This is a more ambiguous result because it forces one to question the adequacy of the experimental operations. Perhaps the wrong area of the brain was removed (functional brain localization may differ from one species to another); perhaps in the course of removing the critical area additional sections were damaged as well (this can usually be determined by histological examination); perhaps the original finding is peculiar to the initially tested species; or it might be that a different method of testing food preferences, more appropriate to the new species, must be found. Each of these interpretations can be converted into specific research questions and operations that will, hopefully, clarify the nature of the problem and permit one to proceed further with the main line of investigation.

Besides those questions aimed at clarifying the results, other questions may extend them or increase their generality. A new species of animal may be studied, or a new population of humans, to find out how the same variables appear there. Increased generality might occur in two different forms. The first, and simplest, is when the relations established in one population can be replicated exactly in another. Quite a different outcome is presented when the new relations are not identical to the old, but the difference can be accounted for systematically by a difference between the two populations. This implies that a new interactive variable is added to the interpretation, thus permitting prediction of a wider range of phenomena, though with a modified, more general, theory.

In the same way, one might wish to extend the generality of results, not across populations of subjects but across populations of measuring instruments and operations. Is the superior effect on learning of distributed practice (as opposed to massed practice) displayed in situations involving "insight" as well as in those requiring "rote" learning, or is a more general (interactive) principle required which takes into account the nature of the task?

Finally, in addition to questions involving clarification or generalization of the results, one may pose questions about antecedents and consequences that involve entirely new variables. If students with flexible minds are shown to be superior problem solvers, then how does one go about inculcating flexibility? If mentally deficient persons can be trained by appropriate procedures to perform a specified kind of task, then how does one analyze (or construct) jobs to be relatively certain that only this kind of task is required? Problems such as these are sometimes relegated to the domain of "applied research," if the new variables they suggest are not part of the theoretical system that accounts for the original relationships. But there is no reason why they cannot provide the basis for a new theoretical framework, or perhaps an extension of the old one, if the relevant variables are appropriately formulated.

The implications of any research project, imaginatively viewed, can thus extend well beyond the problem it was originally designed to investigate. From the scientific point of view, the most important implications are those involving researchable questions. The sponsor or consumer may ask himself, "How can I apply these results to my situation? What new course of action do these findings suggest for me?" The dedicated researcher will be more concerned with what else he needs to know before such questions of application can be intelligently answered, about the implications the findings have for other theoretical issues, and about how to pin down the findings and his interpretation of them even more unequivocally.

REPORTING THE STUDY

The habits of researchers being what they are, it is likely that the volume of unanalyzed or unpublished data buried in files exceeds that available in the literature. A healthy dose of compulsiveness comes in handy in many phases of research; it is particularly useful in seeing to it that the results of a study are made available to others in a comprehensible form. Unpublished findings are not of much use to science.

Some beginners have the impression that once the study is completed it takes a day or two to write up the report. This impression is unrealistically optimistic. We know of no data on the matter, but we suspect that typically somewhere around one fourth of the time spent on a research project is spent in writing it up—though there are wide variations. For the average psychologist, not endowed with inordinate skill in writing, it often takes three, four, or even ten drafts of a paper before it is ready for publication. So one should leave plenty of time for preparing the final report; it is almost certain to take longer than initially anticipated.

A second widespread misconception is that authors of scientific papers get paid for their manuscripts. Although this may be true of a few trade journals, encyclopedias, and some popular magazines, none of the technical scientific journals in psychology pays its authors for their trouble. In fact, part of the publication cost is often assumed by the author: he must actually pay to get his paper published. Many journals charge the author the full cost of special material, such as tables and figures, some charge him a flat page rate if he wants the paper to appear earlier than it normally would ("early publication"), and others charge a regular fixed page fee for all papers. Of course, this situation does not reflect a mercenary streak in editors and publishers. Publishing scientific journals is an expensive enterprise, and, since the audience is specialized and narrow, costs of publication are rarely covered by subscription income. Subsidy is the rule, and, be cause even this is often not enough, authors may have to be charged to help make ends meet. (At the present writing, though, none of the APA journals charges costs to authors, except in the case of early publication, for which the fee is fixed at $30 per printed page.)

The Ethics of Publishing

Throughout these chapters we have frequently made reference to ethical principles governing a psychologist's professional conduct. Among the more important are several having to do specifically with publication. We have already mentioned the one that is perhaps most frequently violated: that the researcher's duties to his field are not fulfilled until his findings are made available in public form. This principle is double-edged; some would hold that premature publication is fully as unethical, if not more so, than withholding findings. It is often not easy to know what is the correct course of action in a concrete instance. Decisions about what constitutes ethical conduct are easier in relation to two other issues: proper assignment of credit and the injunction against publishing the same material more than once.

The APA code of ethics has some explicit rules for assigning credit to the proper people in the appropriate way. If a person has made a substantial professional contribution to a study, he should be included as an author. If he has made a lesser contribution, he should be cited either in a footnote or in the text. If two or more researchers have made substantial professional contributions, warranting coauthorship, the names are given in the order of the significance of their contributions. The person with primary responsibility is listed first (he is usually referred to as "senior author," whether or not he is older than the others), the one who contributed next most is listed second, and so on; if the contributions are equal the names are presented in alphabetical order. Details of these procedures can be found in the original APA code of ethics (1953) and in the later briefer versions (1958, 1959). As a general rule, for the sake of graciousness and to avoid unpleasantness, it is probably better to err on the side of giving too much credit than too little.

"Double reporting" refers to the practice of formally publishing substantially the same paper or the same results in more than one written outlet. This practice is considered unethical both for a moral and for a practical reason. In professional psychology an individual's competence and accomplishment in the field are often judged at least superficially by the length of his publication list rather than on the basis of quality; double reporting would expand such a list illegitimately. Second, journal editors are already hard pressed to find sufficient space for all the articles that seem to warrant it; double reporting in effect robs another article of the space that it might have filled.

Although double reporting is not acceptable practice in most cases, there are a few rare circumstances under which it may be considered appropriate. If an investigator feels that two widely disparate groups provide reasonable audiences for his paper, he might try to publish simultaneously in journals of two very different fields, whose readerships presumably do not overlap. Also, editors of a journal or a book of readings may wish to reprint a paper published elsewhere; if an editor explicitly solicits such an article, no one would consider it unethical for the author to permit its reprinting, if credit is given to the original source.

Nor is it considered unethical to follow the very common practice of presenting the report first in oral form at a meeting of a professional society and then writing it up for formal publication in a professional journal. This serves the purpose of making the material available before the printed version appears (given normal publication lags, this may be quite a while), and it also permits others to discuss the report with the researcher himself, thus facilitating interchange among people working in a common research area. Almost never, though, is it appropriate to read a paper at a meeting in the form prepared for journal publication, if for no other reason than that the stylistic requirements of the two media are very different. One can put a great deal more information into a given number of printed words than into words that are to be followed by the ear alone.

Choosing the Outlet

The way to write a report depends to a large extent on the audience for which it is intended. Level, formality, and other details of style must be different for oral and written presentation; furthermore, various journals have their own particular outline and style requirements as well as their own particular "flavor." If the investigator has an early idea of the outlet for his report and gauges his writing as far back as the preliminary research proposal accordingly, much less modification and revision will be necessary in later phases.

At how wide and what kind of an audience should the researcher aim? The final report should, of course, be disseminated in such a way that the material becomes at least potentially available to everyone who is likely to be interested in it. Usually, intimate discussion with friends and colleagues is insufficient; for some studies a paper read at a local, regional, or national professional association meeting may be all that is warranted. Sometimes a mimeographed report can be sent to investigators who might be interested; most often complete formal publication in a journal is advisable. On rare occasions one may wish to consider a monograph or a book.

If the research is limited in scope and likely to be of interest to only a small number of people, the investigator might well choose one of the simpler forms of "publication." Mimeographing, dittoing, photocopying, and various other processes will produce duplicate copies of the paper to send to interested people. Many technical reports of government contract research are handled this way. Very often, also, mimeographing is used to produce an interim form of a paper that is eventually intended for fuller publication. The preliminary form can be shown to one's colleagues for criticisms and suggestions; after it has been revised, a final draft is submitted to a journal.

If a journal article seems to be the best medium, the researcher must consider which of the many possible journals affords the most appropriate audience. A close acquaintance with the available outlets (many of which were listed briefly in the supplement to Chapter 2) is essential in arriving at such a decision. Choice of journal affects not only matters of length, style, level of presentation, and so forth, but also such technicalities as the forms of reference and the use of abbreviations. When preparing a paper for an APA journal, the writer must follow the detailed specifications of the American Psychological Association *Publication Manual* (1957). For non-APA journals the same specifications can often be used as a general rule, but the best thing to do is to get a copy of the journal and note the details of style and format used in its papers. Frequently, also, editors list manuscript specifications on the covers or elsewhere in the journal; some, on request, will send a "style sheet" to potential contributors. To spare both the author's and the editor's time, the manuscript should conform as exactly as possible with the practices of the journal. Some of these requirements may strike one as very minor and arbitrary, and the novice may wonder why the journal editors do not themselves bear the burden of assuring conformity to their formats by appropriate editing and retyping. The volume of manuscripts submitted, and the insufficiency of editorial assistance in most journal offices, make it impossible for the editor to take care of these details. If the manuscript as submitted does not conform to stylistic standards, he must return it to the author for retyping, and this can result only in a longer publication delay than usual.

It is often particularly difficult to find a willing publisher for a book-length report of research. Commercial publishers are generally unable to accept such a manuscript because of the economics of publishing; the sales of a technical volume are likely to be too few to make its publication defensible as a business venture. A frequently used alternative is publication by one of the university presses, which are generally heavily subsidized and which are often set up explicitly for the purpose of making such technical material available in published form. The investigator may also wish to consider one of the monograph series in psychology. Whatever outlet he chooses, the problems encountered in preparing monographs and books are similar to those associated with writing journal articles, except that they are greatly magnified. (Various publishers will send an "author's guide" to the potential author; this provides specific information on format, organization, style, details of production, etc.) Before one decides on a lengthy printed report, he should ask himself whether the material really warrants so much space and whether it might not be possible to reduce its length radically. In publishing a long manuscript, the cost to the investigator in time and money is likely to be quite great, even if a regular monograph series or a university press is used as the outlet. Furthermore, a lengthy report is unlikely to be read as widely as a brief one.

Outlining

The formal details of the write-up will to a large extent depend on the requirements of the intended outlet. Whatever specifications one follows, whether those of the APA *Publication Manual* or some other set, it is generally wise to make a full and detailed outline of the entire report before writing any of it. This will reduce the likelihood of general disorganization, of discussing things in unreasonable order, of omitting essential points, etc. If the outline is prepared conscientiously and fully, the job of writing a comprehensible report is made a great deal easier.

Usually the outline can be conceived in six major sections; and although these will vary somewhat depending on the nature of the paper, almost all technical reports of research follow this general form. First is a short introductory section, in which the area is specified, perhaps a quick overview of the history of the problem is provided, and the immediately relevant literature is cited briefly. The second section presents the theoretical framework (when relevant) and usually culminates in a statement of the specific hypotheses to be tested or relationships to be explored. The third section consists of the methodology and techniques of the research, including operational definitions, design, and often a restatement of the hypotheses (or problem) in operational terms. The outline up to this point follows that suggested for the final research proposal (Chapter 2). In section four the results are presented as succinctly and clearly as possible. One must decide which of several possible data displays would be the most informative—that is, whether to use tables, figures, or neither; also, how to present the tables and figures to make them as comprehensible as possible. In this results section, especially if new instruments have been employed, it is often advisable to include some indication of the reliability of the measures (see Chapters 6, 7, and 8). The fifth section is a discussion of the findings. Here the investigator offers his interpretation of their meaning, tries to integrate the results with those of other studies, and sometimes suggests their implications for theory, practice, or further research. In particular, the results are interpreted in terms of whatever theoretical framework may have been presented in section two. The sixth and final section of the write-up is a very brief summary and conclusion, generally a one- or two-paragraph abstract of the essentials of the study.

In some reports the first two sections may be combined, and sometimes the results and discussion are made into one section, in which case the writer should be careful to keep the results clearly distinct from his interpretation of them so that the reader will not confuse fact with speculation.

Some Writing Hints

The aim of scientific writing is primarily to communicate, not to express. It is unnecessary—and irrelevant—in scientific writing for the author to express his feelings about a problem or to go into the history of his own abortive attempts to get the study under control.

The important thing is to get across to the reader what the problem was, how it was attacked, and what the results were. Although all of this sounds very obvious, it may prove an arduous task indeed to get the write-up into such a shape that it does communicate clearly to the reader, who is not as familiar with the study as the writer is. The writer may feel that the paper is clear, but unless it can be readily understood by other readers it is inadequate.

There are no simple rules to assure an adequate write-up, and the present text attests to the fact that even if considerable effort is applied to trying to make material readable one all too rarely achieves a really satisfactory product. For most writers, words are reluctant servants; some of them seem purposefully to obscure meanings, to demand inordinate attention to convey the intended content clearly and succinctly. Some general suggestions may be of use in making words do what you want them to.

First, and perhaps foremost, write for the reader. If you constantly keep the audience in mind, you are unlikely to present materials without the background or assumptions necessary to make them understandable to a reader who is unfamiliar with your reasoning. Some things may not require the detailed discussion that at first seemed needed; conversely, you may end up explaining in detail things that are very clear to you but which require spelling out to somebody else. If while writing you always try to keep the reader in mind, the manuscript is far more likely to be comprehensible to him.

Aim for brevity and simplicity. The use of long, pedantic, Latin-root words where simple one-syllable Teutonic words will do is wasteful and confusing. If it can be put more clearly or more simply, put it that way. Thurstone (1935) wrote, "Psychology has three defense mechanisms which frequently serve to hide the absence of ideas, namely correlations and probable errors, unnecessary instrumentation, and verbiage, all of which help to make the obvious seem profound and scientific." Verbiage can indeed do this; more likely, it can make the obvious obscure. Often a sentence is not fully clear until it has reached a level that appears almost too simple to the writer. But though the author's own impression of the paper is, of course, important, even more important is that the reader be able to understand it.

A third principle is to make use of the criticisms of others. Give the paper, once you think it is in its final form, to a friend who will not be too timid to show you where it is unclear to him. Better yet, get comments from several different people. Their reactions are almost certain to show up all kinds of weaknesses in the paper. Incidentally, it is inappropriate to try to defend the manuscript against criticisms; the function of the critic is to show you where the paper did not do what was intended, and your job is to fix it so that the difficulties the readers see (though you may not see them yourself) are remedied. Before you approach others, though, be sure the paper is in a form as good as you can make it. Do not wear out your critics prematurely by asking their help before you yourself have done all you can to make it comprehensible.

Another useful practice which may help the writer see his paper as it looks to others is to lay it aside awhile—two or three weeks or a month—after he considers it finished. Having let it mellow and having gained some perspective, the author may on returning to it discover all kinds of deficiencies not previously noticed. Sometimes it is also profitable to let some time pass between the final analyses and the "discussion" or "interpretation" part of the writing, to permit the often vague ideas suggested by the results to jell and become communicable.

One final minor suggestion which may save some exasperation is that the early drafts of a paper be prepared in legible form. It is useful to type them triple-spaced, so that there is ample room between lines for corrections.

Seeing a Paper through the Press

Once the last changes and corrections have been made, the next step is to get a finished draft to send to the editor of the journal. This includes the text, complete references, footnotes, tables, and (preferably) glossy high-contrast photographs of the figures that have previously been drawn in India ink on white cardboard.

Preparing tables and figures can be an intricate matter. For tables, there are such details as setting them up appropriately, formulating headings, seeing to it that they contain neither more information than is warranted nor so little that they are unnecessary, devising an informative but brief title, and so on. Diagrams and graphs may require the services of a draftsman and a photographer; many departments and research institutes have facilities and personnel for such purposes; sometimes a university graphic service or bureau of audiovisual aids can help.

There is also the question whether to present the findings in a table or figure or in the text. (It is only rarely appropriate for the same results to be presented both in a figure and a table.) Often a figure can present a great deal of information at a glance more efficiently than a table, but figures are more expensive to produce and print. The APA's *Publication Manual* will help in arriving at such decisions and will also help the writer to prepare his figures and tables in acceptable form.

Two double-spaced, typewritten copies (using one side of each sheet only) of the finished manuscript are sent to the editor with a brief cover letter; and the author keeps a third carbon copy himself. (The editor receives two copies rather than just one so that he can quickly get the reactions of several editorial consultants.) As soon as the editor receives the manuscript, he typically sends a form postcard notifying the author. This, and subsequent procedures, will vary from journal to journal and from editor to editor, but the following considerations will apply to most papers.

The next stage is one of waiting to hear from the editor. It may be anywhere from several weeks to almost a year before he can obtain the opinions of various consultants on the advisability of publishing the paper. When the author does get a reply, it will be either (1) that the paper is flatly rejected, (2) that the paper will be acceptable subject to various changes; or (3) that the paper has been accepted in its present form.

If the editor rejects a paper, he can usually be expected to extend the courtesy of providing reasons for his decision or suggesting an alternative outlet. If the author genuinely feels that a mistake has been made, he might (on a rare occasion) write a tactful letter requesting reconsideration and indicating specifically where the consultant seemed in error. Errors, however, should be distinguished from matters of judgment; it is pointless to engage in extended correspondence about every manuscript that cannot be published. Editors are generally very busy, and any further inquiry is only likely to irritate them. (Most editors do their editorial work on a part-time basis and often can scarcely find time even for correspondence on papers they intend to publish.) Rather than write to the editor, the author might well ask himself whether the paper is worth publishing at all. If he feels it is, he must decide whether revisions or a different publishing outlet, or both, are necessary.

In the event that the paper is acceptable on condition of certain changes, it is only reasonable to make the changes quickly in order to have the repaired manuscript back in the editor's hands as soon as possible. Almost invariably the editor's or reviewer's suggestions will prove highly constructive; if, however, the author feels that they are inappropriate or should not be followed, he may engage in further correspondence with the editor concerning his objections to certain of the suggested revisions. A fairly extensive correspondence may have to take place before the provisionally accepted manuscript is considered fit to be set in type.

On occasion, the editor may ask the author to make available certain supplementary material, such as raw data, by depositing them with the American Documentation Institute. This material, which must be prepared as carefully as the manuscript, is then sent to the editor, who sees that it is sent to the proper place and adds a footnote to the paper stating that the material is available from the A.D.I. This procedure gives readers ready access to considerably more detail than could reasonably be included in the paper itself.

Once a manuscript is accepted, it may be quite some time before the author receives the proofs. These usually consist of galleys in which the manuscript has been set in type, without being broken down into separate pages. The galley proof and the manuscript typically arrive with the admonition to have both back to the editor within a few days. It is the author's job at this point to proofread the galleys for errors in typesetting or in other respects. He may scarcely recognize his manuscript, with all of the instructions to the printers scribbled on it, but generally he need not worry about his product's being seriously altered (unless the editor indicates that this is so). On occasion, the scribbles may include queries regarding placement of tables, completion of references, and other matters, which the author must try to answer as rapidly and thoroughly as he can. Care in answering these queries, in proofreading, and in use of standard proofreaders' marks will save time and avoid errors. Sometimes a card or folder defining the various proofreading symbols will be enclosed with the proofs and manuscript; the meaning of the marks can also be found in many standard reference sources.

Proofreading can often be made a less tedious—and more efficient —chore if done with someone else, the author reading the proofs aloud (including all punctuation, capitalization, etc.) while the other person follows the manuscript; for some people it works better to have the proofreading team alternate reading aloud by paragraphs. After reading the material through once this way, watching for minute details, the author may wish to go over it silently a second time, with greater attention to the meaning. On very rare occasions (rare because of the inconvenience, the additional delay, and the cost to the author, who typically must foot the bill for such alterations), he may decide to make some changes in the paper, adding or deleting material; if such alterations are required, they should never be made on the manuscript itself but only on the proof so that it is clear that the changes were made *after* the manuscript was set in type. At any rate, rapid action on reading proofs is essential; it is a good idea on anything other than a very lengthy manuscript to try to have galleys and manuscript back in the mail within twenty-four hours of their initial receipt. In the case of journal articles, at least, delays in returning proof may mean that an entire issue will be held up; an author who is responsible for such delays is being extremely inconsiderate and discourteous to the editor and the contributors of other articles in the issue in which his paper is scheduled to appear.

A reprint order form generally accompanies the galleys. On this the author indicates how many extra copies of the paper he would like and whether or not he wishes the reprints to have covers. (Some people feel that if anything is worth publishing in the first place, it is worth putting inside covers; others feel that covers just make additional unnecessary expense.) The reason for asking the author to place his order this early is that after the journal has been printed and the various additional reprints run off the type is usually torn down. Estimating the number of reprints needed is often difficult; a study which the investigator considers very important may be ignored, whereas in a few months he may run out of reprints of a study he considers minor. It is perhaps wise to err on the side of purchasing more reprints than one initially thinks he will need, as it is troublesome to get a new order filled. Should the author underestimate his need and require additional copies of the reprints at a later date, it is generally not economical to have type set up again for printing. Instead, the article could be reproduced by some photographic process (e.g., The Reprint Co., 1025 Connecticut Avenue, Washington 6, D. C., uses a Xerox process); often the cost per copy will not be much greater than it was in the first order of reprints. One must not forget, however, that if the article is to be reproduced later in any form—photo offset, mimeograph, or otherwise—written permission must be obtained from the agency holding the copyright, usually the publisher. There is hardly ever any problem in getting such a request fulfilled.

Although the wait between submission of a manuscript and acceptance of a final version may be as long as a year or more, it may be another year between acceptance and its appearance in proof. Finally, there may be quite a few months intervening between return of the proofs and mailing of the journal issue in which the paper is published. Thus the publication lag between the initial submission and the final appearance of a journal paper may be as long as two and a half or even three years, although typically most editors try hard to keep it under one year.

Presenting a Paper at a Meeting

Presenting a paper at a professional society meeting serves two major purposes. First, since the publication lag is generally long, and since some results of the research may be of interest even before a final report is written, meetings can provide a means for telling other people in the area about the research one has just completed or in which one is currently engaged. Secondly, they afford an opportunity for researchers with common interests to discuss them.

There are many different kinds of professional society meetings held in the United States. Aside from the International Congresses of Psychology, which assemble in various places in the world every four years or so, annual meetings are held by the American Psychological Association, by the Psychonomic Society, and by the regional affiliates of APA—the Eastern Psychological Association, Midwestern Psychological Association, Rocky Mountain Psychological Association, Southeastern Psychological Association, Southern Society for Philosophy and Psychology, Southwestern Psychological Association, and Western Psychological Association. There are also many state and county societies which hold meetings to disseminate research results and some still more local meetings in the larger cities. Further, societies like the American Association for the Advancement of Science, the Acoustical Society of America, and the American Psychiatric Association and various academies of science (such as the New York or the Colorado-Wyoming Academy of Science) may hold sessions at which psychological papers are read.

Whatever the meeting, the scientific presentations are generally of two kinds: technical papers and symposia. The papers are usually ten- to twenty-minute reports of original research; most of the time the symposia are discussions by several participants on the current status of research in some particular area. The principles of presenting a contribution at either type of session are essentially the same, although symposium papers are more likely to offer broad coverage of an area than detailed reports of single research projects.

The outline of technical papers read at professional meetings is typically similar to that used in writing a journal article. However, the style called for is quite different. The author must keep in mind that it is harder for an audience to obtain information from listening to a lecture than from reading it. It is good practice, in any technical report, to limit the number of points to two or three and to prune off as many unessential details as possible. Getting a couple of ideas across in ten or fifteen minutes is difficult enough as it is; it becomes particularly so if the paper is one among several hundred presented at a meeting.

The style of writing for oral presentation should generally be quite different from that used in a journal article; probably the redundancy rate should be higher, the emphasis clearer, and possibly the presentation should be somewhat less formal. As in the case of written articles, the author is wise always to keep the audience and the circumstances of presentation in mind when he is writing his paper; the same holds true during the reading of the paper.

Every effort is required to make the material comprehensible to the audience. This means, among other things, avoiding a monotonous or rushed reading; it means reasonable and considered differential emphasis; and it also means a judicious use of audio-visual supports. Often slides are useful, especially if there are not too many and if the figures presented on them are simple enough to comprehend at a glance. There is no point in presenting an elaborate table in a slide, since such materials tend only to confuse rather than to clarify. Dittoed handouts of tables, figures, etc., are sometimes used as an alternative to slides; they may distract the audience, but they involve fewer administrative headaches for the officials responsible for the meeting and make it possible for an interested listener to take some of the material with him to study after the meeting.

Announcement of a meeting, with a call for papers, is usually published in the sponsoring association's house organ (e.g., the *American Psychologist*) several months before the meeting date; some societies send out mimeographed or separately printed requests for papers. Every month the *American Psychologist* lists the dates and locations of most international, national, and regional psychological meetings, with the names and addresses of people to write to for information about them.

When proposing to read a paper, the investigator submits an abstract to the appropriate official of the association or to a program committee. Deadlines for receipt of abstracts are generally three or four months before the date of the meeting. Since a committee must evaluate it in a relatively brief time, it is important to prepare the abstract with great care. It may run from one hundred to three hundred words, depending on the society; some associations require both a long and a short abstract; on occasion—especially for theoretical papers—the author must submit the entire article so that a committee can decide upon the appropriateness of including it in the program. The American Psychological Association requests authors to submit some copies of the abstract without the name of the author or his institutional connection, so that choice of program will not be influenced by such considerations; some other societies follow a similar policy.

There are many other details that constitute the know-how and mechanics of presenting papers at meetings. The reader is urged to become acquainted with Schlosberg's article (1956), which provides many helpful hints on this matter. But the best way to develop skill is to practice. The neophyte might start by presenting material orally at a local, state, or regional meeting before attempting to present at an APA convention. If he has read papers at several minor meetings, he will find himself more competent and more comfortable when reporting at a major one. For that matter, practicing "role playing," or undertaking a "dress rehearsal" by presenting the paper before an audience of colleagues, in a setting as realistic as possible, can serve as a useful preliminary to presenting the paper at any meeting, whatever its level.

Using the Mass Media

On rare occasions the results of a research project may be of sufficient interest to the general public to warrant an account in newspapers, over the radio, or on television. Generally, news coverage of professional meetings is reasonably good, so that the decision whether to use such media for the further communication of one's findings may to some extent be made by others than the researcher himself. But if the professional report is made only in a journal, it is up to the investigator to decide whether to talk to a reporter. Sometimes the news bureau at the institution where the research was performed may help in making the decision and also in preparing an appropriate press release. On occasion, a representative of the mass media may approach the researcher without his solicitation; it is then up to both of them to decide whether the study is "newsworthy."

The problem of writing press releases or of providing appropriate material in a news interview is basically one of teaching. The audience, whether the reporter himself, the newspapers' readership, the television viewers or the radio listeners, is very different from one's professional colleagues, who, of course, have a background and a familiarity with technical jargon that cannot be assumed for the layman. Hence the communication problem is made much more difficult. One must be prepared to simplify to at least some degree, to explain findings and technical background material in everyday terms, while at the same time not doing an injustice to the material through exaggeration or excessive modesty. The APA's *Public information guide* (1954) includes a variety of practical advice on such matters.

Sometimes a report in a "middle level" medium like the magazine *Scientific American* may seem called for. Preparing a paper for such an outlet is a time-consuming task; the researcher must ask himself whether he is doing his duty to himself and to his science best by spending his time in writing a semipopular article or whether he would make better use of it instead by improving his professional report or by engaging in further research.

Obviously it is not every study that warrants wider dissemination than to the professional audience. On the other hand, a judicious use of the mass media is a part of public relations practices which will help in developing a reasonably accurate public image of behavioral scientists and what they do and which may in the long run prove useful in obtaining support for further work.

SUMMARY

Once the data have been analyzed, the researcher is faced with the task of interpreting their meaning. Usually there will be not just one meaning but several, each of which appears equally well supported by the data. The problem then is to decide whether the various plausible alternatives are clear enough and other clear ones are implausible, so that one can legitimately say that something specific has been learned. If so, he is ready to publish. If not, he is presumably at least in a position to design new research either to replicate the unanticipated findings or to permit selection among competing interpretations. In any case, with clear or muddy findings, the curious researcher can now think up a host of new questions that he did not have in the beginning; some of them may prove susceptible of investigation in subsequent studies.

If a relation has been clearly pinned down, or has clearly been shown not to hold, the investigator's obligation to his discipline cannot be considered fulfilled until he has made a report of his research available to others. Generally, an oral presentation at a professional society meeting is followed by formal publication in a technical journal; for effectiveness in communication, the style and content of the report vary with the medium and the audience.

Preparing a published report usually takes a long time and a great deal of effort, both for writing an adequate draft in the first place and for handling the various technical matters involved in seeing a paper through the press. The processes are facilitated if a detailed outline (usually including introduction, hypothesis, method, results, discussion, conclusion) is followed carefully and if one realistically anticipates the chores of making revisions, producing a polished final manuscript complete with figures and tables, and proofreading on short notice.

A public report through the mass media may, in rare instances, be desirable. This requires care in putting the material into everyday language without exaggeration or excessive simplification.

REFERENCES

American Psychological Association. *Ethical standards of psychologists.* Washington, D. C.: American Psychological Association, 1953.

American Psychological Association. *Public information guide.* Washington, D. C.: American Psychological Association, 1954.

American Psychological Association Council of Editors. *Publication manual of the American Psychological Association.* (Rev. Ed.) Washington, D. C.: American Psychological Association, 1957.

American Psychological Association, Inc. Committee on Ethical Standards of Psychologists. Report of the Committee. *Amer. Psychologist,* 1958, 13, 266–271; and *Amer. Psychologist,* 1959, 14, 279–282.

Schlosberg, H. Hints on presenting a paper at an APA convention. *Amer. Psychologist,* 1956, 11, 345–346.

Thurstone, L. L. Preface to Thurstone, L. L. *The reliability and validity of tests.* Ann Arbor, Mich.: Edwards Bros., 1935. (Also cited in Guilford, J. P. *Psychometric methods.* New York: McGraw-Hill, 1936, p. 12.)

Appendix

TABLE A

Random Numbers

	00–04	05–09	10–14	15–19	20–24	25–29	30–34	35–39	40–44	45–49
00	54463	22662	65905	70639	79365	67382	29085	69831	47058	08186
01	15389	85205	18850	39226	42249	90669	96325	23248	60933	26927
02	85941	40756	82414	02015	13858	78030	16269	65978	01385	15345
03	61149	69440	11286	88218	58925	03638	52862	62733	33451	77455
04	05219	81619	10651	67079	92511	59888	84502	72095	83463	75577
05	41417	98326	87719	92294	46614	50948	64886	20002	97365	30976
06	28357	94070	20652	35774	16249	75019	21145	05217	47286	76305
07	17783	00015	10806	83091	91530	36466	39981	62481	49177	75779
08	40950	84820	29881	85966	62800	70326	84740	62660	77379	90279
09	82995	64157	66164	41180	10089	41757	78258	96488	88629	37231
10	96754	17676	55659	44105	47361	34833	86679	23930	53249	27083
11	34357	88040	53364	71726	45690	66334	60332	22554	90600	71113
12	06318	37403	49927	57715	50423	67372	63116	48888	21505	80182
13	62111	52820	07243	79931	89292	84767	85693	73947	22278	11551
14	47534	09243	67879	00544	23410	12740	02540	54440	32949	13491
15	98614	75993	84460	62846	59844	14922	48730	73443	48167	34770
16	24856	03648	44898	09351	98795	18644	39765	71058	90368	44104
17	96887	12479	80621	66223	86085	78285	02432	53342	42846	94771
18	90801	21472	42815	77408	37390	76766	52615	32141	30268	18106
19	55165	77312	83666	36028	28420	70219	81369	41943	47366	41067
20	75884	12952	84318	95108	72305	64620	91318	89872	45375	85436
21	16777	37116	58550	42958	21460	43910	01175	87894	81378	10620
22	46230	43877	80207	88877	89380	32992	91380	03164	98656	59337
23	42902	66892	46134	01432	94710	23474	20423	60137	60609	13119
24	81007	00333	39693	28039	10154	95425	39220	19774	31782	49037
25	68089	01122	51111	72373	06902	74373	96199	97017	41273	21546
26	20411	67081	89950	16944	93054	87687	96693	87236	77054	33848
27	58212	13160	06468	15718	82627	76999	05999	58680	96739	63700
28	70577	42866	24969	61210	76046	67699	42054	12696	93758	03283
29	94522	74358	71659	62038	79643	79169	44741	05437	39038	13163
30	42626	86819	85651	88678	17401	03252	99547	32404	17918	62880
31	16051	33763	57194	16752	54450	19031	58580	47629	54132	60631
32	08244	27647	33851	44705	94211	46716	11738	55784	95374	72655
33	59497	04392	09419	89964	51211	04894	72882	17805	21896	83864
34	97155	13428	40293	09985	58434	01412	69124	82171	59058	82859
35	98409	66162	95763	47420	20792	61527	20441	39435	11859	41567
36	45476	84882	65109	96597	25930	66790	65706	61203	53634	22557
37	89300	69700	50741	30329	11658	23166	05400	66669	48708	03887
38	50051	95137	91631	66315	91428	12275	24816	68091	71710	33258
39	31753	85178	31310	89642	98364	02306	24617	09609	83942	22716
40	79152	53829	77250	20190	56535	18760	69942	77448	33278	48805
41	44560	38750	83635	56540	64900	42912	13953	79149	18710	68618
42	68328	83378	63369	71381	39564	05615	42451	64559	97501	65747
43	46939	38689	58625	08342	30459	85863	20781	09284	26333	91777
44	83544	86141	15707	96256	23068	13782	08467	89469	93842	55349
45	91621	00881	04900	54224	46177	55309	17852	27491	89415	23466
46	91896	67126	04151	03795	59077	11848	12630	98375	52068	60142
47	55751	62515	21108	80830	02263	29303	37204	96926	30506	09808
48	85156	87689	95493	88842	00664	55017	55539	17771	69448	87530
49	07521	56898	12236	60277	39102	62315	12239	07105	11844	01117

Reproduced by permission from George W. Snedecor, *Statistical methods* (Fifth Edition, 1956), copyright the Iowa State University Press, Ames, Iowa.

TABLE A (*Continued*)

	50-54	55-59	60-64	65-69	70-74	75-79	80-84	85-89	90-94	95-99
00	59391	58030	52098	82718	87024	82848	04190	96574	90464	29065
01	99567	76364	77204	04615	27062	96621	43918	01896	83991	51141
02	10363	97518	51400	25670	98342	61891	27101	37855	06235	33316
03	86859	19558	64432	16706	99612	59798	32803	67708	15297	28612
04	11258	24591	36863	55368	31721	94335	34936	02566	80972	08188
05	95068	88628	35911	14530	33020	80428	39936	31855	34334	64865
06	54463	47237	73800	91017	36239	71824	83671	39892	60518	37092
07	16874	62677	57412	13215	31389	62233	80827	73917	82802	84420
08	92494	63157	76593	91316	03505	72389	96363	52887	01087	66091
09	15669	56689	35682	40844	53256	01872	35213	09840	34471	74441
10	99116	75486	84989	23476	52967	67104	39495	39100	17217	74073
11	15696	10703	65178	90637	63110	17622	53988	71087	84148	11670
12	97720	15369	51269	69620	03388	13699	33423	67453	43269	56720
13	11666	13841	71681	98000	35979	39719	81899	07449	47985	46967
14	71628	73130	78783	75691	41632	09847	61547	18707	85489	69944
15	40501	51089	99943	91843	41995	88931	73631	69361	05375	15417
16	22518	55576	98215	82068	10798	86211	36584	67466	69373	40054
17	75112	30485	62173	02132	14878	92879	22281	16783	86352	00077
18	80327	02671	98191	84342	90813	49268	95441	15496	20168	09271
19	60251	45548	02146	05597	48228	81366	34598	72856	66762	17002
20	57430	82270	10421	05540	43648	75888	66049	21511	47676	33444
21	73528	39559	34434	88596	54086	71693	43132	14414	79949	85193
22	25991	65959	70769	64721	86413	33475	42740	06175	82758	66248
23	78388	16638	09134	59880	63806	48472	39318	35434	24057	74739
24	12477	09965	96657	57994	59439	76330	24596	77515	09577	91871
25	83266	32883	42451	15579	38155	29793	40914	65990	16255	17777
26	76970	80876	10237	39515	79152	74798	39357	09054	73579	92359
27	37074	65198	44785	68624	98336	84481	97610	78735	46703	98265
28	83712	06514	30101	78295	54656	85417	43189	60048	72781	72606
29	20287	56862	69727	94443	64936	08366	27227	05158	50326	59566
30	74261	32592	86538	27041	65172	85532	07571	80609	39285	65340
31	64081	49863	08478	96001	18888	14810	70545	89755	59064	07210
32	05617	75818	47750	67814	29575	10526	66192	44464	27058	40467
33	26793	74951	95466	74307	13330	42664	85515	20632	05497	33625
34	65988	72850	48737	54719	52056	01596	03845	35067	03134	70322
35	27366	42271	44300	73399	21105	03280	73457	43093	05192	48657
36	56760	10909	98147	34736	33863	95256	12731	66598	50771	83665
37	72880	43338	93643	58904	59543	23943	11231	83268	65938	81581
38	77888	38100	03062	58103	47961	83841	25878	23746	55903	44115
39	28440	07819	21580	51459	47971	29882	13990	29226	23608	15873
40	63525	94441	77033	12147	51054	49955	58312	76923	96071	05813
41	47606	93410	16359	89033	89696	47231	64498	31776	05383	39902
42	52669	45030	96279	14709	52372	87832	02735	50803	72744	88208
43	16738	60159	07425	62369	07515	82721	37875	71153	21315	00132
44	59348	11695	45751	15865	74739	05572	32688	20271	65128	14551
45	12900	71775	29845	60774	94924	21810	38636	33717	67598	82521
46	75086	23537	49939	33595	13484	97588	28617	17979	70749	35234
47	99495	51434	29181	09993	38190	42553	68922	52125	91077	40197
48	26075	31671	45386	36583	93459	48599	52022	41330	60651	91321
49	13636	93596	23377	51133	95126	61496	42474	45141	46660	42338

TABLE A (Continued)

	00–04	05–09	10–14	15–19	20–24	25–29	30–34	35–39	40–44	45–49
50	64249	63664	39652	40646	97306	31741	07294	84149	46797	82487
51	26538	44249	04050	48174	65570	44072	40192	51153	11397	58212
52	05845	00512	78630	55328	18116	69296	91705	86224	29503	57071
53	74897	68373	67359	51014	33510	83048	17056	72506	82949	54600
54	20872	54570	35017	88132	25730	22626	86723	91691	13191	77212
55	31432	96156	89177	75541	81355	24480	77243	76690	42507	84362
56	66890	61505	01240	00660	05873	13568	76082	79172	57913	93448
57	48194	57790	79970	33106	86904	48119	52503	24130	72824	21627
58	11303	87118	81471	52936	08555	28420	49416	44448	04269	27029
59	54374	57325	16947	45356	78371	10563	97191	53798	12693	27928
60	64852	34421	61046	90849	13966	39810	42699	21753	76192	10508
61	16309	20384	09491	91588	97720	89846	30376	76970	23063	35894
62	42587	37065	24526	72602	57589	98131	37292	05967	26002	51945
63	40177	98590	97161	41682	84533	67588	62036	49967	01990	72308
64	82309	76128	93965	26743	24141	04838	40254	26065	07938	76236
65	79788	68243	59732	04257	27084	14743	17520	95401	55811	76099
66	40538	79000	89559	25026	42274	23489	34502	75508	06059	86682
67	64016	73598	18609	73150	62463	33102	45205	87440	96767	67042
68	49767	12691	17903	93871	99721	79109	09425	26904	07419	76013
69	76974	55108	29795	08404	82684	00497	51126	79935	57450	55671
70	23854	08480	85983	96025	50117	64610	99425	62291	86943	21541
71	68973	70551	25098	78033	98573	79848	31778	29555	61446	23037
72	36444	93600	65350	14971	25325	00427	52073	64280	18847	24768
73	03003	87800	07391	11594	21196	00781	32550	57158	58887	73041
74	17540	26188	36647	78386	04558	61463	57842	90382	77019	24210
75	38916	55809	47982	41968	69760	79422	80154	91486	19180	15100
76	64288	19843	69122	42502	48508	28820	59933	72998	99942	10515
77	86809	51564	38040	39418	49915	19000	58050	16899	79952	57849
78	99800	99566	14742	05028	30033	94889	53381	23656	75787	59223
79	92345	31890	95712	08279	91794	94068	49337	88674	35355	12267
80	90363	65162	32245	82279	79256	80834	06088	99462	56705	06118
81	64437	32242	48431	04835	39070	59702	31508	60935	22390	52246
82	91714	53662	28373	34333	55791	74758	51144	18827	10704	76803
83	20902	17646	31391	31459	33315	03444	55743	74701	58851	27427
84	12217	86007	70371	52281	14510	76094	96579	54853	78339	20839
85	45177	02863	42307	53571	22532	74921	17735	42201	80540	54721
86	28325	90814	08804	52746	47913	54577	47525	77705	95330	21866
87	29019	28776	56116	54791	64604	08815	46049	71186	34650	14994
88	84979	81353	56219	67062	26146	82567	33122	14124	46240	92973
89	50371	26347	48513	63915	11158	25563	91915	18431	92978	11591
90	53422	06825	69711	67950	64716	18003	49581	45378	99878	61130
91	67453	35651	89316	41620	32048	70225	47597	33137	31443	51445
92	07294	85353	74819	23445	68237	07202	99515	62282	53809	26685
93	79544	00302	45338	16015	66613	88968	14595	63836	77716	79596
94	64144	85442	82060	46471	24162	39500	87351	36637	42833	71875
95	90919	11883	58318	00042	52402	28210	34075	33272	00840	73268
96	06670	57353	86275	92276	77591	46924	60839	55437	03183	13191
97	36634	93976	52062	83678	41256	60948	18685	48992	19462	96062
98	75101	72891	85745	67106	26010	62107	60885	37503	55461	71213
99	05112	71222	72654	51583	05228	62056	57390	42746	39272	96659

TABLE A (*Continued*)

	50-54	55-59	60-64	65-69	70-74	75-79	80-84	85-89	90-94	95-99
50	32847	31282	03345	89593	69214	70381	78285	20054	91018	16742
51	16916	00041	30236	55023	14253	76582	12092	86533	92426	37655
52	66176	34047	21005	27137	03191	48970	64625	22394	39622	79085
53	46299	13335	12180	16861	38043	59292	62675	63631	37020	78195
54	22847	47839	45385	23289	47526	54098	45683	55849	51575	64689
55	41851	54160	92320	69936	34803	92479	33399	71160	64777	83378
56	28444	59497	91586	95917	68553	28639	06455	34174	11130	91994
57	47520	62378	98855	83174	13088	16561	68559	26679	06238	51254
58	34978	63271	13142	82681	05271	08822	06490	44984	49307	62717
59	37404	80416	69035	92980	49486	74378	75610	74976	70056	15478
60	32400	65482	52099	53676	74648	94148	65095	69597	52771	71551
61	89262	86332	51718	70663	11623	29834	79820	73002	84886	03591
62	86866	09127	98021	03871	27789	58444	44832	36505	40672	30180
63	90814	14833	08759	74645	05046	94056	99094	65091	32663	73040
64	19192	82756	20553	58446	55376	88914	75096	26119	83898	43816
65	77585	52593	56612	95766	10019	29531	73064	20953	53523	58136
66	23757	16364	05096	03192	62386	45389	85332	18877	55710	96459
67	45989	96257	23850	26216	23309	21526	07425	50254	19455	29315
68	92970	94243	07316	41467	64837	52406	25225	51553	31220	14032
69	74346	59596	40088	98176	17896	86900	20249	77753	19099	48885
70	87646	41309	27636	45153	29988	94770	07255	70908	05340	99751
71	50099	71038	45146	06146	55211	99429	43169	66259	97786	59180
72	10127	46900	64984	75348	04115	33624	68774	60013	35515	62556
73	67995	81977	18984	64091	02785	27762	42529	97144	80407	64524
74	26304	80217	84934	82657	69291	35397	98714	35104	08187	48109
75	81994	41070	56642	64091	31229	02595	13513	45148	78722	30144
76	59537	34662	79631	89403	65212	09975	06118	86197	58208	16162
77	51228	10937	62396	81460	47331	91403	95007	06047	16846	64809
78	31089	37995	29577	07828	42272	54016	21950	86192	99046	84864
79	38207	97938	93459	75174	79460	55436	57206	87644	21296	43395
80	88666	31142	09474	89712	63153	62333	42212	06140	42594	43671
81	53365	56134	67582	92557	89520	33452	05134	70628	27612	33738
82	89807	74530	38004	90102	11693	90257	05500	79920	62700	43325
83	18682	81038	85662	90915	91631	22223	91588	80774	07716	12548
84	63571	32579	63942	25371	09234	94592	98475	76884	37635	33608
85	68927	56492	67799	95398	77642	54913	91853	08424	81450	76229
86	56401	63186	39389	88798	31356	89235	97036	32341	33292	73757
87	24333	95603	02359	72942	46287	95382	08452	62862	97869	71775
88	17025	84202	95199	62272	06366	16175	97577	99304	41587	03686
89	02804	08253	52133	20224	68034	50865	57868	22343	55111	03607
90	08298	03879	20995	19850	73090	13191	18963	82244	78479	99121
91	59883	01785	82403	96062	03785	03488	12970	64896	38336	30030
92	46982	06682	62864	91837	74021	89094	39952	64158	79614	78235
93	31121	47266	07661	02051	67599	24471	69843	83696	71402	76287
94	97867	56641	63416	17577	30161	87320	37752	73276	48969	41915
95	57364	86746	08415	14621	49430	22311	15836	72492	49372	44103
96	09559	26263	69511	28064	75999	44540	13337	10918	79846	54809
97	53873	55571	00608	42661	91332	63956	74087	59008	47493	99581
98	35531	19162	86406	05299	77511	24311	57257	22826	77555	05941
99	28229	88629	25695	94932	30721	16197	78742	34974	97528	45447

TABLE B

Areas in the Tail of the Normal Curve

(Probability of obtaining a CR of given size or greater)

CR	.00	.01	.02	.03	.04	.05	.06	.07	.08	.09
0.0	.5000	.4960	.4920	.4880	.4840	.4801	.4761	.4721	.4681	.4641
0.1	.4602	.4562	.4522	.4483	.4443	.4404	.4364	.4325	.4286	.4247
0.2	.4207	.4168	.4129	.4090	.4052	.4013	.3974	.3936	.3897	.3859
0.3	.3821	.3783	.3745	.3707	.3669	.3632	.3594	.3557	.3520	.3483
0.4	.3446	.3409	.3372	.3336	.3300	.3264	.3228	.3192	.3156	.3121
0.5	.3085	.3050	.3015	.2981	.2946	.2912	.2877	.2843	.2810	.2776
0.6	.2743	.2709	.2676	.2643	.2611	.2578	.2546	.2514	.2483	.2451
0.7	.2420	.2389	.2358	.2327	.2296	.2266	.2236	.2206	.2177	.2148
0.8	.2119	.2090	.2061	.2033	.2005	.1977	.1949	.1922	.1894	.1867
0.9	.1841	.1814	.1788	.1762	.1736	.1711	.1685	.1660	.1635	.1611
1.0	.1587	.1562	.1539	.1515	.1492	.1469	.1446	.1423	.1401	.1379
1.1	.1357	.1335	.1314	.1292	.1271	.1251	.1230	.1210	.1190	.1170
1.2	.1151	.1131	.1112	.1093	.1075	.1056	.1038	.1020	.1003	.0985
1.3	.0968	.0951	.0934	.0918	.0901	.0885	.0869	.0853	.0838	.0823
1.4	.0808	.0793	.0778	.0764	.0749	.0735	.0721	.0708	.0694	.0681
1.5	.0668	.0655	.0643	.0630	.0618	.0606	.0594	.0582	.0571	.0559
1.6	.0548	.0537	.0526	.0516	.0505	.0495	.0485	.0475	.0465	.0455
1.7	.0446	.0436	.0427	.0418	.0409	.0401	.0392	.0384	.0375	.0367
1.8	.0359	.0351	.0344	.0336	.0329	.0322	.0314	.0307	.0301	.0294
1.9	.0287	.0281	.0274	.0268	.0262	.0256	.0250	.0244	.0239	.0233
2.0	.0228	.0222	.0217	.0212	.0207	.0202	.0197	.0192	.0188	.0183
2.1	.0179	.0174	.0170	.0166	.0162	.0158	.0154	.0150	.0146	.0143
2.2	.0139	.0136	.0132	.0129	.0125	.0122	.0119	.0116	.0113	.0110
2.3	.0107	.0104	.0102	.0099	.0096	.0094	.0091	.0089	.0087	.0084
2.4	.0082	.0080	.0078	.0075	.0073	.0071	.0069	.0068	.0066	.0064
2.5	.0062	.0060	.0059	.0057	.0055	.0054	.0052	.0051	.0049	.0048
2.6	.0047	.0045	.0044	.0043	.0041	.0040	.0039	.0038	.0037	.0036
2.7	.0035	.0034	.0033	.0032	.0031	.0030	.0029	.0028	.0027	.0026
2.8	.0026	.0025	.0024	.0023	.0023	.0022	.0021	.0021	.0020	.0019
2.9	.0019	.0018	.0018	.0017	.0016	.0016	.0015	.0015	.0014	.0014
3.0	.0013	.0013	.0013	.0012	.0012	.0011	.0011	.0011	.0010	.0010
3.1	.0010	.0009	.0009	.0009	.0008	.0008	.0008	.0008	.0007	.0007

Abridged from A. L. Edwards, *Statistical methods for the behavioral sciences.* New York: Rinehart, 1954, by permission of the author and publisher.

TABLE C

Distribution of t

n	P = .1	.05	.02	.01	.001
1	6.314	12.706	31.821	63.657	636.619
2	2.920	4.303	6.965	9.925	31.598
3	2.353	3.182	4.541	5.841	12.941
4	2.132	2.776	3.747	4.604	8.610
5	2.015	2.571	3.365	4.032	6.859
6	1.943	2.447	3.143	3.707	5.959
7	1.895	2.365	2.998	3.499	5.405
8	1.860	2.306	2.896	3.355	5.041
9	1.833	2.262	2.821	3.250	4.781
10	1.812	2.228	2.764	3.169	4.587
11	1.796	2.201	2.718	3.106	4.437
12	1.782	2.179	2.681	3.055	4.318
13	1.771	2.160	2.650	3.012	4.221
14	1.761	2.145	2.624	2.977	4.140
15	1.753	2.131	2.602	2.947	4.073
16	1.746	2.120	2.583	2.921	4.015
17	1.740	2.110	2.567	2.898	3.965
18	1.734	2.101	2.552	2.878	3.922
19	1.729	2.093	2.539	2.861	3.883
20	1.725	2.086	2.528	2.845	3.850
21	1.721	2.080	2.518	2.831	3.819
22	1.717	2.074	2.508	2.819	3.792
23	1.714	2.069	2.500	2.807	3.767
24	1.711	2.064	2.492	2.797	3.745
25	1.708	2.060	2.485	2.787	3.725
26	1.706	2.056	2.479	2.779	3.707
27	1.703	2.052	2.473	2.771	3.690
28	1.701	2.048	2.467	2.763	3.674
29	1.699	2.045	2.462	2.756	3.659
30	1.697	2.042	2.457	2.750	3.646
40	1.684	2.021	2.423	2.704	3.551
60	1.671	2.000	2.390	2.660	3.460
120	1.658	1.980	2.358	2.617	3.373
∞	1.645	1.960	2.326	2.576	3.291

Abridged from R. A. Fisher and F. Yates, *Statistical tables for biological, agricultural, and medical research,* published by Oliver & Boyd, Ltd., Edinburgh, by permission of the authors and publishers.

TABLE D

Transformation of r to z

r	z	r	z	r	z
.01	.010	.34	.354	.67	.811
.02	.020	.35	.366	.68	.829
.03	.030	.36	.377	.69	.848
.04	.040	.37	.389	.70	.867
.05	.050	.38	.400	.71	.887
.06	.060	.39	.412	.72	.908
.07	.070	.40	.424	.73	.929
.08	.080	.41	.436	.74	.950
.09	.090	.42	.448	.75	.973
.10	.100	.43	.460	.76	.996
.11	.110	.44	.472	.77	1.020
.12	.121	.45	.485	.78	1.045
.13	.131	.46	.497	.79	1.071
.14	.141	.47	.510	.80	1.099
.15	.151	.48	.523	.81	1.127
.16	.161	.49	.536	.82	1.157
.17	.172	.50	.549	.83	1.188
.18	.182	.51	.563	.84	1.221
.19	.192	.52	.577	.85	1.256
.20	.203	.53	.590	.86	1.293
.21	.214	.54	.604	.87	1.333
.22	.224	.55	.618	.88	1.376
.23	.234	.56	.633	.89	1.422
.24	.245	.57	.648	.90	1.472
.25	.256	.58	.663	.91	1.528
.26	.266	.59	.678	.92	1.589
.27	.277	.60	.693	.93	1.658
.28	.288	.61	.709	.94	1.738
.29	.299	.62	.725	.95	1.832
.30	.309	.63	.741	.96	1.946
.31	.321	.64	.758	.97	2.092
.32	.332	.65	.775	.98	2.298
.33	.343	.66	.793	.99	2.647

TABLE E

Distribution of Chi-Square

n	.30	.20	.10	.05	.02	.01	.001
1	1.07	1.64	2.71	3.84	5.41	6.64	10.83
2	2.41	3.22	4.60	5.99	7.82	9.21	13.82
3	3.66	4.64	6.25	7.82	9.84	11.34	16.27
4	4.88	5.99	7.78	9.49	11.67	13.28	18.46
5	6.06	7.29	9.24	11.07	13.39	15.09	20.52
6	7.23	8.56	10.64	12.59	15.03	16.81	22.46
7	8.38	9.80	12.02	14.07	16.62	18.48	24.32
8	9.52	11.03	13.36	15.51	18.17	20.09	26.12
9	10.66	12.24	14.68	16.92	19.68	21.67	27.88
10	11.78	13.44	15.99	18.31	21.16	23.21	29.59
11	12.90	14.63	17.28	19.68	22.62	24.72	31.26
12	14.01	15.81	18.55	21.03	24.05	26.22	32.91
13	15.12	16.98	19.81	22.36	25.47	27.69	34.53
14	16.22	18.15	21.06	23.68	26.87	29.14	36.12
15	17.32	19.31	22.31	25.00	28.26	30.58	37.70
16	18.42	20.46	23.54	26.30	29.63	32.00	39.25
17	19.51	21.62	24.77	27.59	31.00	33.41	40.79
18	20.60	22.76	25.99	28.87	32.35	34.80	42.31
19	21.69	23.90	27.20	30.14	33.69	36.19	43.82
20	22.78	25.04	28.41	31.41	35.02	37.57	45.32
21	23.86	26.17	29.62	32.67	36.34	38.93	46.80
22	24.94	27.30	30.81	33.92	37.66	40.29	48.27
23	26.02	28.43	32.01	35.17	38.97	41.64	49.73
24	27.10	29.55	33.20	36.42	40.27	42.98	51.18
25	28.17	30.68	34.38	37.65	41.57	44.31	52.62
26	29.25	31.80	35.56	38.88	42.86	45.64	54.05
27	30.32	32.91	36.74	40.11	44.14	46.96	55.48
28	31.39	34.03	37.92	41.34	45.42	48.28	56.89
29	32.46	35.14	39.09	42.56	46.69	49.59	58.30
30	33.53	36.25	40.26	43.77	47.96	50.89	59.70

Abridged from R. A. Fisher and F. Yates, *Statistical tables for biological, agricultural, and medical research,* published by Oliver & Boyd, Ltd., Edinburgh, by permission of the authors and publishers.

TABLE F

Distribution of F for Three Levels of Significance:
.05 (roman), .01 (*italic*), and .001 (**boldface**)

n_2 \ n_1	1	2	3	4	5	6	8	12	24	∞
1	161	200	216	225	230	234	239	244	249	254
	4052	*4999*	*5403*	*5625*	*5724*	*5859*	*5981*	*6106*	*6234*	*6366*
	405284	**500000**	**540379**	**562500**	**576405**	**585937**	**598144**	**610667**	**623497**	**636619**
2	18.51	19.00	19.16	19.25	19.30	19.33	19.37	19.41	19.45	19.50
	98.49	*99.01*	*99.17*	*99.25*	*99.30*	*99.33*	*99.36*	*99.42*	*99.46*	*99.50*
	998.5	**999.0**	**999.2**	**999.2**	**999.3**	**999.3**	**999.4**	**999.4**	**999.5**	**999.5**
3	10.13	9.55	9.28	9.12	9.01	8.94	8.84	8.74	8.64	8.53
	34.12	*30.81*	*29.46*	*28.71*	*28.24*	*27.91*	*27.49*	*27.05*	*26.60*	*26.12*
	167.5	**148.5**	**141.1**	**137.1**	**134.6**	**132.8**	**130.6**	**128.3**	**125.9**	**123.5**
4	7.71	6.94	6.59	6.39	6.26	6.16	6.04	5.91	5.77	5.63
	21.20	*18.00*	*16.69*	*15.98*	*15.52*	*15.21*	*14.80*	*14.37*	*13.93*	*13.46*
	74.14	**61.25**	**56.18**	**53.44**	**51.71**	**50.53**	**49.00**	**47.41**	**45.77**	**44.05**
5	6.61	5.79	5.41	5.19	5.05	4.95	4.82	4.68	4.53	4.36
	16.26	*13.27*	*12.06*	*11.39*	*10.97*	*10.67*	*10.27*	*9.89*	*9.47*	*9.02*
	47.04	**36.61**	**33.20**	**31.09**	**29.75**	**28.84**	**27.64**	**26.42**	**25.14**	**23.78**
6	5.99	5.14	4.76	4.53	4.39	4.28	4.15	4.00	3.84	3.67
	13.74	*10.92*	*9.78*	*9.15*	*8.75*	*8.47*	*8.10*	*7.72*	*7.31*	*6.88*
	35.51	**27.00**	**23.70**	**21.90**	**20.81**	**20.03**	**19.03**	**17.99**	**16.89**	**15.75**
7	5.59	4.74	4.35	4.12	3.97	3.87	3.73	3.57	3.41	3.23
	12.25	*9.55*	*8.45*	*7.85*	*7.46*	*7.19*	*6.84*	*6.47*	*6.07*	*5.65*
	29.22	**21.69**	**18.77**	**17.19**	**16.21**	**15.52**	**14.63**	**13.71**	**12.73**	**11.69**
8	5.32	4.46	4.07	3.84	3.69	3.58	3.44	3.28	3.12	2.93
	11.26	*8.65*	*7.59*	*7.01*	*6.63*	*6.37*	*6.03*	*5.67*	*5.28*	*4.86*
	25.42	**18.49**	**15.83**	**14.39**	**13.49**	**12.86**	**12.04**	**11.19**	**10.30**	**9.34**
9	5.12	4.26	3.86	3.63	3.48	3.37	3.23	3.07	2.90	2.71
	10.56	*8.02*	*6.99*	*6.42*	*6.06*	*5.80*	*5.47*	*5.11*	*4.73*	*4.31*
	22.86	**16.39**	**13.90**	**12.56**	**11.71**	**11.13**	**10.37**	**9.57**	**8.72**	**7.81**
10	4.96	4.10	3.71	3.48	3.33	3.22	3.07	2.91	2.74	2.54
	10.04	*7.56*	*6.55*	*5.99*	*5.64*	*5.39*	*5.06*	*4.71*	*4.33*	*3.91*
	21.04	**14.91**	**12.55**	**11.28**	**10.48**	**9.92**	**9.20**	**8.45**	**7.64**	**6.76**
11	4.84	3.98	3.59	3.36	3.20	3.09	2.95	2.79	2.61	2.40
	9.65	*7.20*	*6.22*	*5.67*	*5.32*	*5.07*	*4.74*	*4.40*	*4.02*	*3.60*
	19.69	**13.81**	**11.56**	**10.35**	**9.58**	**9.05**	**8.35**	**7.63**	**6.85**	**6.00**
12	4.75	3.88	3.49	3.26	3.11	3.00	2.85	2.69	2.50	2.30
	9.33	*6.93*	*5.95*	*5.41*	*5.06*	*4.82*	*4.50*	*4.16*	*3.78*	*3.36*
	18.64	**12.97**	**10.80**	**9.63**	**8.89**	**8.38**	**7.71**	**7.00**	**6.25**	**5.42**

Abridged from R. A. Fisher and F. Yates, *Statistical tables for biological, agricultural, and medical research,* published by Oliver & Boyd, Ltd., Edinburgh, by permission of the authors and publishers.

TABLE F (*Continued*)

n_2 \ n_1	1	2	3	4	5	6	8	12	24	∞
13	4.67	3.80	3.41	3.18	3.02	2.92	2.77	2.60	2.42	2.21
	9.07	*6.70*	*5.74*	*5.20*	*4.86*	*4.62*	*4.30*	*3.96*	*3.59*	*3.16*
	17.81	**12.31**	**10.21**	**9.07**	**8.35**	**7.86**	**7.21**	**6.52**	**5.78**	**4.97**
14	4.60	3.74	3.34	3.11	2.96	2.85	2.70	2.53	2.35	2.13
	8.86	*6.51*	*5.56*	*5.03*	*4.69*	*4.46*	*4.14*	*3.80*	*3.43*	*3.00*
	17.14	**11.78**	**9.73**	**8.62**	**7.92**	**7.43**	**6.80**	**6.13**	**5.41**	**4.60**
15	4.54	3.68	3.29	3.06	2.90	2.79	2.64	2.48	2.29	2.07
	8.68	*6.36*	*5.42*	*4.89*	*4.56*	*4.32*	*4.00*	*3.67*	*3.29*	*2.87*
	16.59	**11.34**	**9.34**	**8.25**	**7.57**	**7.09**	**6.47**	**5.81**	**5.10**	**4.31**
16	4.49	3.63	3.24	3.01	2.85	2.74	2.59	2.42	2.24	2.01
	8.53	*6.23*	*5.29*	*4.77*	*4.44*	*4.20*	*3.89*	*3.55*	*3.18*	*2.75*
	16.12	**10.97**	**9.00**	**7.94**	**7.27**	**6.81**	**6.19**	**5.55**	**4.85**	**4.06**
17	4.45	3.59	3.20	2.96	2.81	2.70	2.55	2.38	2.19	1.96
	8.40	*6.11*	*5.18*	*4.67*	*4.34*	*4.10*	*3.79*	*3.45*	*3.08*	*2.65*
	15.72	**10.66**	**8.73**	**7.68**	**7.02**	**6.56**	**5.96**	**5.32**	**4.63**	**3.85**
18	4.41	3.55	3.16	2.93	2.77	2.66	2.51	2.34	2.15	1.92
	8.28	*6.01*	*5.09*	*4.58*	*4.25*	*4.01*	*3.71*	*3.37*	*3.00*	*2.57*
	15.38	**10.39**	**8.49**	**7.46**	**6.81**	**6.35**	**5.76**	**5.13**	**4.45**	**3.67**
19	4.38	3.52	3.13	2.90	2.74	2.63	2.48	2.31	2.11	1.88
	8.18	*5.93*	*5.01*	*4.50*	*4.17*	*3.94*	*3.63*	*3.30*	*2.92*	*2.49*
	15.08	**10.16**	**8.28**	**7.26**	**6.61**	**6.18**	**5.59**	**4.97**	**4.29**	**3.52**
20	4.35	3.49	3.10	2.87	2.71	2.60	2.45	2.28	2.08	1.84
	8.10	*5.85*	*4.94*	*4.43*	*4.10*	*3.87*	*3.56*	*3.23*	*2.86*	*2.42*
	14.82	**9.95**	**8.10**	**7.10**	**6.46**	**6.02**	**5.44**	**4.82**	**4.15**	**3.38**
21	4.32	3.47	3.07	2.84	2.68	2.57	2.42	2.25	2.05	1.81
	8.02	*5.78*	*4.87*	*4.37*	*4.04*	*3.81*	*3.51*	*3.17*	*2.80*	*2.36*
	14.59	**9.77**	**7.94**	**6.95**	**6.32**	**5.88**	**5.31**	**4.70**	**4.03**	**3.26**
22	4.30	3.44	3.05	2.82	2.66	2.55	2.40	2.23	2.03	1.78
	7.94	*5.72*	*4.82*	*4.31*	*3.99*	*3.76*	*3.45*	*3.12*	*2.75*	*2.31*
	14.38	**9.61**	**7.80**	**6.81**	**6.19**	**5.76**	**5.19**	**4.58**	**3.92**	**3.15**
23	4.28	3.42	3.03	2.80	2.64	2.53	2.38	2.20	2.00	1.76
	7.88	*5.66*	*4.76*	*4.26*	*3.94*	*3.71*	*3.41*	*3.07*	*2.70*	*2.26*
	14.19	**9.47**	**7.67**	**6.69**	**6.08**	**5.65**	**5.09**	**4.48**	**3.82**	**3.05**
24	4.26	3.40	3.01	2.78	2.62	2.51	2.36	2.18	1.98	1.73
	7.82	*5.61*	*4.72*	*4.22*	*3.90*	*3.67*	*3.36*	*3.03*	*2.66*	*2.21*
	14.03	**9.34**	**7.55**	**6.59**	**5.98**	**5.55**	**4.99**	**4.39**	**3.74**	**2.97**

TABLE F (Continued)

n_2 \ n_1	1	2	3	4	5	6	8	12	24	∞
25	4.24	3.38	2.99	2.76	2.60	2.49	2.34	2.16	1.96	1.71
	7.77	5.57	4.68	4.18	3.86	3.63	3.32	2.99	2.62	2.17
	13.88	9.22	7.45	6.49	5.88	5.46	4.91	4.31	3.66	2.89
26	4.22	3.37	2.98	2.74	2.59	2.47	2.32	2.15	1.95	1.69
	7.22	5.53	4.64	4.14	3.82	3.59	3.29	2.96	2.58	2.13
	13.74	9.12	7.36	6.41	5.80	5.38	4.83	4.24	3.59	2.82
27	4.21	3.35	2.96	2.73	2.57	2.46	2.30	2.13	1.93	1.67
	7.68	5.49	4.60	4.11	3.78	3.56	3.26	2.93	2.55	2.10
	13.61	9.02	7.27	6.33	5.73	5.31	4.76	4.17	3.52	2.75
28	4.20	3.34	2.95	2.71	2.56	2.44	2.29	2.12	1.91	1.65
	7.64	5.45	4.57	4.07	3.75	3.53	3.23	2.90	2.52	2.06
	13.50	8.93	7.19	6.25	5.66	5.24	4.69	4.11	3.46	2.70
29	4.18	3.33	2.93	2.70	2.54	2.43	2.28	2.10	1.90	1.64
	7.60	5.42	4.54	4.04	3.73	3.50	3.20	2.87	2.49	2.03
	13.39	8.85	7.12	6.19	5.59	5.18	4.64	4.05	3.41	2.64
30	4.17	3.32	2.92	2.69	2.53	2.42	2.27	2.09	1.89	1.62
	7.56	5.39	4.51	4.02	3.70	3.47	3.17	2.84	2.47	2.01
	13.29	8.77	7.05	6.12	5.53	5.12	4.58	4.00	3.36	2.59
40	4.08	3.23	2.84	2.61	2.45	2.34	2.18	2.00	1.79	1.51
	7.31	5.18	4.31	3.83	3.51	3.29	2.99	2.66	2.29	1.80
	12.61	8.25	6.60	5.70	5.13	4.73	4.21	3.64	3.01	2.23
60	4.00	3.15	2.76	2.52	2.37	2.25	2.10	1.92	1.70	1.39
	7.08	4.98	4.13	3.65	3.34	3.12	2.82	2.50	2.12	1.60
	11.97	7.76	6.17	5.31	4.76	4.37	3.87	3.31	2.69	1.90
120	3.92	3.07	2.68	2.45	2.29	2.17	2.02	1.83	1.61	1.25
	6.85	4.79	3.95	3.48	3.17	2.96	2.66	2.34	1.95	1.38
	11.38	7.31	5.79	4.95	4.42	4.04	3.55	3.02	2.40	1.56
∞	3.84	2.99	2.60	2.37	2.21	2.09	1.94	1.75	1.52	1.00
	6.64	4.60	3.78	3.32	3.02	2.80	2.51	2.18	1.79	1.00
	10.83	6.91	5.42	4.62	4.10	3.74	3.27	2.74	2.13	1.00

TABLE G

n	$\log_2 n$	n	$\log_2 n$	n	$\log_2 n$
1	0	36	5.16992	71	6.14975
2	1.00000	37	5.20945	72	6.16992
3	1.58496	38	5.24793	73	6.18982
4	2.00000	39	5.28540	74	6.20945
5	2.32193	40	5.32193	75	6.22882
6	2.58496	41	5.35755	76	6.24793
7	2.80735	42	5.39232	77	6.26679
8	3.00000	43	5.42626	78	6.28540
9	3.16993	44	5.45943	79	6.30378
10	3.32193	45	5.49185	80	6.32193
11	3.45943	46	5.52356	81	6.33985
12	3.58496	47	5.55459	82	6.35755
13	3.70044	48	5.58496	83	6.37504
14	3.80735	49	5.61471	84	6.39232
15	3.90689	50	5.64386	85	6.40939
16	4.00000	51	5.67243	86	6.42626
17	4.08746	52	5.70044	87	6.44294
18	4.16993	53	5.72792	88	6.45943
19	4.24793	54	5.75489	89	6.47573
20	4.32193	55	5.78136	90	6.49185
21	4.39232	56	5.80736	91	6.50780
22	4.45943	57	5.83289	92	6.52356
23	4.52356	58	5.85798	93	6.53916
24	4.58496	59	5.88264	94	6.55459
25	4.64386	60	5.90689	95	6.56986
26	4.70044	61	5.93074	96	6.58496
27	4.75489	62	5.95420	97	6.59991
28	4.80736	63	5.97728	98	6.61471
29	4.85798	64	6.00000	99	6.62936
30	4.90689	65	6.02237	100	6.64386
31	4.95420	66	6.04439	101	6.65821
32	5.00000	67	6.06609	102	6.67243
33	5.04439	68	6.08746	103	6.68650
34	5.08746	69	6.10852	104	6.70044
35	5.12928	70	6.12928	105	6.71424

Reproduced by permission of Edmund T. Klemmer and the Electronics Systems Division, United States Air Force.

TABLE G (*Continued*)

n	$\log_2 n$	n	$\log_2 n$	n	$\log_2 n$
106	6.72792	141	7.13955	176	7.45943
107	6.74147	142	7.14975	177	7.46761
108	6.75489	143	7.15987	178	7.47573
109	6.76818	144	7.16992	179	7.48382
110	6.78136	145	7.17991	180	7.49185
111	6.79442	146	7.18982	181	7.49985
112	6.80735	147	7.19967	182	7.50779
113	6.82018	148	7.20945	183	7.51570
114	6.83289	149	7.21917	184	7.52356
115	6.84549	150	7.22882	185	7.53138
116	6.85798	151	7.23840	186	7.53916
117	6.87036	152	7.24793	187	7.54689
118	6.88264	153	7.25739	188	7.55459
119	6.89482	154	7.26679	189	7.56224
120	6.90689	155	7.27612	190	7.56986
121	6.91886	156	7.28540	191	7.57743
122	6.93074	157	7.29462	192	7.58496
123	6.94251	158	7.30378	193	7.59246
124	6.95420	159	7.31288	194	7.59991
125	6.96578	160	7.32193	195	7.60733
126	6.97728	161	7.33092	196	7.61471
127	6.98868	162	7.33985	197	7.62205
128	7.00000	163	7.34873	198	7.62936
129	7.01123	164	7.35755	199	7.63662
130	7.02237	165	7.36632	200	7.64386
131	7.03342	166	7.37504	201	7.65105
132	7.04439	167	7.38370	202	7.65821
133	7.05528	168	7.39232	203	7.66534
134	7.06609	169	7.40088	204	7.67243
135	7.07682	170	7.40939	205	7.67948
136	7.08746	171	7.41785	206	7.68650
137	7.09803	172	7.42626	207	7.69349
138	7.10852	173	7.43463	208	7.70044
139	7.11894	174	7.44294	209	7.70736
140	7.12928	175	7.45121	210	7.71425

TABLE G (*Continued*)

n	log₂n	n	log₂n	n	log₂n
211	7.72110	246	7.94251	281	8.13443
212	7.72792	247	7.94837	282	8.13955
213	7.73471	248	7.95420	283	8.14466
214	7.74147	249	7.96000	284	8.14975
215	7.74819	250	7.96578	285	8.15482
216	7.75489	251	7.97154	286	8.15987
217	7.76155	252	7.97728	287	8.16491
218	7.76818	253	7.98299	288	8.16992
219	7.77479	254	7.98868	289	8.17493
220	7.78136	255	7.99435	290	8.17991
221	7.78790	256	8.00000	291	8.18487
222	7.79442	257	8.00562	292	8.18982
223	7.80090	258	8.01123	293	8.19476
224	7.80735	259	8.01681	294	8.19967
225	7.81378	260	8.02237	295	8.20457
226	7.82018	261	8.02791	296	8.20945
227	7.82655	262	8.03342	297	8.21432
228	7.83289	263	8.03892	298	8.21917
229	7.83920	264	8.04439	299	8.22400
230	7.84549	265	8.04985	300	8.22882
231	7.85175	266	8.05528	301	8.23362
232	7.85798	267	8.06070	302	8.23840
233	7.86419	268	8.06609	303	8.24317
234	7.87036	269	8.07146	304	8.24793
235	7.87652	270	8.07682	305	8.25267
236	7.88264	271	8.08215	306	8.25739
237	7.88874	272	8.08746	307	8.26209
238	7.89482	273	8.09276	308	8.26679
239	7.90087	274	8.09803	309	8.27146
240	7.90689	275	8.10329	310	8.27612
241	7.91289	276	8.10852	311	8.28077
242	7.91886	277	8.11374	312	8.28540
243	7.92481	278	8.11894	313	8.29002
244	7.93074	279	8.12412	314	8.29462
245	7.93664	280	8.12928	315	8.29921

TABLE G (*Continued*)

n	$\log_2 n$	n	$\log_2 n$	n	$\log_2 n$
316	8.30378	351	8.45533	386	8.59246
317	8.30834	352	8.45943	387	8.59619
318	8.31288	353	8.46352	388	8.59991
319	8.31741	354	8.46761	389	8.60363
320	8.32193	355	8.47168	390	8.60733
321	8.32643	356	8.47573	391	8.61103
322	8.33092	357	8.47978	392	8.61471
323	8.33539	358	8.48382	393	8.61839
324	8.33985	359	8.48784	394	8.62205
325	8.34430	360	8.49185	395	8.62571
326	8.34873	361	8.49585	396	8.62936
327	8.35315	362	8.49985	397	8.63299
328	8.35755	363	8.50383	398	8.63662
329	8.36194	364	8.50779	399	8.64024
330	8.36632	365	8.51175	400	8.64386
331	8.37069	366	8.51570	401	8.64746
332	8.37504	367	8.51964	402	8.65105
333	8.37938	368	8.52356	403	8.65464
334	8.38370	369	8.52748	404	8.65821
335	8.38802	370	8.53138	405	8.66178
336	8.39232	371	8.53528	406	8.66534
337	8.39660	372	8.53916	407	8.66888
338	8.40088	373	8.54303	408	8.67242
339	8.40514	374	8.54689	409	8.67596
340	8.40939	375	8.55075	410	8.67948
341	8.41363	376	8.55459	411	8.68299
342	8.41785	377	8.55842	412	8.68650
343	8.42206	378	8.56224	413	8.69000
344	8.42627	379	8.56605	414	8.69349
345	8.43045	380	8.56986	415	8.69697
346	8.43463	381	8.57365	416	8.70044
347	8.43879	382	8.57743	417	8.70390
348	8.44294	383	8.58120	418	8.70736
349	8.44708	384	8.58496	419	8.71081
350	8.45121	385	8.58871	420	8.71425

TABLE G (*Continued*)

n	$\log_2 n$	n	$\log_2 n$	n	$\log_2 n$
421	8.71768	456	8.83289	491	8.93958
422	8.72110	457	8.83605	492	8.94251
423	8.72451	458	8.83920	493	8.94544
424	8.72792	459	8.84235	494	8.94837
425	8.73132	460	8.84549	495	8.95128
426	8.73471	461	8.84862	496	8.95420
427	8.73809	462	8.85175	497	8.95710
428	8.74147	463	8.85487	498	8.96000
429	8.74483	464	8.85798	499	8.96290
430	8.74819	465	8.86109	500	8.96578
431	8.75154	466	8.86419	501	8.96867
432	8.75489	467	8.86728	502	8.97154
433	8.75822	468	8.87036	503	8.97441
434	8.76155	469	8.87344	504	8.97728
435	8.76487	470	8.87652	505	8.98014
436	8.76818	471	8.87958	506	8.98299
437	8.77149	472	8.88264	507	8.98584
438	8.77479	473	8.88570	508	8.98868
439	8.77808	474	8.88874	509	8.99152
440	8.78136	475	8.89178	510	8.99435
441	8.78463	476	8.89482	511	8.99718
442	8.78790	477	8.89784	512	9.00000
443	8.79116	478	8.90087	513	9.00281
444	8.79442	479	8.90388	514	9.00562
445	8.79766	480	8.90689	515	9.00843
446	8.80090	481	8.90989	516	9.01123
447	8.80413	482	8.91289	517	9.01402
448	8.80735	483	8.91588	518	9.01681
449	8.81057	484	8.91886	519	9.01959
450	8.81378	485	8.92184	520	9.02237
451	8.81698	486	8.92481	521	9.02514
452	8.82018	487	8.92778	522	9.02791
453	8.82337	488	8.93074	523	9.03067
454	8.82655	489	8.93369	524	9.03342
455	8.82972	490	8.93664	525	9.03617

TABLE G (*Continued*)

n	$\log_2 n$	n	$\log_2 n$	n	$\log_2 n$
526	9.03892	561	9.13186	596	9.21917
527	9.04166	562	9.13443	597	9.22159
528	9.04439	563	9.13699	598	9.22400
529	9.04712	564	9.13955	599	9.22641
530	9.04985	565	9.14211	600	9.22882
531	9.05257	566	9.14466	601	9.23122
532	9.05528	567	9.14720	602	9.23362
533	9.05799	568	9.14975	603	9.23601
534	9.06070	569	9.15228	604	9.23840
535	9.06340	570	9.15482	605	9.24079
536	9.06609	571	9.15735	606	9.24317
537	9.06878	572	9.15987	607	9.24555
538	9.07146	573	9.16239	608	9.24793
539	9.07414	574	9.16491	609	9.25030
540	9.07682	575	9.16742	610	9.25267
541	9.07948	576	9.16993	611	9.25503
542	9.08215	577	9.17243	612	9.25739
543	9.08481	578	9.17493	613	9.25974
544	9.08746	579	9.17742	614	9.26209
545	9.09011	580	9.17991	615	9.26444
546	9.09276	581	9.18239	616	9.26679
547	9.09540	582	9.18487	617	9.26913
548	9.09803	583	9.18735	618	9.27146
549	9.10066	584	9.18982	619	9.27379
550	9.10329	585	9.19229	620	9.27612
551	9.10591	586	9.19476	621	9.27845
552	9.10852	587	9.19722	622	9.28077
553	9.11114	588	9.19967	623	9.28309
554	9.11374	589	9.20212	624	9.28540
555	9.11634	590	9.20457	625	9.28771
556	9.11894	591	9.20701	626	9.29002
557	9.12153	592	9.20945	627	9.29232
558	9.12412	593	9.21189	628	9.29462
559	9.12670	594	9.21432	629	9.29691
560	9.12928	595	9.21675	630	9.29921

TABLE G (Continued)

n	$\log_2 n$	n	$\log_2 n$	n	$\log_2 n$
631	9.30150	666	9.37938	701	9.45327
632	9.30378	667	9.38154	702	9.45533
633	9.30606	668	9.38370	703	9.45738
634	9.30834	669	9.38586	704	9.45943
635	9.31061	670	9.38802	705	9.46148
636	9.31288	671	9.39017	706	9.46352
637	9.31515	672	9.39232	707	9.46557
638	9.31741	673	9.39446	708	9.46761
639	9.31967	674	9.39660	709	9.46964
640	9.32193	675	9.39874	710	9.47167
641	9.32418	676	9.40088	711	9.47370
642	9.32643	677	9.40301	712	9.47573
643	9.32868	678	9.40514	713	9.47776
644	9.33092	679	9.40727	714	9.47978
645	9.33315	680	9.40939	715	9.48180
646	9.33539	681	9.41151	716	9.48382
647	9.33762	682	9.41363	717	9.48583
648	9.33985	683	9.41574	718	9.48784
649	9.34207	684	9.41785	719	9.48985
650	9.34430	685	9.41996	720	9.49185
651	9.34651	686	9.42207	721	9.49385
652	9.34873	687	9.42417	722	9.49585
653	9.35094	688	9.42626	723	9.49785
654	9.35315	689	9.42836	724	9.49985
655	9.35535	690	9.43045	725	9.50184
656	9.35755	691	9.43254	726	9.50383
657	9.35975	692	9.43463	727	9.50581
658	9.36194	693	9.43671	728	9.50779
659	9.36414	694	9.43879	729	9.50978
660	9.36632	695	9.44087	730	9.51175
661	9.36851	696	9.44294	731	9.51373
662	9.37069	697	9.44501	732	9.51570
663	9.37286	698	9.44708	733	9.51767
664	9.37504	699	9.44915	734	9.51964
665	9.37721	700	9.45121	735	9.52160

TABLE G (*Continued*)

n	$\log_2 n$	n	$\log_2 n$	n	$\log_2 n$
736	9.52356	771	9.59059	806	9.65464
737	9.52552	772	9.59246	807	9.65643
738	9.52748	773	9.59432	808	9.65821
739	9.52943	774	9.59619	809	9.66000
740	9.53138	775	9.59805	810	9.66178
741	9.53333	776	9.59991	811	9.66356
742	9.53527	777	9.60177	812	9.66534
743	9.53722	778	9.60363	813	9.66711
744	9.53916	779	9.60548	814	9.66888
745	9.54110	780	9.60733	815	9.67066
746	9.54303	781	9.60918	816	9.67242
747	9.54496	782	9.61102	817	9.67419
748	9.54689	783	9.61287	818	9.67596
749	9.54882	784	9.61471	819	9.67772
750	9.55075	785	9.61655	820	9.67948
751	9.55267	786	9.61839	821	9.68124
752	9.55459	787	9.62022	822	9.68299
753	9.55651	788	9.62205	823	9.68475
754	9.55842	789	9.62388	824	9.68650
755	9.56033	790	9.62571	825	9.68825
756	9.56224	791	9.62753	826	9.69000
757	9.56415	792	9.62936	827	9.69174
758	9.56605	793	9.63118	828	9.69349
759	9.56796	794	9.63299	829	9.69523
760	9.56985	795	9.63481	830	9.69697
761	9.57175	796	9.63662	831	9.69870
762	9.57365	797	9.63844	832	9.70044
763	9.57554	798	9.64025	833	9.70217
764	9.57743	799	9.64205	834	9.70390
765	9.57932	800	9.64386	835	9.70563
766	9.58120	801	9.64566	836	9.70736
767	9.58308	802	9.64746	837	9.70908
768	9.58496	803	9.64926	838	9.71081
769	9.58684	804	9.65105	839	9.71253
770	9.58872	805	9.65284	840	9.71425

TABLE G (*Continued*)

n	$\log_2 n$	n	$\log_2 n$	n	$\log_2 n$
841	9.71596	876	9.77479	911	9.83131
842	9.71768	877	9.77643	912	9.83289
843	9.71939	878	9.77808	913	9.83447
844	9.72110	879	9.77972	914	9.83605
845	9.72281	880	9.78136	915	9.83763
846	9.72451	881	9.78300	916	9.83920
847	9.72622	882	9.78463	917	9.84078
848	9.72792	883	9.78627	918	9.84235
849	9.72962	884	9.78790	919	9.84392
850	9.73132	885	9.78953	920	9.84549
851	9.73301	886	9.79116	921	9.84706
852	9.73471	887	9.79279	922	9.84862
853	9.73640	888	9.79442	923	9.85019
854	9.73809	889	9.79604	924	9.85175
855	9.73978	890	9.79766	925	9.85331
856	9.74147	891	9.79928	926	9.85487
857	9.74315	892	9.80090	927	9.85643
858	9.74483	893	9.80252	928	9.85798
859	9.74651	894	9.80413	929	9.85953
860	9.74819	895	9.80574	930	9.86109
861	9.74987	896	9.80735	931	9.86264
862	9.75154	897	9.80896	932	9.86419
863	9.75322	898	9.81057	933	9.86573
864	9.75489	899	9.81218	934	9.86728
865	9.75656	900	9.81378	935	9.86882
866	9.75822	901	9.81538	936	9.87036
867	9.75989	902	9.81698	937	9.87190
868	9.76155	903	9.81858	938	9.87344
869	9.76321	904	9.82018	939	9.87498
870	9.76487	905	9.82177	940	9.87652
871	9.76653	906	9.82337	941	9.87805
872	9.76818	907	9.82496	942	9.87958
873	9.76984	908	9.82655	943	9.88111
874	9.77149	909	9.82814	944	9.88264
875	9.77314	910	9.82972	945	9.88417

TABLE G (*Continued*)

n	$\log_2 n$	n	$\log_2 n$	n	$\log_2 n$
946	9.88570	981	9.93811		
947	9.88722	982	9.93958		
948	9.88874	983	9.94105		
949	9.89026	984	9.94251		
950	9.89178	985	9.94398		
951	9.89330	986	9.94544		
952	9.89482	987	9.94691		
953	9.89633	988	9.94837		
954	9.89785	989	9.94983		
955	9.89936	990	9.95128		
956	9.90087	991	9.95274		
957	9.90237	992	9.95420		
958	9.90388	993	9.95565		
959	9.90539	994	9.95710		
960	9.90689	995	9.95855		
961	9.90839	996	9.96000		
962	9.90989	997	9.96145		
963	9.91139	998	9.96290		
964	9.91289	999	9.96434		
965	9.91438	1000	9.96578		
966	9.91588				
967	9.91737				
968	9.91886				
969	9.92035				
970	9.92184				
971	9.92333				
972	9.92481				
973	9.92630				
974	9.92778				
975	9.92926				
976	9.93074				
977	9.93221				
978	9.93369				
979	9.93517				
980	9.93664				

TABLE H

n	n log$_2$ n	n	n log$_2$ n	n	n log$_2$ n
0	0				
1	0	36	186.11730	71	436.63205
2	2.00000	37	192.74977	72	444.23460
3	4.75489	38	199.42125	73	451.85719
4	8.00000	39	206.13069	74	459.49955
5	11.60964	40	212.87712	75	467.16140
6	15.50977	41	219.65963	76	474.84249
7	19.65148	42	226.47733	77	482.54256
8	24.00000	43	233.32938	78	490.26137
9	28.52932	44	240.21499	79	497.99868
10	33.21928	45	247.13339	80	505.75425
11	38.05375	46	254.08385	81	513.52785
12	43.01955	47	261.06568	82	521.31926
13	48.10572	48	268.07820	83	529.12827
14	53.30297	49	275.12078	84	536.95466
15	58.60336	50	282.19281	85	544.79823
16	64.00000	51	289.29369	86	552.65877
17	69.48687	52	296.42287	87	560.53608
18	75.05865	53	303.57978	88	568.42998
19	80.71062	54	310.76393	89	576.34028
20	86.43856	55	317.97478	90	584.26678
21	92.23867	56	325.21188	91	592.20931
22	98.10750	57	332.47473	92	600.16770
23	104.04192	58	339.76290	93	608.14177
24	110.03910	59	347.07594	94	616.13135
25	116.09640	60	354.41344	95	624.13628
26	122.21143	61	361.77498	96	632.15640
27	128.38196	62	369.16017	97	640.19155
28	134.60594	63	376.56864	98	648.24156
29	140.88145	64	384.00000	99	656.30631
30	147.20672	65	391.45391	100	664.38562
31	153.58009	66	398.93001	101	672.47936
32	160.00000	67	406.42798	102	680.58738
33	166.46501	68	413.94747	103	688.70955
34	172.97374	69	421.48819	104	696.84573
35	179.52491	70	429.04981	105	704.99578

Reproduced by permission of Edmund T. Klemmer and the Electronics Systems Division, United States Air Force.

TABLE H (*Continued*)

n	n log$_2$ n	n	n log$_2$ n	n	n log$_2$ n
106	713.15957	141	1006.67674	176	1312.85996
107	721.33697	142	1015.26409	177	1321.76618
108	729.52785	143	1023.86160	178	1330.68055
109	737.73209	144	1032.46920	179	1339.60302
110	745.94957	145	1041.08682	180	1348.53356
111	754.18016	146	1049.71439	181	1357.47210
112	762.42375	147	1058.35183	182	1366.41862
113	770.68022	148	1066.99910	183	1375.37307
114	778.94946	149	1075.65611	184	1384.33540
115	787.23136	150	1084.32280	185	1393.30557
116	795.52579	151	1092.99911	186	1402.28354
117	803.83267	152	1101.68498	187	1411.26926
118	812.15188	153	1110.38034	188	1420.26270
119	820.48331	154	1119.08513	189	1429.26382
120	828.82687	155	1127.79928	190	1438.27256
121	837.18245	156	1136.52275	191	1447.28891
122	845.54995	157	1145.25546	192	1456.31280
123	853.92928	158	1153.99736	193	1465.34421
124	862.32034	159	1162.74839	194	1474.38309
125	870.72304	160	1171.50849	195	1483.42941
126	879.13727	161	1180.27762	196	1492.48313
127	887.56295	162	1189.05570	197	1501.54421
128	896.00000	163	1197.84269	198	1510.61261
129	904.44832	164	1206.63853	199	1519.68830
130	912.90782	165	1215.44316	200	1528.77124
131	921.37841	166	1224.25654	201	1537.86139
132	929.86002	167	1233.07862	202	1546.95872
133	938.35256	168	1241.90933	203	1556.06319
134	946.85595	169	1250.74862	204	1565.17477
135	955.37010	170	1259.59646	205	1574.29342
136	963.89495	171	1268.45278	206	1583.41911
137	972.43039	172	1277.31754	207	1592.55180
138	980.97637	173	1286.19068	208	1601.69146
139	989.53281	174	1295.07217	209	1610.83806
140	998.09962	175	1303.96194	210	1619.99156

TABLE H (Continued)

n	n log$_2$ n	n	n log$_2$ n	n	n log$_2$ n
211	1629.15193	246	1953.85857	281	2285.77380
212	1638.31914	247	1963.24671	282	2295.35348
213	1647.49315	248	1972.64069	283	2304.93828
214	1656.67394	249	1982.04048	284	2314.52818
215	1665.86146	250	1991.44607	285	2324.12316
216	1675.05570	251	2000.85743	286	2333.72320
217	1684.25662	252	2010.27454	287	2343.32829
218	1693.46418	253	2019.69737	288	2352.93840
219	1702.67837	254	2029.12591	289	2362.55352
220	1711.89914	255	2038.56013	290	2372.17364
221	1721.12647	256	2048.00000	291	2381.79872
222	1730.36032	257	2057.44551	292	2391.42877
223	1739.60068	258	2066.89663	293	2401.06376
224	1748.84750	259	2076.35335	294	2410.70367
225	1758.10077	260	2085.81563	295	2420.34849
226	1767.36045	261	2095.28347	296	2429.99820
227	1776.62651	262	2104.75683	297	2439.65278
228	1785.89892	263	2114.23569	298	2449.31222
229	1795.17767	264	2123.72005	299	2458.97650
230	1804.46271	265	2133.20987	300	2468.64561
231	1813.75403	266	2142.70513	301	2478.31952
232	1823.05159	267	2152.20581	302	2487.99823
233	1832.35537	268	2161.71190	303	2497.68172
234	1841.66534	269	2171.22338	304	2507.36996
235	1850.98148	270	2180.74021	305	2517.06296
236	1860.30376	271	2190.26239	306	2526.76068
237	1869.63215	272	2199.78989	307	2536.46312
238	1878.96663	273	2209.32270	308	2546.17025
239	1888.30717	274	2218.86079	309	2555.88208
240	1897.65374	275	2228.40415	310	2565.59857
241	1907.00633	276	2237.95275	311	2575.31971
242	1916.36490	277	2247.50658	312	2585.04549
243	1925.72944	278	2257.06562	313	2594.77590
244	1935.09991	279	2266.62985	314	2604.51092
245	1944.47630	280	2276.19924	315	2614.25053

TABLE H (*Continued*)

n	n log$_2$ n	n	n log$_2$ n	n	n log$_2$ n
316	2623.99472	351	2967.81985	386	3316.68842
317	2633.74347	352	2977.71993	387	3326.72544
318	2643.49678	353	2987.62410	388	3336.76618
319	2653.25462	354	2997.53237	389	3346.81065
320	2663.01699	355	3007.44470	390	3356.85882
321	2672.78387	356	3017.36110	391	3366.91070
322	2682.55524	357	3027.28155	392	3376.96626
323	2692.33108	358	303 7.20605	393	3387.02550
324	2702.11140	359	3047..13457	394	3397.08842
325	2711.89617	360	3057.06711	395	3407.15499
326	2721.68538	361	3067.00366	396	3417.22522
327	2731.47901	362	3076.94421	397	3427.29909
328	2741.27706	363	3086.88874	398	3437.37660
329	2751.07950	364	3096.83725	399	3447.45773
330	2760.88633	365	3106.78972	400	3457.54248
331	2770.69753	366	3116.74614	401	3467.63083
332	2780.51309	367	3126.70650	402	3477.72278
333	2790.33300	368	3136.67080	403	3487.81832
334	2800.15723	369	3146.63902	404	3497.91744
335	2809.98579	370	3156.61114	405	3508.02013
336	2819.81865	371	3166.58717	406	3518.12638
337	2829.65581	372	3176.56708	407	3528.23619
338	2839.49725	373	3186.55087	408	3538.34954
339	2849.34296	374	3196.53853	409	3548.46643
340	2859.19292	375	3206.53004	410	3558.58684
341	2869.04712	376	3216.52541	411	3568.71077
342	2878.90556	377	3226.52461	412	3578.83822
343	2888.76822	378	3236.52764	413	3588.96916
344	2898.63508	379	3246.53448	414	3599.10360
345	2908.50613	380	3256.54513	415	3609.24152
346	2918.38137	381	3266.55958	416	3619.38292
347	2928.26077	382	3276.57781	417	3629.52779
348	2938.14434	383	3286.59982	418	3639.67612
349	2948.03205	384	3296.62560	419	3649.82790
350	2957.92389	385	3306.65513	420	3659.98312

TABLE H (*Continued*)

n	n log$_2$ n	n	n log$_2$ n	n	n log$_2$ n
421	3670.14177	456	4027.79785	491	4389.33339
422	3680.30386	457	4038.07501	492	4399.71714
423	3690.46936	458	4048.35534	493	4410.10381
424	3700.63827	459	4058.63881	494	4420.49341
425	3710.81059	460	4068.92542	495	4430.88593
426	3720.98630	461	4079.21518	496	4441.28137
427	3731.16540	462	4089.50806	497	4451.67971
428	3741.34787	463	4099.80406	498	4462.08096
429	3751.53372	464	4110.10318	499	4472.48511
430	3761.72293	465	4120.40541	500	4482.89214
431	3771.91549	466	4130.71074		
432	3782.11140	467	4141.01917		
433	3792.31065	468	4151.33069		
434	3802.51324	469	4161.64529		
435	3812.71914	470	4171.96297		
436	3822.92837	471	4182.28371		
437	3833.14090	472	4192.60752		
438	3843.35673	473	4202.93438		
439	3853.57586	474	4213.26430		
440	3863.79827	475	4223.59726		
441	3874.02397	476	4233.93326		
442	3884.25293	477	4244.27228		
443	3894.48516	478	4254.61433		
444	3904.72064	479	4264.95940		
445	3914.95938	480	4275.30749		
446	3925.20136	481	4285.65857		
447	3935.44657	482	4296.01266		
448	3945.69501	483	4306.36974		
449	3955.94666	484	4316.72981		
450	3966.20154	485	4327.09285		
451	3976.45961	486	4337.45888		
452	3986.72089	487	4347.82787		
453	3996.98536	488	4358.19982		
454	4007.25301	489	4368.57473		
455	4017.52384	490	4378.95259		

Index

Bibliographic references are in **boldface;** references to footnotes are indicated by n following the page number.

427